P9-CFX-633

Revolutionary Education in China

DOCUMENTS AND COMMENTARY

Peter J. Seybolt

This volume illustrates and analyzes recent revolutionary changes in the Chinese educational system and provides background and perspective.

The material translated from the current period focuses on the radical departure of Chinese education from both traditional and Western goals and methods and offers insight into why the Chinese regard the transformation of their educational system as indispensable for the transformation of their society.

Documents from the Yenan period (1937-1945) offer valuable insight into the genesis of many Maoist educational ideas. The Yenan period was the precursor of, and explicit model for, much that is taking place today.

Professor Seybolt's extensive introduction puts the transformation of education in the context of the total Chinese situation, giving some historical background but concentrating mainly on contemporary events and trends.

A biographical guide and a glossary are appended.

utionary
tion in China

PETER J. SEYBOLT

Revolutionary Education in China

DOCUMENTS AND COMMENTARY

Peter J. Seybolt is an assistant professor of history at the University of Vermont.

Professor Seybolt received a Ph.D in History and Far Eastern Languages from Harvard University in 1970. He has published several journal articles on China and is the editor of the journal *Chinese Education.* Professor Seybolt is currently preparing a book on cadre training and mass education in the Yenan period.

INTERNATIONAL ARTS AND SCIENCES PRESS, INC. iasp WHITE PLAINS, N.Y.

Library of Congress Catalog Card Number: 72-77204
International Standard Book Number: 0-87332-007-7

901 North Broadway, White Plains, New York 10603

Printed in the United States of America

For Jean Bond Seybolt and Crosby Jordan Seybolt

Whoever wants to know a thing has no way of doing so except by coming into contact with it, that is, by living (practicing) in its environment. . . . If you want knowledge, you must take part in the practice of changing reality. If you want to know the taste of a pear, you must change the pear by eating it yourself. . . . If you want to know the theory and methods of revolution, you must take part in revolution. All genuine knowledge originates in direct experience.

MAO TSE-TUNG

Contents

INTRODUCTION xvii

I. HISTORY OF THE STRUGGLE OVER EDUCATIONAL POLICY

1. Chronology of the Two-Road Struggle on the Educational Front in the Past Seventeen Years
   Educational Revolution 5

II. GENERAL DIRECTIVES

2. Quotations from Chairman Mao
   Red Flag 63

3. Universities and Middle and Primary Schools Should All Resume Classes and Make Revolution
   People's Daily 65

4. Shorten the Period of Schooling and Revolutionize Education
   People's Daily 69

5. The Working Class Must Exercize Leadership in Everything
   Yao Wen-yüan 74

III. EDUCATING THE ELITES

6. The "May 7" Cadre School
   Peking Review 83

7. On the Reeducation of Intellectuals
People's Daily and Red Flag Commentators 91

8. Wholeheartedly Complete "Reeducation" Work
Investigation Team of the Kirin Provincial Revolutionary Committee and the Pai-ch'eng Special District Revolutionary Committee 97

IV. CONTROL OF THE SCHOOLS

9. Chairman Mao's [March 7] Directive Concerning the Great Strategic Plan for the Great Proletarian Cultural Revolution
People's Daily 107

10. Thoroughly Implement the Latest Directive of Our Great Leader Chairman Mao, and Firmly Execute the Battle Orders Issued by the Proletarian Headquarters
People's Daily 109

11. School Management by Poor and Lower-Middle Peasants as Shown by the Practice of Three Production Brigades in the Educational Revolution
People's Daily 117

12. Consolidate the Leadership of the Working Class Over the Educational Revolution
CCP Committee of Liaoning University 128

V. TEACHERS AND TEACHING

13. Taking a Joyous Step Forward in the Educational Revolution
Kuo T'ung 147

14. Strengthen the Building of the Ranks of Urban Primary and Middle School Teachers
CCP Kiangsu Provincial Committee Writing Group 155

15. A "Mobile University" for the Training of Teachers with Greater, Faster, Better, and More Economical Results
Red Flag 166

VI. SHORT-TERM TRAINING CLASSES

16. Four New Kinds of Schools
Red Flag 181

VII. ELEMENTARY EDUCATION, RURAL SCHOOLS

17. A Primary School Run by the People Under the Control of the Poor and Lower-Middle Peasants
Red Flag 191

18. The Poor and Lower-Middle Peasants Have Acquired Socialist Culture
Red Flag 200

19. A Network for Popularizing Socialist Education
Red Flag 210

VIII. MIDDLE SCHOOLS, PHYSICAL EDUCATION

20. A Middle School Serving the Three Great Revolutionary Movements
Red Flag 229

21. How Did We Initiate "Industrial Studies" Activities?
Tientsin No. 42 Middle School Revolutionary Committee 239

22. Mass Physical Training
Peking Review 247

IX. HIGHER-LEVEL TECHNICAL TRAINING

23. The Way to Train Engineering and Technical Personnel as Viewed from the Shanghai Machine-Tool Plant
People's Daily 259

24. Strive to Build a Socialist University of Science and Engineering
Workers' and PLA Mao Tse-tung Thought Propaganda Team Stationed at Tsinghua University 272

X. LIBERAL ARTS COLLEGES

25. Liberal Arts Universities Must Carry Out Revolutionary Mass Criticism
Shanghai Revolutionary Mass Criticism Writing Group 303

26. Reform Liberal Arts Universities Through Revolutionary Mass Criticism
Red Flag 313

XI. THE YENAN BACKGROUND

27. Educational Method at K'angta
The Situation at the Resist Japan Military and Political University 333

28. The Problem of Transforming General Education in the Base Areas
Liberation Daily 349

29. On Regulations and Curriculum in General Education
Liberation Daily 355

30. Border Region Government Directive on Promoting the Study of Model Schools and on Experimentation with Popular-Management Primary Schools (April 18, 1944)
Educational Policy in the Shen-Kan-Ning Border Region 365

31. Regarding the New Curriculum for Middle Schools
Liberation Daily 372

32. Yenan University Educational Policy and Temporary Regulations (May 21, 1944)
Educational Policy in the Shen-Kan-Ning Border Region 376

APPENDIX

Biographical Guide 387

Glossary 399

Acknowledgments

This book is a product of the work of many people. I am particularly indebted to Douglas Merwin for his excellent advice and careful editorial work.

I would also like to thank Fred Ablin, editorial director of International Arts and Sciences Press, for promoting the publication of this volume and offering criticism and encouragement along the way.

Students in my course on the history of modern China at the University of Vermont contributed a number of helpful suggestions for improving the introduction, as did my colleagues in a faculty seminar. Special thanks are due to Robert V. Daniels, Harvey Salgo, Harold Schultz and David Shiman for carefully reading the manuscript and commenting on style and content.

Some of the documents included in the volume were originally selected for publication in the journal *Chinese Education* by its former editors Leo Orleans, Chi Wang, Robert Barendsen and Yi Tsien. I am grateful for their contribution, as I am for that of the translators who have helped to make the materials in this volume available to a Western audience. They include Lewis Cook, Alison B. Huey, Douglas Merwin, Akira Odani, A. W. Sariti, and the translation staff of the U. S. Consulate General in Hong Kong.

The admirable Chinese caligraphy on the jacket is the work of Zunvair J. Yue.

Finally, I would like to thank my wife, Cynthia, for her very perceptive criticism and advice.

Introduction

The educational theory and practice of a society is one of the best indicators of its values and future direction. For the past several years the Chinese have placed extraordinary emphasis on the transformation of their educational system as a requisite for continuing the transformation of their society. The documents in this book on the educational revolution should therefore be of interest to students of contemporary China, and to those engaged in comparative study of societies, as well as to teachers and other educators. The latter will find in the Chinese experience a valuable tool for reexamining their own current practice, for the innovations which have emerged from the turmoil of the Cultural Revolution directly challenge conventional educational wisdom and test basic assumptions which long have been taken for granted.

The materials translated and presented here were first published in the Chinese press. With two exceptions they were written originally for domestic use and constitute official instructions and models for emulation rather than a description of widespread practice. As such, they give an excellent picture of what the Chinese leadership would like to achieve and what it wishes to abolish or avoid.

This introduction is intended to provide background to the material in the documents, and particularly to give readers unfamiliar with contemporary China, and with the conventions peculiar to the Chinese press, a point of reference.

Five topics will be discussed: the broad objectives of Chinese communism under the leadership of Mao Tse-tung; the conditions in China which particularly affect education; the "struggle between two lines," or the basic differences that divided China's leadership before 1966 and provoked the Cultural Revolution; the events of the early years of the Cultural Revolution as they affected education; and, finally, a more detailed description of current educational principles which are now being applied.

I. General Objectives

The general objectives outlined here encompass every aspect of social endeavor, as well as objectives particular to education. They are the ostensible goals of all Marxists regardless of the means employed to realize them or of measures taken at various times which seem clearly dysfunctional to their accomplishment.

There are, of course, those who contend that the professed motives of the Chinese Communists simply mask a desire for power for its own sake, uncomplicated by principle or purpose. Without engaging in a necessarily lengthy discussion of that view, the stated objectives are presented here on the premise that it is impossible to make sense of the current educational revolution in China without reference to them.

The long-term goal of Marxism in China is to realize an egalitarian society in which there is no more exploitation: a classless society in which the economic, social and political fruits of human endeavor are distributed on a basis of approximate equality.

The socialist ideal of equality differs fundamentally from the liberal ideal of equal opportunity to reach the top. In a fully socialist society, distinctions of top and bottom in regard to privilege (as distinct from talent or achievement) are eliminated.

In addition to collective ownership of the means of production and distribution, this implies reduction and eventual elimination of the disparity of wealth, status and power between urban and rural areas, mental and manual labor, and men and women — divisions which have been particularly acute in China in the past.

Realization of the Marxist ideal also requires the production of more material wealth. Equal distribution of poverty will not bring the happiness to humankind that Marx envisioned. In the Marxist analysis, the adverse ratio of goods to needs (both real, life sustaining needs, and contrived "needs" of the imagination) was responsible for a division of labor, and hence class differentiation, in the first place. It can be argued that desire for possession will always outstrip the capacity to produce, but socialists regard that historically observable phenomenon as behavior peculiar to a particular stage of history and not as human nature. They are confident that when production reaches a certain level vis-à-vis population, a society, for its mutual benefit and preservation, can and indeed will control the rapacity of the few for the well-being of the many. In other words, increasing production is a means to an end and not a goal in itself. Chinese economists do not measure success primarily in terms of gross national product.

Nationalism (the pursuit of principally Chinese state interests), like production, is also seen as a necessary means, at this particular stage of history, for promoting egalitarian ends. Although nationalism contradicts the supranational aim of communism, the Chinese recognize a need to build a defense against the innate expansionist tendency of capitalist countries in search of investment opportunities, markets and raw materials, and the calculated expansionist tendency of social imperialism (i.e., the USSR). It is also thought that a strong nation moving toward socialism will inspire revolutionary movements elsewhere by its example, if not by more concrete forms of assistance, which will lead to the eventual extinction of a world-integrated capitalist system and establish the conditions necessary for international socialism.

II. Conditions Affecting Educational Theory and Practice

The educational measures currently being employed in the People's Republic of China to achieve these universal socialist objectives are shaped by the historical legacy and immediate conditions in China. It will be useful to mention briefly the more outstanding of these before examining educational theory and practice.

Perhaps the most conspicuous feature of Chinese society today, and a major consideration for any endeavor, is the immense size of the population. China is a land of 650-850 million people. The task of educating a population that size is obviously enormous, particularly given the Communists' broad conception of education and their aspiration to see it universally implemented at all age levels.

Second, China is a largely agrarian society; at least 80 percent of the people live in rural areas and engage in agriculture. It is a poor nation on a per capita basis, and the rural areas are the poorest and culturally most backward. This fact is particularly important for educators committed to reducing social disparity based in part on uneven development of city and countryside.

The task is made especially difficult by a poor communications system, the isolation of many areas, and the continuing existence of ignorance, superstition and disease. Much has been done since 1949 to change this situation, but criticisms made during the Cultural Revolution indicate a continuing problem on a fairly large scale.

The contribution that formal education can make toward eliminating these conditions is circumscribed by a still considerable amount of functional illiteracy. Before 1949 at least 70-80 percent of the population was illiterate. In some areas the rate was as high as 99 percent. This was primarily the result of social conditions which have been largely eliminated, but the situation is complicated by a language marvelous in aesthetic value and subtlety, but very difficult to learn. The structure of the script has now been simplified, and the grammar made to conform more with patterns of speech, but the written language remains an obstacle rather than a tool for rapid assimilation of written information.

Another feature of Chinese society affecting progress toward an egalitarian society is a long tradition of ethically sanctioned class domination by a self-designated "virtuous" few. For over two thousand years, class distinctions were fostered and maintained by the official Confucian ideology as well as by political and economic institutions consonant with it. As in almost all societies before the industrial age, class domination was overt, with no apologies. But traditional China was incomparably successful in conserving and reinforcing its elitist system. The Confucian ethic was manifest in a separation between mental and manual laborers, rulers and ruled. Age dominated youth and men dominated women by moral imperative; urban areas dominated rural by the nature of the Confucian bureaucratic system. These characteristics of traditional Chinese society are all antithetical to the goals of new China, but they are still deeply pervasive. A continuity of attitudes for over two thousand years is not easily dispelled.

An influence of shorter duration, but also very powerful and hard to eliminate, is the now rejected USSR model of bureaucratic centralism. The Soviet experience of revolution from the top down and paternalistic elitism, and its history of industrial development based on exploitation of the countryside, are not in accord with China's revolutionary past, or with her future aspirations. Disagreement over the model presented by the USSR is, of course, one of the major factors of the split between Mao Tse-tung and Liu Shao-ch'i that paved the way for the Cultural Revolution.

III. The Struggle Between Two Lines

Given these conditions, how have the Chinese Communists pursued their objectives? Prior to the Cultural Revolution, it was assumed by almost everyone in the West that the top Chinese leadership was united in its goals and methods. But the struggle for leadership which surfaced in 1966 has made explicit two very different approaches to socialism — one identified with Mao Tse-tung, chairman of the Communist Party, and the other with Liu Shao-ch'i, then president of the People's Republic. Both have claimed to seek the same broad socialist objectives, but they have advocated very different means to that end — so different that the Maoists assert that Liu and his followers are really nothing but bourgeois revisionists promoting an essentially capitalist line.

The Maoists have won the struggle, at least for the time being, and it is their policies which are of interest to us in this book of readings on contemporary policy. We will examine the Liuist line only as it is presented to us by the Maoists — as a negative example of what to avoid or eliminate, and as a contrast to the Maoist line serving to sharpen and clarify it.

For the Maoists, the path to revolutionary objectives is revolution — a struggle in which one class seizes power from another and uses it to promote its own ends. The form that such a social revolution takes is determined to a large extent by the material conditions or the economic base of a society. From the Maoist analysis, China was ripe for the Cultural Revolution because the "social relations of production" were not consonant with the "mode of production." In other words, the economic base was socialist because the means of production had been transferred from private ownership to public ownership, but the social institutions built on that base had not been transformed — a controlling elite was using them in its own interest.

Liu Shao-ch'i and his followers are accused of perpetuating a system of class privilege by insisting on a policy of "production above everything." Following essentially bourgeois practice, they were using institutions such as education to create a corps of highly trained professionals and experts who could lead China most rapidly (in theory) toward modernization. Ostensibly they would serve the masses with their expertise and contribute to everyone's welfare. This elitist concept of welfare, however, is unacceptable to the Maoists because, regardless of its intentions, it sustains a dominance-dependency relationship between elite and masses, sharpens class lines, and in effect creates a new ruling class which, history suggests, will not willingly relinquish its power and privilege.

The Maoist line affirms the need for production, but insists that it be inextricably combined with class struggle. It takes the form of an attack on institutions such as education which foster elitism and privilege, on the one hand, and the conversion and use of those institutions to raise the level of the majority, who are relatively backward economically, politically and culturally, on the other. The Maoists argue that their policy is economically more sound as well as socially more just than the elitist line of Liu Shao-ch'i. By using available resources to raise the productive capacity of the many (rather than using them to create an elite technocracy), and concentrating on developing relatively simple skills most immediately applicable to China's labor-intensive economy, they expect to broaden the economic base, strike a better balance between urban and rural production, and create a much sounder foundation for future development. Thus the Maoists reject the very premise underlying the elitist line in education.

Maoist class consciousness and emphasis on class struggle makes the question "for whom?" basic to every endeavor. Do (educational) principles and practice primarily serve the interests of the laboring classes — the industrial workers and the poor and lower-middle peasants (see glossary) who constitute a majority of the population — or are they relatively advantageous to an elite at the expense of those classes? Maoists deny that all interests in a class society can be equally served. A choice must be made.

Even with a firm commitment to serve the interests of the laboring classes, it still remains to determine whether or not a proposed measure helps them seize power and move toward an egalitarian society. Except in the most obvious cases, there is no way of knowing in advance. Mao maintains that ideas have no substance, no truth, until they are tested and proven in practice. The Maoist approach, therefore, is first of all to instill in the entire population, and particularly in those in positions of responsibility, a firm ideological commitment to "serve the people" as an ethical basis for action. That is the reason for the intensive study during the past several years of Mao's writings.

Second, the Maoist approach is to develop in all cadres (see glossary) a mass-line work style — "from the masses to the masses." It is the intrinsic duty of a revolutionary leadership to promote change, to point the way beyond existing consciousness and procedures. Mao has always insisted, however, that movement toward socialist goals is possible only with the voluntary participation of the great majority of the people. Effective leadership must proceed from the immediate needs and desires of the led. Cadres must "learn from the people" before presuming to teach them. They must study the local situation and solicit the opinions of the masses before conceptualizing plans for change. Once a plan is determined, it must be patiently explained until it is accepted, or it must be altered to meet objections. Cadres then work with the people to implement a plan, and finally they must be accountable to the people in mass-criticism and self-criticism sessions.

The mass-line work style is an attempt to balance leadership and mass initiative. Needless to say, it has not always been followed. Cadre "commandism" and separation from the people was one of the principal charges against Liu Shao-ch'i's administration, and some of Mao's own projects during the 1958 Great Leap Forward met considerable resistance from large portions of the population, either because they were ill-conceived or because cadres proceeded incorrectly. The Cultural Revolution, a major effort to reassert the mass-line work style, has resulted in considerable changes in the educational system.

IV. The Cultural Revolution in Education — The Early Years

The revolution in education began in 1966 following an intra-Party debate on literature which exposed sharp ideological divisions among China's leaders. In May a young teacher in the philosophy department of Peking University posted what is now referred to as the first "big character poster" (*ta-tzu pao*) of the Cultural Revolution. It asked why the debates on literature and the Peking press had been suppressed at Peking University. This precipitated, from May to August, a period now known as "fifty days of white terror," a struggle between supporters of the existing educational system and radical critics of it. When in August Mao Tse-tung wrote his own big character poster, "Bombard the Headquarters," attacking the bourgeois dictatorship of those who would suppress the revolutionary movement, the issue was decided in favor of the radicals.

The much publicized Red Guard student organizations, which shut down the schools and brought the Cultural Revolution to the attention of the world, were by no means united organizationally or ideologically. Their main contribution to revolutionary transformation in China was to attack established authority and provoke a reexamination of all existing institutions. Their function was essentially destructive — a necessary phase of revolutionary transformation in accord with Mao's assertion of the historical dialectic: "no construction without destruction." Mao recognizes that there is no such thing as a void. The process of destroying the old is part of the process of building the new. But the various Red Guard and rebel groups were too divided among themselves to keep the new from being anarchic. And many of them ignored or misinterpreted Mao's definition of "destruction." It should be, he said, a process of verbal "criticism and repudiation" of bourgeois tendencies. In his sixteen-point directive for promoting the Cultural Revolution, he particularly eschews violence. This admonition was often ignored as millions of youth, given the mandate to develop revolutionary attitudes and experience by freely making revolution, attacked established authority in the Party and government.

With the fall of Liu Shao-ch'i and repudiation of bureaucratic tendencies in Party and government, criticism in the press shifted to the ultra-leftists for their policy of "remove all, destroy all." Known as May 16 elements [see glossary], they have been held responsible for such acts as burning the British Embassy and subverting the Chinese Foreign Ministry with irresponsible directives. Reportedly abetted by agents provocateurs working to restore Liu Shao-ch'i's establishment (and some proudly acknowledged by Chiang K'ai-shek to be Kuomintang agents), they discredited the revolutionary movement by acts of vandalism and violence.

The situation in the universities was very confused as competing groups of Red Guards and rebels fought for supremacy. At major universities like Tsinghua and Peking, most students had gone on long marches (see glossary) or had simply returned home, but those who remained engaged in pitched battles resulting in loss of life and property. The most ostensibly radical of these factions are now described as being "left in form but right in essence." Their acts are condemned as exemplifying bourgeois individualism taken to the point of nihilism and anarchism. Their undiscriminating attack on all those who represented authority or tradition violated Mao's basic united front principle of "uniting with all possible allies to defeat a handful of enemies." As a result they alienated many people who were in basic agreement with the principles of the Cultural Revolution.

As early as February and March 1967, two CCP Central Committee directives ordered students at all educational levels to return to their schools to make revolution. Classes resumed in many primary and secondary schools, but order was not restored in the universities. In October 1967, schools on all levels were again instructed to resume classes (see Document 3), but animosities were too deep to permit compliance in the universities. Finally, in March 1968, a year after the first directive, Mao Tse-tung ordered units of the People's Liberation Army and workers' Mao Tse-tung thought propaganda teams (see below) to enter the schools and restore order. They were told to reason with the students and on no account to use armed force. It took some thirty thousand workers to end the fighting at Tsinghua University that had escalated to the point of using tanks and bombs. Although some of their number were killed by student combatants, the workers are reported never to have resorted to counterviolence, and eventually, by persuasion and example, they restored order on the campuses and brought the revolution in education into its second stage.

The second stage is expected to be a long period of "struggle-criticism-transformation" in which repudiation of bourgeois tendencies is combined with the creation of new methods to replace them. It is a probing stage, with emphasis on diversity and experimentation. Nothing is yet settled, but certain clear guidelines have emerged.

It should be pointed out that not one of the basic principles of the current educational revolution is new. Almost all of them had been conceptualized by the mid-1940s, as is apparent in documents 27-32. What is new is the way in which the basic principles have been employed since the Cultural Revolution and, in some cases, the fact that they have been employed.

V. The Transformation of the Educational System

Control of the Schools

During the early years of the Cultural Revolution the problem of control of institutions was antecedent to the problem of their transformation. The attack on Liu Shao-ch'i's administrative apparatus resulted in the breakup of central bureaucracies and a diminution of central planning and central control in all fields that had steadily increased under Liu's presidency. The two ministries of education (one for higher education and one for lower levels) and their branch offices were criticized not only for their policies (discussed in subsequent sections) but for the very nature of their operation.

The Maoists subscribe to the theory that a highly rationalized bureaucracy staffed by professionals is innately elitist and conservative. The historical trend of bureaucratic development to increase both the specificity and routinization of particular jobs, and the rules and regulations defining them, is conducive more to static specialization than to flexibility and change. The official as bureaucrat finds that he must spend an increasing amount of time in an office handling paper work, thus reducing his contact with the people and observation of actual conditions — both necessary for implementing the mass line. Furthermore, specialization of function in a particular agency results in a weakened relationship with other agencies and limits the potential for coordinated change.

In a society satisfied with maintaining the status quo, or with gradual incremental change, such a situation is acceptable, even desirable. But in a society dedicated to comprehensive, revolutionary transformation, it is intolerable for any length of time. That is why major innovations in China that have occurred under Mao Tse-tung's leadership have been accomplished through mass mobilization, campaign politics, rather than through normal government channels, and have been accompanied by a denigration of professionalism and expertise.

An example of the bureaucratic mentality in China prior to the Cultural Revolution was the desire by the ministries of education to standardize (<u>cheng-kuei-hua</u>) institutions and procedures. A number of highly innovative schools, such as Kungta (the Worker's University), and many rural mass schools which had been established in 1958 during the Great Leap Forward were condemned as "irregular" and closed down.

Since the Cultural Revolution, the principle has been to recognize local differences and build on local strengths, and to encourage diversity and experimentation in all aspects of the educational system. This has led to a considerable decentralization of administration and a reduction in the number of bureaucrats. When orders were coming from the center and emphasis was on standardization, many officials were needed to see that standard procedures were being maintained. The necessity for that control function has now been considerably reduced.

An interim work group for cultural and educational affairs, set up within the State Council, has replaced the two education ministries, and it functions to keep the whole system moving toward common goals; but its directives are of a more general nature than those of the two ministries, allowing much greater diversity of implementation. Furthermore, the most powerful unifying factor today is not bureaucratic control, but ideology, the thought of Mao Tse-tung. The extent to which the goals and ethics of Mao's thought are internalized by everyone, and particularly by officials, is inversely proportionate to the need for central direction and control. The problem of interpretation of Mao's general principles and directives, however, will probably become increasingly difficult in the future, particularly after the Chairman dies, and may provide impetus for reassertion of administrative controls.

An institution which came into being during the Cultural Revolution to deal with the bureaucratic situation is the May 7 Cadre School. Governmental and Party agencies of all sorts have established these schools as a place where cadres can concentrate on a thorough examination of their work and, through intensive study of Maoist principles and long hours of discussion, criticism and self-criticism, recognize tendencies in their work which contradict the mass line and socialist goals. Study is combined with hard physical labor meant to strengthen their empathy with and understanding of the problems of the great majority of the Chinese people — the laboring classes who do this sort of work every day. Many of the May 7 Cadre Schools, if not most, are located in wasteland areas. The cadres build their own dwellings and other facilities and work to reclaim the land. Often they establish small manufacturing facilities in an attempt to make the schools as self-sustaining as possible.

While at the schools, the cadres draw their regular salaries and many return to their regular jobs after a period varying from six months to several years. Others are reassigned, and a few lose their cadre status and take a regular job either because their former job has been abolished or because they cannot conform to the new demands of leadership.

The May 7 Cadre Schools represent a uniquely Chinese effort to curb the tendency of officialdom to become a special interest group and, in effect, a new ruling class. Indications at present are that the May 7 Schools will continue to function, and periodic attendance at them will be a normal expectation for holding an official position.

Another institution that has played a very important role in the Cultural Revolution in general, and in transforming educational administration in particular, is the People's Liberation Army. Under Defense Minister Lin Piao's direction, the PLA was schooled in Mao Tse-tung's thought before the Cultural Revolution began. The "little red book," Quotations from Chairman Mao Tse-tung, was first compiled by Lin Piao for that purpose. When the conflict between Mao and Liu Shao-ch'i came into the open, Mao was confident that the PLA would support him. This proved to be true despite the recent revelation of factions within the army and Lin Piao's personal ambitions, which ultimately led him to challenge the authority of Mao himself.

During the first phase of the Cultural Revolution the army was directed to avoid the use of violence, but to support the left. When the Red Guards had stopped existing administrative procedure but were unable to replace it, the PLA, as we noted above, was called upon to restore order. PLA intervention was not always direct. In many cases workers' Mao Tse-tung thought propaganda teams from factories, or leaders of production brigades and militia units in the countryside, took over the schools; but their authority was backed by the army.

The task of these teams has been to initiate within the school and within the community a thorough discussion of education and to organize criticism and self-criticism of the former system. They were, however, instructed not to retain sole leadership, but to help establish a school revolutionary committee to take over the administrative function. Referred to as "triple alliance" or "three-in-one" revolutionary committees, the new administrative groups are supposed to represent different age levels — the young (under thirty-five), the middle-aged (thirty-five to fifty-five) and the old (over fifty-five) — and different interests in the community, as well as the interests of the central leadership. They need not always adhere precisely to the three-in-one formula. For instance, the triple alliance in the school in Aihui People's Commune (mentioned in Document 11) consists of four groups: (1) leading members of production brigade revolutionary committees, (2) representatives of the poor and lower-middle peasants, (3) leaders of militia companies, and (4) representatives of teachers and students. They are always supposed to be dominated numerically by those with worker or poor and lower-middle peasant background to ensure that the interests of those favored classes are paramount. Obviously the PLA or workers' propaganda teams, with their extensive ideological training, are there to see that decisions are in accord with the general Maoist line. Particular policies, however, are very much a local option. One of the first acts of newly constituted revolutionary committees is to examine all existing rules and regulations, throw out all but a bare minimum, and make sure that those conform to the needs and resources of each area or institution.

The immediate goal of this new administrative order is to move closer to the mass-line ideal, that is, to strike a better balance between central leadership and local mass initiative. As we have seen, the mass line seeks to avoid both the elitist authoritarianism of Liu Shao-ch'i's apparatus and undirected liberalism, which Mao rejects for its piecemeal, anarchic approach to problems. If the guarantees of leadership seem especially strong, it should be noted that there are substantial safeguards against its becoming authoritarian. In the first place, there is the recently reasserted imperative that those in positions of authority regularly face the masses and hear their criticism. Conducting official school business "behind closed doors" is proscribed. People in the community are urged to become actively involved in the affairs of the school and to freely offer suggestions and complaints.

Second, there is a renewed effort to change the composition of the leadership so that, in terms of class composition at least, it reflects the interests of the workers and poor and lower-middle peasants. New educational principles, which we will now discuss, play an important role in preparing this leadership and enabling it to emerge.

Admissions and Advancement — Whom Shall Education Serve?

Nowhere are the differences in the two lines, Maoist and

turn them down if they are clearly unqualified. Workers, peasants, and soldiers from the ranks are given precedence in the selection process. Everyone chosen to go to a university must have had at least two years of working experience after secondary school, though not all those chosen need be secondary school graduates. Artificial age restrictions have been removed. Older workers who never had an opportunity to attend secondary school are considered for admission on the basis of their demonstrated capacity for learning and performance.

Equally important is the committee's assessment of the candidates' political attitude or ideological stand — the major criterion being whether they are willing to return to the work unit which sent them and "serve the people" with their newly acquired knowledge. Exempted from returning are those few students chosen for further study in the graduate academies, but still the academy must obtain the permission of the sponsoring work unit.

The stipulation that one return to the work unit is designed to circumvent the phenomenon, so common in largely agrarian countries, of having the educated few congregate in the cities, often without jobs commensurate with the kind of education they have received, and contribute little to the welfare of anyone but themselves.

The criteria for advancement have also been considerably altered since the Cultural Revolution. Proceeding from one educational level to the next is not considered the ultimate student achievement. Indeed, university education has been deemphasized, at least for the time being. University attendance is much smaller than before the start of the Cultural Revolution, partly because it is still at a very experimental stage, but mainly because attention has been focused on lower educational levels. As of October 1971, only one-quarter of the universities operating before the Cultural Revolution were admitting students. On the other hand, the number of both schools and students at the elementary and secondary levels has grown enormously since 1968. In keeping with the concept of simplicity and emphasis on basic knowledge, elementary and middle school training have each been reduced from six to five years. In many areas seven-year schools combining elementary and junior middle school have been created where formerly there was little or no schooling at all.

The discrepancy between enrollment figures at higher and lower levels reflects the feeling that China's immediate problems do not require for their solution a large number of university trained experts. On the contrary, what is needed is a much broader educational base at the lower levels which will produce more people with relatively simple technological skills. Since the Yenan period in the 1940s, it has been a Maoist principle that the educational system of a society must be roughly commensurate with the economic base, and that they should advance together in a close dialectical relationship (see Document 29). There are, to be sure, advanced research institutes for high-level research, but the main emphasis in education is on raising the level of those farthest behind, enabling them to more nearly realize their human potential.

Tests and examinations are still given as a means of assessing the effectiveness of teaching and learning, but they too have been deemphasized. No longer are they used as the major criterion for advancement. The Maoist insistance on combining learning and doing has resulted in replacing classroom tests in many technological courses with actual job performance. The new relationship of schools with work units (discussed below) facilitates this process. Classroom tests are still given in subjects such as foreign language in which study and application are not so easily combined. But instead of fostering individual competition among students, they have become a vehicle for cooperative learning. In a typical exam, students are given the questions ahead of time. They study together, the faster learners helping the slower ones. Frequently a fast and a slow learner will become a "red pair" working together. Students take the tests individually and then grade each other's papers. Often the teacher submits a paper also. After grading, all study their mistakes and the exam is given again.

The point of exams, then, is to help everyone learn certain

information or methods and to assess the accomplishments of the whole class. Unlike previous exams, they are not intended to make invidious distinctions. On the other hand, there are no restraints on excellence. Each individual is encouraged to exert maximum effort. But the achieving individual is expected to help others achieve also to the limit of their capacity, not to strive to outdo them simply for his own relative aggrandizement.

There are early indications of some discontent with the new attitude toward examinations. Teachers have complained that the new procedures make it difficult to maintain standards and that classes are being slowed to the pace of the slowest students. In some areas examinations are again being used to make distinctions between students. It is difficult to know at this point how much this discontent reflects residual assumptions and biases of the old intellectual class, and how much it indicates real pedagogical problems, even for those who accept the new approach.

The former education ministries' decision to consolidate the schools has also been reversed by the Cultural Revolution. The order is now to disperse rather than to concentrate. This has affected educational institutions at all levels. For instance, only twenty of the high-level research institutes of the Academy of Sciences (which includes institutes of history, social sciences, and humanities, as well as natural sciences) will remain under the direct control of the Academy in Peking. The rest will be, or have been, shifted to other organizations (such as production units), or will be under provincial authority or under "dual leadership" of the Academy and its local branches. It is thought that decentralization will stimulate initiative from both above and below. Overall policy will still be made at the central Academy in Peking.

Universities are also decentralizing. A number of the larger schools are establishing branches in rural areas, and a variety of high-level technical training institutes of a new type are being run in conjunction with factories and communes.

It is at the lower educational levels that decentralization will ultimately make the greatest difference. During the Yenan period, a number of "popular-management" (min-pan) schools were created which brought formal education to many areas where it had previously been inaccessible. Implementation of the popular-management idea was reasserted in 1958, during the Great Leap Forward, after several years of neglect when China was emulating Soviet models. Between 1960 and 1965, however, many of the popular-management schools were discontinued because they did not conform to standards of quality then in effect (see documents 11, 12, 17, 18). Today they are vigorously promoted once again.

The principle for establishing popular-management schools is self-reliance (tzu-li keng-sheng). Each area is encouraged to rely on its own resources to provide as much education for the local area as possible, and not to be dependent on superior agencies, or restricted by conventional standards of quality. This has resulted in the creation of a tremendous number of new schools, especially in the countryside. Obviously this expansion has been possible only because former conceptions of proper teaching personnel, teaching methods, and course content have been drastically altered.

Teaching Personnel

The attack on professionalism during the Cultural Revolution included a rejection of the idea that only those trained in normal schools and high-level research institutes (or abroad in the case of the prestige universities) are qualified to teach. Full-time, professional teachers have now been joined by tens of thousands of diversely talented workers, officials and others from the community. Some teach part time, some full time. Practical skills are taught by industrial and agricultural workers beyond the confines of school walls, in factories and on farms, as well as in the classroom. Even history and social science are sometimes studied in the community. By making education a concern of the whole community, the former teacher shortage in China has been somewhat alleviated. The professional teachers are still very much needed, however, and are still the most important source of instruction.

The first phase of the Cultural Revolution was very hard on professional teachers. As the assumptions under which they had operated were called into question, many teachers were denounced and humiliated, and some were physically mistreated by the now discredited ultra-left. The feeling that "it is dangerous to be a teacher" and that "teachers have no future" (referred to in numerous documents in this book) caused many teachers to seek other jobs or simply to stand aside and let events take their course. In the past several years, however, there has been a concerted effort by the leadership to make amends and counteract these attitudes. While continuing to assert that teachers are the main problem in educational reform, the official press has publicized the important role of teachers and has repeated time and again that only a small percentage of teachers are incorrigibly bourgeois or feudal in attitude and unsuited to teach. The remaining teachers, well over ninety percent, like everyone else in positions of authority and responsibility in China, have spent long hours discussing goals and methods and through criticism and self-criticism have sought to change their orientation, even while continuing to teach. Teachers have kept their former salaries and a very nonegalitarian wage differential has been maintained. In a university, for instance, an experienced professor might make as much as 360 yuan per month while an instructor makes 60 yuan, one-sixth as much, but still about equal to the average factory worker's wage. No official explanation for this anomaly in socialist society has been offered, but it seems to indicate that material incentive and traditional attitudes still play a role in China, and that experienced teachers are valued highly.

Teaching Methods

The strong emphasis on experimentation in education today has stimulated considerable innovation in teaching methods. They vary with different age levels, locations, courses, and teaching situations. But with all the diversity, certain pedagogical principles are the foundation for all teaching. They are derived from an epistemological theory outlined by Mao Tsetung in a series of lectures at K'angta (The Resist Japan University) in 1937. Known today, in a revised form, as "On Practice" and "On Contradiction," they are required reading for all teachers.

In the first of these essays, Mao distinguishes two stages in the cognitive process. The first stage is one in which the subject perceives the material world by means of his senses. In this perceptual stage, sights, sounds, odors, etc., are received by the brain, which has the innate capacity to make distinctions and organize sensual data into categories. The first stage, then, is a compound process of empirical observation and analysis of the objective world. The analysis is greatly facilitated if the perceiving subject is aware of the dialectical nature of the world and seeks to identify the forces in opposition, or contradictions, that characterize every aspect of being (see "On Contradiction").

In the second stage, the mind synthesizes the perceived data, makes judgments and inferences, and formulates ideas which go beyond material reality. This conceptual stage is rational and subjective. It enables man to change the objective world. He does this through a third, indispensable process: practice (or in Marxist terms, praxis). That is, he implements his ideas and tests their veracity and value with his labor. Labor, by changing material conditions, creates a new reality which occasions renewed perception, conception and practice indefinitely.

The process is not entirely open-ended, or undirected by preconceived goals. Maoists accept the Marxist analysis that history is moving in a certain direction, i.e., toward communism. This movement, they contend, is historically verifiable to the present and strongly indicates the trend of the future — a trend that is desirable but not inevitable. The Cultural Revolution is a strong assertion that there is no predetermined mechanical force leading history inexorably in a particular direction. Man makes his own history, though not under conditions chosen by himself. Marx's prediction about the future, therefore, can be regarded as a hypothesis to be proven by Chinese practice. The Chinese point to the Soviet Union as proof that there can be regress from, as well as progress toward, socialism.

If humans are to guide history by shaping the forces which affect them, rather than just reacting to those forces, they can do so most effectively by consciously using the dialectical method described above. The implications for education are obvious. Once the desired goal is established, education begins with the empirical study of a given situation, proceeds to an analysis of the situation and conceptualization of ideas for changing it, and then to the implementation of those ideas, testing them to see if they work. The next step is to sum up experience to ascertain the quality of the process — the accuracy of the perceptions, the relevance and applicability of the ideas, the effectiveness of the practice.

This method applies to all courses in the curriculum, even though some are less suited to direct practice than are others. The purpose of studying history, for instance, is to use the facts of the past as a foundation for theory and practice that will change the present. A Maoist seeks to know the world in order to change it. Education is very goal-oriented. If learning stops with simply knowing the world as it now exists (i.e., stops at the perceptual stage) it is necessarily conservative. Likewise, if ideas are formulated without proper study of existing conditions they too will be conservative, for their power to change existing reality corresponds to the proximity of their relationship to it. Dogmatism, the adherence to an idea unrelated to current reality, is just as much the enemy of revolution as are ideas based on an accurate perception of reality which seek only to maintain it.

Maoist pedagogy has been facilitated during the Cultural Revolution by a directive that schools on all levels "link up" with factories and farms, and that the latter "guide the specialization" of the former. Factories have been encouraged to establish their own schools, and schools, whenever possible, to set up workshops and agricultural plots. A regular work-study program now applies to all students equally. No longer is there a "dual school system."

To encourage the conceptualization of new ideas, the lecture method of classroom instruction has been deemphasized in favor of small group discussion and the cooperative working out of concrete problems.

In discussion groups, mutual criticism is a normal expectation. It is based on assessment of performance of a specific task, or of adherence to a well-defined principle, and is meant to be a constructive part of the learning process. Students are encouraged to be frank and open in their relationships with each other and with their teachers. Grievances and complaints are to be freely aired so that all problems are brought into the open where they can be discussed and resolved.

Because teachers are subject to constant scrutiny and criticism by students and by the local community, their status in the classroom depends on demonstrated capacity, and not on ascribed considerations of position independent of performance. A number of articles in the press proclaim that a new teacher-student relationship has resulted from the Cultural Revolution (see Document 13).

In discussing teaching methods and teacher-student relationships, it should be emphasized that what is prescribed is not always what is practiced. Recent visitors to China have been struck by the continuing formality and regimentation of classroom teaching and learning, and by the extensive use of rote learning and group recitation still evident in many schools. Study, work, and play seem to be highly structured and closely supervised, with little deviation from previous classroom behavior. These characteristics are deeply imbedded in Chinese educational tradition, long predating the Communist era. To the extent that they contradict the spirit of creativity and innovation implicit in Maoist pedagogy, efforts will no doubt continue to be made to change them. But change may not come easily or soon. The educational methods that have been strongly promoted since the Cultural Revolution are by no means new. The major principles had all been formulated in the Yenan period and tested in the Communist-held areas in the 1940s (see documents 27-32). They continued to affect educational practice in the two decades after 1949, even while countermeasures were sometimes exerting a greater influence. If they are realized now and in the future more completely than in the past, it will be because the Cultural Revolution has given old principles a new life.

Content

Educational content in China today is overtly political, or to use a current expression, politics is in command. This means simply that there is no pretense of moral or political neutrality. Educators work for the accomplishment of well-defined goals by following principles contained in the writings of Mao Tse-tung. Politics, in this context, is indistinguishable from ideology. Mao's thought provides a world view and an ethical orientation that serves both as a guide and as a standard by which particular activities can be assessed. As such it has been used since Mao's triumph in the Cultural Revolution as the foundation for all study.

It is true that since 1949 politics has always been in command and Mao's thought has always been the basis for study, but never has the logic of these principles been pushed so far. In schools no one is exempt from the study of Mao's thought; no one is "born red," nor is anyone hopelessly bourgeois or feudal, regardless of social background or experiences.

While some of Mao's writings are particularly relevant to specific problems, others provide a more general orientation applicable to all situations. Such are the "three constantly read articles" chosen from Mao's works early in the Cultural Revolution as short pieces representative of his ideology. They are "In Memory of Norman Bethune," "Serve the People," and "The Foolish Old Man Who Removed the Mountains." Their message is best illustrated by quoting briefly from each:

Comrade Bethune's spirit, his utter devotion to others without any thought of self, was shown in his great sense of responsibility in his work and his great warm-heartedness toward all comrades and the people. . . . We must all learn the spirit of absolute selflessness from him. With this spirit everyone can be very useful to the people. A man's ability may be great or small, but if he has this spirit, he is already noble-minded and pure, a man of moral integrity and above vulgar interests, a man who is of value to the people.

(From "In Memory of Norman Bethune," December 1939.)

If we have shortcomings, we are not afraid to have them pointed out and criticized, because we serve the people. Anyone, no matter who, may point out our shortcomings. If he is right, we will correct them. If what he proposes will benefit the people, we will act upon it. . . . In times of difficulty we must not lose sight of our achievements, must see the bright future and must pluck up our courage. The Chinese people are suffering; it is our duty to save them and we must exert ourselves in struggle. Wherever there is struggle, there is sacrifice, and death is a common occurrence. But we have the interests of the people and the sufferings of the great majority at heart, and when we die for the people, it is a worthy death.

(From "Serve the People," September 1944.)

There is an ancient Chinese fable called "The Foolish Old Man Who Removed the Mountains." It tells of an old man who lived in northern China long, long ago and was known as the Foolish Old Man of North Mountain. His house faced south and beyond his doorway stood the two great peaks, Taihang and Wangwu, obstructing the way. He called his sons, and hoe in hand they began to dig up these mountains with great determination. Another greybeard, known as the Wise Old Man, saw them and said derisively, "How silly of you to do this! It is quite impossible for you few

> to dig up these two huge mountains." The Foolish Old Man replied, "When I die, my sons will carry on; when they die, there will be my grandsons, and then their sons and grandsons, and so on to infinity. High as they are, the mountains cannot grow any higher and with every bit we dig, they will be that much lower. Why can't we clear them away?" Having refuted the Wise Old Man's wrong view, he went on digging every day, unshaken in his conviction. God was moved by this, and he sent down two angels, who carried the mountains away on their backs. Today, two big mountains lie like a dead weight on the Chinese people. One is imperialism, the other is feudalism. The Chinese Communist Party has long made up its mind to dig them up. We must persevere and work unceasingly, and we, too, will touch God's heart. Our God is none other than the masses of the Chinese people. If they stand up and dig together with us, why can't these two mountains be cleared away?
>
> (From "The Foolish Old Man Who Removed the Mountains," June 1945.)

The essays "On Practice," "On Contradiction," "On the Correct Handling of Contradictions Among the People," and "Concerning Methods of Leadership" contribute a theory of history, an analytical technique, and the mass-line work style to the values presented in the "three constantly read articles." Other essays by Mao, including "Combat Liberalism" and his famous "Talks at the Yenan Forum on Literature and Art," which explicitly addresses the question "for whom?", have also been widely distributed, as have lesser quantities of European Marxist writings. Marx's "Communist Manifesto," <u>Critique of the Gotha Programme</u>, <u>The Civil War in France</u>; Engels' <u>Anti-Dühring</u>; and Lenin's <u>State and Revolution</u> and <u>Left-Wing Communism, An Infantile Disorder</u>, among other works, have been read in conjunction with Mao's works and are quoted with increasing frequency in Chinese journals, showing an ideological continuity from Marx to Mao, "the greatest Marxist-Leninist of our era."

Mao's insistence that theory and practice be closely related applies to study of his works just as it does to all others. In his "Foreword" (now expunged) to the second edition of _Quotations from Chairman Mao Tse-tung_, Lin Piao provides a study guide:

> In studying the works of Chairman Mao, one should have specific problems in mind, study and apply his works in a creative way, combine study with application, first study what must be urgently applied so as to get quick results, and strive hard to apply what one is studying. In order really to master Mao Tse-tung's thought, it is essential to study many of Chairman Mao's basic concepts over and over again, and it is best to memorize important statements and study and apply them repeatedly.

The sterile, pedantic exercise of memorizing and chanting Mao's works without reference to application was a common phenomenon during the earlier years of the Cultural Revolution, and ironically, much of it is now attributed to the ultra-leftist influence of Lin Piao. It contradicts an essential aspect of Mao's thought, cited here from "On Practice," that is repeated time and again, using different language, in Mao's writings:

> If we have a correct theory but merely prate about it, pigeonhole it and do not put it into practice, then that theory, however good, is of no significance.

Mao's thought, then, is meaningful only in conjunction with other courses and with work. In a general discussion of education on all levels it is impossible to describe various courses from elementary school through college, particularly when the emphasis is on local diversity and innovation, but we can indicate principles and practice common to all levels.

To begin with, the number of courses has been reduced in accordance with the principle "few but essential" (_shao erh ching_).

The idea is to concentrate on courses which relate most closely to China's immediate and essential needs. It is better to learn a few things well and build on that knowledge than to be superficially exposed to many subjects.

In elementary schools the basic courses are Chinese language and arithmetic. At higher levels, emphasis has been placed on technical courses, though courses in social science, history, the arts and humanities are being slowly reconstructed to conform with the imperatives of the Cultural Revolution.

Militia training is part of the curriculum in all schools in compliance with Mao's directive that everyone must "prepare for war, prepare for natural disaster, and serve the people." It is primarily a precaution against attack from the Soviet Union, but it also is regarded as a means of engendering a spirit of unity and cooperation.

Much of the technical curriculum follows directly from the association of schools with various work units. In some higher-level schools, students bring problems from their particular factory or commune which the class attempts to analyze and solve. General principles are learned from the study of particular cases.

Course content of a more abstract nature, derived mainly from reading books, has undergone a thorough review in the past several years. Textbooks are all being rewritten to bring them up to date, adjust their political content, and relate them to the needs and interests of those now favored for admission. Foreign textbooks have come under particular scrutiny. The followers of Liu Shao-ch'i in education offices are denounced for indiscriminate borrowing from abroad and uncritically adopting Western (particularly Russian) materials. Their "foreign slave mentality" is blamed for stifling creativity and growth. The Maoists assert that all textual material, regardless of the topic, is the product of a particular society at a particular period of history, and reflects particular class interests. There is no reason why China should follow the same path. She should rather "let foreign things serve China" through a process of critical selection; be self-reliant and not become dependent on either foreign products or foreign expertise. Educational arrangements such as the Cambridge Degree Program, which strives to give a proper British education to Indians and Africans, or American educational programs in countries like the Philippines, which give advanced technological training to a privileged few, are worse than no education at all in the Chinese view, for they often leave the students ill-prepared psychologically and technically to deal with the most pressing and elementary problems in their own country. The "brain drain" is a direct result of these semi-colonial educational programs.

The rewriting of textbooks is a cooperative effort. Students, teachers, workers and others from the community often participate. Major textbooks in some fields are being rewritten under the direction of the various institutes in the Academy of Sciences.

On the elementary and secondary levels much educational material is developed locally so that it will be familiar and applicable to the local situation. In technical courses at higher levels, texts are being rewritten as part of the teaching and learning process. The idea is constantly to improve them — to simplify those parts which "make mysteries of simple things," and always attempt to push theory to a higher level. The attempt to go beyond the given, to change and improve rather than just to accept and use, is crucial to the educational method, as we have seen, and suggests that rewriting textbooks will be a continuing project.

Courses in history and the humanities have been slow to recover from the criticism launched against them in the early years of the Cultural Revolution. The debate on literature and art, which precipitated the Cultural Revolution, continues to be of central importance, but the dimensions of the conflict have been reduced to questions of form and content. The purpose of artistic creation, as defined by Mao's 1942 "Talks at the Yenan Forum on Literature and Art," has been reaffirmed as the definitive guide for writers, artists, and their students. Art and literature regarded as bourgeois has been criticized and repudiated. Henceforth, literature and art must reflect proletarian values and provide revolutionary inspiration. Writers and artists have spent long periods of time in factories and farms working with laboring people and learning from them; and concurrently, working people have been encouraged to express themselves artistically. Both professionals and amateurs are ostensibly engaged in an effort to create a new, proletarian art and literature.

So far, the results have been meager for a country of perhaps 700 million people. The limited number of works published to date are rather stereotyped in form and content and do not indicate an upsurge in mass creativity that is at all commensurate with worker and peasant contributions to applied technology. The teaching of literature and art in the schools puts more emphasis on performance than on creativity. In art and theater classes, for example, children are taught to copy a model rather than to express themselves creatively. Again, this is in accord with Chinese tradition, but not with the Maoist stress on innovation. There seems to be an unresolved contradiction between the desire for mass artistic creativity and the restrictive guidelines placed on it.

History is a subject in which there has been considerable innovation, but little output as yet. Since 1972 there have been a number of articles emphasizing the importance of historical study. Historical research has proceeded from the premise that the masses are the makers of history. The relationship between master and slave, ruler and ruled, and hypotheses on their role in history have been debated and explored, and they have produced numerous insights that were ignored or deliberately obfuscated in earlier histories. Historical studies have been mainly focused on the recent past, but archaeology, which continued without interruption during the Cultural Revolution and which has benefited greatly from "basic construction" projects in the past several years, has contributed significantly to knowledge and interpretation of the more distant past.

Historical studies in China since 1949 have been circumscribed by certain conventions shared by other communist nations — for instance, the Marxist conjecture that society passes through a series of historical stages characterized as primitive communist, slave, feudal, bourgeois, socialist, and eventually communist. A good argument can be made that this schema applies only to Europe and does not fit Chinese tradition without considerable distortion, and that indeed Marx recognized that when he characterized Chinese society as oriental despotism. It can also be argued that Marx's stage analysis was only a hypothesis subject to refinement or change after further historical research. It was not until Stalin suppressed the concept of the "Asiatic mode of production" and decreed in the 1930s that the stage theory be definitive for the world that it was so applied.

If this convention has inhibited Chinese historical studies, other Marxist historical tools have been very productive. Class analysis has put the majority of the population into history for the first time as acting human beings and not just mindless objects in the hands of a few rulers and heroes. The historical dialectic and economic analysis have broken the spell of the old Chinese cyclical theory of history and moralistic interpretations of growth and decay that served the interests of the Confucian ruling classes, and bound historical interpretation as tightly as the Marxist stage theory. The prospects for substantial contributions by Chinese historians in the next several years are very good.

Probably the greatest innovation in nontechnical subjects stems from the directive that students in liberal arts colleges should "take the whole society as their factory." Students and teachers have conducted social surveys in communities and work units, identifying aspects of class struggle, learning from the people and, in turn, teaching them revolutionary theory, and writing survey reports and criticism articles. The reports are usually read to the group surveyed and revised on the basis of their comments.

Social surveys are not limited to any particular aspect of society. They range from investigation of literary and theatrical production in one area (see Document 26) to the daily life in a production brigade in another. By combining sociological investigation with teaching and with learning to write, they constitute a rather full course of study on contemporary society. The ultimate objective, as always, is to change society. Learning is directly related to application. The survey results are published or used in some other way to point out problems and suggest remedies.

There is little doubt that more courses will be added in the next several years; foreign language study, for instance, will become much more important, but unless there is a counter-revolution, the objectives and the methodology which shape the curriculum will continue to make it very unorthodox from a Western point of view. And that is just the point — China is going her own way. Educational principles and policies differ from those of industrially advanced countries because conditions differ, but even more, because China's goals differ fundamentally.

* * *

It is too early to assess the results of the recently implemented changes in China's educational system, but it is certain that the forecasters of doom who, in the early years of the Cultural Revolution, asserted that the attack on the educational system had irreparably damaged China from every rational viewpoint, were wrong. Even those who think of education as essentially a vehicle for developing "manpower" have had to reassess their earlier dour predictions. They may not approve of the ultimate objectives or the methods of the Maoists, but insofar as their concern is with increased production of material wealth, they are confronted by the apparent contribution of the new educational system in accomplishing that aim, even while pursuing social goals by means originally thought to be antithetical to it.

Unquestionably a number of problems and uncertainties remain which could upset the current social-economic synthesis and the mass-line attack on elitism and class privilege. The relationship between political, vocational and traditional academic courses is still in flux, as is the relationship between the personnel representing these three interests in the schools. The relationship between local self-reliance and central aid and control is another delicate issue where no firm guidelines are appropriate or possible at present or for a long time to come. Numerous problems will undoubtedly arise as China industrializes and her educational system, in accordance with the dialectic described above, becomes more complex. It may then become more difficult to keep an elite of specialists and professionals from taking control and asserting their own interests again. Mao Tse-tung himself has stated that there will probably have to be several cultural revolutions before the socialist ideal is realized.

What one thinks of the current revolution in education depends, in the final analysis, on the degree to which one is sympathetic with the ultimate objectives of Maoist Communism, and on the subsidiary question of how effective the methods now being employed are in promoting those objectives. But regardless of the conclusions individuals may reach, Chinese theory and practice is bound to be provocative and stimulating for everyone seriously interested in education or in social reform, for it is the most radical approach to problems endemic in the world today.

Revolutionary Education in China

DOCUMENTS AND COMMENTARY

Peter J. Seybolt

I

History of the Struggle Over Educational Policy

1

CHRONOLOGY OF THE TWO-ROAD STRUGGLE ON THE EDUCATIONAL FRONT IN THE PAST SEVENTEEN YEARS*

Educational Revolution

> "Wind and rain enshroud Mount Chung in yellowish green,
> A grand army of one million crosses the Yangtze."

Chairman Mao, our great teacher, leader, commander, and helmsman, commands a formidable revolutionary army of hundreds of millions to unleash a general offensive against Liu Shao-ch'i, who is the foremost authority in the Party taking the capitalist road. Hundreds of millions of people concentrate their fire to pursue and attack in order to criticize thoroughly the revisionist line Liu Shao-ch'i has promoted in politics, economics, culture, and education. The Great Proletarian Cultural Revolution has entered a brand new stage of decisive war!

In the seventeen years since the founding of the nation, there has existed on China's educational front, as on the other fronts, the struggle between two classes, two roads, and two command headquarters, as well as the struggle between Chairman Mao's proletarian educational line and the counterrevolutionary revisionist educational line represented by Liu Shao-ch'i. This

---

*"Shih-ch'i nien lai chiao-yü chan-hsien shang liang t'iao lu-hsien tou-cheng ta-shih-chi." Chiao-yü ke-ming, May 6, 1967.

struggle is quite complex, devious, and violent.

With a view to enabling the comrades to have a brief understanding of the general status of the two-road struggle in educational work so that they may further expose the counterrevolutionary revisionist educational line represented by Liu Shao-ch'i and defend Chairman Mao's educational line, we have compiled this "Chronology." Because of the insufficiency of data at our disposal and our low level of ideology and understanding, defects, errors, and omissions are inevitable. We welcome criticisms and corrections from our comrades.

1. The Period of Rehabilitation and Growth of People's Education (1949-1952)

The east is red; the sun rises. In 1949, the motherland, in the abyss of distress, stood up like a giant!

The period from 1949 to 1952 was the period of China's national economic rehabilitation. Under Chairman Mao's leadership, such political movements as the resist-America and aid Korea campaign, land reform, suppression of counterrevolutionaries, and the ideological transformation of intellectuals were launched throughout the nation. At the same time, industrial and agricultural production was rehabilitated actively in order to heal the wounds of war and to make preparations for the planned development of the national economy.

In what direction is the education of new China headed? Chairman Mao suggested that "the old educational system, educational contents, and pedagogy be reformed systematically" and that the "new educational experience of the old Liberated Areas should form the basis." On the other hand, Liu Shao-ch'i, Lu Ting-i, etc., did their utmost to uphold the old educational system and transplanted the Soviet Union's revisionist educational system to resist Chairman Mao's directives concerning educational revolution. This was the first engagement of the struggle between two classes, two roads, and two command headquarters on the educational front.

1. The people of China have stood up! On June 15, 1949, Chairman Mao pointed out in his speech at the preparatory meeting of the new Political Consultative Conference: "Once the destiny of China is in the hands of the people, China will, like the sun rising in the east, use its splendorous light to illuminate the great earth, thus rapidly washing off the mud and polluted waters left by the reactionary regime, healing the ravages of war, and constructing a strong and prosperous People's Republic both in name and in fact." After the inauguration of new China, it would be necessary "to devote maximal energy to rehabilitate and develop people's economic enterprises and, at the same time, to rehabilitate and develop people's cultural and educational enterprises."

On September 21 Chairman Mao further pointed out in his inaugural address at the Chinese People's Political Consultative Conference: "With the advent of the high tide of economic construction, there is bound to emerge a high tide of cultural construction. The era in which the Chinese people were considered by others as uncivilized has passed; we will appear before the world as a people with a high degree of culture."

2. Chairman Mao pointed out the direction for new China's education. In what direction is the education of new China headed? Our great helmsman Chairman Mao has pointed out the direction. In September 1949 it was pointed out in the "Common Program of the Chinese People's Political Consultative Conference": "The People's Government should systematically reform the old educational system, educational contents, and pedagogical methods."

In the summing up of the First National Educational Work Conference, convened in the latter part of December 1949, it was clearly pointed out, pursuant to Chairman Mao's direction: "The education of new China should use the new educational experiences of the old Liberated Areas as the basis, should absorb the useful experiences of the old education, and should make use of the experiences of the Soviet Union."

To use the new educational experiences of the old Liberated Areas as the basis and to develop schools of the "K'angta"

[Anti-Japanese University] type was then the direction for the development of new China's education.

Based on Chairman Mao's directive, K'angta type schools were established in the large Liberated Areas and in some of the provinces and municipalities (such as North China University, East China Military and Political University), thus inheriting the educational experience of the old Liberated Areas.

In 1950 Chairman Mao wrote in his message for the inaugural issue of People's Education [Jen-min chiao-yü]: "To rehabilitate and develop people's education is one of the important tasks at the present time."

On June 6, in his report entitled "Struggle to Secure a Basic Favorable Turn of the Nation's Financial and Economic Conditions" to the Third Plenum of the Central Committee of the Seventh Party Congress, Chairman Mao again mentioned the task of reforming the old education. He said: "[We must] systematically and persistently undertake the work of reforming the original school educational enterprises and the old social and cultural enterprises in order to win over all patriotic intellectuals to serve the people. On this question, the idea of procrastination and reluctance to reform is not right; nor is the idea of trying to launch reform by crude methods because of impatience.

This, then, was the bugle to open fire on the old educational system!

3. Beginning of educational reform. Once Mao Tse-tung thought was grasped by the masses, it immediately produced stupendous material strength.

Beginning in 1950, we took over from the imperialists and the Kuomintang reactionaries some 310,000 universities and colleges, middle schools and primary schools, thus recovering the power of education.

The Kuomintang reactionaries' fascist administrative system in the schools was abolished; fascist education and the domination of special agents over the students were also eliminated.

Such courses as "Party Doctrine" [tang-i] in the schools

during the period of Kuomintang reactionary rule were abolished; courses on Marxism-Leninism were opened to launch revolutionary ideological and political education among the students.

Adjustments of institutes and departments and pedagogical reforms were made in higher institutions.

Extension [rapid-course] middle schools for industry and agriculture were established so that worker and peasant cadres, industrial workers, and demobilized soldiers might have the opportunity to enter higher institutes for further education.

The number of resident students in higher, middle and primary schools increased rapidly.

All these achievements were scored under the guidance of Chairman Mao's proletarian educational line.

4. With a view to reforming the old education and bringing about the healthy growth of the new generation, Chairman Mao has advanced the policy of "health first and study second."

In most of the schools under the influence of the old-style regularization there was a proliferation of courses; the teaching tasks were heavy and the burdens of the students were unduly great, thus resulting in poor health conditions. With respect to this question, Chairman Mao wrote on June 19, 1950, to the Minister of Education Ma Hsü-lun: "It is necessary for the schools to pay attention to health first and study second. Where nutrition is insufficient, funds should be increased. The time for study and meetings should be curtailed drastically." Nonetheless, the leadership of the Ministry of Education blocked the chairman's directive; it did not convey it downward and failed to take any measures, and the problem was thus unsolved.

On January 15, 1951, Chairman Mao wrote Ma Hsü-lun again, pointing out: "The problem of the health of students that I discussed with you before deserves attention; I suggest that administrative measures by adopted to resolve this problem specifically." "I deem that the policy of health first and study second is correct."

Because of Chairman Mao's repeated emphasis on the question

of student health, Minister of Education Ma Hsü-lun and Vice Minister Ch'ien Chun-jui had no alternative but to discuss it. However, Ma Hsü-lun continued to resist Chairman Mao's directive. At the National Middle School Education Conference held in March 1951, he mentioned only "health first," but omitted "study second." He also said: "To consummate teaching work forms the central phase of school work. It behooves all organizations, personnel, and activities of the school to revolve around this center, to cater to the demands of pedagogy, and to strive for the satisfactory fulfillment of the pedagogical plan."

5. Liu Shao-ch'i and company boycotted Chairman Mao's correct directive on the reform of the old education. Contrary to Chairman Mao's proletarian educational line, China's number one authority taking the capitalist line, Liu Shao-ch'i, was bent on leading new China's education onto the sinister road of capitalism.

a) Advocacy of "all-out Sovietization."

Liu Shao-ch'i opposed Chairman Mao's correct policy of using the educational experience of the old Liberated Areas to serve as the basis to reform old education; he advocated the thorough adoption of the Soviet Union's revisionist educational line.

Even as early as the eve of national liberation, Liu Shao-ch'i, during his meeting with the Central Committee of the Soviet Communist Party, asked the Soviet Union to send a group of experts to help China set up the Harbin Polytechnic University and the China People's University. These two schools would be used as "models" for the reform of China's higher education, thus completely abandoning the educational experience gained in the old Liberated Areas.

On the question of learning from the Soviet Union, Liu Shao-ch'i advanced the policy of "transplanting first and transforming later" [hsien-pan hou-hua]. On October 3, 1950, in his speech at the inauguration ceremony of China People's University, Liu advocated the study of Russian and said this was "replete with decisive significance"; he stressed reliance on

Soviet experts, "without whose help our university cannot be consummated; without Soviet faculty it would be impossible to garner so much new knowledge."

Counterrevolutionary revisionist Lu Ting-i has always held that there was no university in the old Liberated Areas, thereby negating K'angta's educational experience. When Liu Shao-ch'i introduced the revisionist educational line of learning from the Soviet Union in toto, he was supported fully by Lu Ting-i.

Counterrevolutionary revisionist Lin Feng (then serving as chairman of the Northeast Administrative Committee) was even more enthusiastic in advocating complete emulation of the education of the Soviet Union. He directed the vice director of the education department of the Northeast region, who was then Tung Chun-ts'ai, to first of all transplant to China the Soviet Union's teaching material, educational system, and pedagogical methods, which were later promoted in all of China through the advocacy of Lu Ting-i and Ch'ien Chun-jui.

b) All kinds of obstructions were applied to the reform of the old educational system, educational contents, and pedagogical methods.

Chairman Mao's directive concerning the "systematic reform of old educational systems, contents, and pedagogical methods" has been consistently obstructed by Liu Shao-ch'i and others so that it could not be implemented.

In the drafts of the "Temporary Plan of Pedagogy for Middle Schools" and the "Temporary School Calendar for Middle Level Schools," promulgated by the Ministry of Education on August 1, 1950, with the exception of abolishing such reactionary courses as "Citizenship" and increasing political courses, in all disciplines the courses established during the Kuomintang period were basically followed. It was further stipulated that productive labor and social activities "be geared systematically to the regular classes in order to achieve the aim of consummating the regular courses."

As for the contents of instruction, according to the "Decision on Textbooks for Middle and Primary Schools for the Fall of 1950," promulgated by the Ministry of Education on July 5, 1950, it was stipulated that except in language and history disciplines the old textbooks of the Kuomintang period were to continue to be used.

In March 1951 Liu Shao-ch'i stated in his directive to the Ministry of Education: "It is necessary to emphasize teaching in the school; administrative work is to serve teaching; the system of the school principal assuming the responsibility should be changed to the system of the principal's responsibility system." He further directed that "the contents of political courses should teach more comprehensive political knowledge," and teaching materials should "be based on Soviet textbooks," thus harping on a theme that was totally opposed to Chairman Mao's.

With Liu Shao-ch'i's support, the "Decision Concerning the Reform of the School System," drafted by the Ministry of Education, was promulgated by the State Council. It basically upheld the old educational system, and no basic reforms were made therein.

On March 18, 1952, the "Draft of Temporary Regulations for Middle Schools" and the "Draft of Temporary Regulations for Primary Schools" were promulgated by the Ministry of Education for experimental implementation. These regulations clearly prescribed that the schools implement the policy of "overall development of intellect, morality, physique, and esthetics," thus further establishing the bourgeois old-style regularized educational system and beginning to transplant the pedagogical plans of the Soviet Union for middle and primary schools as well as Soviet teaching materials for some of the disciplines.

On November 15 the Ministry of Education further issued the "Directive on the Rectification and Development of Popular-Management Primary Schools," in which it was stipulated that when the masses establish any schools they would be approved only after they have found sufficient funds to maintain operations for three years, thus restricting the development of popular-management educational enterprises.

At the instigation of Liu Shao-ch'i and Lu Ting-i, the old

Chinese bourgeois educational system and the Soviet revisionist educational system began to join forces, and the educational system of the old Liberated Areas was completely negated.

c) Opposition to education serving proletarian politics.

Chairman Mao has always stressed that education must serve proletarian politics and revolutionary struggle. In the "Directive Concerning the Problem of Revamping K'angta," he pointed out: "Political education forms a central phase; there must not be too many courses; class education and Party education and work must be greatly strengthened."

At the beginning of liberation, the broad masses of revolutionary teachers and students responded to the appeals of the Party Central Committee and Chairman Mao by actively participating in social and political activities and in the resist-America and aid-Korea campaign, as well as by doing propaganda work for the land reform and the suppression of counterrevolutionaries. This had important significance in accelerating the revolutionary struggle then, in training revolutionary successors, and in reforming the old educational system.

Nevertheless, Liu Shao-ch'i and company were opposed to the emphasis on politics. At a cadre conference in Tientsin in 1949, Liu Shao-ch'i said: "For the time being, it is important to study culture and technology, while politics will be studied in the future." In 1951, in his directive to the Ministry of Education, he said: "It is necessary to stress pedagogy," thus opposing participation in social and political activities on the part of the students. Based on Liu Shao-ch'i's black directive, Ma Hsü-lun publicly criticized the students for their participation in political activities at the National Middle-Level Educational Conference held in March 1951. He said: "At present there is a prevalent phenomenon that is detrimental to and even hampers the teaching of classes, and this must be firmly overcome."

The editorial of the August 1, 1951, issue of *People's Education* also regards student participation in political activities as a deviation and slanders it as a "chaotic phenomenon," thus opposing political commandership.

6. Chairman Mao personally unleashed criticisms on the motion pictures The Life of Wu Hsün and The Secret History of the Ch'ing Palace in order to unleash the struggle between two roads and two classes in the ideological sphere.

After criticism of The Life of Wu Hsün, a struggle was also waged on the educational front. The slave ideology of "begging to develop education" disseminated by The Life of Wu Hsün was criticized; this was tantamount to surrendering to the feudal landlords. Also criticized was the "life education" promoted by T'ao Hsing-chih, the bourgeois educator who had lauded the "Wu Hsün spirit" before, and also the "living education" of compradore bourgeois educator Ch'en Hao-ch'in. This was the first attack on bourgeois educational ideology.

Thereafter, from November 1951 to September 1952, teachers of colleges and middle and primary schools throughout China launched the ideological transformation movement to criticize bourgeois individualist ideology and to establish the ideology of serving the people. Most of the teachers of higher institutions were also organized to take part in such political movements as the land reform, suppression of counterrevolutionaries, and the three-anti and five-anti campaigns.

2. The Period of Affirmation of Socialist Educational Policy (1953-1957)

At the end of 1952 Chairman Mao advanced the General Line for the transitional period. Beginning with 1953, China entered the period of the First Five-Year Plan of construction. In 1956 China had completed the socialist transformation of agriculture, the handicraft industry, and capitalist industry and commerce. In 1957 the all-people's antirightist struggle and the rectification movement were launched, thus bringing the socialist revolution to the political and ideological fronts.

On the educational front a handful of people in authority in the Party, who were headed by Liu Shao-ch'i and took the capitalist line with a view to consolidating the "new democratic order" and restoring capitalism, advocated all-out and systematic emulation of the Soviet Union, energetically promoted the revisionist educational line, and boycotted basic reforms in educational enterprises. The contraband of the Soviet Union's revisionist education became rampant in China. Geared to these problems, Chairman Mao advanced in 1957 a proletarian educational policy, creatively developed the Marxist educational theory, and pointed out the correct direction for China's education.

1. In order to adapt to the needs of the socialist revolution, Chairman Mao again gave directives on educational reform.

On May 17, 1953, Chairman Mao convened a meeting of the Central Committee Politburo, during which he issued a series of important directions for educational work.

Chairman Mao said: "To develop a school properly, the problem of leadership backbone in the school must be resolved. With a strong principal, good teachers will be produced.

"The so-called teaching reform is the reform of educational contents and teaching methods. Consequently, it is necessary to revise and compile teaching materials and to compile pedagogical methods.

"In primary school education, labor education should be stressed."

At the meeting, Chairman Mao sharply criticized Hsi Chung-hsün, who was vice director of the State Council's Cultural and Educational Committee and also one of Liu Shao-ch'i's followers. Hsi Chung-hsün opposed the curriculum reform; he stopped the promotion of the five-year primary school system and did away with the popular-management primary schools, which were to enable the children of poor and lower-middle peasants to attend school locally. With respect to these problems, the chairman pointed out: "The document concerning the consecutive five-year primary school system is not bad. It is necessary to develop schools with diversified methods, and one should not try to have uniformity. Popular-management primary schools should be allowed.

2. Chairman [Mao] issued the "three good" appeal.

At the Third National Congress of the Youth League held in June 1953, Chairman Mao issued the "three-good" appeal.

Chairman Mao said: "I wish to say a few words on the youth: first, to congratulate them on their good health; second, to congratulate them on their good study; third, to congratulate them on their good work.

"It is incumbent on the new China to think of the youth and to be concerned with the growth of the young generation. Youth want to study and work, but the period of youth is also one in which the body grows. Thus, one must give ample regard to the two facets of their work and study and their recreation, physical education, and rest."

3. Liu Shao-ch'i and company wanted to promote the Soviet revisionist educational system and attempted to lead China's education onto the revisionist road.

In 1953, at the rally to celebrate the third anniversary of the signing of the Sino-Soviet Treaty of Friendship, Alliance, and Mutual Assistance, Liu Shao-ch'i did his best to laud and support the Soviet Union. He said: "China has already dispatched hundreds of students to study in the Soviet Union and more will be sent there later. Many Soviet professors are also teaching in higher institutions in China. The courses offered in Chinese schools will also be revamped gradually, applying the advanced experience of the Soviet Union."

Under Liu Shao-ch'i's black directive of "transplanting first and transforming later" in regard to emulation of the Soviet Union, Ch'ien Chün-jui, who was then the responsible Party and group person in the Ministry of Education, went even further by advancing the revisionist slogans "In order to learn comprehensively the experience of the Soviet Union, let us transplant it here first," and "Dogmatism first and then coordinate it with the practice of China.

In July 1953 the Ministry of Education promulgated teaching plans for middle schools and teaching outlines in which the teaching plans and outlines of related disciplines for middle schools of the Soviet Union were adopted in their entirety.

At the meeting of the responsible cadres of higher institutions in China, held under the auspices of the Ministry of Higher Education in April 1954, the counterrevolutionary revisionist Yang Hsiu-feng said that the fact that great achievements have been garnered by the China People's University was due "mainly to its all-out and systematic as well as wholehearted emulation of the Soviet Union." Under the guidance of this ideology, the teaching plans of some 300 special courses and the teaching outlines for 3-4,000 courses used by higher institutions of the Soviet Union were used in higher institutions in China, and enormous numbers of textbooks and teaching materials were translated. Beginning with 1954, all college students had to study Russian, and the teaching of English was suspended.

Thereafter, China's school system was also prolonged comparatively. In 1955 most of the higher institutions had changed from the four-year system to a five-year system, while some schools stretched their program to six years. Lu Ting-i personally launched an eight-year medical college. The worker and peasant rapid-course middle schools were also suspended.

In 1956 the Ministry of Education further imitated the Soviet Union by revising teaching plans, teaching outlines, and textbooks for middle and primary schools. Under the advocacy of the counterrevolutionary revisionist Hu Ch'iao-mu, the Soviet system was followed in language teaching in middle schools by teaching "literature" and "Han language" as separate disciplines. Even in teaching geography in middle schools, the Soviet system was copied by dividing it minutely into physical geography, world geography, Chinese geography, Chinese economic geography, and foreign economic geography. The courses in middle schools were also increased further: the class with the most courses might have as many as fifteen, who attended thirty-three hours each week.

During the period 1954-1956, the Ministry of Higher Education also introduced a set of the Soviet Union's revisionist rules and regulations. Among the regulations drafted were "Temporary Measures for the Workloads and Working Days of Teachers of Higher Institutions," "Regulations for Academic Degrees, Academic Titles, and Honorary Titles," "Regulations on the Training of Associate Doctors [fu-po-shih] and Research Fellows (Postgraduates)," thus engaging in material stimulations, enlarging the three great differentiations, and implementing all-out Sovietization.

In July 1956 Liu Shao-ch'i stated in a speech at the Higher Party School that "to learn socialist experiences there is only the Soviet Union."

In 1957 the Ministry of Education sponsored the "Exhibition of the Soviet Union's National Education," thus further peddling the black contraband of the Soviet Union.

4. Resisting Chairman Mao's directive, Liu Shao-ch'i allowed bourgeois intellectuals to dominate the schools.

At a meeting of the Politburo in 1953, Chairman Mao pointed out that it was necessary to strengthen the basic leadership in higher institutions and that a large number of cadres should be recruited to compile new teaching materials. Nonetheless, people like Liu, Teng, and Lu were reluctant to carry out the directive; they also took the opportunity to give the leadership power to bourgeois intellectuals. Both Lu Ting-i and Lin Feng supported the Ministry of Education's action to recruit middle and primary school teachers whose ideology had not yet been successfully remolded. Yeh Sheng-t'ao, who before liberation was the proprietor of the K'ai-ming Bookstore, was asked to recommend some bourgeois specialists who had compiled textbooks for middle and primary schools in old China and also some bourgeois reactionary academic authorities to form the People's Educational Publishing Society and revise the teaching materials.

In March 1956, when Liu Shao-ch'i was being briefed on the work of the Ministry of Higher Education, he said that "professors may also be appointed as vice presidents." Thereafter, many bourgeois authorities were appointed college presidents. A great many of them were classified as rightists in 1957. Yang Hsiu-feng also did his best to advocate "educational development by depending upon veteran teachers."

5. Rampancy of the bourgeois educational ideology of "intellect first."

Following the revisionist tide of the blind introduction of Soviet experience, the Soviet revisionist educational theory — the education of K'ai-lo-fu [?] — also spread to China and became widely disseminated. The bourgeois educational ideology of "intellect first" and "teaching overrides everything" became rampant in China, thereby causing education to be alienated from politics and to become a tool for capitalist restoration.

On March 1, 1953, People's Education published an editorial entitled "Teaching Work Is the Central Task Which Overrides All." It charged participation in social activities by students with being a "chaotic phenomenon," thereby restricting the students from taking part in social struggle.

On November 26 of the same year, the State Council adopted the "Directive Concerning Rectification and Revamping of Primary Education," drafted by the Ministry of Education; it reiterated that "teaching is the central task which overrides everything else" and stated that "the deviation of excessive participation in social activities and nonteaching activities inside the schools by teachers and students must be corrected."

On June 23, 1954, the Peking black municipal Party committee under P'eng Chen's domination fabricated a revisionist educational program entitled "Decision Concerning the Enhancement of the Quality and Quantity of Peking's Middle and Primary Education." In this decision every effort was made to advocate "intellect first" and "material stimuli." It also stated that the salary of the teachers should be appraised on the basis of the study records of students. On August 7 this black program was circularized throughout the nation by the Ministry of Education for implementation. This was the black program of the counterrevolutionary clique of the old municipal committee to bring about capitalist restoration on the educational front.

In June 1956 this set of measures was completely affirmed by Liu Shao-ch'i in his directive to the Ministry of Education. He further said that "without educational national salvation there can be no industrial national salvation"; "universal education is still not too urgent now; the question now is still higher education and the need for specialists." "Dogmas should be studied, classics should be read," and "even The General History of China may also be read." Thus he upheld the old and opposed any reform.

During 1956 the handful of men in authority in the Party who took the capitalist road also distorted the Party's policy on intellectuals and its appeal for scientific pursuit by advocating that the youth should "seek the title of associate doctoral degree," thus guiding young students to become expert but not red, as well as to pursue personal fame and profit only.

6. Abolition of political classes.

The Soviet revisionist educational line opposed an emphasis on politics and would not launch proletarian political and ideological education among the students. Thus, during this period, Liu Shao-ch'i and those in authority in the educational circle who took the capitalist road utilized the Soviet revisionist educational system to oppose the use of education to serve proletarian politics.

During the early period after liberation, political classes were set up extensively in the schools. After the emulation of the Soviet Union, the politics class for the first year of junior middle school was abolished in 1953; in 1954 that of the second year in junior middle schools was cut; in 1955 political classes for the first and second years of senior high school were successively eliminated. By 1956, with the exception of the third year of senior middle school, in which a section of the "Constitution" class was opened each week as having been learned from the Soviet Union, political classes for all other years were entirely cancelled.

On February 10, 1955, the Ministry of Education issued the "Order Concerning the Promulgation of Regulations to Be Observed by Primary School Students." This order introduced a series of petty study disciplines and regulations of daily life to shackle the students, thus leading them to the sinister road of political apathy and meticulousness in small matters.

The State Council and the Ministry of Education, under Liu Shao-ch'i's aegis, decreed time and again "to rectify the deviation in which teachers and students participate excessively in social activities and in nonteaching activities of the school." As a result, students shut themselves up to read books; they failed to approach workers and peasants, did not participate in the practice of the Three Great Revolutionary Movements, and became detached from politics and from social class struggle.

7. Adoption of "general technological education."

On May 17, 1953, Chairman Mao suggested at a meeting of the Central Committee Politburo that "labor education should be stressed" in schools. Nonetheless, Liu Shao-ch'i and those in authority in educational circles who took the capitalist road used the revisionist educational line of the Soviet Union to oppose Chairman Mao's view that education should be coordinated with productive labor.

On August 8, 1954, Tung Chun-ts'ai published in People's Daily [Jen-min jih-pao] his article entitled "Endeavor to Train Fully Developed Members of Socialist Society." In it he peddled the revisionist educational theory of the Soviet Union by saying that "study per se should be regarded as a principal form of labor; through the teaching in the various disciplines, the labor viewpoint and labor habit of students should be trained. They should also acquire basic knowledge and techniques in industrial and agricultural production."

In 1955, at the cultural and educational work conference convened by the second staff office of the State Council, Lin Feng did his best to advocate the Soviet Union's general technological education. Under the pretext of "systematically implementing basic education of productive technology," he used technological education to replace Chairman Mao's labor education. Thereafter the "sinister style" of the so-called implementation of basic education on productive technology prevailed. In the primary school teaching plan promulgated by the Ministry of Education in September, with a view to carrying out technical education on basic production, manual labor classes were added to all classes of the primary school. In October a Chinese middle and primary school teachers' delegation was sent to the Soviet Union, led by Vice Minister of Education

Ch'en Tseng-ku, in order to study the methods of implementing general technological education.

In February 1956 Ch'en Tseng-ku wrote his "Report on a Visit to the Soviet Union and Its Achievements," in which he praised glowingly the "advanced experience" of the Soviet Union. Members of the delegation also went out to all parts of China to give reports, thus further stirring up a high tide for blind emulation of Soviet experience.

In March the Ministry of Education revised its plan for middle schools, in which "political classes" were cut; with a view to introducing the general [polytechnic] technological education of the Soviet Union, "practice classes" [shih-hsi k'o] were opened from the first year of junior middle to the third year of senior middle school.

8. Phenomenal development of educational enterprise following the advent of the high tide of socialist transformation.

In the latter half of 1955 a high tide of socialist transformation appeared in China's rural villages.

On December 27, 1955, Chairman Mao pointed out in the preface to his book The High Tide of Socialism in China's Rural Villages: "During the second half of 1955 a basic change arose in China's conditions.... The scope and speed of China's industrialization, the scope and speed of the development of such enterprises as science, culture, education, public health, etc., are such that they can no longer be carried out in accordance with what has been conceived originally. There should be considerable expansion and acceleration in all these areas." Chairman Mao's direction greatly pushed the development of educational work during 1956.

On January 25, 1956, Chairman Mao convened the supreme State Council meeting to discuss the program for agricultural development. He proposed the task of "basically eliminating illiteracy within five to seven years" and "popularizing compulsory primary education within seven to twelve years."

These directives from Chairman Mao gave immense encouragement to the masses. After the opening of the fall term in 1956, there was great positiveness in the development of schools on the part of the masses; there emerged the new pattern in which primary schools in rural villages were "padded" to become middle schools. In that year the number of middle school students rose 32.3 percent over the 1955 figure; the number of primary school students increased 19.4 percent.

9. Liu Shao-ch'i "opposed adventurism" in the hope of preventing the development of education.

In 1957 Liu Shao-ch'i and Teng Hsiao-p'ing, geared to the crosscurrent of capitalist restoration both internationally and domestically, launched a strong opposition against Chairman Mao. They seized upon some of the new problems stemming from the Great Leap Forward in 1956 to exaggerate errors and shortcomings and thus to brew the sinister wind of anti-adventurism.

In March 1957 Liu Shao-ch'i said: "One important error was that too many students were enrolled last year, thus introducing considerable difficulties in our work." This was an attack on Chairman Mao's wise directive to oppose rightist deviation at the end of 1955.

At the Third National Administrative Conference convened in March of the same year, in keeping with Liu Shao-ch'i's tune of "opposing adventurism," Vice Ministers of Education Tung Chun-ts'ai and Liu Shih charged that the growth of educational enterprise during 1956 was too fast and alleged that it "exceeded the possible prerequisites."

10. The counterrevolutionary revisionist Lu Ting-i proposed the revisionist educational policy of "coordination between overall development and teaching according to talents."

During 1956 discussions on educational policy were held among educational circles in China.

In June, at a round table conference of directors of propaganda and cultural and educational departments of provincial and municipal Party committees, Lu Ting-i arbitrarily used "coordination between overall development and teaching according to talents" as educational policy, thus causing ideological chaos in educational circles.

11. Chairman Mao advanced a socialist educational policy.

On February 27, 1957, Chairman Mao convened the Supreme State Affairs Conference and released his splendid work "On the Correct Handling of Contradictions Among the People."

In this splendid work, Chairman Mao ingeniously developed the class struggle theory of Marxism-Leninism by pointing out: "In China, although in regard to the system of ownership socialist transformation has been basically completed and the turbulent class struggle among the masses during the revolutionary period has been basically concluded, the remnants of the overthrown landlords and compradores continue to exist, the bourgeoisie still exists, and the petty bourgeoisie is being transformed. Class struggle has not yet been ended. Class struggle between proletariat and bourgeoisie, class struggle among the political forces of the various parties, and class struggle in the ideological sphere between proletariat and bourgeoisie are still protracted, devious, and even very violent at times. The proletariat wants to transform the world according to its own world outlook; the bourgeoisie also wants to do the same. In this connection, the question of who will win between socialism and capitalism has not yet been resolved truly."

From the viewpoint of class and class struggle, Chairman Mao proposed: "Our educational policy should enable the educated to gain development morally, intellectually, and physically in order to become laborers with socialist awareness and culture." This concluded the dispute on educational policy which has been in existence for many years and pointed out the direction for China's socialist education. This is also Chairman Mao's creative development of Marxist-Leninist educational theory.

With respect to the bourgeois educational line promoted by Liu Shao-ch'i and those in authority in educational circles who took the capitalist road, which was separated from politics and advocated intellect first, Chairman Mao pointed out sharply: "Having no correct political viewpoint is tantamount to having no soul." "All departments should be responsible for ideological and political work. This should be the duty of the Communist

Party, the Youth League, the various ministries and departments of the government, and especially the principals and teachers of all schools."

12. Chairman Mao also gave a series of important directives on educational work at the Party's National Propaganda Work Conference.

On March 6, 1957, Chairman Mao pointed out in his talk to the directors of educational departments and bureaus of seven provinces and municipalities:

"There should not be too many courses with such exalted standards; one-half could be reduced, and eight courses would be sufficient.

"Political and ideological education should be strengthened. There is a director of propaganda in each provincial committee; there is a director of education to be in charge of ideological education work; it is important to grasp ideological leadership.

"Political classes should be strengthened in junior and senior middle schools, and textbooks on politics should be compiled.

"It is necessary to curtail teaching materials, reduce the number of courses, and deemphasize classical literature.

"In regard to the problem of commune- and popular-management schools, they should be developed wherever circumstances permit.

"The teaching material should have some local color; some local teaching materials should be added. Agricultural textbooks should be compiled by the respective provinces in which they are used. Some indigenous literature should be taught; this applies also to natural sciences."

In this talk, Chairman Mao sharply criticized Liu Shao-ch'i and his ilk for blind adoption of the Soviet system:

"You are in charge of the Ministry of Education: is this a Soviet Ministry of Education or a Chinese one? Why don't you then use the things of the old Liberated Areas as the blueprint for teaching materials?"

On July 7 Chairman Mao wrote in a letter to Premier Chou: "In both colleges and middle schools it is necessary to strengthen ideological and political leadership as well as to revamp ideological and political education. It is also necessary to cut down the curriculum, restore political classes for middle schools, abolish the constitution class, and compile new textbooks on ideology and politics."

On March 12 Chairman Mao released his "Talk at the National Propaganda Work Conference of the Chinese Communist Party." In his talk Chairman Mao analyzed the conditions of some five million intellectuals in China and pointed out:

"If the intellectuals cannot rid themselves of whatever is improper in their head, they will not be able to assume the task of teaching others. Of course, we can only teach while we learn, serve as teachers while we make ourselves pupils. In order to be a good teacher, one must first be a good pupil. There are many things which cannot be learned merely from books; one must learn from producers, workers, and the poor and lower-middle peasants. While in schools, it is necessary to study from the students and from the objects of one's own education."

In July Chairman Mao gave directions concerning the strengthening of class education in his talk with the leadership cadres of the Shanghai Motive Power Institute. He said: "We must strengthen ideological and political work for youth; we must teach them not to despise labor so that they will be able to construct our nation successfully! Even if the youth is a young worker, because he has not undergone the hardships of the old society it is all the more necessary to strengthen class education in order to enhance his ideological awareness."

13. Liu Shao-ch'i joined the battle to oppose Chairman Mao's educational policy.

In March 1957, after Chairman Mao's educational policy had been announced for less than a month, Liu Shao-ch'i went out personally to grasp educational work, visiting the five provinces of Honan, Hupeh, Hunan, Hopeh, and Kwangtung on "inspection." He peddled everywhere his revisionist educational viewpoint, harping on a theme that was contrary to Chairman Mao's.

He vigorously advocated the theory of the extinction of class struggle to oppose Chairman Mao's thesis on class and class struggle. He said at Shih-chia-chuang: "We must know that the landlords have already been eliminated, counterrevolution has been basically liquidated, and imperialism has also been ousted. Thus, our contradiction with the enemy is no longer the principal contradiction."

He did his utmost to oppose Chairman Mao's educational policy; he opposed the training of "laborers with socialist awareness and culture" but encouraged people to become famous and authorities. At a students' forum discussion in Hsü-ch'ang, Honan, he said: "I would advise you that instead of serving as cadres when you return to your village, you should earnestly till the land for three or five years. . . . Because you have culture while the peasants do not have it, once you have developed good relations with the masses, you will be able to serve as cadres on the hsiang, hsien, and provincial level; you may also go to the central government, depending on your individual talents. . . . You are the first generation of Chinese peasants who have had culture. It is also more advantageous for the first generation. I am the first generation in participating in revolution, and I am now a member of the Central Committee. This will be impossible for the second and third generations."

Liu Shao-ch'i also publicly opposed Chairman Mao's directive concerning the strengthening of political and ideological educational work. On March 22, at a discussion forum of the representatives of middle school students in Changsha, he said: "I suggest to you to be prepared for these two points: one is to strengthen your studies 'by being unconcerned about everything which happens outside of your window as well as by concentrating your attention on reading the books of sages and savants' in order to be prepared for higher education. . . . If I am to congratulate you, then it is to congratulate all of you for entering higher institutions, which is the best course."

On April 8 he got Yang Shang-k'un to send his lecture draft to the People's Daily, which revised and published it as the editorial entitled "Concerning the Problem of the Participation in Agricultural Production by Middle and Primary School Graduates." This editorial failed to mention Chairman Mao's educational policy and openly proselytized the bourgeois knavish philosophy of suffering little losses to gain greater profit in order to corrode youth. This is a big poisonous weed opposed to Mao Tse-tung thought and must be criticized thoroughly.

In June Liu Shao-ch'i disregarded Chairman Mao's criticism, as well as the sinister results stemming from the emulation of Soviet revisionism, and continued to tell Yang Hsien-chen: "It is definitely not enough for us to have solidarity with the Soviet Union and emulate its experience. Only in the Soviet Union can socialist experience be learned."

On November 6, in his speech at the rally celebrating the fortieth anniversary of the October Revolution held in Peking, Liu said: "It is incumbent on all our Party and League members and revolutionary intellectuals to study arduously, learn their business assiduously, and acquire all kinds of special techniques and scientific knowledge. Where there are prerequisites, one must try to make oneself into a red expert who is 'both red and expert.'" This was also contrary to Chairman Mao's educational policy.

14. Chairman Mao personally led and unleashed the antirightist struggle in order to prepare for the great educational revolution of 1958 politically and ideologically.

On April 27, 1957, the Party Central Committee issued a directive concerning the rectification movement. The bourgeoisie and its intellectuals seized the opportunity to unleash a frantic attack. Rightists of the educational circle tried to seize the right of educational leadership from the Party; they clamored that "professors should rule the school, that "laymen cannot lead experts," and that "the Communist Party be withdrawn from schools."

On June 8 the People's Daily published an editorial entitled "What Is This For?" in order to sound the bugle of the antirightist struggle, thus beginning a nationwide antirightist struggle. This was socialist revolution on the political and ideological front. Through the antirightist struggle, the awareness of the broad masses of revolutionary teachers and students was enhanced, thus further consolidating Party leadership in the schools.

The victory of the antirightist struggle and the rectification movement prepared the political and ideological conditions for the great educational revolution of 1958.

On November 17 Chairman Mao received Chinese students who were studying and practicing in Moscow, and he gave these important directions: "The world is yours as well as ours; it is yours in the final analysis. You are young and exuberant, being at a stage of flourishing like the sun at eight or nine o'clock in the morning. Our hope is placed in you."

3. The Period of Great Educational Revolution and Development (1958-1960)

In 1958 Chairman Mao enacted the General Line of "building socialism by going all out, aiming high, and achieving greater, faster, better results at lower costs." There emerged a great leap forward in China's industry, agriculture, and other enterprises. People's communes were formed in rural areas. In 1959 the antirightist movement was launched, smashing the frantic attack of right opportunism led by P'eng Te-huai and realizing the sustained leap of the national economy.

During this stage, under Chairman Mao's leadership, a resounding educational revolution was launched against the revisionist educational line represented by Liu Shao-ch'i and the vestigial educational systems millenniums old. This has destroyed all domestic and foreign dogmas and opened up the brand new road for education to serve politics and for coordination between education and productive labor. This was a period in which Mao Tse-tung's educational thought shone brilliantly!

1. Chairman Mao personally ignited the flames of educational revolution.

On January 31, 1958, Chairman Mao pointed out a clear direction for educational revolution in the "Sixty Articles on Work Methods":

"The relation between being red and expert and between politics and business is the unity of two opposite things. We must criticize the tendency of political apathy. On the one hand, we have to oppose the empty-headed politicians; on the other hand, we must oppose pragmatists who have lost their compass.

"In all middle-level technical schools and polytechnic schools, where possible, factories or farms should be launched experimentally to engage in production in order to be self-sufficient and semi-self-sufficient. The students should perform half-work and half-study.

"In laboratories and workshops of all higher engineering institutes where production can be undertaken, besides ensuring the needs of teaching and scientific research, production should be implemented as much as possible. Additionally, it may also be possible for students and teachers to enter into labor contracts with the local factories.

"In all agricultural schools, besides undertaking production in their own farms, it may also be possible for them to sign contracts with local agricultural cooperatives for labor participation. Also, teachers may live in these cooperatives so that theory and practice can be coordinated. Cooperatives should send some qualified persons to enroll in agricultural schools.

"All rural middle and primary schools should sign contracts with local agricultural cooperatives to participate in productive labor for agriculture and subsidiary industry. Rural students should also utilize their vacations and holidays or extracurricular time to return to their own villages to participate in production.

"In the case of colleges and urban middle schools, wherever possible, several schools may establish a factory or workshop jointly; they may also sign labor contracts with factories, construction sites, or service enterprises."

In March, at the Chengtu Conference, Chairman Mao sharply

criticized Liu Shao-ch'i for introducing the Soviet system. He said: "[We have adopted] the one principal system, five-consecutive-year system, five-points system, and even in journalism have borrowed the system of Pravda. Some comrades have forgotten their historical lessons and refused to think independently. In emulating the experience of the Soviet Union, we must choose what is good and disregard what is bad. We have borrowed a great many systems and regulations without analyzing them, thus completely losing our independent thinking. Some comrades feel dismayed when they do not borrow. Why should we borrow the superstructure of others?" Thus, he called on us to take our own road, to shatter the shackles of all foreign dogmas, and to establish our own socialist educational system.

In May, at the second session of the Eighth Party Congress, Chairman Mao issued the great appeal "to destroy superstition and to liberate ideology," to be unafraid of bourgeois professors and "to hoist the red flag and distinguish the direction."

Chairman Mao's wise directive has sounded the bugle call for educational revolution.

2. Revolutionary teachers and students responded to Chairman Mao's appeal to launch the educational revolution.

In the spring of 1958 the broad mass of teachers and students of China, under the guidance of Mao Tse-tung's invincible thought, launched intensive debates on being red and expert. They criticized the bourgeoisie who once occupied positions of dominance in schools and were merely expert but not red. These people pursued the bourgeois educational line, which was interested only in personal fame and prestige. Thus, an important victory was scored by the proletarian educational line represented by Chairman Mao.

Thereafter, responding to Chairman Mao's appeal, the broad mass of teachers and students imaginatively and bravely launched criticisms against bourgeois reactionary academic authorities, and many regulations and systems which shackled revolutionary teachers and students were abolished. Under the leadership of the Party, they implemented the three-in-one combination of Party committee, teachers, and students, and compiled their own textbooks, teaching plans, and teaching outlines. They also adopted the system of blooming and contending, published wall posters, and criticized the old educational system. In the form of school development, the methods of state schools and popular-management schools were adopted simultaneously; full-day schools and work-and-study as well as after-work schools were also developed side by side, thus bringing about the phenomenal growth of educational enterprises.

3. Chairman Mao inspected Tientsin University and Wuhan University and enthusiastically supported the half-work and half-study launched by revolutionary teachers and students.

In August 1957 Chairman Mao, during his visit to Tientsin University, directed: "Hereafter schools must manage factories, and factories must manage schools. Even teachers must also participate in labor; they should not merely talk without using their hands." He further said: "Higher institutions must first grasp these three things: Party committee leadership, mass line, and coordination between education and productive labor."

In September Chairman Mao inspected Wuhan University and pointed out: "It is a good phenomenon when students consciously demand the implementation of half-work and half-study. This is the inevitable trend when schools launch factories. This kind of demand should be granted; they should be given active support and encouragement."

Chairman Mao's sincere concern and important directive greatly heartened the revolutionary students and teachers in China. They actively joined the all-people's steel smelting movement and the three-autumn movement, thus linking education to politics and productive labor. A new high tide emerged in the educational revolution.

The "Directive Concerning Educational Work," promulgated by the Central Committee and the State Council, further stirred the high tide of educational revolution.

4. From April to June 1958 the Central Political Bureau convened conferences to discuss the problem of educational policy.

On September 8 Chairman Mao pointed out in his talk at the Supreme State Affairs Conference: "If the school should launch a factory and the factory should launch a school, if the school maintains a farm, if communes develop schools for half-work and half-study, then both study and labor would be coordinated. It is a basic principle that we must coordinate education with labor. Generally, there are these conditions: one is coordination between education and labor; one is Party leadership; there is also the mass line."

In the "Directive Concerning Educational Work" issued by the Central Committee and State Council on September 19, the policy of "education to serve politics and of coordination between education and productive labor" was prescribed. It criticized the errors of education, in which it is alienated from production and practice and neglects politics and Party leadership.

5. Liu Shao-ch'i, Teng Hsiao-p'ing, and Lu Ting-i played counterrevolutionary double-faced tricks to oppose the educational revolution unleashed by Chairman Mao.

Teng Hsiao-p'ing said in March 1958: "The most crucial problem in education now is the problem of popularization and elevation, and all problems must be considered from this principle."

On April 15 Lu Ting-i said publicly at the National Educational Work Conference: "K'ai-lo-fu's [?] educational theory is socialistic; unless education is elevated, there will not be scientists, writers, and educators; it is therefore necessary to elevate the quality of education; ordinary schools should not engage in developing half-work and half-study courses."

In May, at the enlarged conference of the Central Committee Politburo, Liu Shao-ch'i advanced his revisionist black program for "two kinds of educational system and two kinds of labor system," thus regarding half-study and half-work as his own innovation and altering the revolutionary content of half-work and half-study.

In June Liu Shao-ch'i disseminated the fallacy that by engaging in half-work and half-study "the quality of study may drop."

On June 8 Liu Shao-ch'i viciously attacked Chairman Mao's educational policy by saying: "The past educational policy did not have a clear purpose and it should be criticized." On June 12 he further charged that in China's education "there is no clear long-range policy, and it has failed to shape a Marxist-Leninist line."

In July, in his directive to the Hopei provincial and Tientsin municipal Party committees, Liu said: "At present you have already launched some schools for half-work and half-study. Your experience is still insufficient and you must observe first and not try to develop them hastily," thus trying his best to obstruct the great educational revolution.

In August Lu Ting-i tried to change the revolutionary content of Chairman Mao's policy that "education must be coordinated with productive labor." He said: "The first duty of education is to teach and learn knowledge"; the significance of the practice of coordinating education with productive labor is to "enable the students to have broader and more comprehensive knowledge"; "overall development embraces this basic content, which is to enable the students to have broader knowledge and to become versatile."

In September, when he was inspecting the Northeast, Teng Hsiao-p'ing said: "When students participate in labor, the basic courses must not be weakened under any circumstances. The most important task of education is to consummate the research and experiments on apogeal sciences geared to the contents of pedagogy." This was to attempt to bring the young, who have just emerged from their bookshelves, back into a dead end, thus strangulating the educational revolution.

In November Lu Ting-i threw out his own black program at the Chengtu municipal-level Party cadres meeting by advocating the system of ten consecutive years for middle and primary schools. He further said: "I am in favor of changing all middle schools to a full-day system; we must not develop half-work and half-study.

6. Crosscurrent of right opportunism in educational circles.

During 1959 a handful of those in authority in the Party who took the capitalist road, geared to bourgeois reactionary forces in society, seized upon certain shortcomings of the Great Leap Forward to attack the Three Red Flags; and Lu Ting-i and his ilk also stirred up the vicious style of right opportunism in educational circles.

In January 1959 Lu began to assail the great educational revolution at the National Educational Work Conference. He said: "The Party's leadership power does not lie in the continued use of mass strength to repress the veteran teachers, but it should lead teaching successfully. Without learning this, Party leadership cannot be consolidated, and it is bound to collapse sooner or later. There are mistakes in the great educational development of 1958. This was due to feverish headlines and inept ideological methods. . . . What has happened to cultural and educational work in the Great Leap Forward? Speaking on the whole, it is a great leap; speaking specifically, some have leapt, others have not, and still others have retrogressed."

In February Lu Ting-i again gave his absurd views at the conference: "There is some reason for the Soviet Union to advocate technology first and cadres first. Though it is necessary to oppose dogmatism, there must also be a united front. One may be a rightist politically but understand something academically; a man like Ch'ien Wei-ch'ang would still be able to teach."

On February 23 Lu Ting-i openly opposed educational reform at the National Educational Work Conference. He said: "Honestly, the question of teaching is not reform; even to reform a little is reformism. It is better not to call it teaching reform."

In March Lu Ting-i negated "the training of common laborers"; he opposed the view that "bourgeois intellectuals are the objects of revolution."

In April Minister of Education and counterrevolutionary revisionist Yang Hsiu-feng stressed in his speech at the

National People's Congress: "It is incumbent on middle and primary schools to spend their utmost efforts on elevating the quality of the teaching of basic disciplines in order to lay a firm foundation for cultural and scientific knowledge." This was to oppose educational revolution.

On May 18 Lu Ting-i, at the meeting of the responsible persons of cultural and educational departments on the central level, viciously attacked educational revolution as "chaotic, sloppy, and slanted" and said "it is bound to collapse if things continue this way."

In June, at a meeting of the Central Cultural and Educational Group, Lu Ting-i said: "Scientific research is excessive; there is also too much labor; though it is right to have political courses, it would seem that they occupied too much time; there are more cases where the regular business is neglected, thus reducing the amount of regular business, which is to read books."

In the "Regulations Concerning the Arrangement for Teaching, Labor, and Living in Full-Day Schools," drafted by the Ministry of Education under the instigation of Lu Ting-i and others, and promulgated by the State Council on May 24, it is stipulated that teaching should be the principal work, thus controlling the time spent by students in productive labor.

On June 5 the Ministry of Education issued the "Circular on Several Problems in the Teaching Work in Middle, Primary, and Normal Schools During the 1959-60 School Year." It further demanded "stabilizing the order of teaching and gradually raising the standard of educational quality." It stipulated that the main courses in primary school are language and arithmetic; in middle schools the main courses are language, foreign languages, mathematics, physics, and chemistry, thus excluding political classes and productive labor from the main disciplines.

7. Chairman Mao issued the great appeal "to oppose rightism and go all out" and educational revolution continued to forge ahead.

In August 1958 Chairman Mao personally convened the

Eighth Plenary Session of the Central Committee of the Eighth Party Congress, smashed the P'eng, Huang, Chang, and Chou counterrevolutionary clique, and issued the great appeal to oppose rightism and fulfill the main targets of the Second Five-Year Plan ahead of schedule. The entire Party held high the Three Red Flags and the great leap was continued.

Stimulated by the slogan of "opposing rightism and going all out," the broad masses on the educational front also actively joined the technological renovation movement and stirred up the high tide of developing the schools. Educational revolution penetrated deeply the sphere of teaching, and a mass experiment for curricular reform was launched. Thus the handful of men in authority in the Party who took the capitalist road, Liu Shao-ch'i, Lu Ting-i, etc., failed to sabotage the educational revolution.

8. Comrade Lin Piao held high the great red flag of Mao Tse-tung thought and called on the entire army to study Chairman Mao's works.

In August 1960 Comrade Lin Piao pointed out: "School education must implement two principles: one is simple but essential, the other is brief and to the point. It is necessary to reform the curriculum, and the time should not be too long."

In October Comrade Lin Piao pointed out: "Mao Tse-tung thought is the apex of Marxism-Leninism." He further said that "in theoretical study, it is not right to talk only about some 'integral' and 'systematic' books, or to prescribe certain courses and how many sections and chapters in each course and how much time should be devoted to them. If this is done and there is a failure to emphasize Comrade Mao Tse-tung's writings, this kind of 'integrity' and 'systematism' is merely a muddled concept."

9. Liu Shao-ch'i and Lu Ting-i continued to conspire to strangle the great educational revolution and to prepare public opinion for the restoration of capitalism on the educational front.

Liu Shao-ch'i and his ilk were not content with their defeat and continued to sabotage the great educational revolution.

On February 16, 1960, Lu Ting-i said at the educational work forum discussion: "Our general [elementary] education is too backward and I do not know to what place it has been relegated in the world," thus describing the educational revolution as completely dismal.

In April Lu Ting-i brought out the revisionist educational program "Teaching Must Be Reformed" at the second session of the Second National People's Congress. He used the signal of "educational revolution" to perpetrate the deed of strangling the educational revolution and shifting the general direction of this revolution, thus attempting to put the educational revolution into the orbit of the "teaching reform" which he has enacted personally. He also used the slogan of "four adequatenesses" to peddle the bourgeois contraband of "pedagogy as the backbone and intellect first" to oppose Chairman Mao's educational policy. In the autumn of that year, a handful of the men in authority in the Party who took the capitalist road and were connected with the cultural office of the State Council and with the Central Propaganda Department and the Ministry of Education, in keeping with Lu Ting-i's black program, designated the Ching-shan School, the Erh-lung-lu School, and the Feng-sheng School, all in Peking, as experimental schools in which to promote revisionist pedagogical reform.

On April 29 P'eng Chen stated at the meeting of the Central Cultural and Educational Group: "In higher institutes it is the proletarian intellectuals who occupy a predominant position; it should be affirmed that the intellectual group is not a revisionist one." This was to obliterate class struggle on the educational front.

On July 7, at the ministerial meeting of the old Ministry of Propaganda, Chou Yang said with respect to the teaching of language and literature in primary schools: "We must stress more writing, writing the characters correctly without making errors, and understanding the grammar. It is also necessary to advocate the reciting of books, which is a Chinese tradition."

On November 28 the counterrevolutionary revisionist Hsi

Chung-hsun, who was also a former vice premier and secretary-general of the State Council, said: "The main function of the school is study; there is too much labor now. . . . Hereafter, whatever interferes with study must be given up."

An evil wind to strangle the great educational revolution was gradually aroused, and a great instability was fermented. There was the desperate struggle of the revisionist educational line represented by Liu Shao-ch'i and Lu Ting-i.

4. The Period of Fluctuations of the Educational Revolution (1961-1963)

From 1961 to 1963, because of several years of continuous natural disasters and because of the sabotage of the Soviet Union, China's national economy encountered temporary difficulties. International imperialism, modern revisionism, and reactionaries of various foreign countries launched a mammoth anti-Chinese campaign. Internally, the handful of persons in authority in the Party who took the capitalist road, led by Liu and Teng, together with the demons and monsters of society, energetically advocated "three freedoms and one contract" [san-tzu i-pao] and "three reconciliations and one reduction" [san-ho i-shao], thus stirring up the style of independent endeavor and attempting to restore capitalism.

In educational circles, since 1958, such counterrevolutionary revisionists as P'eng Chen, Lu Ting-i, Yang Hsiu-feng, and Chiang Nan-hsiang, with the support of Liu Shao-ch'i and Teng Hsiao-p'ing, frantically attacked the educational revolution and Chairman Mao's educational line, thus bringing about a great instability on the educational front.

Our great leader, Chairman Mao, stemmed this countercurrent, insisted on the socialist direction, and issued the great appeal that "one must never forget class struggle." He also unleashed the socialist education movement to rout this countercurrent of capitalist restoration.

1. Lu Ting-i's gang frantically attacked the great

educational revolution.

As a result of two years of serious natural calamities and the sabotage of the Soviet revisionists, temporary difficulties appeared in China's national economy during 1961. In January the Party Central Committee convened the Ninth Plenum of the Eighth Congress, in which the policy of "massive development of agriculture and grain production" was adopted.

On February 7, 1961, the Central Committee approved and transmitted the report of the Central Cultural and Educational Group on the arrangement of cultural and educational work during the coming period. It pointed out that "the current cultural and educational work must implement the policy of adjustment, consolidation, replenishment, and enhancement" and "emphasize the replenishing of contents, energetic enhancement of quality, and suitable control of development."

Lu Ting-i's group used this opportunity to charge maliciously that the great educational revolution led by Chairman Mao in 1958 was "chaotic, sloppy, and slanted," in order to launch their counterattack.

On July 20 the Ministry of Education issued "Opinions on Certain Problems Concerning Full-Day Schools," in which it pointed out that since 1958 "there has been too much productive labor, and political activities were too numerous . . . thus affecting the quality of teaching." The ministry ruled: "It is necessary to control stringently all kinds of social activities." This was to attempt to push the schools back to the old pre-1957 road.

On July 10, 1962, in summing up the past thirteen years of work in general education of the Central Ministry of Propaganda, Lu Ting-i viciously attacked the great educational revolution and Chairman Mao, alleging that "the standard for students has declined steadfastly and that it cannot be compared with the better schools of Peiyang warlordism and the Kuomintang era. The main cause is that the leadership is not firm and that they would reform when someone suggested that reform is needed. When the lower echelons say that the standard is too high, it is lowered immediately. They were still dissatisfied, and it would seem that it was impossible to raise the standard a little bit."

On August 2, in a general report of the Central Ministry of Propaganda to Chairman Mao signed by Lu Ting-i, the great educational revolution was attacked. The report charged that "the pace of growth was too fast and too much power was delegated to the lower echelons; there was too much labor and too few classes; language courses were taught as political classes; the standard has been lowered; chaos prevailed and it has greatly hurt the schools."

2. Liu Shao-ch'i, Teng Hsiao-p'ing, and Lu Ting-i enacted a program for the restoration of capitalism on the educational front.

In January 1961 the Party Central Committee called on the various ministries and departments to summarize their experience and to enact specific directions, policies, and measures under the guidance of Mao Tse-tung thought and based on the general policy and general line of the Party.

Under the pretext of summing up the experience since 1958, Lu Ting-i, supported by Liu and Teng, organized his staff to enact an educational program for restoring capitalism. He designated Lin Feng, Chang Chi-ch'un, and Chiang Nan-hsiang to draft "Sixty Articles on Higher Education" and asked Yang Hsiu-feng and Tung Chun-ts'ai to draft temporary work regulations for regular (full-day) middle and primary schools.

Early in June, one or two Party secretaries from each large administrative region came to discuss the revision of the "Sixty Articles on Higher Education." At the meeting they demanded that the achievements of the educational revolution since 1958 be affirmed fully. However, Lu Ting-i chided them for not daring to admit defects and errors in their work and that like Ah Q, they were afraid others might say they had scabies on their head.

It was in this month that Lu Ting-i asked Lin Feng and Chiang Nan-hsiang to convene a "three-three system" conference (in which school Party secretaries should form one-third of the participants, veteran professors who are new Party members should form one-third, and nonpartisan professors should form one-third) to discuss revision of the "Sixty Articles on Higher Education." Bourgeois reactionary authorities clamored at the conference that "there has been too much productive labor and the level of basic theories has been unduly reduced," that "students do not respect their teachers," etc.

In July Lu Ting-i personally presided over the meeting of the Central Cultural and Educational Group and held three discussions on the "Sixty Articles." Lu was still dissatisfied with the document, deeming that "it was not clear enough as to what should be endorsed and what should be opposed." He then asked T'ung Ta-lin and others to draft a document which proposed implementation of the system of responsibility of college presidents and the adoption of a tutor system in training postgraduate students.

In August, at a conference of the Secretariat under the auspices of Teng Hsiao-p'ing and attended by such counterrevolutionary revisionists as P'eng Chen, Lu Ting-i, Wang Chia-hsiang, Lo Jui-ch'ing, Po I-po, Lin Feng, Yang Shang-k'un, and Chiang Nan-hsiang, revision of the "Sixty Articles on Higher Education" was discussed. Teng Hsiao-p'ing said that "this is a good document" and "rightist teachers can exercise guidance functions."

In September the Central Work Conference adopted the "Sixty Articles on Higher Education." This was the black program for restoration of capitalism on the educational front prescribed by Liu Shao-ch'i, Teng Hsiao-p'ing, P'eng Chen, and Lu Ting-i. The "Sixty Articles on Higher Education" is a big poisonous weed which opposes Mao Tse-tung's ideology and educational line. It used a variety of negative terms, such as "cannot be allowed" and "should not," to negate the achievements of the great educational revolution since 1958 and the leadership of the Party; it obliterated the struggle between two classes and two roads; it proselytized the revisionist view that politics should be realized in business, thus providing facilities for bourgeois intellectuals and causing the students to return to their bookish pursuits and to become detached from politics and labor.

In December Lu Ting-i personally presided over the discussions on the preliminary draft of work regulations for regular middle and primary schools. He dictated that political demands on students should be reduced and said absurdly that "if everyone should be asked to become Marx, this would lead to the opposite."

In September 1962 the final draft of "Temporary Work Regulations for Regular Middle and Primary Schools" was adopted. These two documents negate class struggle and advocate intellect first; they stress teaching as the main thing and oppose the emphasis on politics. This is the black program of Liu Shao-ch'i, Teng Hsiao-p'ing, and Lu Ting-i to restore capitalism on the general educational front.

3. Bourgeois reactionary academic authorities were canvassed to recompile teaching materials and reissue pedagogical plans and outlines, thus implementing a counterattack on the great educational revolution.

In February 1961, in the name of the Secretariat of the Central Committee, Teng Hsiao-p'ing, P'eng Chen, and Lu Ting-i appointed the counterrevolutionary revisionist Chou Yang to lead the work of selecting and compiling liberal arts teaching materials for higher institutions, and Yang Hsiu-feng and Chiang Nan-hsiang to lead the work of selecting and compiling teaching materials for engineering and sciences. They also used such reactionary academic authorities as Feng Ting, Feng Yu-lan, and Chien Po-tsan to compile liberal arts textbooks.

In April, at the conference on teaching materials for liberal arts, Chou Yang again disseminated his revisionist fallacy on the relations between red and expert, history and discourse, Chinese and foreign, and ancient and contemporary, thus making a frantic counterattack against the 1958 great educational revolution and completely negating the ideological criticisms against reactionary academic authorities in 1958. He received the accolade of the bourgeois reactionary academic authorities right there.

At this conference Lu Ting-i openly voiced his fallacious view of two conveyances (that is, both bourgeois and proletarian ideologies must be conveyed and taught) and two long lives (that is, long live idealism and metaphysics, and long live dialectical materialism), thus giving the green light for the rampancy of bourgeois reactionary ideology.

On April 1, during a discussion at the old Ministry of Propaganda on teaching materials for middle and primary schools, Lu Ting-i said: "Language is language and it suffices to grasp some knowledge therein. Political education comprises political classes and labor only."

On May 13, at a meeting of group leaders of liberal arts teaching materials, Chou Yang said: "In compiling teaching materials it is necessary to emphasize the ability of the veteran teachers. Though the revolutionary zeal of youth is admirable, it does not work when one depends only on blatancy. When it is not practical, problems may arise. With one hand stretched toward the ancient and another toward foreign countries, we will be able to accomplish a great deal to surprise the world. If we do not grasp them now, when the old experts die off, losses will be sustained.

In September Lu Ting-i put Chang P'an-shih in command and asked the Ministry of Education's Party group to recruit such reactionary academic authorities as Tai Po-t'ao and others to participate in the compilation and review work group for middle and primary school teaching materials. Under the manipulation of Chang P'an-shih and in keeping with Lu Ting-i's guiding ideology of "intellect first and pedagogy as the backbone," teaching plans for the twelve-year regular middle and primary schools were drafted, teaching outlines were adopted, and new textbooks were compiled.

On June 12, 1962, Lin Feng called together a number of leadership persons to discuss teaching plans for middle and primary schools. T'ung Ta-lin, who was Lu Ting-i's close confidant, said: "It is the main function of middle and primary schools to grasp the tools of study with which knowledge can be acquired. The tools consist mainly of language, foreign languages, and teaching. The purpose of the political class is to acquire some knowledge, and there may be fewer courses on history and geography. The purpose of labor is to garner some basic production techniques."

On July 16 Lin Feng said: "It is necessary to have concentrated courses and to stress the standard. The work done in 1958 was rather messy; we must send someone to ascertain the old curriculum of the first middle school of Peking Normal University. I will compile the curriculum for the middle school of Nan-k'ai University myself. It may also be possible to ascertain the curriculum of Nan-yang Middle School." Thus he conspired to restore the old curriculums and schedules of the Kuomintang era.

On January 21, 1963, the Ministry of Education issued "Opinions on Some Problems Concerning Rural Primary Schools and 'Private (Family) Schools.'" This directive even prescribed that such books as the *Three-Character Classic* [San-tzu ching], *100 Family Names* [Pai-chia hsing], *Miscellaneous Phrases of Four, Five, and Six Words* [Ssu, wu, liu kuan tsa tzu] *Four Books* [Szu shu], and *Five Classics* [Wu ching] may also be used as temporary textbooks, thus clearing the way for the restoration of feudalism.

On May 2 Hsü Li-ch'un, king of the palace of Hades, began to grasp the editing of materials for middle school political textbooks to boycott the use of Chairman Mao's works as the basic teaching matter. The reactionary academic authority Feng Ting was selected as the chief compiler of *Dialectical Materialism*.

On July 31 the Ministry of Education issued the "Circular Concerning Implementation of the Teaching Plan for Regular Middle and Primary Schools (Draft)." This teaching plan was a hodgepodge copied from curricular arrangements of the Kuomintang era, Soviet revisionist countries, and imperialist countries. There were miscellaneous courses, and the number of hours was increased, completely violating Chairman Mao's directive on curricular reform.

On September 1 some of the regular schools began to use

the newly compiled textbooks and the teaching outlines for the various disciplines. These teaching materials are heavy and have excessive contents, and they emphasize the basic knowledge and techniques unilaterally, seriously weaken political and ideological education, and increase the load of both teachers and students. The lively and vivid situation that had emerged after the educational revolution had been strangulated completely.

4. Compromise with and surrender to bourgeois intellectuals so that they have come to dominate the schools once more.

In 1961 Lu Ting-i charged that academic criticism was "muddled criticism and reckless pulling out of the white banner" and it "was even more low-class than the 'Ah Q' type of spiritual victory."

In September, at the conference for leadership cadres of higher institutions convened by the Ministry of Education, Lu Ting-i wantonly slandered the ideological criticism of bourgeois intellectuals launched since 1958 as "ruthless struggle and blows." He said that "the bourgeoisie in China is the most cultured; if we don't study from the bourgeoisie, it will be impossible to realize the intellectualization among the worker and peasant masses."

Lin Feng has also repeatedly proselytized the class reconciliation theory of "combining two into one," saying that "it is only by enabling China's younger generation to study and to inherit the traditions of the veteran cadres, as well as the business expertise of the veteran bourgeois professors, that it will be possible to become both 'red and expert.'"

During January-February 1962, at the scientific planning conference held in Canton, it was decided to implement the policy of "removing the hat" from bourgeois intellectuals (meaning that hereafter they will no longer be called bourgeois intellectuals) and to "coronate" them (meaning that hereafter they will be called laboring intellectuals who serve socialism). Thereafter, in such important work as teaching, scientific research, training of research students, and compilation of teaching materials in the higher institutions, reliance has been placed on bourgeois veteran experts and reactionary academic authorities. This enabled bourgeois intellectuals to dominate our schools and to hamper revolution in our educational institutions.

On November 27, at the National Propaganda and Educational Conference, Lu Ting-i said: "After one has served as a teacher and principal for several decades and has made education a life career, this is an honor; and one who can develop the school and teach the students successfully is also an expert. For good principals and teachers the salary may be raised to one hundred or two hundred yuan a month, and they will be praised at some rallies."

In February 1962, in Shanghai and Tientsin, under the auspices of Yang Hsiu-feng and Liu K'an-feng, the Ministry of Education held round-table conferences on experience in developing middle schools. The so-called famous middle school leadership cadres and veteran teachers from a dozen or more schools were invited. They energetically advocated the style of worshiping what is foreign and restoring what is ancient. They also praised the "teaching experience" of bourgeois intellectuals and treated them royally.

On March 13 the Party organization of the Ministry of Education, pursuant to the wish of Teng Hsiao-p'ing and Lu Ting-i and under the auspices of Chiang Nan-hsiang, submitted a report to the old Ministry of Propaganda on "Our Preliminary Opinions on the Conditions and Problems of Appraising and Selecting Experts in Peking and Shanghai Who Have Engaged in Middle and Primary Educational Work for a Long Time with Outstanding Achievements." Some ninety-nine veteran teachers were chosen and it was decided to confer the title of "Educational Expert" on them and to raise their salaries. The highest raise was from 177 yuan to 261.5 yuan a month.

5. Strong opposition to Mao Tse-tung thought and efforts to stop the broad masses of teachers and students from studying Chairman Mao's works.

In January 1961 Comrade Lin Piao suggested that in studying Chairman Mao's works it is "necessary to bring along the questions, make a living study and living application, coordinate study with application, study what is more urgent first to produce immediate results." The Liberation Army stirred up a high tide of living study and living application of Chairman Mao's writings, thus accelerating ideological revolutionization and setting an example for the entire people.

In February the reactionary revisionist Chou Yang made a vicious attack at the conference on teaching materials for the liberal arts. He said: "Mao Tse-tung thought has been applied recklessly in some places. This means that higher Party schools should use Mao Tse-tung thought as the outline in teaching political classes; it does not mean that all disciplines should use it recklessly. Reckless use is not commandership; it is, rather, for recruiting soldiers."

In April, with the support of Liu and Teng, Lu Ting-i said frantically: "When you write textbooks, you must not misinterpret and must not put on Mao Tse-tung's label." He also used such big sticks as "simplification," "pragmatism," and "vulgarian" to denounce Comrade Lin Piao's directive.

In August 1962 Liu Shao-ch'i revised his black How to be a Good Communist [Hsiu-yang] and issued it on a large scale. He opposed and assailed Mao Tse-tung thought and urged people to "be good students of Marx and Lenin" to oppose Lin Piao's directive on "serving as Chairman Mao's good pupil."

6. With advantage taken of the adjustment of planning, the half-work and half-study system was assailed and an effort was made to develop "small pagodas."

With a view to training bourgeois intellectuals, a handful of men in authority in the Party who took the capitalist road, such as Lu Ting-i and Lin Feng, stressed the importance of developing a group of regular (full-day) colleges and middle and primary schools and of fostering some key schools to engage in the development of "little pagodas." They did everything to harm half-work and half-study, the fruit of the 1958 educational revolution. Since 1961 almost all the colleges and middle schools with half-work and half-study launched since 1958 have been abolished and almost all the factories sponsored by these schools have been suspended.

On October 22, 1962, Lu Ting-i declared openly at the National Cultural and Educational Conference that it was "necessary to develop state-operated regular middle and primary schools. This would be like a pagoda to enable the students to gradually enroll in higher institutions as well as to train diverse experts."

7. The evil wind of seeking higher education; refusal to implement the Party's class line in enrollment work.

At the end of 1959, Lu Ting-i convened a conference of cultural and educational secretaries from the various provinces. He praised Fukien for its highest rate of students studying in higher institutions and arranged a list of the various provinces according to the rate of educational advancement. As a result there emerged in China the sinister style of catching up with Fukien and with the Foochow First Middle School. With a view to improving the rate of pursuit of higher education, many schools even squeezed out politics and labor.

In 1962 the United Front Department, which was dominated by counterrevolutionary revisionists, suggested that in the enrollment of colleges, bourgeois children should "receive equal treatment." Under the instigation of Chiang Nan-hsiang and Yang Hsiu-feng, the method of enrollment "by sections from higher grades to lower grades" was adopted, thus cancelling the provision whereby children of workers and peasants enjoyed priority of enrollment and excluding large numbers of them.

In 1963 Teng Hsia-p'ing reviewed and approved the system of conferring academic titles. In the meantime the Ministry of Education promulgated "Excerpts on the Conference on the Work of Research Students of Higher Institutions" and the "Temporary Regulations (Draft) on the Work of Research Students in Higher Institutions," thus attempting to develop a revisionist high-salaried bracket in China.

8. Chairman Mao grasped the compass of socialism and led the entire people to rout the countercurrent of capitalism.

On July 30, 1961, when Lu Ting-i and others were destroying

the half-work and half-study system, Chairman Mao wrote to the Kiangsi Communist Labor University: "I endorse your enterprise fully. The development of a work-study school does not require a cent from the state, and it is possible to have primary and middle schools as well as colleges which are scattered on the mountaintops in various provinces and a few located on the plains. Such schools are really good."

In 1962, at the Tenth Plenum of the Central Committee of the Eighth Party Congress, Chairman Mao issued the great appeal that "one must never forget class struggle."

In March 1963 Chairman Mao issued the great appeal "to learn from Comrade Lei Feng"; the movement to emulate Lei Feng developed exuberantly in all schools.

In May the "Decision on Certain Problems in Current Rural Work (Draft) (First 10 Articles)" was adopted under Chairman Mao's personal aegis. An urban and rural socialist educational movement was unleashed to repel the frantic attack of the bourgeoisie and to consolidate socialist economic foundations and the proletarian dictatorship.

In his comment on "Seven Good Data from Chekiang Concerning Labor Participation by Cadres," Chairman Mao pointed out clearly that "class struggle, production struggle, and scientific experimentation are the Three Great Revolutionary Movements to construct a socialist power; this forms the real guarantee for Communists to avert bureaucratism, revisionism, and dogmatism, as well as to become invincible. It is also a reliable guarantee for the proletariat to be aligned with the broad laboring masses and to implement democratic dictatorship."

In December Chairman Mao gave important directions concerning art and literature work. He pointed out: "In many sectors the results of socialist transformation are still very thin. Many sectors are still dominated by 'dead people.' Though the economic base of society has changed, the art sector, which is one of the superstructures serving this base, still remains problematical."

Under Chairman Mao's wise leadership, the people began to

rout this countercurrent of capitalist restoration and to insist on the socialist direction.

5. The Period of Intensive Development of the Struggle Between Two Lines and Two Command Headquarters on the Education Front (1964-1965)

In 1964 a new leap forward appeared in China's national economy. The entire Party and people launched the socialist education movement even more intensively and extensively. The people of China responded to Chairman Mao's great appeal that they should study Taching in industry and Tachai in agriculture and that the entire nation should learn from the Liberation Army. There was stirred a high tide for studying Chairman Mao's works. A series of criticisms were launched in philosophy circles, historiography circles, and literature and art circles.

In the area of education, Chairman Mao has given many important directions and pointed out that education must be reformed thoroughly. When Liu Shao-ch'i, the black commander of the educational circle, saw that he could not stem the tide of educational revolution, he came out personally to advance the two kinds of educational systems in order to boycott Chairman Mao's educational line. The struggle entered an unprecedentedly acute stage.

1. Chairman Mao again ignited the flames of educational revolution and issued the great appeal for thoroughly criticizing the revisionist educational line and reforming the old education.

During the spring festival (February 13) of 1962, at the Spring Festival Round-Table Conference convened by the Central Committee, Chairman Mao gave the most comprehensive and systematic directive. He pointed out:

"The existing school system, curriculum, teaching method, and examination method must be revamped. These are detrimental to the people.

"The present methods are detrimental to talent and to youth, and I do not agree with them. One has to read so many books, and examination is what one does to the enemy; it kills and it has to be changed.

"All foreign and native dogmas must be done away with."

On March 10 Chairman Mao further pointed out in his commentary on the Second Railway Middle School's document "Concerning the Problems of School Curriculum and Lectures and the Methods of Examination": "There are now too many courses that impose terrific pressures on students. The lecture methods are poor. The method of examination regards the students as enemies in carrying out sudden blitzkriegs. All three items are inimical to the training of youth so that they may develop naturally in intellect, morality, and physique."

Chairman Mao's directive greatly stimulated the broad masses of revolutionary teachers and students, who strongly demanded thorough reform of the old education.

2. Liu Shao-ch'i, Teng Hsiao-p'ing, and Lu Ting-i did their best to resist Chairman Mao's Spring Festival Directive in order to prevent the educational revolution.

On March 4, 1964, Lu Ting-i was the first to oppose curricular reform. At a meeting of the Central Cultural and Educational Group, he said: "What to do when the curriculum has been cut by one-half?... We are now studying this problem of cutting one-half and will do what we can, but it must be done carefully. If the lower echelons cannot cut the curriculum properly, they must not do it recklessly."

In March Lu Ting-i instigated Liu Chi-p'ing, one of the people in authority in the Party who took the capitalist road in the Ministry of Education, to stringently block Chairman Mao's talk during the Spring Festival. At the national conference of heads of educational departments and bureaus, Liu Chi-p'ing conveyed the talk to only a few persons. Lu Ting-i, however, stated openly at the conference: "A striking problem of class struggle in education is the problem of unilateral pursuit of higher education." Liu Chi-p'ing also talked about "opposition to the unilateral pursuit of higher education" and criticized the "education of motherly love" in order to shift the target and boycott Chairman Mao's directive on the school system, the curriculum, teaching methods, and examination methods, all of which must be reformed.

In April, at the conference of leadership cadres of higher institutions convened by the Ministry of Education, Lu Ting-i viciously attacked Chairman Mao's talk. He said: "Our Party has always advocated that everything must be tested first. Both land reform and agricultural cooperative development have been carried out at experimental points first before they were gradually promoted, thus increasing production. The only exception is the communes, which have been promoted without experimenting. The result was that production diminished and hardships ensued. I feel that the reform of the school system, curriculums, teaching methods, and examination methods should also be experimented with first."

Yang Hsiu-feng, however, advanced the slogan that "ideology must be active and action must be stable." He suggested that the arrangements for special departments (courses) and the general frameworks of the teaching plan should be kept intact, thus resisting Chairman Mao's Spring Festival Directive.

3. Liu Shao-ch'i brought out the black program of "two kinds of educational system and two kinds of labor system."

Less than three months after Chairman Mao's Spring Festival directive, Liu Shao-ch'i advanced "two kinds of educational system." Since May 1964, and within two years, he has gone to some nineteen provinces and municipalities and made some twenty reports, peddling his black contraband.

Liu Shao-ch'i personally formed an educational staff office; he also indicated that a "Second Ministry of Education" and "Second Department of Education" should be formed in order to engage in second-command headquarters.

Liu Shao-ch'i tried to usurp other people's merit as his own by claiming that the half-work, half-study system was adopted by him at Tientsin in 1958. In various talks he linked himself directly with Marx, Engels, Lenin, and Stalin, but did not mention Chairman Mao's educational thought at all, thus deprecating

Chairman Mao's great contributions to Marxist-Leninist educational theory.

Liu Shao-ch'i's "two kinds of educational systems" is thoroughly opposed to Mao Tse-tung thought. He used the bourgeois "half-work and half-study" to resist Chairman Mao's theory on the prevention of capitalist restoration; he used the name of half-work and half-study to uphold the old educational system and oppose the educational revolution; he mutilated the objects of training as suggested by Chairman Mao by declaring that the system of half-work and half-study was to cultivate "technicians," "engineers," "factory managers, plant directors, Party committee secretaries, mayors, and magistrates." He took away the revolutionary soul of the half-work and half-study educational system, peddled the bourgeois educational system of double tracks, and disseminated the poisons of economism.

In October 1965 Liu Shao-ch'i transferred his loyal aide Ho Wei to the Ministry of Education to serve as the minister. After assuming his office, Ho actively promoted Liu Shao-ch'i's black contraband of two kinds of educational system.

In April 1965 Ho Wei, at the instigation of Liu Shao-ch'i and Lu Ting-i, convened the National Rural Half-Work and Half-Study Conference at which Liu peddled his black contraband on a large scale.

In November the National Urban Half-Work and Half-Study Educational Conference was convened, and Liu Shao-ch'i continued to peddle his contraband.

On November 15, at an enlarged session of the Central Committee Politburo, Liu Shao-ch'i attacked Chairman Mao obliquely by saying that if one "could see clearly" in regard to the reform of schools of the full-day system, "one would not give a blind command."

In January 1966 the National Half-Work (agricultural), Half-Study Higher Educational Conference was convened to further promote Liu Shao-ch'i's contraband.

4. Chairman Mao issued the great appeal to the entire Party for "training tens of millions of successors to the proletarian

revolutionary enterprise."

In July 1964 Chairman Mao summed up the painful lesson of the Soviet capitalist restoration. He pointed out that the question of training revolutionary successors "is an extremely important problem affecting the life and death of our Party and the destiny of our state." He mentioned the five prerequisites for the successors of proletarian revolutionary enterprise and pointed out: "Successors to the proletarian revolutionary enterprise are produced in mass struggle and tempered amidst great revolutionary storms. It is therefore necessary to observe and distinguish cadres and to select and train the successors during the protracted mass struggle."

In July Chairman Mao gave important directions on educational work in his conversation with Comrade Mao Yüan-hsin. Chairman Mao pointed out: "Class struggle is one of your main courses. You should not emphasize grades, but must focus your energy on instilling the ability to analyze and resolve problems, and you must not be shackled by following the teachers. The crux of educational reform lies with the teachers; the pedagogical method of infusion of knowledge must be opposed; what is most important is to study from practice."

On August 29 Chairman Mao received the Nepal educational delegation and pointed out in his talk that there exists a struggle between two roads on China's educational front. He said: "I suggest that you should not be superstitious about China's educational system or regard it as good. Reform is needed now; there are many difficulties; some people do not support it." Liu Shao-ch'i and Lu Ting-i were representative figures among them. He also said that "very few people endorse the new methods."

On September 4 Chairman Mao received the head and the principal members of the Laotian Patriotic (Liberation) Front's cultural work group and pointed out in his talk:

"Political education is the center of all education.

"Educating youth is a big problem; if we should be negligent, the bourgeoisie will come to seize power."

5. Chairman Mao issued the "July 3" Directive.

Liu Shao-ch'i and Lu Ting-i stubbornly boycotted Chairman Mao's directives and refused to carry out the school-system and curricular reforms, thus causing heavy curricular burdens.

On July 3, 1965, Chairman Mao gave another directive: "The burdens of students are too heavy, thus affecting their health, making even study useless. It is therefore suggested that one-third be cut from the total amount of activities. Representatives of teachers and students should be invited to discuss this a few times to decide on implementation."

Thereafter Chairman Mao further noted, in his talk with Comrade Wang Hai-jung: "The school should permit its students to rebel." He also encouraged Wang Hai-jung to take the lead in rebellion.

In December, during a talk at Hangchow, Chairman Mao again sharply criticized the old educational system.

Liu Shao-ch'i, Lu Ting-i, and others continued to ignore Chairman Mao's "July 3" Directive and resorted to double-faced tactics to resist his educational line.

In August, with a view to deceiving Chairman Mao, P'eng Chen and Lu Ting-i instigated Ho Wei and Liu Chi-p'ing to convene a so-called round-table conference to implement the "July 3" Directive. They said openly at the conference: "Some people, when they see the word 'cut,' would cut all education. Thus, we will cease to develop education; how can that be done?"

In September, at the political work conference of higher institutions under the Ministry of Higher Education, Lu Ting-i alleged that Chairman Mao's "July 3" Directive was a "partial problem and that the problem must be viewed as a whole."

In October Ho Wei drafted a "Report on the Question of Reducing Student Burdens and Ensuring Student Health." On the one hand, it stressed that the teaching materials must not be reduced; on the other hand, it recommended the reduction of political and militia activities as well as labor, thus boycotting Chairman Mao's directive.

6. Liu Shao-ch'i, Lu Ting-i, and Chiang Nan-hsiang stubbornly opposed the study of Chairman Mao's work by students

and opposed emphasis on politics and emulation of the Liberation Army. In 1964 Chairman Mao made this appeal in his commentary on "Concerning the Directive on Emulating the Liberation Army and Strengthening Political Work": "Now that the entire nation is emulating the Liberation Army and emulating Taching, it also behooves the schools to learn from the Liberation Army. A political department, a political bureau, and political instructions should be established, and the four firsts and the three-eight work style should be implemented.

Lu Ting-i and Chiang Nan-hsiang attacked this by stating that "the experience of the Liberation Army's institutes and schools is not applicable to local schools." As a result, even in higher institutions the establishment of a political department has been deferred.

Responding to Chairman Mao's appeal, during 1964-1965 some 300,000 teachers and students participated in large groups in the urban and rural socialist education movement. Liu Shao-ch'i opposed this and warned that "the quality of study must not be reduced because of participation in these movements."

After Chairman Mao's "July 3" Directive was issued, Lu Ting-i and Ho Wei attributed the unduly heavy burdens of students to the fact that "some things have been launched excessively, such as the study of Mao Tse-tung's selected works, emulation of the Liberation Army, military training, labor, etc." Thus, they began to curtail political activities on a large scale and forced the dissolution of many study groups for studying Chairman Mao's works.

6. The Period of the Great Proletarian Cultural Revolution (1966 to Date)

In 1966, under the personal mobilization by and leadership of our great leader, Chairman Mao, an unprecedented Great Proletarian Cultural Revolution has been launched resoundingly in China! The educational revolution has since entered a broader and more intensive stage.

1. Chairman Mao unleashed a Great Proletarian Cultural Revolution unprecedented in Chinese history.

In November 1965 Chairman Mao personally commented on and released Yao Wen-yüan's article "On the New Historical Play The Dismissal of Hai Jui," thus sounding the bugle for the Great Proletarian Cultural Revolution.

On March 20, 1966, Chairman Mao said: "The Central Propaganda Ministry is the palace of the king of Hades, and so we must overthrow the king and liberate the small devils."

In May Chairman Mao called an enlarged session of the Politburo and exposed the counterrevolutionary clique of P'eng, Lu, Lo, and Yang.

On June 1 Chairman Mao personally approved the broadcasting of the first Marxist-Leninist big-character poster in China, written by Nieh Yüan-tzu and six other comrades of Peking University, thus igniting the flames of the Great Proletarian Cultural Revolution throughout the country.

2. Chairman Mao's important directives on the educational revolution.

On May 7, 1966, Chairman Mao pointed out in his comment on the "Report Concerning Further Implementation of Army Units' Agricultural and subsidiary Industrial Production" submitted by the General Rear Services Department of the National Defense Council: "The same holds true for the students. While their main task is to study, they should also learn other things; that is to say, they should not learn only book knowledge but should learn also about industry, agriculture, and the military. They should also criticize the bourgeoisie. The curriculum should be reduced and there should be an educational revolution. The phenomenon in which our schools are dominated by bourgeois intellectuals cannot be allowed to continue any more."

On August 8, 1966, the "Decision of the Central Committee of the Chinese Communist Party on the Great Proletarian Cultural Revolution," which was adopted under Chairman Mao's personal auspices, pointed out: "To reform the old educational system and the old methods and policy of teaching is an extremely important task of this Great Proletarian Cultural Revolution.

"In this Great Proletarian Cultural Revolution, the phenomenon in which bourgeois intellectuals dominated our schools must be thoroughly changed."

The death-knell of the revisionist educational line represented by Liu Shao-ch'i was sounded! The time to thoroughly smash the old educational system and create a brand new proletarian educational system has arrived!

3. The struggle between two lines in the Great Proletarian Cultural Revolution.

In June 1966 Liu and Teng sent out work groups to promote the bourgeois reactionary line, implement bourgeois dictatorship, and besiege and suppress the revolutionaries, thus attempting to beat down the resounding Cultural Revolution.

On July 13, under the instigation of counterrevolutionary double-faced T'ao Chu, Ho Wei, together with Yung Wen-t'ao and others, drafted and issued the "Circular on the Problems of Enrollment, Examination, Holidays, and Graduation in Middle and Primary Schools." This circular asked middle and primary schools in China to enroll students in the autumn, with the vacation for the first and second year classes in junior middle schools to be given as usual, thus trying to strangle the Great Proletarian Cultural Revolution in the middle and primary schools.

On July 15, under the instigation of Liu Shao-ch'i and T'ao Chu, Ho Wei drafted the "Decision Concerning the Reform of the School System (Draft)," thereby continuing to peddle Liu Shao-ch'i's "half-work and half-study," resisting Chairman Mao's "May 7" Directive, and attempting to shift the general direction of the current struggle.

On August 8 the "Sixteen-Point Decision" were released, announcing the bankruptcy of the Liu and Teng bourgeois reactionary line.

On August 12 Chairman Mao issued the great appeal: "You must be concerned with the important events of the state and push the Great Proletarian Cultural Revolution to its end."

In October the entire nation criticized the bourgeois reactionary line profoundly.

In January 1967 Chairman Mao issued the appeal for the proletarian revolutionaries to form a great coalition to seize power; thus the storm of the "January revolution" engulfed the entire nation.

In April Comrade Ch'i Pen-yü's important article "Patriotism or Renegadism?" was published; hundreds of millions of people unleashed a general offensive against Liu Shao-ch'i — China's No. 1 authority who took the capitalist line. The Great Proletarian Cultural Revolution entered a stage of decisive war to eliminate the root of revisionism!

Now it is time to thoroughly weed out the general root of Liu Shao-ch'i's revisionism! It is time to thoroughly smash Liu Shao-ch'i's revisionist educational line!

Down with Liu Shao-ch'i!

Long live Chairman Mao's proletarian revolutionary line!

Long live our most beloved leader Chairman Mao!!!

II

General Directives

2

QUOTATIONS FROM CHAIRMAN MAO*

Red Flag

"It is still necessary to have universities; here I refer mainly to colleges of science and engineering. However, it is essential to shorten the length of schooling, to revolutionize education, to put proletarian politics in command, and to take the road of the Shanghai Machine Tool Plant in training technicians from among the workers. Students should be selected from among workers and peasants with practical experience, and they should return to production after a few years' study."

"Education must serve proletarian politics and be combined with productive labor."

"Our educational policy must enable everyone who receives an education to develop morally, intellectually, and physically and to become a worker with both socialist consciousness and culture."

"The same holds true for the students. While their main task is to study, they should also learn other things; that is to say, they should not learn only book knowledge but should learn also about industry, agriculture, and the military. They should also criticize the bourgeoisie."

---

*"Mao chu-hsi yü-lu." Hung-ch'i, No. 8 (July 21, 1970), 1-4.

"Besides meeting the needs of teaching and scientific research, all laboratories and affiliated factories of engineering colleges that can undertake production tasks should do so to the best of their ability."

"To accomplish the proletarian educational revolution, it is essential to have working class leadership. The masses of workers must take part in this revolution and, in cooperation with Liberation Army fighters, form a revolutionary three-in-one combination with the activists among the students, teachers, and workers in schools and colleges, who are determined to carry the proletarian educational revolution through to the end. The workers' propaganda teams should stay permanently in the schools and colleges, take part in all the tasks of struggle-criticism-transformation there, and always lead these institutions. In the countryside, schools and colleges should be managed by the poor and lower-middle peasants — the most reliable ally of the working class."

3

UNIVERSITIES AND MIDDLE AND PRIMARY SCHOOLS SHOULD ALL RESUME CLASSES AND MAKE REVOLUTION*

People's Daily

The resumption of classes to make revolution is urgently needed in the current phase of the Great Proletarian Cultural Revolution, and is the common aspiration of the broad masses of revolutionary teachers and students and the broad revolutionary masses. The sixteen-point "Decision of the Central Committee of the Chinese Communist Party Concerning the Great Proletarian Cultural Revolution," which was personally formulated by Chairman Mao, points out that the reform of the old educational system and of the old teaching guidelines and methods is an extremely important task in the current Great Proletarian Cultural Revolution.

In his programmatic directive issued on May 7, 1966, Chairman Mao pointed out the fundamental orientation for the revolution in education: "Students should also do likewise. While their main task is to study, they should also learn other things. They should study not only literature but also industry, agriculture, and military affairs; they should also criticize the bourgeoisie. The period of schooling must be shortened and education must be revolutionized. The atmosphere in which the bourgeois in-

*Ta, chung, hsiao hsüeh-hsiao tou yao fu k'o nao ke-ming." Jen-min jih-pao, October 25, 1967.

tellectuals control our schools must not be allowed to continue any longer."

At present, the Great Proletarian Cultural Revolution has won a decisive victory. In the course of more than one year of the Great Proletarian Cultural Revolution, a handful of counterrevolutionary revisionists on the educational front have been dragged out and the revisionist educational line represented by China's Khrushchev has been criticized and repudiated en masse. This has paved the way for reforming the old educational system and the old teaching guidelines and methods.

Under such circumstances, it is completely possible and necessary for all schools to change from suspending classes to make revolution to resuming classes to make revolution. The broad masses of revolutionary teachers and students must concentrate their efforts in the direction of carrying out the "struggle-criticism-transformation" campaign in their own schools and completing the arduous tasks of teaching reforms. It is necessary to believe in, rely on, and motivate the masses with a free hand, develop the enthusiasm and initiative of the broad masses of revolutionary teachers and students, hold aloft the revolutionary red banner of Mao Tse-tung thought, do some thinking, and devise methods.

To reform teaching, it is necessary to integrate with practice in teaching. We must engage in teaching while conducting reforms. If we departed from practice in teaching, we would not know how to reform. Chairman Mao taught us: "You must have knowledge in order to be able to take part in the real practice in building the country. You must take a bite of the pear in order to know the taste of the fruit." Only in the course of practice in teaching and through mass discussions, criticism, revolution, and creation can we thoroughly implement Chairman Mao's thought on revolution in education, recognize the law of revolution in education under the socialist system, and gradually propose revolutionary plans for an educational system and program.

Resuming classes to make revolution and doing a good job

on "struggle-criticism-transformation" in the schools is the struggle between two classes, two roads, and two lines, and the struggle between two kinds of world outlook. The various schools must conscientiously implement Chairman Mao's great directives concerning "struggle-criticism-transformation," educate every revolutionary teacher or student to vigorously combat self-interest in his mind, with a great sense of proletarian revolutionary responsibility, thoroughly criticize and repudiate the revisionist educational line represented by China's Khrushchev, and vigorously foster Chairman Mao's proletarian educational line. All revolutionary comrades must maintain vigilance against the disruptive activities of the class enemy.

In order to take firm hold of the basic question of "combating self-interest and repudiating revisionism," it is necessary to grasp tightly the political-ideological work of revolutionary teachers and students and to take firm hold of the thoroughgoing criticism and repudiation of the revisionist educational line. In this way the resumption of classes to make revolution can be carried out properly and the revolution in education can be made successfully.

In the course of resuming classes to make revolution, the mass organizations and revolutionary Red Guards in various schools must comply with Chairman Mao's March 7 Directive, learn the experience of the Yenan Middle School in Tientsin, realize the revolutionary great alliance on the basis of grades and departments under the revolutionary principle, and help the revolutionary cadres and teachers in stepping forward and establishing leading groups of the revolutionary three-way alliance.

In the course of resuming classes to make revolution, revolutionary teachers and revolutionary cadres must constantly keep in mind that the undertakings in which they are engaged involve the major undertaking of cultivating successors to the proletarian revolution. They must have the courage and determination to criticize thoroughly the old educational system and completely break away from their bourgeois world outlook.

They must be aware that they are educators and, at the same time, persons being educated. In many cases, the students are more competent. They must go among the students, mingle with them, and establish socialist new-style teacher-student relations.

The principle of relying on one's own efforts and of being diligent and frugal must also be implemented in resuming classes to make revolution. Advocate the easy and simple way. Everyone must help in solving problems involving teaching materials and equipment. We must educate the students to love and protect state property. Parents must also cooperate with the schools and strengthen their children's political-ideological education.

Fulfilling the task of the proletarian revolution in education is a magnanimous and great cause. We must use Chairman Mao's thought on revolution in education as a weapon and become brave forerunners of the revolution in education, be daring and undaunted, have courage and plans, be tough, dare to smash the old stereotypes of the bourgeoisie which oppose Mao Tse-tung thought, and dare to put forward the new socialist educational systems, new teaching programs, and new teaching methods that are in line with Mao Tse-tung thought.

Practice, recognize; again practice, and again recognize. In the course of repeating revolutionary practices, continuously sum up experiences and establish a red proletarian educational system that flashes with the luster of Mao Tse-tung thought.

4

SHORTEN THE PERIOD OF SCHOOLING AND REVOLUTIONIZE EDUCATION*

People's Daily

Our great leader Chairman Mao has long maintained that the period of schooling should be shortened. Since the whole country was liberated, he has issued a number of extremely important instructions on transforming the old educational system. For example, he said in 1966: "The period of schooling should be shortened, education should be revolutionized; the domination of our schools by bourgeois intellectuals should by no means be allowed to continue."

The series of important instructions by Chairman Mao provides a clear-cut direction for the proletarian revolution in education.

But these instructions of Chairman Mao have been frantically resisted by China's Khrushchev and his agents in the educational field, such as Lu Ting-i and company. For instance, China's Khrushchev said: "All the courses must be completed. Do not stipulate the period of schooling." He went so far as to point the spearhead directly at Chairman Mao when he said: "We should not hastily give orders when we are not sure of the

*"Hsüeh-chih yao so-tuan chiao-yü yao ke-ming." Jen-min jih-pao, January 9, 1968.

target." The counterrevolutionary revisionist element Lu Ting-i and others also said: "Generally, the period of schooling for higher schools run on a full-time basis is not shortened."

Taking advantage of the leading positions they had usurped in the field of education, instead of shortening the period of schooling, they prolonged it. Specialized courses requiring a shorter period of schooling and short-term training classes for industry and agriculture were dropped. The four-year university and college courses grew to five, six, or even eight years. They even resisted and opposed the decision which the Central Military Commission made on shortening the period of schooling in the universities and colleges specializing in national defense industries.

China's Khrushchev and Lu Ting-i also spread a host of reactionary fallacies to oppose Chairman Mao's ideas on the proletarian revolution in education and to maintain the old educational system. Among the most poisonous of these was their excuse that "the quality of education should be raised." China's Khrushchev, for instance, insisted that the period of schooling should be determined by the number of years required of particular courses. Lu Ting-i also said that the students "must get comparatively complete knowledge" on the ground that the first and foremost task of education was to impart knowledge.

Beyond any doubt we should raise the quality of education. The question is what kind of "quality of education" it should be and what class it should serve. The "quality of education" desired by China's Khrushchev and company was bourgeois education designed to foster successors for the bourgeoisie. Since China's Khrushchev and company gave first place to devoting long years of study to particular branches of specialized knowledge, they favored prolonging the period of schooling.

The longer years of schooling advocated by China's Khrushchev and Lu Ting-i divorced students from proletarian politics, from reality, from the workers, peasants, and soldiers. The youth, which is "like the sun at eight or nine o'clock in the morning," had to spend its time immersed in books, to become intellectual aristocrats lording it over the working people. Some students complained that after leaving the classroom to become cadres in government offices — direct from the school to government institutions without going to the fields to help peasants plant and harvest crops — they were no longer willing to go to places abounding in hardships. Obviously, the proletariat needs no such raising of the "quality of education."

At the same time that they exerted themselves to prolong the period of schooling, China's Khrushchev and Lu Ting-i also endeavored to instill feudal, capitalist, and revisionist ideas in the students. Lu Ting-i, for instance, said: "The students should first study feudal and capitalist culture before acquiring socialist culture." This is indeed the confession of a counterrevolutionary revisionist, striving to preserve intact all aspects of knowledge.

Let us ask Lu: is it possible for students imbued with ideas of feudal and capitalist culture to assimilate socialist culture? Under the revisionist line espoused by China's Khrushchev and Lu Ting-i, more and more courses were added in many schools; the content of these courses became more and more complicated and students' homework grew much heavier.

Taking advantage of classroom instruction to peddle revisionist stuff to poison the students, some bourgeois intellectuals even misled their pupils into going deep into the origins of the formation of certain Chinese characters, such as the combination of strokes and dots, saying they could acquire extensive "learning" from these studies.

As Lenin said of the old schools, they "compelled their pupils to assimilate a mass of useless, superfluous, and barren knowledge" and were "encumbering young people's minds with an immense amount of knowledge, nine-tenths of which was useless and the remaining one-tenth distorted."

Why did China's Khrushchev and Lu Ting-i work so assiduously to prolong the period of schooling? The reason is they wanted to keep the workers and peasants and their children out of the schools and to exercise bourgeois dictatorship over them. The longer the period of schooling, the less the chance of workers, peasants, and their children attending schools, because they were needed for production and because of economic considerations.

The proletariat has its own standard of educational quality, namely, that education must help to foster reliable successors for the proletarian revolutionary cause. Chairman Mao teaches us: "Successors to the revolutionary cause of the proletariat come forward in mass struggles and are tempered in the great storms of revolution." This is why the period of schooling must be shortened.

Chairman Mao teaches us: "Reading is learning, but application is also learning and the more important kind of learning at that." Therefore, school education must be carried out on the principle of "less but better," with both content and method directed toward a common purpose. In other words, education must be closely integrated with practical needs and circumstances, and study must be combined with application.

After going to school for a comparatively short time, creatively studying and applying Chairman Mao's writings and laying a foundation in moral, intellectual, and physical development, all students require tempering and need to grow up in the midst of actual struggles. The history of China's revolutionary wars shows that commanders and fighters of our armed forces, who had never entered a school and had done very little reading, defeated the military academy graduates of the reactionary Kuomintang, conquered the Japanese militarists who were armed to the teeth, and, in the world-famous war to aid Korea and resist U.S. aggression, outfought and overcame the American imperialists — number one enemy of the people of the world.

The history of the development of China's science and technology also amply proves that young scientific workers, the revolutionary masses, and revolutionary cadres — without any such bourgeois titles as "academician" or "eminent doctor" — in a comparatively short period have successfully produced atom and hydrogen bombs, and at a speed far surpassing that of the U. S. imperialist and the Soviet revisionists, by following the principles laid down by our great leader, Chairman Mao, and Vice Chairman Lin, his close comrade-in-arms, the principles of going all-out and aiming high, of doing things self-reliantly and with great efforts, and with the lofty ambition of catching up with and surpassing the world's most advanced scientific and technological levels.

Fostering successors to the revolutionary cause of the proletariat requires the establishment of a new school system. The world-renowned "K'angta" set an example by introducing a revolutionary new system of education, an extraordinarily revolutionary and extraordinarily militant new type of school for embodying Chairman Mao's ideas on education. "K'angta" fostered a large number of persons of outstanding talent for the proletariat, thus providing important conditions for the victories of the War of Resistance Against Japan and the War of Liberation.

The struggle we have been waging on the educational front against the handful of top Party persons in authority taking the capitalist road on the question of the period of schooling is a struggle between the two classes, the two roads, and the two lines, a struggle between the proletariat and the bourgeoisie for the younger generation. We must therefore firmly grasp this key link, the shortening of the period of schooling, and thoroughly transform the old educational system.

Our great leader Chairman Mao's ideas on revolutionizing education form an important component of Mao Tse-tung thought. It is an ingenious, creative development of Marxism-Leninism, a development of epochal importance for destroying the old bourgeois educational system and establishing a new proletarian educational system. Let us therefore hold high the great red banner of Mao Tse-tung thought, critically condemn and thoroughly repudiate the old educational system, and root out the poisonous fallacies spread by the handful of top Party persons in authority taking the capitalist road for the purpose of upholding the old educational system.

Proletarian Revolutionaries of the Organs
of the National Defense Science Commission

5

THE WORKING CLASS MUST EXERCIZE LEADERSHIP IN EVERYTHING*

Yao Wen-yüan

. . . The workers' propaganda teams are entering the field of education. This is an earth-shaking event. Schools were the monopoly of the exploiting classes and their children from ancient times. Conditions improved somewhat after liberation, but in the main the schools were still monopolized by bourgeois intellectuals. Some students from these schools have been able, for various reasons, to integrate themselves with, and serve, the workers, peasants, and soldiers (generally speaking, because they themselves or their teachers are comparatively good or because of the influence of their families, relatives, or friends, but chiefly of society at large). Some others have not. In a state of the dictatorship of the proletariat, there exists a serious situation — the bourgeoisie contends with the proletariat for leadership. When the young Red Guard fighters rose in rebellion against the handful of capitalist roaders within the Party during the current Great Proletarian

*Peking, Foreign Languages Press, 1968. Original appeared in Hung-ch'i [Red Flag], No. 2 (August 25, 1968), 3-6: "Kung-jen chieh-chi pi-hsü ling-tao i-ch'ieh." The Foreign Languages Press translation has been edited to conform with American spelling and punctuation.

Cultural Revolution, the reactionary bourgeois forces in the schools got hard blows for a while. But shortly afterward, certain people were again active in secret. They incited the masses to struggle against each other, and they set out to sabotage the Great Cultural Revolution, disrupt struggle-criticism-transformation, undermine the great alliance and the revolutionary "three-in-one" combination, and destroy the work of purifying the class ranks and of Party rectification. All this has aroused dissatisfaction among the masses. The facts show us that under such circumstances it is impossible for the students and intellectuals by themselves to fulfill the tasks of struggle-criticism-transformation and a whole number of other tasks on the educational front; workers and People's Liberation Army fighters must take part, and it is essential to have strong leadership by the working class.

Chairman Mao recently pointed out:

"In carrying out the proletarian revolution in education, it is essential to have working-class leadership; it is essential for the masses of workers to take part and, in cooperation with Liberation Army fighters, bring about a revolutionary "three-in-one" combination, together with the activists among the students, teachers, and workers in the schools who are determined to carry the proletarian revolution in education through to the end. The workers' propaganda teams should stay permanently in the schools and take part in fulfilling all the tasks of struggle-criticism-transformation in the schools, and they will always lead the schools. In the countryside, the schools should be managed by the poor and lower-middle peasants — the most reliable ally of the working class."

This instruction of Chairman Mao's indicates the orientation and road for the educational revolution in the schools. It is a sharp weapon for thoroughly destroying the bourgeois educational system. The masses of young students should enthusiastically welcome the working class as it takes over the school position, participates in struggle-criticism-transformation, and assumes permanent leadership of the schools.

The working class has rich practical experience in the Three

Great Revolutionary Movements of class struggle, the struggle for production, and scientific experiment. It shows the utmost enmity for all counterrevolutionary words and deeds opposed to socialism and Mao Tse-tung thought. It most bitterly hates the old educational system, which served the exploiting classes. It most strongly opposes the "civil war" activities of certain intellectuals in damaging state property and obstructing struggle-criticism-transformation. It thoroughly detests the habit of empty talk and the practice of double-dealing, in which words and actions do not match. Therefore, when they combine with fighters of the Chinese People's Liberation Army — the main pillar of the dictatorship of the proletariat — the masses of the working class will be most powerful in stemming all erroneous tendencies contrary to Chairman Mao's revolutionary line and will be most effective in resolving all kinds of problems that have been described as long-standing, big, and difficult. Contradictions that the intellectuals have been quarreling over without end and unable to resolve are quickly settled when the workers arrive. As regards the handful of villains who have been hiding behind the scenes and inciting the masses to struggle against each other, only when the workers and Liberation Army fighters step in is it possible to bare their counterrevolutionary features completely.

"The workers have only to look after their factories, that's enough." This is an anti-Marxist viewpoint. The working class understands that it can achieve its own final emancipation only by emancipating all mankind. Without carrying the proletarian revolution in education in the schools through to the end and without rooting out revisionism, the working class cannot achieve its final emancipation; and the danger of capitalist restoration and of the working class's being exploited and oppressed anew still exists. It is the bound duty of the politically conscious working class to take an active part in the Great Cultural Revolution in all fields and to ensure that Mao Tse-tung thought occupies every position in culture and education.

"Let us liberate ourselves. There is no need for the workers outside school to join in." What the "Decision of the Central

Committee of the Chinese Communist Party Concerning the Great Proletarian Cultural Revolution" states is that the method "is for the masses to liberate themselves." Are the workers not included in the "masses"? Is not the working class made of your own people? All genuine proletarian revolutionaries — not those who pay lip service to deceive people — regard members of the working class as their own people and as the most advanced and the most politically conscious among the masses. The "three-in-one" combination of workers, soldiers, and the revolutionary activists in the schools is the most reliable guarantee for the masses to liberate themselves. Whoever regards the workers as a force alien to himself is, if not muddleheaded, himself an element alien to the working class; and the working class has every reason to exercise dictatorship over him. Some intellectuals who styled themselves "proletarian revolutionaries" oppose the workers whenever the working class touches on the interests of their tiny "independent kingdoms." There are still quite a few such people in China like Lord She,* people who look down upon the workers and peasants, who are inclined to put on airs and think themselves great. As a matter of fact, they are just modern Lord She. It is essential for the workers and People's Liberation Army fighters to go to those places where intellectuals are concentrated, be they schools or other units, to smash the complete domination by intellectuals, occupy the "independent kingdoms," big or small, and take over those places where the advocates of the theory of "many centers," that is, the theory of "no center," are entrenched. In this way, the unhealthy atmosphere, style of work, and thinking that exist among intellectuals concentrated in groups can be changed;

---

*As told by Liu Hsiang (77-6 B.C.), of the Han Dynasty, in his Hsin Hsu, Lord She was so fond of dragons that he adorned his whole palace with drawings and carvings of them. But when a real dragon heard of his infatuation and paid him a visit, he was frightened out of his wits. This betrayed Lord She's fondness for dragons as a sham — Tr.

and thus there is the possibility for intellectuals to remold themselves and achieve emancipation.

"Workers don't understand education." These are the words of some so-called "high-ranking" intellectuals. None of your ugly, bourgeois intellectual airs! There are two kinds of education: bourgeois and proletarian. What you "understand" is the pseudoknowledge of the bourgeoisie. Those who teach science and engineering do not know how to operate or repair machines; those who teach literature do not know how to write essays; those who teach agricultural chemistry do not know how to use fertilizer. Aren't such laughingstocks to be found everywhere? The proletarian educational system characterized by the integration of theory with practice can be gradually brought into being only when the proletariat takes a direct part. This is utterly beyond people like you.

"The workers don't know the situation in the schools and the history of the struggle between the two lines there." Don't worry, comrades. The workers will get to know them. Compared with those shortsighted intellectuals who see only their small mountain-strongholds, the working class stands on a far higher eminence. The workers will not stay in the schools for just a few days; they will keep on working there permanently and always occupy and lead the schools. Everything that exists objectively can be understood. The working class will deepen its recognition of the world through its own revolutionary practice and remake the world in its own image.

Workers' propaganda teams should, step by step and in a planned way, go to universities, colleges, middle schools, and primary schools, to all sectors of the superstructure and to all units in which struggle-criticism-transformation has not been carried out well. Taking Mao Tse-tung thought as the guiding principle, they should unite with and help the activists there who are determined to carry the proletarian revolution in education through to the end; unite with the great majority of the masses, including those intellectuals who can be remolded; and, in the proletarian spirit of thoroughgoing revolution, promote the struggle-criticism-transformation there.

This is a great historical mission of the Chinese working class at the present time. In the course of fulfilling this mission, the working class will itself be profoundly steeled in the class struggle; and a group of outstanding worker-cadres will emerge, not merely to manage schools but to reinforce every sector of the state organs and the revolutionary committees at all levels.

To fulfill this historical mission, the working class must earnestly and thoroughly study Mao Tse-tung thought, learn the mass line and the style of investigation and study that Chairman Mao has always taught us, make ceaseless efforts to raise its political consciousness, heighten its revolutionary sense of discipline, and constantly criticize and repudiate the corrosion and influence of rotten bourgeois ways within the working class. The bourgeoisie has a traditional influence in the cultural and educational institutions. When the working class sets about transforming the world according to the proletarian world outlook, that is, Mao Tse-tung thought, the bourgeoisie invariably makes every effort to use the bourgeois world outlook to corrode the weak sections in the ranks of the workers, including those of their leading cadres. The working class must maintain sharp vigilance against this. It must keep to the firm stand of the proletariat and maintain vigilance against attacks from sugarcoated bullets or by other means against the ranks of the workers. In addition, it must conscientiously do a good job of purifying the class ranks, grasp revolution and promote production, and make a success of struggle-criticism-transformation in factories and other enterprises. . . .

III

Educating the Elites

6

THE "MAY 7" CADRE SCHOOL

Peking Review *

An innovation born in the Great Cultural Revolution, "May 7" cadre schools are all over China. Every province, municipality, and autonomous region, as well as many special administrative regions, counties, and cities, all have this type of school. More than a hundred belong to the departments under the Central Committee of the Chinese Communist Party and the State Council.

Those who have been sent to the school include veteran cadres who went through the Long March, the War of Resistance Against Japan, or the War of Liberation; cadres who joined the revolution after liberation; those who went from their homes to schools and from there to government offices and who were lacking in practical experience; and young cadres who had been Red Guards. While at cadre school, they get their regular wages and the same welfare benefits as when they are on the job. The term generally is for a year or so: the least, six months; the most, two to three years.

---

*Peking Review, No. 19 (May 12, 1972), 5-7. This article has been edited to conform with American spelling and punctuation.

Versatile Activities

Regardless of seniority or how high a post held, everyone is an ordinary student, a "May 7" fighter. At the Chingkou "May 7" Cadre School in Kirin Province, the former director of the agriculture bureau becomes a pig-breeder; the former secretary of the city Party committee, a carpenter; a department head, a cart driver; and a county head, a cook.

Students' lives are many-sided. They do productive manual labor as well as study. They criticize the bourgeoisie and do mass work. The school also organizes militia training and cultural and sports activities. Some schools set aside time for students to study their vocations or raise their general educational level.

The "May 7" cadre school is a school for training cadres at their posts in rotation.

How does the school accomplish its tasks? How do students study? In general the answers are as follows:

Studying Marxist-Leninist Works

In the light of the revolutionary struggle and their ideology, the students study the works of Marx, Engels, Lenin, and Stalin and Chairman Mao's works to raise their level of Marxism and their consciousness of the struggle between the two lines, thereby increasing their ability to distinguish between genuine and sham Marxists.

The students at the Huangho "May 7" Cadre School in Honan spend half a day studying and the other half doing manual labor. In the busy farming season, they work during the day, studying in the morning or evening. Last year they studied the Manifesto of the Communist Party, Critique of the Gotha Programme, and The State and Revolution, as well as "On Practice" and "On Contradiction." They pay special attention to linking theory with practice and often organize group discussions and criticism meetings.

Participating in Class Struggle

Students at cadre schools take part in the class struggle and in criticizing the bourgeoisie to temper themselves. They often link their work and ideological problems with their mass criticism of swindlers like Liu Shao-ch'i and of the theory of the dying out of class struggle, the bourgeois theory of human nature, the theory of productive forces, idealist apriorism, the theory that doing manual labor is a punishment, and the theory of going to school in order to get an official post. Some cadre schools carry out various political movements in step with the movements in the units they belong to. Some have sent students to rural people's communes to take part in or help local people carry out a political campaign such as attacking active counterrevolutionaries, or campaigns against embezzlement and theft, or extravagence, waste, and speculation.

Taking Part in Productive Labor

Cadre schools devote themselves mainly to agricultural production. Where conditions allow, they branch out into forestry, animal husbandry, side occupations, and fisheries. At the same time, they go in for small industries, such as machine-repairing, manufacturing of chemical fertilizers and insecticides, paper- and brick-making, and sugar refining.

Every cadre school has cultivated land — much was once wasteland — ranging from hundreds to thousands of mu, parts of which are reclaimed tracts along seacoasts or lake shores and on barren hillsides and alkaline slopes. Inner Mongolia's Ikh Chao League cadre school converted much sandy land into fertile fields by covering the sand with layers of mud.

"Plain living and hard struggle" and "self-reliance" are the mottoes of all the cadre schools.

The object of students taking part in industrial or agricultural productive labor is not only to create material wealth for the country but mainly to improve their ideology and to transform their subjective world as they transform the objective world.

Cadres of the General Office of the Chinese Communist Party's Central Committee turned the building of their school into a process of edifying their thought. Instead of choosing a ready-made site, they preferred to build it from scratch. They turned 5,000 mu of lake shore and other wasteland into fields and built dormitories and factories on their own. They dug canals, wading knee-deep in mud. They went into icy streams to get sand and braved eye-stinging smoke to burn limestone in the kilns. They fought floods to save people's lives and property. They met all these trials head on to gain the revolutionary spirit of "fearing neither hardship nor death."

Going Among Workers and Peasants

Students often leave their schools for short stays in nearby people's communes or factories. Living, eating, and working alongside workers or peasants, they learn from them and carry out social investigations among them at the same time. They also do mass work, such as organizing workers and peasants to study philosophy, helping them get some general education, and aiding local Party organizations in carrying out Party rectification and Party building. All these activities aim at raising their ideological level and reforming their world outlook.

Transforming Man

Cadres come to the schools in turns. They go back to their original posts after "graduation," or are transferred to new work. Practice has shown that their stay at cadre schools, brief as it is, is excellent training. The great majority of students come out of the schools changed in outlook in more ways than one.

One artist at the Kuantang Cadre School in Hunan Province, who had joined revolutionary work straight from school, had not liked to draw peasants because he considered their weather-beaten faces no objects for art. After entering the cadre school, he had a chance to live and eat with peasants, and made some social investigations into their lives. He found out the tragic histories of many peasant families in the old society under the exploitation of the landlord class. His sentiments changed, and he began to have a great compassion for the once-downtrodden peasants. He said: "Before, I looked at things according to bourgeois esthetic standards; the more I drew, the farther from the laboring people I got. Now, the more I draw peasants, the closer I feel to them."

Lin Hsiang-wei, vice-director and chief engineer at a designing institute in Hunan, had designed a highway bridge that wasted tons of bricks because he wanted it fancy. The workers criticized him, without convincing him he was wrong. After going to the Kuantang Cadre School, he happened to be working at a brick-kiln. A rush assignment in summer had him drenched in sweat and covered with dirt in the sweltering heat day after day. Only then did he fully realize what it meant to make one brick. He said, with genuine feeling: "It's only after you've taken part in labor that you get to feel akin to the workers and peasants." During a fierce rainstorm, Lin ran to the kiln and covered up the clay molds, though he got soaking wet. He often expresses his determination to continue to make revolution and thoroughly transform his old ideas, to become an intellectual welcomed by the workers, peasants, and soldiers.

Veteran cadres with much revolutionary experience also gain a great deal from going to cadre school. It puts them back in the war years and helps them get rid of bureaucratic airs and the inactivity that crept up on them in peacetime. It rejuvenates them.

Fang Fu-chin, a veteran of the 25,000-li Long March of the Chinese Red Army in 1934-35, was one of the first to enroll at the Meitsun Cadre School under the Kwangchow Railway Bureau. Once there, he was reminded of the militant life he used to lead in the Chingkang Mountains, Yenan, and Nanniwan in the early days of the revolution. Invigorated, he joined the rank and file in climbing mountains to fell trees and went wherever the difficulties were greatest. Out of consideration for his years, comrades often told him to take a rest. He refused, saying: "You may replace me in labor, but that will never transform my ideology."

Yang Li-feng is a new cadre from a poor peasant family. She entered college in 1960 wearing a pair of simple cloth shoes her mother had made for her. Under the influence of the revisionist line in education, she developed the bourgeois idea of wanting to get up in the world. So she put the cloth shoes at the bottom of a chest. When schoolmates asked her to tell them her family history, she refused, ashamed of past poverty.

At the Hsiushuihotzu People's Commune in Faku County, Liaoning Province, Yang took part in peasant activities to recall past bitterness and praise the new life. She told commune members how her feelings had changed after going to college. The peasants helped her, saying: "You must understand that you've not only forgotten your family's bitter past, but that of your class. You've not only put away the cloth shoes, but the true qualities of the laboring people." Enlightened, Yang plunged into productive labor with renewed zeal and wore her cloth shoes again.

After coming out of cadre schools, most cadres are full of life, keep in close touch with the masses, and have a good style in their work and way of living. The masses of workers, peasants, and soldiers welcome their progress made in this period of "studying once again." They say: "We have full confidence in cadres who can work both at the top and down at the grass roots, and who keep close to the people."

Origin of Cadre Schools

"May 7" cadre schools were set up in all parts of the country according to Chairman Mao's May 7, 1966, Directive.*

---

*This directive pointed out that the "army should be a great school.... In this school, our army should study politics and military affairs, raise its educational level, and also engage in agriculture and side occupations and run small or medium-

In 1968, when the Proletarian Cultural Revolution was developing in depth, the question of how to carry forward the cadres' ideological revolutionization and revolutionize government institutions was discussed on a wide scale. In October of that year Chairman Mao issued the call: "Going down to do manual labor gives vast numbers of cadres an excellent opportunity to study once again; this should be done by all cadres except those who are old, weak, ill, or disabled. Cadres at their posts should also go down in turn to do manual labor."

Cadres at every level all over the country enthusiastically responded to this call and asked to go to the most difficult places to do manual labor and to "study once again." The "May 7" cadre schools were set up to meet these needs, and in the single month of October alone new ones appeared almost every day.

The guiding thought of these cadre schools, which upholds the system of cadre participation in collective productive labor, was pointed out by Chairman Mao and the Party Central Committee long before 1968.

Cadres doing productive labor are in the fine tradition of the Chinese Workers' and Peasants' Red Army, the Eighth Route Army, the New Fourth Army, and, today, of the People's Liberation Army. In an army of the people, officers and soldiers help the masses in manual labor wherever they are. Since the liberation, cadres in government and Party organizations have learned to carry forward this tradition. The system

---

sized factories. . . . Our army should also do mass work. . . . Also our army should always be ready to participate in the struggles to criticize and repudiate the bourgeoisie in the cultural revolution." It also called on people in other fields to "learn other things" while mainly engaging in their own work. "They should also learn industrial production, agricultural production and military affairs. They also should criticize and repudiate the bourgeoisie." They must study "politics and raise their educational level." "Those working in . . . Party and government organizations should do the same."

of cadre participation in collective productive labor for fixed periods has been in effect since 1958, and cadres have been taking turns in going to the countryside or factories.

In 1964, after summing up the experience of revolutionary struggle in China and studying the positive and negative experiences in the international communist movement, Chairman Mao pointed out: "By taking part in collective productive labor, the cadres maintain extensive, constant, and close ties with the working people. This is a major measure of fundamental importance for a socialist system; it helps to overcome bureaucracy and to prevent revisionism and dogmatism."

7

ON THE REEDUCATION OF INTELLECTUALS*

People's Daily and Red Flag Commentators

The establishment of revolutionary committees in twenty-nine provinces, municipalities, and autonomous regions, that is, the entire country except Taiwan Province, indicates that the whole movement of the Great Cultural Revolution has entered the stage of struggle-criticism-transformation on a nationwide scale. Under the guidance of Chairman Mao's latest instructions, mighty contingents of industrial workers, under leadership and step by step, either have entered or are in the process of entering the schools and colleges, various areas of the superstructure, and all units where struggle-criticism-transformation has not been carried out well, so as to promote struggle-criticism-transformation in these places. This has not only ushered in a completely new situation in the proletarian revolution in education but will inevitably accelerate the remolding of the ranks of intellectuals by China's working

*Peking: Foreign Languages Press, 1968. Originally appeared in Hung-ch'i [Red Flag], No. 3 (September 10, 1968), 2-4: "Kuan-yü chih-shih fen-tzu tsai-chiao-yü wen-t'i." The Foreign Languages Press translation has been edited to conform with American spelling and punctuation.

class in accordance with its own outlook.

When the working class enters cultural and educational institutions, its work is directed primarily toward the intellectuals. Correct grasp of the Party's policy toward intellectuals is therefore an important guarantee for victory in the struggle.

The extremely important editor's note of the journal Hung-ch'i [Red Flag], published in the press on September 5, relays the voice of our great leader Chairman Mao. This editor's note raised a very important question, namely, giving attention to the reeducation of the large number of intellectuals — college and secondary-school graduates who started work quite some time ago as well as those who have just begun to work. The editor's note set forth various proletarian policies toward intellectuals and further pointed out the only correct direction for intellectuals — integrating themselves with the workers and peasants.

The great leader Chairman Mao teaches us that the remolding of the intellectuals remains a question of major significance throughout the course of the socialist revolution and socialist construction. After seizing political power, the proletariat should remold the intellectuals in accordance with its own outlook and build up an army of proletarian intellectuals that serves it. This is essential for consolidating and developing the dictatorship of the proletariat and preventing the restoration of capitalism; it is essential for establishing the proletariat in the position of absolute domination in all spheres of ideology and culture. To build up such a corps of proletarian intellectuals, it is necessary to carry out a thoroughgoing proletarian revolution in education, to take the revolutionary road of training technical personnel and other intellectuals from among the workers, peasants, and soldiers, and to select students from among the workers and peasants with practical experience in production and from among the Liberation Army fighters; at the same time, it is necessary to reeducate the large number of intellectuals who graduated from the old schools and colleges in the past so as to win over and unite the vast numbers of intellectuals. As the Great Proletarian

Cultural Revolution deepens and reaches the stage of struggle-criticism-transformation, people can get an ever-clearer appreciation of the great significance of solving this question.

The editor's note pointed out: "Attention should be paid to reeducating the large number of college and secondary-school graduates who started work quite some time ago as well as those who have just begun to work." This involves not only the schools and colleges but also the vast number of intellectuals on our cultural and educational front and in the ranks of our cadres. Why is it called reeducation? Because what they received in the past was bourgeois education and the education they are receiving now is proletarian. This is one meaning. Another is that in the past, under the pernicious influence of the revisionist line of China's Khrushchev, they received education from bourgeois intellectuals whereas now, under the guidance of Chairman Mao's proletarian revolutionary line, they are being reeducated by the workers, peasants, and soldiers. The remolding of one's world outlook is something fundamental. To educate the intellectuals according to the proletarian world outlook so that they can change the bourgeois ideas they formerly received from bourgeois education — such is the content of this reeducation. The fundamental path toward this reeducation is for them to integrate themselves with the workers, peasants, and soldiers and to serve them.

In conducting reeducation, it is necessary to bring the positive factors into full play. The question of line is the fundamental issue. The line that is followed determines the kind of people that are trained. We should concentrate our hatred on the handful of top capitalist-roaders in the Party and their agents since it is their counterrevolutionary revisionist line in education that poisoned the youth. The thorough repudiation of this reactionary line will impel people to make further efforts to carry out Chairman Mao's proletarian educational line. In socialist new China, the majority, or the vast majority, of the students trained in the old schools will, when educated by Mao Tse-tung thought, be able gradually to integrate themselves with the workers, peasants, and soldiers. In the course of this, there will inevitably be wavering and reversals. But provided these people do follow and advance along Chairman Mao's proletarian revolutionary line, accept reeducation by the workers, peasants, and soldiers, and thoroughly repudiate and continuously change the old bourgeois ideas they brought along from home and school, they will be able to contribute their share in serving the workers, peasants, and soldiers. The workers, peasants, and soldiers welcome such intellectuals. Although there are indeed counterrevolutionaries and diehards, they are very few in number. The vast number of intellectuals who are willing to remold themselves under working-class leadership and to integrate themselves with the workers, peasants, and soldiers have bright prospects under the socialist system.

The editor's note pointed out: "There must be some who have done well in integrating themselves and have made inventions or innovations. These people should be publicized in order to encourage them and others." This means to encourage and in a positive way urge the great number of intellectuals to take firmly the road of integrating themselves with the workers, peasants, and soldiers. People who have made a success of this integration and have made inventions or innovations are to be found everywhere. Their example should be cited to educate those intellectuals who have already gone, or are going, to working posts.

The Great Proletarian Cultural Revolution has opened a broader road for the intellectuals to integrate themselves with the workers, peasants, and soldiers, to remold their world outlook, and to serve the people better. The masses of intellectuals have undergone considerable tempering and testing in the Great Cultural Revolution. They feel their shortcomings acutely — their wavering and lack of thoroughness in revolution — and they urgently want to integrate themselves with the workers, peasants, and soldiers. This is most inspiring. The revolutionary committees in all parts of the country and the workers' Mao Tse-tung thought propaganda teams stationed in various units should be good at discovering instances of such initiative by intellectuals, support them in integrating themselves with the workers, peasants, and soldiers, and guide them in taking an active part in struggle-criticism-transformation in their own units. From now on, in places where intellectuals are in concentrated groups, it is necessary, under working-class leadership, to make a success of struggle-criticism-transformation and to run all types of Mao Tse-tung thought study classes well. It is also necessary to organize the intellectuals to go, group by group, among the workers, peasants, and soldiers to be reeducated by them.

People should be given a way out. "It is not the policy of the proletariat to deny people a way out." Only by emancipating all mankind can the proletariat achieve its own final emancipation. Proletarian policy must indicate the way forward for the masses of people of various classes and strata led by the proletariat and turn negative factors into positive ones as far as possible. The adoption of such a policy will help more in prompting those who have committed serious mistakes to own up to and correct their mistakes. As for the very few die-hard capitalist-roaders and bourgeois technical authorities who have incurred the intense wrath of the masses and must be overthrown, they should also be given a way out, after they have been adequately repudiated. This is a question to which attention should be drawn in the final stage of the movement of the Great Proletarian Cultural Revolution.

We must resolutely carry out every proletarian policy on intellectuals set forth by our great leader Chairman Mao. It is essential to distinguish between the two different kinds of contradictions. The contradictions among the people must be handled by the method of unity — criticism and self-criticism — unity. The way to settle questions of an ideological nature is by setting forth facts and reasoning things out and by painstaking and meticulous ideological-political work.

The excellent situation in the Great Proletarian Cultural Revolution as it approaches all-round victory opens up magnificent prospects to the revolutionary masses. We are convinced that, guided by the brilliant light of the great thought of Mao Tse-tung and led by the working class, China's vast number of revolutionary intellectuals and intellectuals who can be remolded will advance faster along the road of revolutionizing themselves and integrating themselves with the working people. "We hope that they [China's intellectuals] will continue to make progress and that, in the course of work and study, they will gradually acquire the communist world outlook, get a better grasp of Marxism-Leninism, and become integrated with the workers and peasants. We hope they will not stop halfway or, what is worse, slip back; for there will be no future for them in going backward" ("On the Correct Handling of Contradictions Among the People").

8

WHOLEHEARTEDLY COMPLETE "REEDUCATION" WORK

Investigation Team of the Kirin Provincial Revolutionary Committee and the Pai-ch'eng Special District Revolutionary Committee *

How is it that the brilliant directive of our great leader Chairman Mao that "intellectual youths be sent down to the countryside to receive reeducation from the poor and lower-middle peasants" has been realized completely throughout an entire hsien? The experience of Ch'ang-ling hsien in Kirin Province was that the leadership personally took a hand in relying on the poor and lower-middle peasants, in wholeheartedly doing the work, and in applying Mao Tse-tung thought to the elevation of the level of reeducation.

Elevate Understanding of "Reeducation" Work

Since 1968, Ch'ang-ling hsien has accommodated more than 3,100 intellectual youths, who were sent down to the countryside from Peking, Ch'ang-ch'un, and Ch'ang-ling itself. When intellectual youths were sent down to Ch'ang-ling, cadres on all levels warmly welcomed them and engaged in large-scale accommodation work. After a period of time, there were some cadres who began to feel that intellectual youths "only presented knotty

*Chi-lin sheng ke-ming wei-yüan-hui, Pai-ch'eng chuan-ch'ü ke-ming wei-yüan-hui tiao-ch'a tsu, "Man-ch'iang je-ch'ing ti tso hao 'tsai-chiao-yü' kung-tso." Hung-ch'i [Red Flag], No. 8 (July 21, 1970), 61-63.

problems," were "difficult to manage, and always "interfered." This sort of thinking was also reflected in the leadership group of the hsien revolutionary committee.

Because this problem was very serious, the hsien revolutionary committee had to resolve it quickly. After investigative research, they presented to the standing committee data on the wholehearted — and with profound class feelings — education of intellectual youths by the poor and lower-middle peasants of the Main No. 4 Brigade of the former No. 7 Commune. They combined some of the problems that had appeared in the past in the work of intellectual youths sent down to the countryside, and they carried on discussions. They felt that some of the cadres' proletarian feelings for the intellectual youths were not as profound as those of the poor and lower-middle peasants. In dealing with the intellectual youths, the poor and lower-middle peasants first and foremost checked to see whether they were essentially and substantially revolutionary, and they positively and patiently helped them correct their deficiencies. But some of our comrades completely ignored the essence and exaggerated the deficiencies. Why is it that there could be two different kinds of thinking and feeling toward the same thing? They again restudied Chairman Mao's great directive on the receiving of reeducation by intellectual youths, and made some progress in recognizing that the question of whether to warmly and thoroughly advance the work of the ideological education of intellectual youths is in fact the question of attitude toward Chairman Mao's proletarian revolutionary line. Only with a deep understanding of the great significance of Chairman Mao's directive on "reeducation," by recognizing that the sending of intellectual youths down to the countryside is a great revolution and that it is a great event that causes the Party and the nation to be forever immutable, can one bear deep proletarian feelings in dealing with the intellectual youths. This is the ideological foundation for completing reeducation work.

The hsien revolutionary committee consciously assigned reeducation work an important position; during research, planning, investigation, and summation work it always made sending intellectual youths down to the countryside an important priority. Important members of the _hsien_ revolutionary committee leadership separately established their own fixed lines of communication. As a rule, when leadership cadres go down to the countryside, they all go to the collectives to look in on the intellectual youths who have been sent down to the countryside, devoting themselves to resolving their ideological problems and, furthermore, devoting themselves to resolving some of the practical problems of the production and the livelihood of the youths. They devote themselves especially to the needs of their study, helping them subscribe to newspapers and often providing them with study materials.

The _hsien_ revolutionary committee is very interested in the intellectual youths and constantly encourages them to make a living study and living application of Mao Tse-tung thought, and to earnestly reform their world view. A great many intellectual youths also take the initiative in reporting conditions to the _hsien_ revolutionary committee. The No. 30 Commune had a backward team; the _hsien_ revolutionary committee went several times to work on it, but could not resolve the problems. The intellectual youths in this team sent a letter reporting the actual conditions, in which an unregenerate was monopolizing the leadership. The _hsien_ revolutionary committee quickly dispatched someone to make an investigation, to mobilize the masses to expose the unregenerate, and to rebuild the leadership group.

Members of the _hsien_ revolutionary committee leadership produced a model and set in motion the agencies and leadership groups of the communes and the teams. Every important commune and team leader personally persisted in reeducation work. The director of the revolutionary committee of the former No. 7 Commune, at the time of going-down-to-the-countryside work, took reeducation work with him wherever he went. He visited and worked with every one of the twenty collectives of this commune, and he carried on frank discussions with 252 intellectual youths.

Penetrate Reality – Do Careful Work

The Ch'ang-ling hsien revolutionary committee followed Chairman Mao's great instructions "You must do careful work," and "Combine general directives with individual guidance." It did not stop at general directives in the work of intellectual youths sent down to the countryside: members of the leadership personally engaged in investigative research, got a firm grip on the model, and did careful work. When leadership is at the fore, work is done at the fore.

Last March, important members of the hsien revolutionary committee leadership, combining an understanding of conditions of struggle-criticism-transformation, visited six communes and twelve collectives. After investigative research, it came to light that some commune brigades only paid heed to using their hands to teach farm life to the intellectual youths, and neglected to grasp politics and grasp ideology. Or else they merely regarded the youths as being objects of reeducation; they did not conceive of them as being one of the most positive and dynamic forces in the Three Great Revolutionary Movements. In accordance with Chairman Mao's great instruction that "the successors to the proletarian revolutionary enterprise are produced among the masses and are wrought from the great revolutionary storm," the hsien revolutionary committee organized and absorbed the intellectual youths sent down to the countryside to participate in every aspect of struggle-criticism-transformation in the villages – letting them make a living study and living application of Mao Tse-tung thought in the fierce struggle between the two classes, the two roads, and the two lines – and to transform their world view. In the midst of actual struggle, the intellectual youths little by little changed their stand, changed their feelings, and continually heightened their awareness of the class struggle and the struggle between the two lines. Deeply moved, they said: "We must not merely work side by side with the poor and lower-middle peasants; we must also engage in heartfelt fighting before we can turn into fighters defending the battleground of rural socialism."

The *hsien* revolutionary committee paid special attention to grasping the work of backward households and backward people. Tung-sheng Brigade had a backward collective. The director of the *hsien* revolutionary committee went there five times in all and established a Mao Tse-tung thought study class, developed revolutionary mass criticism, and elevated their political awareness. Ten times he patiently helped an intellectual youth who had been poisoned by bourgeois ideology and who had made some mistakes. After he had made some progress, the director invited the youth to sit in on a *hsien* discussion meeting on the role of living study and living application of Mao Tse-tung thought. This youth received a great education and made progress very quickly. From the transformation of this youth, the *hsien* revolutionary committee realized that they needed only to persistently apply Mao Tse-tung thought to education of intellectual youths and bring ideological work into their hearts, and backward households and backward individuals would transform their countenance swiftly. They summarized and expanded this experience in a timely way and carried forward intellectual-youth work on a large scale throughout the *hsien*.

From the penetration of reality, investigative research, and doing careful work, members of the revolutionary committee leadership arrived at three "clearnesses": clearness about the conditions of intellectual youths receiving reeducation; clearness about the conditions of poor and lower-middle peasants' work in reeducating intellectual youths; clearness about the new tendency in the struggle for the youths between class enemies and ourselves. In this way, in every period we can seize the power of initiative in reeducation work. The poor and lower-middle peasants say that we should treat intellectual youths as we treat growing seedlings: either there are weeds growing wild or there is no fertilizer; that which should be weeded out is weeded out at the proper time; that which should be watered is watered at the proper time — causing the intellectual youths to follow the direction pointed out by Chairman Mao and to continually grow and flourish.

Rely on the Poor and Lower-Middle Peasants

The hsien revolutionary committee feels that in order to accomplish the task of the reeducation of intellectual youths it is necessary to take the mass road, to rely on the broad poor and lower-middle peasants — not to rely just on the cadres. After the intellectual youths reached the countryside, the hsien revolutionary committee mobilized the poor and lower-middle peasants to take part in reeducation work on a vast scale. Every production brigade assigned outstanding representatives of the poor and lower-middle peasants to positions as political directors of intellectual youth collectives and generally established small reeducation groups. Many poor and lower-middle peasants carried forward affable class education of intellectual youths, remembering the hardships and recalling the pleasures. Moreover, they formed "one-to-one assistance" teams and developed a "one red pair" existence. In the process of the reeducation of intellectual youths, they made use of them, and in the process of making use of them, they educated them, causing the intellectual youths to be tempered in the Three Great Revolutionary Movements and to play a positive role.

In order to mobilize the poor and lower-middle peasants to achieve reeducation work, the hsien revolutionary committee seriously grasped the following points:

1. Run Mao Tse-tung thought study classes on all levels; profoundly understand Chairman Mao's brilliant directive on intellectual youths receiving reeducation and his instruction on training successors to the proletarian revolutionary enterprise; heighten, starting from the fundamentals, recognition of the great significance of the poor and lower-middle peasants' reeducation work. The broad masses of poor and lower-middle peasants have gone one step forward in realizing that the work of reeducation of the intellectual youths sent down to the countryside is no ordinary matter, but is the tremendous issue of training successors to the proletarian revolutionary enterprise. They unrestrainedly state that this is the glorious task passed on to us poor and lower-middle peasants; that we must

apply Mao Tse-tung thought to the achievement of the education of the intellectual youths, help the intellectual youths learn well this major course in class struggle, and see that they fully exert their positive role in the Three Great Revolutionary Movements in the villages.

2. Together with the poor and lower-middle peasants, sum up the experience of the work of the intellectual youths sent down to the countryside, and help the poor and lower-middle peasants grasp the principles of work with intellectual youths. From two years of practice they realized that when intellectual youths have just arrived in the countryside, serious attention must be paid to solving the problem of the understanding of the leadership groups at every level and of the poor and lower-middle peasants being aware of the great significance of reeducation work, of coping solely with the disposal of erroneous ideology, of consciously rising to the task of understanding the heavy burden of training successors to the proletarian revolutionary enterprise. After the sending of intellectual youths down to the countryside has been properly arranged, they must set right the grasping of politics, teach the relationship between production and the management of life, and pay serious attention to resolving the question of putting ideology and politics to the fore. When intellectual youths have caught on to something of the farming life, and when thought reform has attained a certain success, serious attention must be paid to solving the problem of understanding the protracted and formidable character of reeducation work. Most recently, they again paid serious attention to the question of resolving how to bring into full play the activism of the intellectual youths in the Three Great Revolutionary Movements, of progressing in making a living study and living application of Mao Tse-tung thought in the midst of struggle, and of earnestly transforming their world view. In this way step by step they steeped themselves in reeducation work.

3. Help the poor and lower-middle peasants base themselves on the characteristics of the intellectual youths, to do a solid job of the work of intellectual youths sent down to the countryside

that is both vital and dynamic.

In the last two years the broad ranks of intellectual youths sent down to the countryside, under the care of Mao Tse-tung thought, flourished in the Three Great Revolutionary Struggles, progressed very quickly, and brought into play positive applications. Throughout the hsien, of the intellectual youths sent down to the countryside, 353 underwent criticism and became activists in making a living study and living application of Mao Tse-tung thought in the province, the region, and the hsien; 19 joined the Communist Party; 107 entered the Communist Youth League; 46 became responsible hsien, commune, and team cadres, teachers in people's schools, and "barefoot doctors." The broad ranks of masses of intellectual youths are this very moment marching down the road indicated by Chairman Mao, united with the worker-peasant masses.

IV

Control of the Schools

9

CHAIRMAN MAO'S [MARCH 7] DIRECTIVE CONCERNING THE GREAT STRATEGIC PLAN FOR THE GREAT PROLETARIAN CULTURAL REVOLUTION*

People's Daily

Comrades Lin Piao, Chou En-lai, and comrades of the Cultural Revolution Group:

This document should be distributed to the whole country to be acted upon accordingly. The army should give political and military training in the universities, middle schools, and higher classes of primary schools, stage by stage and group by group.

It should help in reopening school classes, strengthening organization, setting up the leading bodies on the principle of the "three-in-one" combination, and carrying out the task of "struggle-criticism-transformation." It should first make experiments at selected points and acquire experience, and then popularize it step by step.

And the students should be persuaded to implement the teaching of Marx that without emancipating all mankind, the proletariat cannot achieve its own final emancipation, and in political and military training they should not exclude those teachers

*"Mao chu-hsi kuan-yü wu-ch'an chieh-chi wen-hua ta ke-ming ti wei-ta chan-lüeh pu-shu ti chih-shih." Jen-min jih-pao, March 8, 1968.

and cadres who have made mistakes.

Apart from the aged and the sick, these people should be allowed to take part so as to facilitate their remolding. Provided all this is done conscientiously, it is not difficult to solve the problems.

10

THOROUGHLY IMPLEMENT THE LATEST DIRECTIVE OF OUR GREAT LEADER CHAIRMAN MAO, AND FIRMLY EXECUTE THE BATTLE ORDERS ISSUED BY THE PROLETARIAN HEADQUARTERS*

People's Daily

Maintain the Great Tide of Struggle-Criticism-Transformation Brought About Under the Proletarian Leadership of the Workers

Under the guidance of the extremely important recent instructions of our great leader Chairman Mao, a large number of workers' Mao Tse-tung thought propaganda teams are rapidly entering colleges and universities and other units which have failed to conduct a successful struggle-criticism-transformation campaign. Thus, a high tide in the struggle-criticism-transformation campaign, under the leadership of the working class and participated in by millions of revolutionary people, is being fiercely launched with a force strong enough to overthrow mountains and upset seas. After they have studied

*"Ch'üan-mien lo-shih wei-ta ling-shou Mao chu-hsi tsui-chin chih-shih, chien-chüeh chih-hsing wu-ch'an chieh-chi ssu-ling-pu chan-tou hao-ling." Jen-min jih-pao, August 28, 1968.

Chairman Mao's latest directives and Comrade Yao Wen-yüan's important article, "The Working Class Must Exercise Leadership in Everything," the broad masses of workers across the nation courageously and without restraint say: "Whenever Chairman Mao waves his hand, we march forward! Under the leadership of the proletarian headquarters, with Chairman Mao as its commander and Vice Chairman Lin Piao as its deputy commander, we must make a living study and living application of Mao Tse-tung thought. The working class should always raise its political consciousness in the course of struggle, unite with the broad masses of revolutionary people of all levels to march forward along Chairman Mao's proletarian revolutionary path, persist in carrying out the great historical mission of the struggle-criticism-transformation campaign, and win a complete victory in the Great Proletarian Cultural Revolution!"

Recently, our great leader Chairman Mao pointed out: "In carrying out the proletarian revolution in education, it is essential to have working class leadership; it is essential for the masses of workers to take part and, with the cooperation of Liberation Army fighters, to bring about a revolutionary three-in-one combination together with the activists among the students, teachers, and workers in the schools who are determined to carry the proletarian revolution in education through to the end. The workers' propaganda teams should stay permanently in the schools and take part in fulfilling all the tasks in the schools of struggle-criticism-transformation, and they will always lead the schools. In the countryside, the schools should be managed by the poor and lower-middle peasants — the most reliable ally of the working class."

In the last several days, the broad masses of workers in large cities and industrial and mining enterprises across the nation, with unlimited excitement and abandon, and with the force of thunder and strong wind, have brought about a great tide to study and to carry out our great leader Chairman Mao's latest directives. Under the unified leadership of revolutionary committees in provinces, cities, and autonomous regions, rapidly elected outstanding workers' representatives, who were organized into thousands of workers' Mao Tse-tung thought propaganda teams, were immediately sent to colleges and universities and other units that have failed to conduct a successful struggle-criticism-transformation campaign. These teams have received a warm welcome and firm support from the broad masses of the revolutionary people.

In Peking, the nation's capital, workers' Mao Tse-tung thought propaganda teams have already entered forty-nine colleges and universities, and they will gradually enter other units where there are many intellectuals, or units that so far have failed to conduct a successful struggle-criticism-transformation campaign. These teams conscientiously explain the series of Chairman Mao's latest directives, thus making a significant contribution in bringing about the great revolutionary alliance and the revolutionary "Three-in-One Combination" [a group consisting of representatives of workers, revolutionary cadres, and the local People's Liberation Army units]. In Shanghai, workers' Mao Tse-tung thought propaganda teams, with the great leader in all their hearts, marched into twenty-six institutions of higher learning. The workers' Mao Tse-tung thought propaganda team, which only yesterday entered Futan University, has today, with the assistance of the little revolutionary Red Guards, revolutionary teachers, students, and employees, already begun Mao Tse-tung thought study classes in order to carry out his latest instructions, and has held mass rallies to take oaths to implement Chairman Mao's latest directives. In Tientsin, as of today, workers' Mao Tse-tung thought propaganda teams have entered sixteen colleges and universities. With deep proletarian feeling toward Chairman Mao, the broad masses of workers say that "even in 10,000 songs we still cannot express our unlimited loyalty to Chairman Mao. Under the invincible guidance of Mao Tse-tung thought, our working class must exercise leadership in everything, and we definitely can provide good leadership in everything."

Elsewhere in the country, for example, in the northeastern industrial base of Mukden, in the cities of Wuhan and Canton with their glorious revolutionary traditions, in the industrial cities of Sian in the northwest and Chungking in the southwest, and in many other large cities, some areas have already sent a large number of workers' Mao Tse-tung thought propaganda teams into colleges and universities, and others are now in the process of doing so. In the Nanchang area, workers' Mao Tse-tung thought propaganda teams, with a brave and militant spirit, have consecutively entered thirty-eight colleges, universities and secondary schools, literary and art groups, scientific research offices, and other units. Veteran workers who are members of the Kailan mine workers' Mao Tse-tung thought propaganda team said that "in the past, bourgeois intellectuals and counterrevolutionary revisionists contemptuously called us uneducated people who could not do this or that. They were really too wild and crazy! But today we have Chairman Mao to back us up. He wants us to lead everything, and we must do a good job so as to open the eyes of those bourgeois intellectuals." As soon as they had put down their bags, the workers' Mao Tse-tung thought propaganda teams that entered Kwangsi University went right into the classrooms, mixed with the masses of people, and chatted with teachers, students, and employees. They taught the latter about proletarian education from their experiences in both the old and the new societies. In Changsha, Hunan Province, members of workers' Mao Tse-tung thought propaganda teams that had entered colleges and universities firmly pledged that they would, under the guidance of the series of orders issued by the proletarian headquarters with Chairman Mao as its commander and Vice Chairman Lin Piao as its deputy commander, firmly unite and educate all forces that could be united, drag out all the hidden rebels, enemy secret agents, and all the die-hard capitalist-roaders, and carry the Great Proletarian Cultural Revolution through to the very end.

In Nanking, Tsinan, Taiyuan, Changchow, Hangchow, Hofei, Harbin, Changchun, Foochow, Kweiyang, Huhehot, Urumchi, Yingchuan, Sinin, Lhasa, and other places, the broad masses of workers pointed out: "The movement of the working class into the field of education is a great strategic arrangement made by Chairman Mao. This is an event unprecedented in human history. We must courageously carry out this great responsibility that Chairman Mao has assigned to us. While transforming the objective world, we must always use his ideology to change the subjective world. We must raise our political consciousness; we must be unlimitedly loyal to Chairman Mao, to his ideology, and to his revolutionary line, so as to better carry out the great historical mission of providing leadership in doing everything."

Recently, our great leader Chairman Mao pointed out: "Generally, the struggle-criticism-transformation campaign in a factory consists of the following several stages: establishing a three-in-one revolutionary committee, holding mass criticism and repudiation meetings, purifying the class ranks, rectifying the Party organization, simplifying organizational structure, changing unreasonable rules and regulations, and sending office workers to lower level units." When the broad masses of workers elect outstanding workers to be their representatives, who are in turn organized into thousands of workers' Mao Tse-tung thought propaganda teams, they are determined to follow Chairman Mao's great instructions to immediately launch a struggle-criticism-transformation campaign in factories, mines, and other enterprises, and to convert factories into great red schools of Mao Tse-tung thought. In the Shantiaoshih area in the city of Tientsin, some sixty factories have begun all kinds of Mao Tse-tung thought study classes to learn to implement his latest instructions. The broad masses of revolutionary workers and employees state that they will certainly use Mao Tse-tung thought to struggle, criticize, and transform and to create a red, proletarian world. At the Lanchow Petrochemical Machine Tool Plant, various production shifts and teams made arrangements ensuring that they would better "grasp revolution and promote production" after they sent some workers from their regular production assignments to join Mao Tse-tung thought propaganda teams. At the Yunnan Mining Machine Repair and

Assembly Plant, revolutionary workers made many recommendations to the revolutionary committee at the plant to better conduct the struggle-criticism-transformation campaign within their own organization. At the Peking General Knitwear Factory, revolutionary workers are determined to raise the great red banner of Mao Tse-tung thought higher and higher and to make persistent efforts to win the struggle-criticism-transformation campaign.

In order to most resolutely and most rapidly implement Chairman Mao's latest directives, leading organs at all levels of the People's Liberation Army, and Army units assigned to assist the leftists, to aid industry and agriculture, to exercise military control, and to provide political and military training, have dispatched thousands of commanders and fighters to assist the workers' propaganda teams entering institutions of higher learning in all parts of the nation. These commanders and fighters are determined to unite closely with the working class, to struggle together, to firmly support the working class in exercising its leadership in everything, and to conduct a successful struggle-criticism-transformation campaign in the several areas of the superstructure. They pledge that they will defeat the schemes of the handful of class enemies to shake and weaken the leadership of the working class, and help win a complete victory in the Great Proletarian Cultural Revolution. Commanders of Air Force and Naval units, who joined the workers' Mao Tse-tung thought propaganda teams that entered Peking Mechanical Engineering College and Peking Language Institute, actively helped the workers explain Chairman Mao's instructions in classrooms and dormitories, and helped the broad masses of revolutionary teachers and students to run Mao Tse-tung thought study classes, thus thoroughly repudiating the reactionary theory of "many centers, meaning no center." As a result, they have strengthened the great revolutionary alliance and brought about the three-in-one revolutionary combination. Commanders of the People's Liberation Army, in assisting the workers' Mao Tse-tung thought propaganda teams that entered Tsinghua University,

Peking University, People's University of China, Futan University of Shanghai, Tungchi University, Tientsin Engineering College, Nankai University, and other institutions of higher learning, are humbly learning from the working class and firmly supporting their revolutionary pioneer spirit in order to carry the proletarian revolution in education to the end.

After having studied Chairman Mao's latest instructions and Comrade Yao Wen-yüan's important article, the broad masses of poor and lower-middle peasants across the nation have unanimously expressed their firm support for working class leadership in everything and have pledged to serve as the reliable ally of the working class. Ku Ah-tao, an activist making a living study and living application of Mao Tse-tung thought, said: "Under the command of our great leader Chairman Mao and under the leadership of the working class, we have overthrown three great mountains. During the Great Proletarian Cultural Revolution, the working class led us in the destruction of the bourgeois headquarters commanded by Liu Chao-ch'i. During the current great struggle-criticism-transformation campaign, only when we insist on maintaining the leadership of the working class can we win a complete victory in the Great Proletarian Cultural Revolution and guarantee that our socialist state will never change its political color." Li Shun-ta and Wu Chun-an, two of our national model peasants, said: "The struggle-criticism-transformation campaign carried out in the superstructure under the leadership of the working class is a serious class struggle, which inevitably will run into opposition. We, the poor and lower-middle peasants, are the most reliable ally of the working class, and we firmly support the leadership of the working class in everything. Who ever opposes this leadership is our enemy, and we will overthrow him." Nung Chun-ying, an assistant instructor of the Kai-feng Peasant Militia Battalion in Ping-chang *hsien*, Kwangsi Province, very excitedly stated: "Since Chairman Mao wants us poor and lower-middle peasants to manage rural schools, we must handle this assignment well, and with the help of Mao Tse-tung thought, convert these schools into a real battlefield to train the successors of the proletarian revolution."

The broad masses of revolutionary teachers and students, revolutionary Red Guard "little generals," and revolutionary intellectuals in the nation must thoroughly carry out Chairman Mao's latest instructions regarding deeds. Revolutionary teachers and students of many institutions of higher learning have held solemn meetings to warmly welcome workers' Mao Tse-tung thought propaganda teams entering their schools and have exercised direct leadership in the revolution in education and other related matters in these schools. They affectionately call the members of these propaganda teams "our relatives sent to us by Chairman Mao," and insist that these teams remain in their schools permanently so as to lead the schools forever. Revolutionary teachers and students of many institutions of higher learning where there are no workers' Mao Tse-tung thought propaganda teams stationed have quickly requested that such teams enter their campuses as soon as possible. Meanwhile, they have been using Chairman Mao's latest directives as weapons to firmly struggle against and to criticize all the fallacies that show no respect for workers and peasants; they are determined to discard their privileged and superior status as intellectuals, to take the road pointed out by Chairman Mao, to integrate with workers and peasants, and to thoroughly change their bourgeois world outlook. They do not want to become a modern Lord She [one who liked dragons but was frightened by a real dragon], afraid of workers and peasants. They definitely want, under the leadership of the working class, to begin a struggle-criticism-transformation campaign as strong as a roaring tide, and to carry the proletarian revolution in education through to the end.

11

SCHOOL MANAGEMENT BY POOR AND LOWER-MIDDLE PEASANTS AS SHOWN BY THE PRACTICE OF THREE PRODUCTION BRIGADES IN THE EDUCATIONAL REVOLUTION

Heilungkiang Province Investigation Report*

People's Daily

Resolutely carrying out Chairman Mao's instructions on the proletarian revolution in education, the poor and lower-middle peasants of the Layaotzu, Sungshukou, and Waisantaokou production brigades of the Aihui People's Commune in Aihui *hsien*, (Heilungkiang Province) entered the schools in November of last year, taking back the power in education in rural areas and smashing complete domination of the schools by bourgeois intellectuals. The poor and lower-middle peasants are masters of culture; they have become the main force in the proletarian revolution in education in the rural areas. They have carried out the recent directive issued by our great leader Chairman Mao: "In the countryside, schools and colleges should be managed by the poor and lower-middle peasants – the most reliable ally of the working class."

*"Ts'ung san-ko ta-tui chiao-yü ke-ming ti shih-chien k'an p'in hsia-chung nung tsen-yang kuan-li hsüeh-hsiao – Heilung-chiang sheng ti tiao-ch'a pao-kao." *Jen-min jih-pao* October 28, 1968.

Smash Domination of the Schools by Bourgeois Intellectuals

Under the rule of the revisionist educational line of China's Khrushchev after the founding of our People's Republic, the leadership of the schools in the countryside was mainly in the hands of bourgeois intellectuals. Take the Sungshukou Primary School as an example. Section chiefs were changed on five occasions after liberation, but all of them came from families of landlords and rich peasants. The poor and lower-middle peasants said: "We are liberated politically and economically but not culturally. In these years we have grasped the hoe but not the pen."

The rural schools dominated by bourgeois intellectuals opened their doors wide for landlords and rich peasants. Four members of the twelve landlord and rich peasant families in the Sungshukou Production Brigade went to college after liberation; some of them work in important organizations of the state, and some are engineers in factories. Of the twelve sons of landlords and rich peasants remaining in the village, six are middle school students and not one is illiterate. On the other hand, the fifty-four families of poor and lower-middle peasants in the brigade do not have a single college student, and only one entered a secondary technical school. In the eighteen to twenty-eight-year-old age group of poor and lower-middle peasants, there is not a single junior middle school graduate, and more than thirty are illiterate or semiliterate.

Kuan Shih-hou, the son of a rich peasant, went from the fifth grade in primary school to the completion of a middle school free of charge or with stipends. However, forty-four sons and daughters of the poor and lower-middle peasants discontinued their studies because of economic difficulties. Only four sons and daughters of the fifty-one families of poor and lower-middle peasants in the second production team of Waisantaokou entered junior middle school after 1956, but all of them dropped out because they could not afford the school fees. However, three of the five sons and daughters of the rich peasant Kuan Tung-shih completed junior middle school, another is studying in senior middle school, and yet another is a college graduate. The poor and lower-middle peasants said angrily: "The schools after liberation were not for us; they still served the sons and daughters of the landlords and rich peasants, bringing up a younger generation for them and exercising dictatorship over us poor and lower-middle peasants."

The schools dominated by bourgeois intellectuals inculcated feudal, capitalist, and revisionist rubbish, bringing up successors for the bourgeoisie. A teacher from a rich peasant family openly spread this kind of pernicious stuff among the students during class: "There are no landlords and rich peasants now. Just as the films show, landlords have mustaches and big bellies and walk with canes." "Landlords and rich peasants never can lead the revolution."

Poisoned by the revisionist educational line, sons and daughters of the poor and lower-middle peasants would not return to the countryside but wanted to remain in the cities after finishing middle school. Eighteen educated young people of the second production team of Waisantaokou have left their village since 1956 and gone to town, making it very difficult for the team to find a bookkeeper.

The poor and lower-middle peasants said sadly: "The students studying in the cities are fed up with the countryside. They don't want to speak to us; they steer clear of us if we meet on a path. Our children have been ruined by such education."

The masses of poor and lower-middle peasants bitterly hate the revisionist educational line, which did harm to them and their sons and daughters. They demanded angrily: "Why is it that our children get less schooling and why can't they go to college?" This puzzle was solved only in the Great Cultural Revolution. It was sabotage by China's Khrushchev that prevented the poor and lower-middle peasants from grasping power in the field of culture and education.

Chairman Mao says: "The domination of our schools by bourgeois intellectuals should by no means be allowed to continue." Like a clap of spring thunder, this militant call roused the masses of poor and lower-middle peasants. They said firmly: "We'll take hold not only of the rifle and the seal of power but also of the pen. If we failed to do a good job in grasping the pen, we would lose the seal of power and the rifle." Using the mighty weapon of Mao Tse-tung thought, they smashed the revisionist educational line, took back power in the field of culture and education, and occupied the position in the schools.

School Management by the Poor and Lower-Middle Peasants Is a Struggle to Seize Power

The entry of the poor and lower-middle peasants into the schools to grasp cultural power is a profound ideological and political revolution, an acute struggle to seize power on the educational front. The unreformed bourgeois intellectuals in the schools worked hand in glove with monsters and freaks in society to create dissension in desperate opposition to management of the schools by the poor and lower-middle peasants. With complete loyalty to the great leader Chairman Mao, the masses of the poor and lower-middle peasants resolutely carried out and courageously defended Chairman Mao's line for the proletarian revolution in education and waged a tit-for-tat struggle against them.

The bourgeois intellectuals said: "Imagine the poor and lower-middle peasants grasping cultural power! It's no easy thing to grasp! How can illiterates manage schools!" The poor and lower-middle peasants answered firmly: "Backed by Chairman Mao, we will hold the power in education forever!" "With Mao Tse-tung thought as our weapon, we will surely do a good job in grasping cultural power and managing the schools! Our minds will never be at ease if you manage the schools."

The bourgeois intellectuals said: "You don't understand how schools are run. Educational work in the schools brooks no intervention!" The poor and lower-middle peasants said unequivocally: "Away with your old rules and regulations. Now you have to obey the poor and lower-middle peasants! We are resolute in smashing revisionist rubbish!"

Adhering to Chairman Mao's "May 7" directive, the poor and lower-middle peasants started to lead the struggle-criticism-transformation in the schools, inflicting mortal wounds on the revisionist educational line and upsetting their plans. The bourgeois intellectual gentlemen stirred up troubles everywhere, saying: "The students are too young to do physical labor"; "the children will stay interested in caring for the pigs for no more than three days"; and "production is held back because students are learning to drive tractors in the fields."

They held secret meetings and spread rumors. They clamored viciously: "The poor and lower-middle peasants won't be able to manage the schools long — it'll be as short as a rabbit's tail. For sure we'll teach again in the future."

They incited the students, saying: "Your school study will amount to nothing." Hoodwinked by them, many of the thirty-eight students at the agricultural middle school of Waisantaokou wavered at the beginning of this year; some cut classes, and six even stopped studying and went home.

All these flurries and vicious storms were aimed at strangling the new in its cradle. Faced by this, the poor and lower-middle peasants, armed with Mao Tse-tung thought, at once saw through the schemes and plots. What to do? Chairman Mao says: "Running study classes is a good method and many problems can be solved in them." The revolutionary committees of the three production brigades sponsored study classes in Mao Tse-tung thought on the revolution in education. In the schools and production teams, special places were set aside for big-character posters on the revolution in education. The masses were organized to vigorously study and disseminate Chairman Mao's latest directives on the revolution in education, and to accuse and repudiate the revisionist educational line.

All these activities enabled the poor and lower-middle peasants to see that our era requires that they manage the schools, for this is a great historic task entrusted to the poor and lower-middle peasants by the great leader Chairman Mao; whether the schools are managed well or not is a big question relating to the struggle for successors and to whether the state changes its political color. They said proudly: "The schools in the countryside belong to the poor and lower-middle peasants. We must occupy the educational positions in the schools and take hold of power in the schools."

They went on to launch revolutionary mass criticism and repudiation and a fierce attack on the class enemies. Finally they exposed the sinister hand at work to sabotage Chairman Mao's proletarian educational line and the Great Proletarian Cultural Revolution. The Sungshukou brigade dragged out a rightist clique set up to reverse correct decisions.

This clique was headed by a primary school teacher named Meng Hsien-chun, who is a son of a rich peasant and obstinately sticks to the reactionary stand. The Waisantaokou brigade ferreted out a primary school teacher named Wu Wen-hsu, former head of the propaganda department of a regional committee of the Kuomintang and a revisionist agent, and Chiang Wei-pin, an active counterrevolutionary. Eliminating the enemies has educated the masses, bringing victory in the struggle to seize power. Going step by step along the bright road opened up by Chairman Mao for the revolution in education, the masses are managing the schools better and better.

The "May 7" Directive Is the Beacon Light of the Poor and Lower-Middle Peasants in Managing the Schools

The poor and lower-middle peasants have followed the road indicated by Chairman Mao's "May 7" directive. They have closely adhered to Chairman Mao's great strategic plan, firmly carried out his latest directives on the revolution in education, and thus transformed the schools.

1. Hold high a banner — the great red banner of Mao Tsetung thought.

The first thing the poor and lower-middle peasants did after starting to run the schools was to grasp the attitude of the teachers and students toward Chairman Mao and Mao Tse-tung thought, and ensure that Mao Tse-tung thought occupies the classrooms and commands everything.

In the past the first words the students said after entering the classroom were: "Good morning, teacher"; now their first words are: "We wish Chairman Mao a long life!" In the past the students saluted their teacher when class began; now they salute Chairman Mao. In the past the first lesson each day was language or mathematics; now it is the fixed daily reading of Chairman Mao's works. In the past it was the bookworms who got high marks who were considered "good students"; now it is those who study and apply Mao Tse-tung thought in a living way who are considered good students. In the past the students did not pay attention to what was happening in the world, but concentrated on reading; now they go out of the school gates among the masses and enthusiastically publicize Mao Tse-tung thought. In the past there were morning meetings, class meetings, and weekend meetings; now there are meetings on the creative study and application of Chairman Mao's works and meetings to fight self and repudiate revisionism.

In the past six months the schools of the three production brigades have held twenty-four meetings on the creative study and application of Chairman Mao's works and eighty meetings to fight self and repudiate revisionism, and thirty-five activists in the creative study and application of Mao Tse-tung thought have come forward. The Sungshukou Middle School has become an outstanding collective in the creative study and application of Mao Tse-tung thought in the province, administrative region, and county.

2. Persevere on a road — the road of integration with the workers and peasants.

Run by the poor and lower-middle peasants, the schools have maintained their principles that education must serve proletarian politics and be combined with productive labor, and have followed the road of integration with the poor and lower-middle peasants. The poor and lower-middle peasants led the students in going out of the schools to face the world and brave the storms in the Three Great Revolutionary Movements — class struggle, the struggle for production, and scientific experiment.

The poor and lower-middle peasants of the Waisantakou Production Brigade ran Mao Tse-tung thought study classes with the revolutionary teachers and students for the study of Chairman Mao's works and to fight self and repudiate revisionism so that the revolutionary teachers and students could learn still better from the poor and lower-middle peasants. This promoted the revolutionization of the training of teachers and students. The revolutionary committee of the Sungshukou Production Brigade drew two students into the work of the leading group to ferret out the class enemies. Its purpose was to give the revolutionary teachers and students a better education in classes and class struggle and enable them to be tempered and to mature in great storms.

Through fighting along with the poor and lower-middle peasants, the revolutionary teachers and students have fostered their boundless loyalty to Chairman Mao. The three production brigades also regularly organize the revolutionary teachers and students to take part in collective labor in the production teams.

In the last six months everyone did thirty-nine days of collective productive labor on the average. In the course of this, many students have basically grasped a set of farming skills.

The schools of the three production brigades have built their own bases for production. This year they have cultivated twenty hectares of land. The revolutionary teachers and students do manual labor in their production bases, undertake on-the-spot teaching and learning, and carry out scientific experiments. Now that the schools are run by the poor and lower-middle peasants, they are production teams and centers for scientific experiment as well as schools. Poor and lower-middle peasants say with elation: "The students trained in the past were not of one heart with us and would not think, act, and speak with us. Now they are both students and commune members, and really are our reliable successors."

3. Build a contingent – remold, reorganize, and rebuild the contingent of teachers in the countryside.

The poor and lower-middle peasants, after taking over the schools, on the basis of purifying the original contingent of teachers, have selected ten educated young people of poor and lower-middle peasant origin with proletarian consciousness and practical experience in production to become teachers. These young people have returned to the countryside and taken part in labor for at least a year or two, some for as long as ten years, after finishing school.

At the same time, twenty poor and lower-middle peasants have been invited to be part-time teachers and regularly give lectures to the students. Old poor peasants who were the most oppressed before liberation give lectures on class struggle. Activists in the creative study and application of Mao Tse-tung thought give lectures on Chairman Mao's works. Revolutionary cadres give lectures on politics. Veteran peasants with experience give lectures on farming skills. Workers give lectures on farm machinery. Militia cadres give lectures on military affairs. Bookkeepers of production brigades give lectures on mathematics for the countryside. Rural health workers give lectures on medical knowledge. Penetrating and lively, popular and understandable, the lectures given by these comrades are closely combined with practice in the Three Great Revolutionary Movements.

The students have learned much more than they could have learned in books. By entering the schools and mounting the lecture platform, poor and lower-middle peasants have strengthened the contingent of teachers, brought in teachers of good class origin, fundamentally taken back power in education, and ended the domination of schools by bourgeois intellectuals. To improve the remolding of the contingent of teachers, revolutionary teachers have been organized, along with the students, to join the poor and lower-middle peasants in the Three Great Revolutionary Movements, and to take the road of integrating with the poor and lower-middle peasants, so that the bourgeois educational ideas they received from their bourgeois education in the past can be completely changed.

4. Practice unified universal education — smooth the way for the sons and daughters of the poor and lower-middle peasants to enter school.

The children of poor and lower-middle peasants faced various obstacles in going to school in the past: entrance examinations for primary schools, six-year primary schools, and middle schools; school fees; examinations for promotion; school-age limits; and so forth.

The children of poor and lower-middle peasants were kept out of school. The poor and lower-middle peasants, having taken over the schools, smashed these obstacles and conventions and paved the way for the children to go to school.

Investigations made in three production brigades show that three methods have been used to solve the question of the children of poor and lower-middle peasants entering school: (1) adding junior middle school classes to primary schools so that the students can receive middle school education right in the villages; (2) reducing the burden on the poor and lower-middle peasants by the following means: exempting the students from school fees and other expenses, giving subsidies from the welfare funds of the production teams to students from households with special difficulties, and carrying out mass mutual aid by poor and lower-middle peasants who voluntarily accumulate money to buy clothing, shoes, and hats for the children of those poor and lower-middle peasants who have difficulties; (3) abolishing the old regulations and conventions that hampered the children of the poor and lower-middle peasants from going to school, such as examinations for enrollment and promotion, the six-year system of primary schools, and the three-year system of junior middle schools.

An uninterrupted seven-year system of education has been instituted to enable all school-age children to go to school. Furthermore, the Layaotzu Production Brigade organized eighteen preschool-age children, gave them two classes every day, and thus brought their education into the school system. Unified universal education has been warmly welcomed by the masses of poor and lower-middle peasants.

5. Organize a group — the leading group for educational revolution with the poor and lower-middle peasants as the main force.

In November of last year, the three production brigades set up leading groups for the proletarian revolution in education consisting of leading members of the brigade revolutionary committees, representatives of poor and lower-middle peasants, leaders of the militia companies, and representatives of revolutionary teachers and students, thus ensuring that rural educational power was firmly in the hands of the poor and lower-middle peasants. The brigades' revolutionary committees put the work of managing schools on their agendas and regularly discuss and study the work of the schools. Leading members of the revolutionary committees go to the schools to exercise leadership and take every school as a team of the brigade and a militia platoon.

The past relationship between the schools and production teams has been changed; it is no longer that of not visiting each other all their lives, though the crowing of their cocks and the barking of their dogs are within hearing of each other." Teachers and students now say: "The production teams are our teams." And poor and lower-middle peasants say: "The schools are our schools."

Combined Investigation Team of the
Hei-ho District Revolutionary Committee,
the Ai-hui Hsien Revolutionary Committee, and
the Ai-hui Commune Revolutionary Committee

12

CONSOLIDATE THE LEADERSHIP OF THE WORKING CLASS OVER THE EDUCATIONAL REVOLUTION

CCP Committee of Liaoning University*

Summary of the Contents

This article discusses the way in which to build a leading body. In places where the intellectuals and the worker-peasant-soldier students form the principal objects of work, the question of how to raise the leading body's consciousness with respect to line, enforce the mass line, and carry out the Party policy so as to consolidate further the political leadership of the working class is a key one that bears on carrying the revolution in education through to the end along Chairman Mao's revolutionary line.

The article sums up the experience gained in this connection and points up the need for the correct handling of the relationship between unity and struggle, the relationship between employment and transformation, and the need to adhere firmly to democratic centralism, thus answering the

*Chung-kuo kung-ch'an-tang Liao-ning ta-hsüeh wei-yüan-hui, "Kung-ku kung-jen chieh-chi tui chiao-yü ke-ming ti ling-tao ch'üan." Hung-ch'i [Red Flag], No. 6 (June 1, 1971), 59-66.

questions raised by certain people. So long as we carry out Chairman Mao's proletarian line in education, rely on the masses in practice and are good at study, we certainly can accomplish gradually the glorious historical mission of the proletarian revolution in education.

* * *

Through studying the advanced experiences of Peking University and Tsinghua University in the practice of the proletarian revolution in education, we have gradually come to understand that in order to transform the old universities according to the outlook of the working class and consolidate its leadership over the revolution in education, it is imperative to study seriously, transform the world outlook with Marxism-Leninism-Mao Tsetung thought, raise the level of consciousness in carrying out Chairman Mao's revolutionary line, and strengthen the ideological construction of the leading body. The higher the degree of the leading body's ideological revolutionization is, the higher its level of consciousness in carrying out Chairman Mao's revolutionary line, the greater its energy in transforming the old universities, and the stronger the leadership of the working class over the schools.

Boldly Arouse the Masses and Ceaselessly Raise the Leading Body's Level of Consciousness in the Struggle Over Line

The Liaoning University Revolutionary Committee was set up in October 1968. In accordance with Chairman Mao's great teaching that "the workers' propaganda teams should stay permanently in the schools and take part in fulfilling all the tasks of struggle-criticism-transformation there," the workers' and People's Liberation Army Mao Tse-tung thought propaganda team took part in the "three-in-one combination" leading body. Our determination to transform the old university was very great, but there were still many misconceptions as to how Mao Tse-tung thought should be used to occupy this front firmly and transform it. Some comrades declared: "Since we are clodhoppers, it doesn't matter if we do things with a strong arm, because any mistake made can be pardoned." Others were complacent and painstakingly and busily exercising ordinary leadership. As the revolution in education deepens, we are required to solve many problems which we did not understand. Since we had business to attend to from morn to dusk and were constantly beset with routine work, we soon felt the revolution in education was really tough. Under the new situation, we were sharply confronted by the question of what should be relied on to exercise leadership and how leadership should be exercised.

In the spring of 1970, in the "one-strike and three oppose" movement, the leadership instructed that we must boldly arouse the masses to air their views, write wall posters, debate in a big way, and "set both extremes on fire" — the question of right and wrong concerning the line on the part of the leading body ideologically at one end, and the monsters and demons at the other. At the time, we put up wall posters to solicit the views of the masses, but as soon as we went indoors, we began to doubt: "In the first place, we are not greedy; in the second place we take nothing, and in the third place we violate no law and discipline. What problems can the fire ferret out?" We adopted a noncommittal attitude toward the mass movement. Since the attitude was incorrect, problems arose.

On one occasion, asked to give us his views, a teacher criticized the representatives of the workers and the Army in the leading body for adopting a provisional attitude and not having made any long-term planning for the school in the revolution in education. He went on: "The views I have put forward may possibly be those which the bourgeois intellectuals hold but dare not express." No sooner had he said this than a member of the leading body started to violently criticize the teacher.

Afterward, with this problem in mind, members on the

leading body studied Chairman Mao's teaching concerning the correct handling of mass criticism. It was felt that what one should fear is not mass criticism but the absence of such, because it is believed to be a great risk if no one will dare to reveal one's view to us. In the final analysis, because we were accustomed to being the driving force and because of our low level of consciousness in the continuation of the revolution, we "feared" the mass movement and "resented" mass criticism. To make revolution, we should fear neither the masses nor criticism. Mass criticism could only rid our thought of undesirable tendencies and make us stronger. With this clearly in mind, everybody decided to substitute the word "fear" with the word "dare": go to the first line of struggle, face the world and brave the storm, face the masses and hear their criticism.

One day the university's revolutionary committee chairman went to the Foreign Languages Department to hear the views of the masses. A wall poster, written by six new students of the class for conducting experiments at selected points, to expose problems in teaching, taught him a profound lesson.

He had come to the Foreign Languages Department twice in the hope of grasping problems in the revolution in education. On the first occasion he went there to attend class, but he failed to understand any of the foreign languages. After class, however, the teacher and students came around to him and gave him their views. Afterward, he discussed this matter with others in the leading body. Some comrades said: "Since we understand neither foreign languages nor mathematics, physics and chemistry, how are we going to grasp them?" The discussion brought no result.

On the second occasion he learned that the department wanted to assign some work to a teacher of the class for conducting experiments at selected points, but a section of students insisted on keeping him in the class, saying: "It is entirely because of this teacher that we have been able to gain some knowledge these few months." The revolutionary committee chairman felt there was something wrong with this, and he criticized the students. However, he did not look at the essence through the phenomenon, nor did he investigate and study why these new students had acquired this kind of feeling.

The wall poster written by the six students served precisely to expose this problem. The problem exposed in the wall poster was found precisely in the person of the teacher whom certain students considered to be most "satisfactory." When this teacher taught in the class for conducting experiments at selected points, he wanted to show himself off by offering his students some "extra dishes." When he coached the students after class, he uncritically discussed in English certain bourgeois works. After hearing this, instead of criticizing the teacher, some students felt that their teacher was "very learned." The wall poster by the six students sharply criticized us, saying: "Why is it that the leadership knows nothing of the grave struggle in the domain of teaching? Why is it that the leadership does not actively exercise a good grip on the occupation of such a position as the classroom with Mao Tse-tung thought?" This wall poster enabled us to dispassionately consider a question: "Why was the class for conducting experiments at selected points affected by the pernicious influence of renegade, hidden traitor, and scab Liu Shao-ch'i's "first place to intellectual culture"? This showed that we had no concrete knowledge of the fact that the struggle between the two lines was still going on. Work involved the question of which line was carried out, and it could never be thought that a new leading body definitely can carry out the correct line.

In the practice of the revolution in education at the former stage, because of our low level of consciousness in the struggle over line, we spent more time in the domain of teaching and grasping vocational work and less time in grasping political work, more time in grasping routine work and less time in grasping ideological work, more time in grasping concrete problems and less time in grasping the question of line. This caused problems to crop up at the lower level. The wall poster by the six students pointed out for us what and how problems should be grasped in the revolution in education. The fire set by the masses burned away our blindness and brought out our consciousness in grasping the class struggle in the domain of teaching, our consciousness in making a success of the revolutionization of the leading body and in raising our awareness of the struggle over line.

Although the representatives of the workers and the Liberation Army in our leading body do not understand or are not familiar with many vocational problems in teaching and are laymen in this connection, this is of no importance and the question is how to exercise leadership. No matter whether we are laymen or those who know the ropes, we cannot give leadership if we do not give prominence to proletarian politics, do not energetically grasp the fundamental principles but are busy with routine work, thus losing our bearings. On the contrary, by grasping the orientation and the line, it is possible to arrive at a correct perception of everything, and the laymen certainly can also lead those who know the ropes. This is to enforce the political leadership of the proletariat.

Study Materialist Dialectics, Raise the Level of Consciousness in Carrying Out the Party Policy on Intellectuals

In the practice of revolution in education, our leading body has gradually come to understand that the transformation of the teachers' world outlook bears on the implementation of Chairman Mao's proletarian line in education. Lenin pointed out: "In any school, the ideological and political orientation of the curriculum is most important. By what is this orientation determined? It can only be determined by teaching personnel" ("Letter to the Students of K'e-p'u-li [?] Party School"). Chairman Mao pointed out: "The question of teaching reform is principally a question of teachers." Therefore, consciously carrying out the Party policy on intellectuals and maintaining a firm hold on the transformation of the teaching ranks offers an important guarantee to winning, in the true sense, the leadership over the revolution in education.

Among our schoolteachers, many are old intellectuals who

are deeply affected by feudal, bourgeois, and revisionist ideas, and the changing of their world outlook is by no means easy. Due to the presence of idealism and metaphysics in the minds of some comrades, they look at the intellectuals in a one-sided way. Because of their deviation in understanding, they show impatience in attitude and imprudence in work, and when they carry out a policy, they waver between the "left" and the right. When they carry out the proletarian policy, they often separate strengthening the leadership of the working class over the revolution in education from uniting, educating, and relying on the majority of the intellectuals. They seek to transform the intellectuals through employment, but once the latter show signs of reversal, they often order them to "stand aside." We understand that in order to transform the bourgeois world outlook of the intellectuals, we must continuously wage struggle to rid our minds of idealism and metaphysics.

When preparations were made for setting up the new Party committee of the school, we further intensified the ideological construction of the leading body in accordance with the great leader Chairman Mao's teaching that "to reorganize things organizationally, it is first necessary to reorganize things ideologically." Following the example of Peking University and Tsinghua University, we boldly aroused the masses, and in close conjunction with the practice of revolution in education, we adopted the method of integrating those inside with those outside and the higher level with the lower level. With the number one as the key link, we waged struggle ourselves and were spurred on by the masses and helped by the leadership to expose contradictions level by level. We discovered that the most important problem of the leading body in ideological revolutionization was that it was unable to correctly handle itself and the intellectuals because it is arrogant and self-complacent.

With this problem in mind, we studied the relevant works of Marx, Lenin, and Chairman Mao and made a class, historical, and dialectical analysis of the intellectuals. We came to understand that most problems of the intellectuals are ideological problems, and that the great majority of the intellectuals can be, and must be, united, educated, and transformed. The proletarian revolution in education is a revolutionary mass movement, and unless the broad masses of the revolutionary intellectuals are mobilized to the full extent to participate in it, it is not possible to properly implement the Party's general and specific policies and line in education. There is struggle in our talk of unity with the intellectuals, and this is just what Chairman Mao has taught us: "It means starting from the desire for unity, resolving contradictions through criticism or struggle, and arriving at a new unity on a new basis" ("On the Correct Handling of Contradictions Among the People"). Our talk of reliance has its class character and, as stated by Chairman Mao, "In carrying out the proletarian revolution in education, it is essential to rely on the broad masses of revolutionary students, revolutionary teachers, and revolutionary workers in the schools, the activists among them, that is, the proletarian revolutionaries who are determined to carry the Great Proletarian Cultural Revolution through to the end." So long as we correctly handle the masses of intellectuals, we can further promote their ideological transformation, unite them most extensively, isolate and hit at a handful of the most obstinate class enemies, more effectively wage struggle against the old ideas and habits of the bourgeoisie, and carry out with greater success Chairman Mao's series of instructions on the revolution in education.

After the formation of the new Party committee, the members of the leading body separately went down to the various departments to investigate and study the problems found when the Party policy on intellectuals was implemented. They also linked these problems with the ideological revolutionization of the leading body and transformed the process of implementing the Party's policy on intellectuals into one of continuously ridding our minds of idealism and metaphysics, of continuously combating self and criticizing revisionism, and of translating ideological revolutionization into reality. The two relationships were thus better handled, and a new atmosphere prevailed in the revolution in education in schools.

1. Correctly handle the relationship between unity and struggle.

In the past, because of our plain class feeling, we abhorred from the depth of our hearts the feudal, bourgeois, and revisionist things bared by the intellectuals themselves. We were therefore alienated from them and could not correctly handle the relationship between unity and struggle. Because of this, we also had no chance whatsoever to transform them and carry out to the letter Chairman Mao's policy on intellectuals.

An associate professor of the Chinese Department had spread in the past considerable feudal, bourgeois, and revisionist poison in the process of teaching. We analyzed and studied his condition together with other comrades in the department, and decided to send him to a factory so that he could get reeducated on the one hand, and take part in the compilation of the supplementary teaching material "History of the Struggle Between the Two Lines on the Literary and Art Front After Liberation," on the other. In the section about the "anti-Hu Feng struggle," drafted by him, he cited a profusion of materials on the negative side, but did not give prominence to Chairman Mao's literary and art line. When this was put to discussion, the workers sharply criticized him. However, this associate professor failed to arrive at a correct perception of the matter, and he held that this was a question of methodology.

Together with the comrades of this department, we studied Chairman Mao's great teaching: "The bourgeoisie and petty bourgeoisie are bound to give expression to their ideologies. It is inevitable that they should stubbornly persist in expressing themselves in every way possible on political and ideological questions" ("On the Correct Handling of Contradictions Among the People"). We understood that the problems bared by this associate professor in the process of compiling the teaching material expressed precisely the class struggle in the ideological sphere, and it would mean deviation to the right if this contradiction were not exposed and active ideological struggle were not unfolded. However, this was also a question of ideology among the people, which "can only be settled by the democratic method, the method of discussion, of criticism, of persuasion and education, and not by the method of coercion or repression" ("On the Correct Handling of Contradictions Among the People"). We convened four meetings for the compilation group, and inspired the associate professor to criticize and repudiate, together with the masses, renegade, hidden traitor, and scab Liu Shao-ch'i's counterrevolutionary revisionist black line in literature and art as well as the "four fellows," including Chou Yang, thus giving him a profound course of education. With the painstaking help of others, he was deeply moved, and he expressed his intention to stand on the side of the workers, peasants, and soldiers, to change his stand, thought, and feeling, and to make an effort to transform his own world outlook.

Because we correctly handled the relationship between unity and struggle, other teachers were also educated. Many teachers took the initiative to bare their own ideological problems in the practice of revolution in education, fiercely criticized and repudiated the baneful influence of the counterrevolutionary revisionist line, and strove to transform their world outlook. This gave us great enlightenment. The bourgeois world outlook of the intellectuals was formed in several decades of life, and we cannot attempt to transform them in a single day. We must overcome our eagerness for success. Only by proceeding from the aspiration for unity and waging consistent and untiring struggle against their old ideas can they be led onto Chairman Mao's revolutionary line.

2. Correctly handle the relationship between employment and transformation.

Having studied Chairman Mao's teaching on "transforming the objective world as well as one's own subjective world," we came to understand that we must adopt the policy of "simultaneously employing and transforming" the original teaching ranks.

A lecturer in the Physics Department was sent by the

department to a factory to teach the students a course on the electric motor. Because he was "divorced from politics, actual production, and the masses" for a long time, he made a clown of himself by mixing up the positions of the stator and the rotor in the electric motor. After that, the department argued that he no longer could teach, and he was allowed to "stand aside."

Together with the general Party branch of the Physics Department, we made a complete analysis of him. He came down to the factory for the first time in twenty years, and this was progress. The exposure of contradictions in practice was the inevitable outcome of his prolonged "divorce from politics, actual production, and the masses." By allowing him to "stand aside," we actually allowed him to continue with his "divorce from politics, actual production, and the masses." After understanding was unified, the department again let him take part in the practice of revolution in education, and he was sent to a factory to handle a new product which was rather difficult to handle. Because the pernicious influence of the philosophy of the foreign slave and the doctrine of trailing behind at a snail's pace had not been thoroughly eliminated in him, his thought underwent another reversal in practice. The general Party branch of the Physics Department still insisted on intensifying his transformation through employment. After several months in which he studied again vocationally and was reeducated by the working class, through working together with the master workmen, he made contributions toward the trial manufacture of this new product of an advanced level in the world.

The long-term character of the ideological transformation of the intellectuals is determined by the long-term, complex, and devious character of the class struggle in the socialist society. The transformation of old ideas by the intellectuals in the Three Great Revolutionary Movements will certainly lead to the appearance of reversal. When a reversal appears, to implement the policy of transformation in the course of employment it is imperative to surmount wavering. We must grasp ideological work well in the reversal, rest our confidence on the unsurpassed power of Mao Tse-tung thought, do painstaking and meticulous work in the education of people with Mao Tse-tung thought, and continuously and firmly adhere to the policy of transformation in the course of employment before we can make the ideological transformation of the intellectuals take another step forward after every reversal.

Simultaneously with exercising a good grip on reeducating the intellectuals, in accordance with Chairman Mao's teaching — "in order to be a good teacher, one must first be a good pupil" — we paid attention to learning from those who underwent reeducation. Besides sending members of the leading body to various departments to stay at selected points and constantly listen to the criticisms and demands of the teachers and students, conferences of representatives of the masses were held periodically to listen to mass criticism. This not only can help us to improve opportunely the style of leadership, but also enables us to carry out effectively Chairman Mao's policy on the intellectuals under the constant supervision of the masses.

In order to carry out to the letter the policy on intellectuals of the Party, we must have a high sense of political responsibility and link every piece of work with Chairman Mao's revolutionary line. Chairman Mao's various proletarian policies represent the concrete embodiment of his revolutionary line. Whether or not the policy of the Party can be carried out to the letter in real earnest is an important hallmark of the high or low level of consciousness of the leading body in the struggle between the two lines. Only by reading seriously, taking Marxism-Leninism-Mao Tsetung thought as a weapon, and overcoming idealism and metaphysics in thought can Chairman Mao's various proletarian policies be carried out to the letter.

Firmly Adhere to Democratic Centralism, Strengthen the Unified Leadership of the Party

In leading the revolution in education in a school, firm adherence to democratic centralism and enforcement of the unified leadership of the Party guarantee the implementation of Chairman Mao's revolutionary line and constitute an important subject in the ideological construction of the leading body.

In order to adhere firmly to democratic centralism in the Party and to enforce the unified leadership of the Party, it is first necessary to achieve unified thinking, policies, plans, command, and actions on the basis of Mao Tse-tung thought, and strengthen the revolutionary unity of the leading body. For this purpose, we regard the repeated study and practice of Chairman Mao's great teaching "Unite and win greater victories " as an important task in the construction of the leading body, and have raised the realization of unity on the basis of Mao Tse-tung thought to the plane of consolidating the proletarian dictatorship in understanding.

In order to adhere firmly to democratic centralism in the Party and uphold the unified leadership of the Party, it is imperative to unfold seriously a positive ideological struggle within the Party. To make revolution, one must talk in terms of class struggle and struggle over line, and cannot advocate the bourgeois theory of human nature and eclecticism. The struggle between the two classes, the two lines, and the two kinds of ideology would inevitably be reflected in the leading body, and differences in opinion constantly arise. When there is difference, there is contradiction. We must dare to expose and be good at solving contradictions, lay divergent views on the table, and let people look for answers in Chairman Mao's works with problems in mind. Only through study and discussion can differences be unified and contradictions be solved.

In December 1969, we went to the countryside to set up bases for learning farming and carrying out Chairman Mao's "May 7 Directive" to the letter. But when we arrived there it was very cold, and the conditions were quite bitter. For a while the teachers and students were rather confused in thinking, and the struggle between the two kinds of ideology was most acute. Seeing that there were so many contradictions and the difficulties were so great, some people in the leading body also questioned "whether this is the proper way to operate a university." This essentially showed lack of clarity in understanding with respect to implementation of the "May 7 Directive." Should we brave the difficulties and charge forward or retreat in the face of difficulties? There lay before us the two roads.

Our leading body especially convened a conference to discuss the situation and the ways people looked at things, and to enable people to express their opinions to the full extent. After that, we studied with problems in mind Chairman Mao's brilliant "May 7 Directive" and his teaching: "At present we study as we are engaged in production, and in the future we shall fight as we carry out production; this is the K'angta work style that is able to overcome any enemy." We reviewed history and looked at the present. Proceeding from the promotion of full-scale "divorce from politics, actual production and the masses" by a handful of capitalist-roaders in the former Liaoning University, we came to see the necessity for intellectuals to take the "May 7" road. Proceeding from the vacillation and reversal in the ideological transformation of the intellectuals, we came to see the importance of changing the standpoint of the intellectuals through labor. Proceeding from the weakness of the intellectuals in fearing hardship and fatigue, we came to see the urgency of sending the intellectuals to a hard and bitter environment to temper their revolutionary will and world outlook. Only through firmly and steadfastly carrying out Chairman Mao's "May 7 Directive" could a school be truly operated as a socialist university. On the basis of unified understanding, we implemented with greater firmness and steadfastness Chairman Mao's policy of "education must serve proletarian politics and be combined with productive labor," and decided to grasp arduous training through labor as an important link of political and ideological work for the intellectuals.

In the process of strengthening the ideological construction of the leading body and realizing the unified leadership of the Party, we have also paid attention to bringing into play the enthusiasm of the representatives of various elements in the leading body. The experience in struggle, ideological level, and capacity for work of the members of the leading body differ, and in the struggle for building a socialist university, attention must be paid to bringing into full play the activism of each comrade before unified leadership can truly be enforced. The representatives of the workers and the army in the leading body must guard against monopolizing all activities at all times, see to it that the role of the representatives of the revolutionary cadres is brought into play and new-born forces are trained, show concern for and take good care of comrades with the revolutionary sense of responsibility, and with wholehearted eagerness unite them together in work.

In our Party committee there is a deputy secretary who is a schoolteacher with very high enthusiasm for work. On one occasion he got hold of some information from the lower level, felt that the revolution in education made rather slow progress in the school, and actively advocated setting a date for the fulfillment of a number of tasks in the revolution in education. The secretary of the Party committee agreed with this view. Later, the secretary of the Party committee went to the departments to do an investigation and study, and he discovered that due to the one-side emphasis on time limit, the teachers were so busy that there was a break in political work, and this was disadvantageous to the deep-going development of the revolution in education. He made known his way of thinking when he chatted with the comrade in question, but the latter was unable to turn around right away. He therefore suggested that this comrade go to the departments to do an investigation and and study afresh.

This comrade studied Chairman Mao's teaching — "in studying a problem, we must shun subjectivity, one-sidedness, and superficiality." He once again went deep into the various departments to make an investigation and study, and came to understand that one-sidedly setting a time limit for the fulfillment of a task actually could not bring proletarian politics to the fore. He therefore took the initiative to suggest that the work plan of the school for the revolution in education be revised. Because the young comrades have insufficient experience, the appearance of certain shortcomings and mistakes in work is unavoidable. We must trust them and boldly entrust them with work. We must support them, offer them advice, think of ways to do things for them and hold ourselves responsible when problems arise. We must help them and lead them to study and apply creatively Mao Tse-tung thought and continuously raise the level of consciousness in class struggle, the struggle over line, and the continuation of the revolution.

In the leading body, in order to implement democratic centralism and strengthen the unified leadership of the Party, the No. 1 man must boldly make self-criticism. When the No. 1 man is in disagreement with other members, he must do meticulous ideological work, must not shift the blame to others when problems arise, and must pay greater attention to looking for the causes in his own person. When making mistakes, he must not complain but take the initiative to hold himself responsible for such mistakes. The No. 1 man shoulders a very heavy responsibility in the leading body, and he exercises a great influence whenever he suggests anything, does anything, agrees or disagrees, or takes the lead in anything. He must therefore "guard against arrogance," against dictating things, and against the patriarchal system. Only in this way can he create in the leading body a democratic atmosphere in which everybody dares to speak. The presence of only one kind of opinion in the leading body does not necessarily mean the realization of unified leadership. There is true unified leadership only when everybody makes known his view fully and when everything is seriously discussed and unified on the basis of Mao Tse-tung thought and Chairman Mao's revolutionary line.

Guided by Chairman Mao's proletarian revolutionary line, we have scored over the past few years some success in the ideological construction of the leading body, but there are still problems. From now on, we are resolved to study painstakingly Marxism-Leninism-Mao Tse-tung thought, make an effort to transform our world outlook, and carry the proletarian revolution in education through to the end along the path charted by the great leader Chairman Mao.

V

Teachers and Teaching

13

TAKING A JOYOUS STEP FORWARD IN THE EDUCATIONAL REVOLUTION

A Visit to Peking's Shih-ching-shan Middle School

Kuo T'ung*

In the clamor surrounding the "return to class and make revolution" movement that has begun in Peking universities, middle schools, and primary schools, the revolutionary students and teachers of Shih-ching-shan Middle School have, with the aid and support of the Chinese People's Liberation Army Military Advisory Group, raised high the great red flag of the thought of Mao Tse-tung, conscientiously studied Chairman Mao's writings, resolutely and thoroughly carried out the latest instructions of Chairman Mao relative to the educational revolution and, in the midst of the educational revolution, have taken a joyous step forward.

After it was announced to the public by Pei-ching jih-pao [Peking Daily News] and Jen-min jih-pao [People's Daily], this joyous achievement by Shih-ching-shan Middle School attracted wide and serious attention in Peking academic circles. In the belief that a large number of foreign readers would also be extremely interested in this happy piece of news,

---

*Kuo T'ung, "Tsai chiao-yü ke-ming chung mai-ch'u k'o-shan i-pu — Fang Pei-ching Shih-ching-shan chung-hsüeh." Chung-kuo hsin-wen [China News], February 16, 1968.

this present writer made a special visit to get a firsthand look at this new success in the educational revolution.

The Great Study of Chairman Mao's Writings

"When navigating on the high seas, we depend on the helmsman; when making revolution, we depend on the thought of Mao Tse-tung." After they returned to class to make revolution, the revolutionary students and teachers of Shih-ching-shan Middle School first resumed the course in Mao Tse-tung thought. Each and every class and section in the school drew up guidelines for the study of Chairman Mao's writings. They placed the propagation of Mao Tse-tung thought and the study of Chairman Mao's writings on a level of unequaled importance and greatness. To date, the school has set up more than 270-odd study groups devoted to the writings of Chairman Mao. A whole series of changes has already taken place in both instructional theory and content. In addition to such courses as "The Writings of Chairman Mao," "Subjectivism and Revisionism," "Class Education," all of which study the writings of Chairman Mao, instruction in liberal arts courses — literature, foreign language, etc. — also makes use of Chairman Mao's writings as teaching material. Similarly, mathematics, physics, and other courses in the science department take Mao Tse-tung thought as their guiding light. In the past, teachers were fond of students who got high marks and were obedient. Now, those who apply themselves to the living study and practice of Chairman Mao's writings and who have a high degree of ideological awareness have become the students who are most esteemed.

In the midst of study of the living study and living application of the writings of Chairman Mao, the revolutionary students and teachers of the school have created many lively and active study methods. For example: "First seek instruction; later, make a report." In the morning, with all kinds of questions on their minds, they study Chairman Mao's writings and manifest their firm resolution to him. Then, in the afternoon, they make a report to Chairman Mao on the good and bad points of the day's work and study. This study method, according to all reports, has met with excellent results. Some students express it this way: "Every day we seek instruction from Chairman Mao. Our faith is great, our will is strong, and as we advance we have direction. Every day we make a report to Chairman Mao. We speak our minds, hold nothing back, and will forever be the red generals of our Chairman."

At a Meeting of a Study Group

On the day I visited Shih-ching-shan Middle School, I joined in the study activities of a first-year study group on Mao Tse-tung thought. This study group was composed of nine female students. The teachers also participate in these study activities. Today it was the government instructor, Mr. Wang, who joined in. The central question discussed by the study group was: Why have an educational revolution? To tell the truth, I was apprehensive at first. How would they be able to discuss such a deep question? What followed proved, however, that my fears had been unwarranted. The children did not at all talk in empty phrases but, on the basis of their own personal experience, exposed, accused, and criticized the revisionist educational line and the old education system, and explained that an educational revolution was absolutely necessary. They said, "The revisionist educational revolution was not dominated by proletarian politics but by 'grades'; it trained people who were to take over the leadership of the capitalist class." The old school administration spared no means in their attempt to produce so-called "honor students." Some teachers even divided their students into ranks on the basis of high and low grades; they threatened that if they failed to study hard, they would be sent out to do farm labor. The students in the study group also criticized and accused the old, so-called inviolable rule that "the teacher's opinion is always right." They said that in the past a student did not dare criticize the teacher; if he did, he was likely to suffer retaliation from the teacher, get a low mark, and fail his course. In those days the teachers liked students who were obedient and submissive. When this point was broached, a student in the group recounted with great anger the following incident: There was a certain primary school student who, because he had violated classroom discipline, was thrown out of class by the teacher. This pupil was so frightened that he did not dare return home, and as a result there were some frightful consequences. This tragic story aroused the students' hatred of the old education system to an even higher degree. They all condemned the damage done to the younger generation by this slave education that had been promoted by China's Khrushchev [Liu Shao-ch'i]. The students said that "the revisionist education line carried on by China's Khrushchev was for the furtherance of his wild scheming to restore capitalism in China. Our implementation of the educational revolution is aimed at seizing the great power over education that was usurped by China's Khrushchev, resolutely guarding and carrying out Chairman Mao's proletarian education line, and ensuring that our red rivers and mountains will never change color."

During the discussion, the teachers and students, acting on the basis of the instructions of Chairman Mao on combating subjectivism and criticizing revisionism, joined together their own ideological realities and struggled against their individual subjective attitudes. One student said, "Certainly the damage and injustice done to us by the revisionist educational line has been very great, but how was it possible that such a line could be taken? The answer to this is inseparable from the problem of our individual subjective attitudes. In the past I used to be intent on getting high marks so that I could get awards and citations."

This was really a lively class. According to various reports, after returning to classes to make revolution, the teachers and students of the school encountered some difficulty in deciding just how to change the direction of the old instruction, reform the old education system, revolutionize the old instruction methods, and cope with a whole series of similar problems. With the help of comrades from the People's Liberation Army

Military Advisory Group, however, they seriously studied Chairman Mao's instructions on the educational revolution and started on a great program of criticism, accusation, and exposure directed toward the old education system and the revisionist education line promoted by China's Khrushchev. As a result, they grew to understand even more profoundly that Chairman Mao's thought on education is a beacon for those who assume the task of accomplishing the proletarian revolution, and that full confidence can be placed in it for the creation of a proletarian education system. Now, with strong support and aid from every side, and having carried on a thorough investigation, they have concluded a preliminary agreement on a draft plan for the educational reform and have put together new course outlines and some new teaching material for mathematics, physics, and other such subjects.

Students Teach in the Classroom

Of the newly created instruction methods, student teaching is one of the outstanding examples. This has been a new attempt by the revolutionary students and teachers of Shih-ching-shan Middle School to carry out Chairman Mao's instructions that "officers teach soldiers, soldiers teach officers, and soldiers teach soldiers." On the day of my visit I listened to a first-year student speak on chemistry. The student's name was Sun Chia-feng. From his dark complexion and simple manner of speech, one could tell at a glance that he was the son of a working-class man. The subject of his talk was: what is a mixed substance and what is a pure substance? He first explained the significant points that would be dealt with in this particular class; he covered the general method and steps to be taken in the experiment, and then performed the "table salt purification experiment." During the demonstration he used Chairman Mao's thought on dialectical materialism to explain that an absolutely pure substance was nonexistent.

After he had finished his talk, Sun Chia-feng asked his fellow students for their criticism. One after the other, his classmates raised quite a number of questions and criticisms. One student asked: "What is the use of doing this kind of experiment? Is there much practical application? If there is not very much practical significance, then the educational reform should eliminate it." Sun Chia-feng answered every one of these questions. When Sun's answers were not able to satisfy his classmates, the classroom suddenly became very noisy. In this kind of situation our young student, Sun Chia-feng, responded with exceptional humility, "Quiet, please, my fellow students. You'll all have a chance to present your criticism. Our educational revolution encourages us all to enter into discussions. Only in this way can we improve our education." That a teen-ager could, with such humility, receive criticism from the masses and put the interests of the revolution above all else without worrying about comparisons of "face," is a full manifestation of the incomparable power of Mao Tse-tung thought.

After class was over, I had a conversation with several students. They all said that there were many advantages in the student-teaching system. It eliminated the "lecture" method and was able to open up the students to independent thinking. Judging by the results, this new method makes it easier for students to understand and remember, and they also like to listen.

According to newspaper accounts, the school already has many courses — such as language, government, mathematics, and physics — in which students are taking part in the teaching. The teacher functions principally as a guide for the student before class. They prepare the lesson together, discuss it, help each other, and also study together. After the student has presented the lesson, the teacher may add some additional explanation or give a recapitulation to help raise the level of instruction. This is truly a new form of instruction.

The New Teacher-Student Relationship

In the midst of the educational revolution, the teacher-student relationship at Shih-ching-shan Middle School has also taken on a brand-new appearance. I heard many moving examples with respect to this development.

In the past there had been a barrier between Miss Liang, a second-year teacher, and her students; this was especially true during the Great Cultural Revolution when, owing to the evil influence of the capitalist reactionary line in education, this barrier became even more difficult to penetrate. This greatly distressed Miss Liang, to the point that she had even once thought of giving up her position as faculty member. The students' criticisms were also quite severe. After the newest instructions of Chairman Mao on "combating subjectivism and criticizing revisionism" had been passed down, the students of this class organized a "united heart society." These students then invited Miss Liang to attend their meetings. Miss Liang was so moved by this gesture on the part of her students that she could not hold her tears back. At the meeting she enthusiastically reviewed her own past errors: upholding the revisionist education line, practicing favoritism among her students, and devoting herself to "professionalism." The students were very moved by this, and all proceeded to make their own self-criticism. In examining their past, some of the students who had been treated coolly by Miss Liang said, "Before, when Miss Liang was not close to us, we did not take any initiative to correct the matter. We are also in the wrong." After this meeting of the "united heart society," the barrier between teacher and student disappeared. Now Miss Liang is often with her students; they study together, work together, struggle together, and have fun together.

Another story is told of Mr. Hu, a third-year teacher. In the study of "combating subjectivism and criticizing revisionism," he has taken the lead in putting the spotlight on "subjectivism"; he has also taken the initiative in seeking out some students who used to be considered undesirable to talk with and to make "home visits" to. The students think very highly of this action. They say, "If we never 'unite our hearts,' then we will never know each other; but once we have, we are closely tied together."

"Mr. Hu is a good teacher."

Similar examples are too numerous to mention. In the past, one thing the students feared most was that the teacher might make a "home visit" and "report" on them. They have a saying: "We're not afraid of heaven or earth, only of the teacher coming to see our fathers." Now, when the teacher makes a home visit, it's not for the purpose of making a bad report but to study the writings of Chairman Mao with the students. Some students say, "The teacher's home visit brings to us the thought of Mao Tse-tung." From fearing the "home visit," the students have now changed to welcoming it. It has gone so far that on holidays some teachers do not even return home but are invited by their students to go home with them to spend their vacation happily.

This visit to Shih-ching-shan Middle School made a deep impression on me. It fully manifested the boundless power of Mao Tse-tung thought. Beneath the dazzling glory of Mao Tse-tung thought, Shih-ching-shan Middle School has carried through the "return to classes and make revolution" movement, has carried out all kinds of investigations, is currently engaged in reforming the old education system and, in turn, is being remade into a great blast furnace that will cast the future leaders of the proletariat, imbuing them with Mao Tse-tung thought. A great, brand-new crimson red school devoted to Mao Tse-tung thought has gradually taken shape.

14

STRENGTHEN THE BUILDING OF THE RANKS OF URBAN PRIMARY AND MIDDLE SCHOOL TEACHERS

CCP Kiangsu Provincial
Committee Writing Group*

Summary of the Contents

This article emphasizes that in strengthening the building of the ranks of urban primary and middle school teachers we should, on the one hand, conscientiously select fine workers to join the ranks of teachers according to Chairman Mao's proletarian line; and, on the other, we should organize the original teachers to remold their world outlook in the practice of the Three Great Revolutionary Movements, correctly handle the relationship between the use and the reform of teachers, and overcome the two deviations, i.e., using them without reforming them and reforming them without using them. In this process it is imperative to grasp the struggle between the two lines and the two world outlooks and to unfold revolutionary mass criticism in a deep-going and protracted manner.

* * *

*Chung-kuo kung-ch'an-tang Chiang-su sheng wei-yüan-hui hsieh-tso hsiao-tsu, "Chia-ch'iang ch'eng-shih chung hsiao-hsüeh chiao-shih tui-wu ti chien-she." Hung-ch'i [Red Flag], No. 6 (June 1, 1971), 9-13.

Great leader Chairman Mao teaches: "The question of educational reform is mainly one concerning the teachers." In order to carry out Chairman Mao's proletarian educational line, implement the shining "May 7 Directive," and train "socialist-awakened and cultured laborers," the intensive reform and building of the ranks of urban primary and middle school teachers remain as important tasks to be fulfilled in the proletarian revolution in education.

The struggle between the two classes, the two roads and the two lines has always run onto the question of how to deal with the ranks of teachers. The series of guiding principles and policies laid down by Chairman Mao point out the fundamental direction in which the ranks of teachers are to be reformed and built. Yet, political charlatans like the renegade, hidden traitor, and scab Liu Shao-ch'i kept on opposing Chairman Mao's proletarian education line from both the right and the extreme "left" in order to restore capitalism. At one time they shouted "Long live the teachers" and "Regard teachers as the key figures," praising them to the skies and denying the necessity of reforming the ranks of teachers. At another, they clamored for "doing away with the teacher system and with the teaching material," denying the role of teachers, negating the importance of selecting fine workers to join the ranks of teachers, and dampening teachers' enthusiasm for the educational revolution. Under the pernicious influence of the revisionist line, some teachers belittled ideological remolding or took the wrong view that one who becomes a teacher "will run a risk" and "lose out." Some people took an incorrect view of the teaching ranks. Even to this day this remnant pernicious influence of the counterrevolutionary revisionist line in education still impedes the deep-going development of revolution in education. This being so, only by roundly criticizing and repudiating the reactionary fallacies spread by Liu Shao-ch'i's group and overcoming the erroneous tendencies and ideas can we ensure that the building of the ranks of urban primary and middle school teachers will take on a healthy development in accord with Chairman Mao's proletarian education line.

Under the guidance of Chairman Mao's revolutionary line, we have seriously grasped the building of the ranks of urban primary and middle school teachers in recent years. Beginning in 1968, the localities concerned selected and transferred groups of fine workers as full-time and part-time teachers. These worker-teachers were selected and transferred mainly in the following ways: (1) By rotation. That is, the workers are transferred to the schools as teachers in rotation. This method insures a relative stability, helps the worker-teachers preserve their true class color, and facilitates the training of more worker-teachers. (2) By exchanging personnel. That is, factory and school established a link, with the former sending workers to the school as teachers and the latter arranging labor training for the teachers in the factory. This method helps the laboring people to acquire knowledge and the intellectuals to become laborers. (3) Over a long period of time. That is, fine workers are selected and appointed to teaching posts over a long period of time. For example, Nanking has selected and transferred more than 520 workers as full-time teachers; Wusih has increased the worker-teachers at middle schools to 30 percent of the total number of middle school teachers. This has greatly changed the class composition in the ranks of teachers and augmented the forces for revolution in education.

Selecting and appointing workers to teaching posts is a new thing on the education front as well as a profound social revolution. This work has all along involved a struggle between the two ideologies and the two world outlooks. At the outset, some factory leaders regarded selection of worker-teachers as an "extra burden." They hated to dispense with the services of their key elements. They were afraid that to transfer their workers as teachers would adversely affect their factory operation. This attitude was determined by their departmentalism.

To appoint workers to teaching posts is an important problem bearing on the training of the successors to the proletarian revolutionary cause. Some comrades have said aptly: Under no circumstances should we concern ourselves only with rolled steel and timber and not with the training of revolutionary personnel. If we should lose state power, then whatever rolled steel and timber we produced would slip out of our hands. It is in the course of struggle that factory activists continue to emerge and raise their level. With one group of key elements gone, a new group will emerge. As long as we bring proletarian politics to the fore, we are sure that appointing workers to teaching posts will promote the development of factory operations and production instead of adversely affecting the factory operation.

With their understanding raised, leading comrades of many factories voluntarily put the selection of worker-teachers in an important position, roused the masses, created revolutionary public opinion and carried out this assignment, conforming to high standards and good quality.

After the worker-teachers moved into the schools some people expressed the opinion that a few workers appointed to teaching posts would not serve any great purpose in reforming the teachers. They used worker-teachers as ordinary teachers, "letting each worker-teacher fill the vacancy of an ordinary teacher." In some cases, worker-teachers were used as substitutes, "filling vacancies and serving as stand-ins."

This approach is wrong in the extreme. Chairman Mao teaches us: "The working class must exercise leadership in everything." Appointing workers to teaching posts is of momentous significance because it is one of the important measures for extending the working class leadership deep into the teaching sphere. It is noted that in some schools certain teachers display new teaching material but teach old content and, in some cases, even peddle the feudal, capitalist, and revisionist stuff. This shows that without extending its leadership into the teaching sphere and without reforming the ranks of teachers the working class will be unable to gain an all-round hold on the school leadership. In various localities of our province, the wrong ideas and methods adopted in dealing with the question of worker-teachers have been criticized and it has been emphasized that worker-teachers should be regarded as "red seeds" in practical work. Many schools have assigned worker-teachers to definite political work, taking into account the specific conditions of the worker-teachers. For example, after being admitted to the school revolutionary committee, worker-teachers were appointed as persons responsible for leading the courses of study and as grade supervisors. Attention was paid to displaying their political role. This contingent served as the backbone to lead all the teachers forward.

Years of practice have proved that worker-teachers are the most vigorous and militant revolutionary force among the ranks of teachers. They have brought the fine ideas, fine style and fine quality of the working class to the schools and have brought about a revolutionary change in the teachers' ranks. Many worker-teachers conscientiously studied and applied Marxism-Leninism-Mao Tse-tung thought in a living way, brought pro-proletarian politics to the fore, and took the lead in grasping the class struggle and two-line struggle. They remained loyal to the Party's educational cause. They vied with one another in carrying the heavy burden in the educational revolution and advanced in the teeth of difficulties. In these circumstances, those teachers who had taken the view that one who became a teacher "will lose out and run a risk" and who had persisted in "struggle-criticism-departure " were made to raise their thinking and understanding and gradually to make up their minds to devote their lifetime to the Party's cause of education. Worker-teachers had deep proletarian affection for the students. They set an example by words and deeds, persisted in positive education, and learned from the students. In these circumstances, the original teachers were made to consciously repudiate such theories as "regard teachers as the key figures" and "uphold the dignity of teachers," and build a new relationship between the teachers and the students. In the course of teaching, worker-teachers strove to integrate theory with practice and taught in language popular and easy to understand. This helped the original teachers to change their former teaching method, which was marked by "three separations." With worker-teachers joining in, the teaching ranks were full of vitality. All this was the best answer to those who belittled the role played by the worker-teachers.

"The working class, too, should constantly heighten its political awakening in the course of struggle." Being part of the ranks of teachers, worker-teachers are also confronted with the problem of intensive ideological revolutionization.

There is a theory that "having red hearts and good class origin and being free from remnant pernicious influence, worker-teachers will not degenerate." This is a metaphysical viewpoint. Worker-teachers do not live in a vacuum. In their minds there is also a struggle between the two education lines and the two ideas on teaching. Bourgeois and revisionist influence and the force of tradition are strong in urban primary and middle schools. "The proletariat seeks to transform the world according to its own world outlook, and so does the bourgeoisie." The bourgeoisie is bound to corrupt worker-teachers with a bourgeois world outlook through various channels. For this reason, worker-teachers must also firmly grasp the remolding of their world outlook. Political and ideological work among worker-teachers should be grasped as an important task. The leading bodies of many factories criticized the erroneous concept that "those who left the factory no longer belong to the factory." They emphasized the need to take care of the worker-teachers politically and ideologically, to know their state of mind, and to make arrangements whereby worker-teachers can periodically come back to the factory for political activity and labor training so that their ties with the factory can be strengthened and their true working class color can be preserved. At the same time that it brought the role of worker-teachers into play, the school leadership actively organized worker-teachers to read Marxist-Leninist works and Chairman Mao's works, and unfolded revolutionary mass criticism in light of the history and reality of struggle between the two classes, the two roads, and the two lines on the education front. The school leadership helped some worker-teachers gradually overcome their notion that "it is difficult to be a teacher."

They were helped to heighten their critical awareness in carrying out Chairman Mao's revolutionary line and to improve their ability to distinguish true Marxism from pseudo-Marxism. In school work the school leadership, by combining teaching and learning, holding exchange-experience meetings, and running "red teachers' classes," helped worker-teachers to elevate their rich practical experience to the theoretical plane and made them play a greater role in the educational revolution. Appointing workers to teaching posts is an important aspect of strengthening the building of the ranks of urban primary and middle school teachers. Another aspect of equal importance involves organizing the original teachers to join the Three Great Revolutionary Movements and move onto the road of becoming one with the worker and peasant masses and remolding the world outlook of the teachers.

Kiangsu has large numbers of old cities, old schools, and old teachers. Many urban primary and middle school teachers come from the families of nonworking people or from the old society. In their case, the influence of feudalism, capitalism, and revisionism is strong, the phenomenon of "three separations" is serious, and the world outlook is basically bourgeois. During the Great Proletarian Cultural Revolution this contingent of teachers was reorganized and a handful of class enemies were purged. The masses of teachers underwent training and heightened their consciousness of class struggle, line struggle, and continuous revolution. Nevertheless, if we want to reform the majority of these teachers to meet the needs of proletarian education, we must firmly put them into the Three Great Revolutionary Struggles and let them take part in collective productive labor and be reeducated by the workers, peasants, and soldiers in the fiery class struggle. Chairman Mao repeatedly teaches us: "We encourage the intellectuals to go among the masses and into the factories and rural districts." Taking part in collective productive labor and keeping in close contact with the worker and peasant masses is the road the masses of teachers must traverse in their ideological revolutionization. Some people think in these terms: "Our teaching assignment is so heavy and our teaching staff is so small that we cannot spare teachers for factories and rural districts." "No useful purpose will be served by sending them down to do manual labor for a few months." Actually, this way of thinking denotes neglect of the remolding of the teachers' world outlook, and must be firmly overcome. Many schools in our province took positive measures to cope with the shortage of teachers. As regards labor time and organizational form, they combined short term and long term and centralization and decentralization and integrated teaching with labor. In this way, they maintained the system of teachers taking part in productive labor and smoothly fulfilled their teaching tasks.

Some hold that it is simple to organize the teachers to do manual labor, saying that all that is required is to send them down. Some teachers expressed their views in these terms: "One who does manual labor is relaxed and happy because one does not have to rack one's brains or worry about things." All these ideas reflect the remnant pernicious influence of the theories advocated by Liu Shao-ch'i's group — "manual labor is a form of punishment" and "manual labor is light and free." Going into the thick of realities and taking part in collective productive labor in the rural districts and factories will create the prerequisites for remolding the teachers' world outlook. But arduous and meticulous political-ideological work will have to be done before the goal of remolding world outlook can be really achieved. It will be necessary to rouse the teachers to study Marxism-Leninism-Mao Tsetung thought conscientiously and to fight self and repudiate revisionism critically. It will be necessary to unfold revolutionary mass criticism purposefully to counter their living ideas and eliminate the "Liuist poison." If organizing teachers to do manual labor is simply regarded as a matter of sending them down to work or if the process of doing manual labor is regarded as one of spending leisure time, it will be impossible to achieve the effect of remolding world outlook.

In organizing teachers to do manual labor at the lower level, it will be necessary to grasp education in ideology and political line conscientiously. It will be necessary to grasp the "question of 'for whom,'" to rouse the teachers to learn from the workers, peasants, and soldiers their devotion to revolution, to change the teachers' stand, to make the teachers gain a more clear-cut view of the school operation. It will be necessary to seize upon the weakness of the teachers, i.e., the "three divorces," and to guide them to go into the thick of realities, learn from the workers, peasants, and soldiers their revolutionary style of study, and to prompt them to establish the idea of integrating theory with practice. It will be necessary to seize upon the bourgeois idea and style of some teachers, i.e., shunning hardship and seeking an indolent life, and to help them undergo tempering in a difficult environment and learn from the workers, peasants, and soldiers their revolutionary spirit of fearing neither hardship nor death. Practice proves that after being steeled in manual labor and reeducated by the workers, peasants and soldiers, the masses of teachers have made up their minds further to teach in the interest of revolution and for the consolidation of the proletarian dictatorship, and that a strong impetus has been given to their ideological revolutionization.

Great leader Chairman Mao teaches us that intellectuals must "gradually establish the communist outlook on the world in the course of their work and study." The teachers spend the longest time and engage in many teaching activities in the schools. The struggle between the two ideologies and the two world outlooks of the teachers is frequently brought into full play in their teaching practice. This being so, just as we attach great importance to sending them down to do manual labor, we are required to attach great importance to grasping the remolding of the teachers' outlook in the process of their teaching practice. On this question, there are two erroneous tendencies that must be subjected to criticism.

One tendency is to lay emphasis on using the teachers without reforming them. "As long as the teachers are able to teach, everything will be all right." There are different methods of teaching. One is to put teaching under the command of Mao

Tse-tung thought, to integrate teaching with practice, and to "open up the students' minds." The other is to peddle the feudal, capitalist, and revisionist stuff in the bourgeois way, to teach from books and to "cram." These are two different methods of teaching. The former is the proletarian method of teaching, while the latter is the bourgeois method of teaching. In the final analysis, these two methods are reflections of two world outlooks. Whatever the world outlook, so goes the line of education and the method of teaching. Only a revolutionized teacher can carry out Chairman Mao's revolutionary line and give revolutionary lessons. Chairman Mao teaches us: "Intellectuals, if they do not rid their minds of undesirable things, will be unable to assume the task of educating others." Using the teachers without reforming them — such an idea and approach will do every sort of harm and no good to the proletarian cause of education.

The other tendency is to reform the teachers without using them. Some people are afraid that "to use the teachers who have many old ideas in their heads will detract from the teaching quality." They prefer to "use them after they have been well reformed." This approach is not correct either. Teaching practice will reveal the teachers' outlook on the world and will provide a chance to criticize and rectify the old ideas in the heads of the teachers. Teaching practice will enable the teachers concerned to overcome the wrong things, develop the correct things, and remold their world outlook. As to the quality of teaching, the teachers will have to go through practice over and over again before their teaching quality can be improved. Remolding the intellectuals' outlook on the world is a protracted process and will have to be conducted step by step; too much haste will result in divorcing the remolding of world outlook from the realities. Chairman Mao teaches us: "Intellectuals must be united, educated and used according to the circumstances of each case." To advocate "reform before use" is contrary to Chairman Mao's policy on intellectuals.

We criticized these two erroneous tendencies drawing a distinction between the use and the reform of teachers. Pursuant to Chairman Mao's policy on intellectuals, we persisted in reforming the ranks of original teachers while using them. We used them freely and encouraged them to intensify their reform in the course of teaching. While using them we organized them to study and apply Mao Tse-tung thought in a living way, "to read and study conscientiously to master Marxism," and to heighten their critical awareness in carrying out Chairman Mao's revolutionary line. As to the problems brought to light in their teaching practice, we made a concrete analysis of them and dealt with them correctly. At the same time, we unfolded revolutionary mass criticism in a deep-going and protracted manner, prompted them to identify what is materialism, what is idealism, what is proletarian ideology, what is bourgeois ideology, what is a fragrant flower and what is a poisonous weed. In this way, they constantly rid themselves of the remnant pernicious influence of revisionism. Further, we organized them to step up the activity of learning from those they educated, developed the four-good movement, promptly cited those teachers who had remolded their world outlook with success, and set typical examples. In this way, the teachers' critical awareness in remolding their world outlook was raised higher and higher. Chairman Mao teaches us: "In the entire course of socialist revolution and socialist construction, the reform of intellectuals is a question of the greatest importance." Intensive building of the ranks of urban primary and middle school teachers is a long-term task. We should hold higher the great red banner of Mao Tse-tung thought, guard against arrogance and rashness, undertake meticulous work, and strive to build new proletarian ranks of primary and middle school teachers.

15

A "MOBILE UNIVERSITY" FOR THE TRAINING OF TEACHERS WITH GREATER, FASTER, BETTER, AND MORE ECONOMICAL RESULTS

The Work Methods and Experience of the Mobile Tutorial Teams of Kwangtung Normal College*

Red Flag

Summary of the Contents

With a view to meeting the need for rapid development of educational services and breaking down the old rules and conventions, this college implements the educational policy of "walking on two legs." In succession, it organized a number of mobile tutorial teams and sent them deep into the countryside and mountainous regions, where they assist, in various ways, the different localities in training teachers. Immense results have been obtained and at, the same time, normal education has been closely combined with the Three Great Revolutionary Movements, thus promoting the revolutionization of the teachers.

* * *

*"To-k'uai hao-sheng pei-yang shih-tzu ti 'liu-tung ta-hsüeh' — Kuang-tung shih-fan hsüeh-yüan hsün-hui fu-tao ti tso-fa yü t'i-hui." Hung-ch'i, No. 6 (June 1, 1971), 84-88.

Kwangtung Normal College, acting in accordance with the great leader Chairman Mao's teaching that "education has to be revolutionized," is carrying out the educational policy of "walking on two legs." While making preparations to set up ordinary classes, beginning from July 1969, it has in succession, and for four terms, sent out 31 mobile tutorial teams to the 40 hsien and municipalities of the eight districts of the province. They assisted the districts, hsien, and communes in setting up 31 middle school teacher training courses, which were attended by more than 8,000 middle and primary school teachers. They also went to 91 communes to provide instruction to nearly 10,000 teachers on the job. This has promoted the development of the educational revolution in various localities and at the same time furnished some initial experiences in the transformation of the old normal colleges. The teams were warmly welcomed by the masses of workers and peasants and the revolutionary teachers and students.

Growing Up in the Midst of the Struggle Between the Two Lines

The Great Proletarian Cultural Revolution smashed the counterrevolutionary revisionist line of the renegade, hidden traitor, and scab Liu Shao-ch'i. With the cultural power in the hands of the working class and the poor and lower-middle peasants, education has developed rapidly in the countryside. Universal primary education has in the main been achieved in the province, while the number of middle school students has doubled. In most of the areas "children need not leave the production team when going to a primary school, or need not leave the commune when going to a middle school." In order to meet the needs of educational development, the various areas have broken down the old rules and selected a number of primary school teachers for teaching in middle schools. Moreover, they are investigating teacher corps that have been strengthened by educated youths and demobilized armymen. Under these conditions, a quantitative rise in the level of the reeducation of teachers is a pressing task in the educational revolution.

In light of the exceedingly favorable situation in the development of the educational revolution, how should the normal college be run? After a portion of the revolutionary teachers and students have gone into the countryside to study, it would seem to be imperative that the normal college keep in close touch with the situation, serve proletarian politics, organize mobile tutorial teams, and go into the countryside and up into the mountains to operate. This revolutionary initiative has won the support of the leadership and the broad ranks of revolutionary teachers and students. However, there are some who still believe that mobile tutorial teams are "irregular" and "cannot guarantee quality," and who go on about how this "doesn't put a stop to the painful needle, and is a very long-range scheme." A big debate directed at this confusing question of whether or not to operate mobile tutorial teams is being unfolded at the college. The broad ranks of revolutionary teachers and students earnestly study Chairman Mao's directives on educational revolution and fiercely criticize Liu-Shao-ch'i's counterrevolutionary revisionist educational line. Everyone realizes that the normal college has to follow Chairman Mao's revolutionary line and, with consolidation of the proletarian dictatorship as the starting point, implement the policy of "walking on two legs" in running schools; go to the rural villages and the mountain areas to operate; train proletarian teachers on the basis of greater, faster, better, and more economical results; and reform, in the practice of educational revolution, the teachers' world view. Only in this way can it be possible to alter thoroughly the "three separations" situation of the old normal college and transform the normal college into an educational battleground for the consolidation of the proletarian dictatorship. With their understanding raised, the teachers and students, full of revolutionary valor, put on their backpacks and walk off the campus and into the countryside to run schools.

Is walking out of the school and engaging in mobile tutorial instruction the realization of Chairman Mao's thought on educational revolution, or is it engaging in purely professional tutoring? Some people say: "If we can be of some use in our own work, then that is enough." In accord with Chairman Mao's instruction that "politics is the commander, the soul," organize the teachers and students to repeatedly study the two "resolutions," criticize the purely professional viewpoint, carry out education on the struggle between the lines, and further eradicate the residual poison of the revisionist "intellectual education first." Everyone realizes that all the work of the tutorial teams, every class, must apply proletarian ideology to the education of the students. If one grasps mathematics, physics, and chemistry, but forgets revolutionization, then one is bound to go down the evil road of capitalism. The original teachers and students must not only forcefully reform their world view but must at the same time also use Mao Tse-tung thought to command tutorial work and propagandize Mao Tse-tung thought.

After a period of such mobile instruction, these teams were lauded by the poor and lower-middle peasants. At this point a few teachers had the feeling that they had done enough and were reluctant to penetrate deeper into the countryside and remote mountain areas to provide mobile instruction. Some said that such instruction was in the "form of handicraft production," and advocated that it was better to establish more "regular" training classes in the city. This posed the question of whether the revolution should be carried through to the end or stop halfway. As soon as this fear of hardship came to light, we organized everyone to study Chairman Mao's theory on continuing the revolution under the dictatorship of the proletariat and the "three constantly read articles." We carried out a small-scale rectification campaign with a view to establishing the idea of serving the people "entirely" and "thoroughly" and the revolutionary spirit of "fearing neither hardship nor death." This enabled everyone to raise his consciousness of the struggle between two lines and strengthened his confidence and determination to implement Chairman Mao's ideas on the educational revolution. As a result, the road has become wider for the teams to operate on.

For the past year and more, these teams have been formed

and developed amid the struggle between the two lines. It is our deep realization that positively developing the education on the struggle between lines is crucial for the penetrating development of the educational revolution. Only by holding high the great red banner of Mao Tse-tung thought, using the "May 7 Directive" as the guideline, putting proletarian politics to the fore, and developing revolutionary mass criticism in a penetrating and sustained manner will it be possible to build these teams into study teams that accept reeducation from the workers, peasants, and soldiers propaganda teams that actively propagate Mao Tse-tung thought, and fighting teams that carry out Chairman Mao's ideas on the educational revolution.

Turning to the Rural and Mountain Areas, It Is Necessary to Conduct Teaching in a Variety of Forms

In turning to the rural and mountain areas, mobile tutorial teams, under the leadership of local revolutionary committees, with the help of the broad masses of poor and lower-middle peasants, and proceeding from the reality of the countryside, have operated mainly in the following three forms:

1. Hold classes at fixed points. With district and hsien teacher-training schools as points, teachers' study courses are run for concentrated training. During the new upsurge of the socialist revolution and socialist construction, the various hsien had established health, teacher-training, and other new-type schools. The mobile tutorial teams took it as their main task to assist in the proper operation of the teacher training schools. Most of the students of the teacher training schools come from among primary and junior middle school teachers, while a number of them are demobilized armymen and educated youths. In general, after receiving three to six months of training, they go back to take up teaching in junior middle or senior middle schools. While attending these training classes, their main task is to study Chairman Mao's ideas on the educational revolution, sum up and exchange the practical experi-

ences in the educational revolution, learn some necessary professional knowledge, and raise their level of using Mao Tse-tung thought to command cultural studies. While giving instruction, the teams bring proletarian politics to the fore, learn those things which should be learned first, combine learning with application, and they have achieved relatively good results. For instance, a mobile tutorial team assisted the Ch'üchiang hsien teacher training school in setting up a second teacher training class. Most of the students of the class were originally teachers of primary schools having a junior middle school cultural level. After two and a half months of training, they raised to a certain extent their ideological consciousness and cultural level. The overwhelming majority of them went back to take up teaching in junior middle classes.

2. Instruction given in scattered places. The teams go deep among the communes and production brigades to provide mobile instruction. In particular, they go to mountainous areas and also the more remote mountainous areas to teach the people there. In view of the rapid development of secondary education at the present time, it is quite difficult to assign large numbers of teachers to concentrated studies, leaving their jobs during the period of their study. Proceeding from reality, therefore, the teams adopt a variety of forms to enable teachers to take up studies during half of their teaching hours or in their spare time, so that they may teach and learn at the same time in order to improve themselves where they work. Such instruction given in scattered places must be conducted with local conditions taken into account. For instance, to solve individual difficult problems in teaching, the teams go to the schools to provide instruction. But in case there are problems of a general nature in teaching, the teams will gather the teachers together in a commune for instruction. Some of these courses last three to five days, some, ten days, and some, half a month. In general, short-term training is conducted by making use of the holidays during busy farm seasons and the teachers' spare time or by making use of the method of 'substitute classes' (namely, teachers teaching different subjects take part in the short-term

training class on a rotational basis, in which case a teacher attending the class will have another teacher take over his class without affecting the studies of the students). During its three-month stay in Hsüwen hsien, a team trained more than a thousand persons through short-term training classes. The short-term training classes study Chairman Mao's ideas on the educational revolution, exchange the practical experiences of the educational revolution, and study some professional knowledge that is urgently required in teaching. In addition, through the criticism of old teaching materials and the introduction of the new, the question of how to use Mao Tse-tung thought to command cultural classes was solved on a priority basis. The students generally reported that such instruction enabled them not only to study Chairman Mao's ideas on the educational revolution but also to solve the difficulties of learning. The teams, in coordination with their investigations of the educational revolution, also go deep into schools to provide them with individual instruction. Teams operating on Hainan Island and in the mountain areas in northern Kwangtung have to climb mountains or wade through rivers to go to the villages inhabited by the people of Li and Yao nationalities in order to teach the people there on the spot. They are praised by the masses.

3. Set up spare-time instruction networks. Mobile tutorial teams cannot possibly stay in a place for a long time. After they are gone, how can the spare-time instruction be maintained? The teams, acting in accordance with Chairman Mao's teaching that "having two positive factors is much better than having one positive factor," help the communes to set up and strengthen instruction networks for the educational revolution. These instruction networks must achieve "five fixes": fix the leadership, fix the instructors, fix the systems, fix the spots, and fix the content of activities. Instructional activities are carried out in many forms: discussing new teaching materials, preparing lessons, holding experimental classes, holding instructional classes, holding meetings to discuss application, holding meetings to exchange experiences, etc. In assisting the Nant'ang Commune of Lufeng hsien in setting up a tutorial net-

work, a mobile tutorial team, under the direct leadership of the commune revolutionary committee, organized those teachers who were good politically and ideologically and had a relatively high level of teaching to carry out tutorial activities, so that in the course of practice they could temper and improve themselves together. Also, a group of key elements was developed for the tutorial network. Welcoming the tutorial network, the masses called it "the tutorial team that stays." Over the past year and more since the tutorial network was set up in Pait'u Commune in Ch'üchiang hsien, the teachers have consistently adhered to the tutorial system, actively developing all kinds of tutorial activities. Practice shows that the network plays a useful role in promoting the teachers' ideological revolutionization and impelling the penetrating development of the educational revolution, and that it is a good form for making such instruction a regular part of the teachers' work by relying on the masses, as well as the basis of self-reliance.

Persistently putting proletarian politics to the fore, all these teams, wherever they go, make a practice of studying and propagating Chairman Mao's ideas on the educational revolution. They go deep into the lower level to carry out investigation and studies and formulate plans for the holding of classes. They organize "three-in-one combination" preparations of lessons, using Mao Tse-tung thought to command cultural classes. They make a success of teaching classes and solve the difficult problems of a general nature in teaching. In addition, they organize experimental classes. After practice a number of times, relatively good results were obtained. Mobile tutorial teams composed of from ten to twelve teachers of various subjects conduct tutorial activities within a hsien in the form of combining points with the whole area and of using points to lead the whole area. Experiences gained at the points are popularized throughout the whole area while problems of the whole area are studied at the points. In this way, points and the whole area are combined and prove mutually complementary. This is a good way of training teachers with greater, faster, better, and more economical results.

An Effective Way of Reforming the Old Normal University

Chairman Mao taught us: "Reforming the old educational system and reforming the old teaching policies and methods is an extremely important task of the present Great Proletarian Cultural Revolution." By going deep into the countryside and mountains to teach the people, and by assisting various localities in training teachers, these mobile tutorial teams enable the teachers joining the teams to undergo reeducation from the workers, peasants, and soldiers in the course of practice, to restudy professionally, to promote their ideological revolutionization, and to motivate the educational revolution in the old normal universities.

"The problem of teaching reform is largely the problem of teachers." Rapidly building up a contingent of proletarian teachers is an extremely important task during the educational revolution. In the light of the Party's policy of uniting, educating, and transforming intellectuals, we have arranged, according to plan and by separate stages, for a number of teachers to teach in ordinary classes, a number of them to participate in teaching in mobile teams, and a number of them to be sent to cadre schools for training. These three groups of teachers are to change place at regular intervals. For the past year and more, more than 180 teachers and cadres have participated in the revolutionary practice of these mobile teams. They go deep into the rural and mountainous areas, place themselves among the masses of workers, peasants, and soldiers, and participate in the practice of the Three Great Revolutionary Struggles. Wherever they go, they join the local poor and lower-middle peasants in labor, in accusing the old society of depriving them of cultural power, and in criticizing Liu Shao-ch'i's counterrevolutionary revisionist line on education. They study the revolutionary spirit of the local poor and lower-middle peasants in managing schools, keeping the cultural power firmly, and consolidating the political power. They learn from the advanced experiences of the local masses in creatively studying and applying Mao Tse-tung thought. They strive arduously to transform their world outlook, criticize the "theory that teachers are doomed," and gradually establish the idea of "being loyal to the Party's educational cause." As a result, their mentality has undergone a tremendous change.

Practice shows that sending these teams to teach in the midst of the Three Great Revolutionary Movements, to receive reeducation from the poor and lower-middle peasants, and to achieve unity of politics and profession and unity of theory and practice during tutorial activities is an effective measure for transforming and improving the existing teachers during employment.

The practice of the educational revolution by these teams has exerted positive effects on the transformation of the old normal university. The syllabuses and teaching methods of the old normal university were to a serious extent separated from the practice of the Three Great Revolutionary Movements, and the students it produced had "trunkloads of books and data; their heads were full of formulas and principles, but they made bad teachers in middle schools." Mobile tutorial teams operate the university in the whole society, organize teaching in close coordination with the practice of the Three Revolutionary Movements, and break down the set of mysterious and complex teaching systems of the bourgeoisie. The team that went to Shaokuan district selected an area marked for the prevention of schistosomiasis as a teaching point. Within two weeks' time they invited the poor and lower-middle peasants to attend the course on class education. In conjunction with the surveying of a water conservacancy project aimed at prevention of schistosomiasis, measuring more than 4,000 meters in length and involving more than 30,000 meters of earth to be moved, it held a class on mathematics. In coordination with the erection of nearly 2,000 meters of power lines and the installation of lighting, it held a class on physics. Through an investigation of the history of blood and tears of the "ghost-house village" where schistosomiasis used to rage during the period of the Kuomintang reactionary rule, it organized the study of Chairman Mao's poem "Farewell to the God of Plague." The students reported that such studies were flexible and useful. Teachers of the department of mathematics, while giving instruction, included in their lessons "surveying," "map production," "study of middle school mathematics," which were excluded from the curriculum by the bourgeois "authorities" in the past. When they went back to their college, they took up practice again with the teachers of the ordinary classes and, by making use of the experiences of open-door teaching in various aspects, made it possible for teaching to be directly integrated with productive labor and serve the practice of the Three Great Revolutionary Movements. The teachers and students of that department separately went to two communes where they took up the task of carrying out surveys for three proposed reservoirs and channels. While doing practice and studying "rural surveying" at the same time, the students were not only able to learn the structural principles of such surveying apparatus as surface plates and leveling and measuring instruments and the methods of using them, but they also were able to gain the practical techniques of surveying highland, channels, and reservoirs.

Going deep into the Three Revolutionary Movements and starting from the reality of middle schools, the instruction teams have compiled some teaching materials of a specialized nature. These new teaching materials have had certain effects on the reform of teaching materials in the college. For instance, together with the teachers of the ordinary classes, they compiled a textbook on "rural surveying." This textbook was written on the basis of the most frequently used methods of flat land surveying, highway surveying, and reservoir surveying in rural production and construction, the practical experiences of the masses of workers and peasants gained in surveying, and certain useful theoretical knowledge contained in the old teaching materials.

The new situation of the development of the educational revolution not only demands that we take up the task of training teachers for middle schools but also requires us to assist the middle schools in solving problems of teaching materials and teaching aids (namely, training middle school teachers, examining middle school teaching materials, and operation of a factory by the college to produce teaching aids). By conducting such mobile classes in the entire province, the tutorial teams become well acquainted with the conditions of the educational revolution in middle schools and study the problems related to it. They become a bridge linking the normal college with the middle schools. This facilitates the fulfillment of the above tasks. For instance, after a team teaching geography made an investigation and did its practice, it compiled a report entitled "Opinions on the Geography Curriculum in Middle Schools." The report contained some good recommendations concerning the revision of teaching materials for geography in middle schools. On top of this, the team, in the light of the practical requirements of the rural middle schools, experimentally produced indigenous teaching aids that can be used for a variety of purposes, and revised the teaching materials while doing practice.

For the past year and more, guided by Chairman Mao's ideas on the educational revolution, the mobile tutorial teams have gained certain experiences for the educational revolution in our college. But there still remain many problems which must be dealt with further as these teams continue to make progress. We are determined to hold high the great red banner of Mao Tse-tung thought, put proletarian politics to the fore, and carry the proletarian educational revolution through to the end.

The Revolutionary Committee of Kwangtung
Normal College

VI

Short-Term Training Classes

16

FOUR NEW KINDS OF SCHOOLS

Comprehensive Report on Four Kinds of Schools in Industry, Agriculture, Health, and Teacher Education Being Managed by Every Hsien (Municipality) in Kwangtung Province*

Red Flag

Following Chairman Mao's great strategic policy and great directive for the educational revolution to "prepare for war, prepare for natural calamities, and serve the people," all the hsien (shih) of Kwangtung Province, during the high tide of socialist revolution and socialist construction, exhibited a revolutionary spirit of self-reliance; they established 298 short-term industrial, agricultural, health, and normal schools, which break down into 59 industrial schools, 60 agricultural schools, 72 health schools, and 107 normal schools. More than 26,000 students were selected from among workers with practical experience, poor and lower-middle peasants, and teachers in active service.

The new schools, guided by Chairman Mao's "May 7 Directive," firmly stress proletarian politics, practice of the Three Great Revolutionary Movements, hard struggle, and frugality in actively training a corps of proletarian scientists, technicians and teachers. They are warmly welcomed by the

*"Ssu-chung hsin-hsing ti hsüeh-hsiao — Kuang-tung sheng ko hsien (shih) ch'uang-pan kung-yeh, nung yeh, wei-sheng, shih-fan ssu-chung tuan-ch'i hsüeh-hsiao ti tsung-ho pao-kao." Hung-ch'i, No. 8 (July 21, 1970), 55-57.

broad mass of workers and poor and lower-middle peasants.

Urgent Needs of the Three Great Revolutionary Movements

Following the development of socialist revolution and socialist construction, a problem in the whole struggle-criticism-transformation campaign that urgently needs resolution is the rapid training of a corps of proletarian scientists and technicians, and a corps of proletarian teachers. The revolutionary committee of each hsien (shih) of Kwangtung Province has discovered by research and study that at present various areas are operating a number of local industries, engaging in technical innovation, carrying out agricultural mechanization, starting scientific agriculture, practicing a cooperative medical system, and developing socialist educational enterprises. They need a great many scientific technicians and teachers of a new type. The existing corps of scientists, technicians, and teachers is far from able to satisfy the need. Cheng-t'ien Brigade of Shih-t'an Commune in Tseng-ch'eng hsien had more than twenty pieces of agricultural machinery, but there was not a single person who could repair them. Therefore, whenever the machines were out of order they had to take them to the hsien capital to be fixed. Last year, Fu-ch'eng Commune of Shih-hsing hsien built nine elementary schools with attached lower-middle school classes; but because there were not enough teachers, six classes had to be temporarily cancelled. The poor and lower-middle peasants are very anxious to run schools for industry, agriculture, health, and education to meet the needs of the Three Great Revolutionary Movements.

In the past, because of the counterrevolutionary revisionist line promoted by the renegade, hidden traitor, and scab Liu Shao-ch'i, in some places technological power did not rest in the hands of the workers and the poor and lower-middle peasants. In 1963, when Pai-pu Commune in Tzu-chin hsien was repairing the water-conduit system, the "experts" of the bourgeois class drew up a plan that was totally unrealistic. It took six years, a tremendous amount of labor, and a state investment of funds that reached 300,000 yuan, but after all this the whole scheme turned out to be obsolete. In Ya-pu Brigade of Tung-feng Commune in Tseng-ch'eng hsien, the former agricultural technicians maintained a reactionary position. When the electric lights of a landlord went off, they voluntarily went to make repairs, but when the machinery of a production team went wrong, they ignored it. The poor and lower-middle peasants said angrily, "Unless we seize for ourselves the important right of technology, and unless we train our own technical personnel and teachers, we cannot thoroughly defeat the bourgeois class, and the political power of the proletariat will never be consolidated."

This vivid truth made the revolutionary committees of each level and the masses realize that fulfilling the needs of the Three Great Revolutionary Movements depends on the creation of four new types of schools, and that they had to strive to establish them.

Good Management of the Four New Kinds of Schools Is a Profound Revolutionary Act

Chairman Mao teaches us: "Education must serve proletarian politics and must be united with productive labor." These schools endeavor to manage themselves according to this guideline.

1. Maintain and stress proletarian politics.

Following Chairman Mao's teaching that "politics is the commander, the soul," we gave primacy to making a living study and living application of Mao Tse-tung thought. The most basic task of the school is to change the students' thought. The very first lesson when school opened was the brilliant "three constantly read articles" of Chairman Mao, which helped the students implant the thought that study is for revolution. To confront the thought still held by the students that one should "emphasize technology and take politics lightly," every school organized its students to make a living study and living application of the great theory of Chairman Mao on continuing the revolution under proletarian dictatorship; to listen to the workers and the poor and lower-middle peasants lecture on the "three histories"; to open a debate on "for whom do we study?"; to relentlessly criticize the absurd ideas of Liu Shao-ch'i that "one studies in order to become an official," "technology first," and "vocation first," so that the students would raise their consciousness of continuing the revolution and forever maintain the characteristics of laboring people. The industrial school of Tseng-ch'en hsien has sixty-nine students, forty-eight of whom have been judged "five-good" students. The poor and lower-middle peasants happily said, "The students of the new schools are making a living study and living application of Mao Tse-tung thought. This we greatly welcome!"

2. Teaching and learning oriented toward the Three Great Revolutionary Movements.

Schools are operating on the front line of the Three Great Revolutions. Industrial schools are operating in progressive factories. Agricultural schools are operating in progressive communes and brigades. Health schools are operating in hospitals or in progressive places that are implementing a cooperative medical system. Normal schools are operating in progressive units involved in the educational revolution. This is advantageous not only for having teachers and students receive re-education from the workers and the poor and lower-middle peasants, but also for enabling them to use society thoroughly as a vast classroom for conducting education.

The old technical schools studied "Western textbooks." What was studied was not applicable. At present the teaching content of the four kinds of schools is based on practicality, and it directly serves the Three Great Revolutions. The Fou-kang hsien Industrial School, based on the needs of the "four transformations" in agriculture in that area, opened classes on Mao Tse-tung thought, on industrial knowledge, on productive labor, and on military affairs and physical activities. It demanded that the students strive to raise their consciousness of continuing revolution, to grasp basic knowledge of mechanical and electrical matters, to concentrate on learning to use the ten kinds of machines that were commonly used in their area, and to serve in the construction of a new socialist countryside.

Tse-chin hsien Health School stresses in its teaching Chinese herbal medicine, new acupuncture therapy, and identification of common rural diseases. It is actively serving to consolidate the cooperative medical system.

Most of the new types of schools are on a three to six month schedule. In their teaching they emphasize thoroughly carrying out the principle of uniting theory and reality and reforming the phenomenon of "dead chanting of books" practiced by schools in the past. In the Tseng-ch'eng hsien Industrial School, after the students learned to use, maintain, and repair the commonly used agricultural machinery in the classroom and the machine shop, the workers and teachers led them into the villages, moving classes into the fields and the machine factories. During the day they repaired the machines there for the poor and lower-middle peasants. At night the workers explained the difficult problems that they had encountered in the process of repair, thus enabling the students to acquire real ability in practice.

Tseng-ch'eng hsien Industrial School has not only been managing an agricultural plot, where it has carried out twenty scientific experiments, but has also made these advanced techniques available to the production teams. It thus has accomplished both learning and practice. Many schools also invite local experts to the classes and develop mutual teaching and mutual learning activities.

3. Depend on the masses, be self-reliant, run the schools with diligence and frugality.

The masses' own school must depend on the masses for its operation. They manage the revolutionary schools with a revolutionary spirit. If there are neither school buildings nor facilities, the masses use their own hands to build them. Their means are simple, in keeping with the paucity of resources. Yang-shan hsien Health School in Pai-wu Brigade, Huang-ch'a Commune, utilized an old gun-turret, a storage room, and a pigpen to start a school. The poor and lower-middle peasants of Shan-k'an Brigade of Lung-wo Commune in Tzu-chin hsien heard that a health school was going to be opened. They wove grass cushions day and night for the school and ran against a cold wind for more than thirty li [ten miles] to deliver them to the school. The workers and the poor and lower-middle peasants have directly grasped the great power of determining school admissions. They themselves select the students. The living expenses of the students who come to school to study are divided proportionately among the communes and brigades that select and send the students to school, according to an accounting of their labor power. From admission to graduation, no state funds are used. In this way, there is good management and little expense.

Merits of the Four New Kinds of Schools

Although the four new kinds of schools have been open only for a short time, their merits are already evident.

Of the thirty-three students who graduated in the first semester from Tseng-ch'eng hsien Industrial School and returned to the villages, twenty-seven became brigade agricultural technicians, four became technicians at commune factories and farms, and one became the deputy chief of a commune processing factory. What is more, most of them became leaders in learning the works of Chairman Mao and basic cadres in militia units. They have three special characteristics: first, their ideas are firm as they strive to make a living study and living application of Mao Tsetung thought, joining their hearts and minds with those of the poor and lower-middle peasants; second, they are truly competent and able to perform various technical and agricultural tasks, everywhere taking the lead; third, they are not divorced from productive labor. They go to the fields and engage in labor during the agricultural busy season, and they go to the factory to work when farming is slack. Thus they sustain the true character of the working people.

Yüan-chou Brigade of Shih-tan Commune in the past had upper-middle peasant technicians. They not only demanded high wages but also did mediocre work. A son of a poor peasant, after graduating from an industrial school, came back to the brigade and became a technician of a water drainage station. Not only was he able to handle many kinds of agricultural machines, he also gave the poor and lower-middle peasants all the knowledge he had acquired without withholding anything. In addition, he actively propagated Mao Tse-tung thought among the commune members. The poor and lower-middle peasants happily said, "That new industrial school is excellent. Best of all, it puts technological power in the hands of the poor and lower-middle peasants." In Ch'an-ling Brigade of La-pu Commune, a son of a poor peasant, after graduating from the industrial school, was not only able to use and repair various kinds of agricultural machinery but was also able to rebuild the sugarpress, thus raising the production of sugar. At one time, when the brigade generator broke down, he was so concerned about the anxiety of the poor and lower-middle peasants that he struggled all night and finally repaired it, making possible the watering and transplanting of the young rice shoots on time in the brigade's field of more than 600 mou. The poor and lower-middle peasants praised him as a "red technician."

Two poor peasant students of Lan-hsi Brigade, Ch'ien-chin Commune, not only could handle many kinds of agricultural machines but also, using wood from the mountains, could make a wooden footpedal threshing machine.

The four kinds of schools have also become battlefields for expanding advanced techniques. When long rains caused an overripening of grains this spring, Fou-kang hsien Agricultural School studied methods of saving overripened grains and started to test and promote them in all the communes and brigades throughout the hsien. The school thus saved the overripened grain in a field of more than 2,000 mou.

The students of Tzu-chin hsien Health School have had classes for less than three months, and they already understand the usage of more than 300 Chinese herbal drugs, to the extent that they can recognize, collect, refine, and use them to cure poor and lower-middle peasants of what were previously believed to be "incurable diseases."

The veterinary class of Tseng-ch'eng *hsien* Agricultural School holds class wherever there are sick livestock. The students learn about the sick animals while treating them. In three months of study they have cured 110 sick pigs and 18 sick cows, and have received enthusiastic praise from the poor and lower-middle peasants.

VII

Elementary Education, Rural Schools

17

A PRIMARY SCHOOL RUN BY THE PEOPLE UNDER THE CONTROL OF THE POOR AND LOWER-MIDDLE PEASANTS

The Direction in Which Rural Education Is Heading Can Be Seen from the Experience of Sung-shu Primary School

(Liaoning Province Investigation Report)*

Red Flag

Red Flag Editor's Note

In our No. 3 issue this year, we introduced the experience in the development of revolutionary education at Suiyuan Commune in Yingkow hsien. Now we introduce to our readers the experience of a primary school run by the people established by the Sung-shu Production Brigade of the Chien-yi Commune of the hsien. Here is a comparison: it shows how a "regular" primary school supported by the state was controlled by the bourgeoisie, and how a primary school run by the poor and the lower-middle peasants of a production brigade on the basis of Chairman Mao's instructions has been warmly welcomed by

*"I so p'in hsia-chung nung chang-ch'üan ti min-pan hsiao-hsüeh — Ts'ung Sung-shu hsiao-hsüeh ti ch'eng-ch'ang k'an nung-ts'un pan-hsüeh ti fang-hsiang (Liao-ning sheng ti tiao-ch'a pao-kao)." Hung-ch'i, No. 5 (November 24, 1968), 46-51.

the poor and lower-middle peasants. This school discarded all the old rules and traditions in order to thoroughly serve the poor and lower-middle peasants. Now there is no age limit for admission; youngsters may start school in any season; they may come late and leave early. Students whose parents have too much to do and have no way to take care of the smaller children may bring their brothers and sisters to the school. In addition, this school has established four teaching centers for the eight production teams. Teachers of this school do manual labor to support their school, and in the last four years the school has not charged the students one cent in tuition. The poor and lower-middle peasants say: "With such a school and such teachers, our younger generation will not change its color."

The Hope of the Poor and Lower-Middle Peasants Has Materialized

Sung-shu Primary School is located in the Sung-shu Production Brigade of the Chien-yi Commune of Yingkow hsien. There are 231 families scattered among Liang-ko, Wu-peng, and the banks of the Yi-tao River. In prerevolution days there was only one school within the general vicinity of five production brigades. It had fifty-three students, of which only two were from the Sung-shu area, and they were children of landlord and bourgeois families. At that time, seventy-five percent of the poor and lower-middle peasants over thirty-five years old in the brigade were illiterates.

After liberation, as a result of domination by the revisionist educational policy, there was a so-called "regular" primary school, supported by the state, and about two and a half miles away from the Sung-shu Production Brigade area. In addition to tuition, there were fees for books as prescribed by regulations of the school; and there were various kinds of expenses, charged under the pretext of practicing the work-study policy, such as calling for the students to collect firewood, food, etc.; there were also unwarranted demands as to what the students should wear to the school. All this made it impossible for many children of the poor and lower-middle peasants to go to school. Thus, the poor and lower-middle peasants complained that the school was too far for their children to walk to; that the school expenses were too high for them to pay; that the school was too foreign for their children to attend; and that the ideology of the teachers was too impure for their children to learn. They angrily said: "To run such a school means to keep our children out of school." Even as late as 1964 over forty-five percent of the school-age children of the members of this brigade could not attend this school.

In 1964, the text of Chairman Mao's "Speech at the New Year's Forum" and other directives on education were received at the Sung-shu Production Brigade. After they learned about Chairman Mao's instruction, "As far as schools being run by communes or production brigades is concerned, if they have the resources, they are permitted to do so," the broad masses of the poor and lower-middle peasants were greatly excited, and they decided to open their own schools. To be sure, there were a few spoilers who said: "For peasants to run a school is sheer bunk. It will be such a weak thing that a breeze can sweep it away." And there were even a few cadres who made discouraging wisecracks.

But the poor and lower-middle peasants were not a bit ruffled by these smart remarks. An old poor peasant named Li Sen-wen said: "When Chairman Mao says we can start our own school, we will surely be able to do so." All other peasants responded: "We peasants will run a school for peasants. We know what kind of people we want our children to grow up to be. If there are no classrooms, then every place will become our classroom. If there are no teachers, everybody will become a teacher." It was precisely in this way that the peasants started their school. In 1964, when they first opened the school, there was only one class with 14 students. Today the school has four grades, seven classes, and 155 students, who amount to over ninety percent of the school-age children of the members of the production brigade.

The Poor and Lower-Middle Peasants Have Complete Control of the School

From the very beginning, the poor and lower-middle peasants have had complete control of Sung-shu Primary School. At that time a school committee was created under the direction of the Communist Party branch headquarters of the production brigade. Now, under the leadership of the brigade revolutionary committee, there is an Educational Reform Committee consisting of representatives of the poor and lower-middle peasants, which exercises power in three areas of the school: personnel, educational policy, and finance.

During the last four years, how have the poor and lower-middle peasants of the Sung-shu Production Brigade run the school?

They selected teachers from among the young intellectuals who had returned to the village. In the past there were many bad elements who wormed their way into the ranks of teachers in the so-called "regular" school, about which the poor and lower-middle peasants had made many suggestions for change. But nothing was ever done to correct the situation. They became very angry and said: "If we can select our own animal husbandry specialists, why can't we also select our own teachers?" Therefore, when they started to establish their own school, they conducted thorough discussions and careful investigations to make sure the potential teachers were good revolutionaries who also loved manual labor and had strong affection for the poor and lower-middle peasants, before they decided on whom to hire. They said: "We feel safe leaving our children to teachers we selected ourselves."

They have basically changed the content of the curriculum and the teaching method. In accordance with Chairman Mao's instruction that our education must be reformed, the poor and lower-middle peasants got rid of the rigid, unreasonable rules that were made by the revisionist educators. When there were no teaching materials, they edited and printed their own materials, including as the first lesson the simplified version of an article entitled "Long Live Chairman Mao"; they also included the "Eight-Character Constitution" and a list of names of farm instruments. At the same time, they discarded the worn-out feudal stories and the black stuff of the bourgeoisie and revisionists. In addition, they increased the number of classes in Chairman Mao's writings, proletarian politics, and agricultural production techniques, thus implementing Chairman Mao's directive that "teaching materials must be local in nature." As far as the teaching methods are concerned, they are closely integrated with real life, i.e., students go to class for half a day, and they do manual work for half a day; and on top of all this, students regularly get involved in socialist activities. During the busy season in farming, classroom instruction gives way to farm production. In classes in proletarian politics and agricultural production techniques, a policy of "going out to invite outside teachers" has been followed. As a result, many poor and lower-middle peasants have lectured in these classes. Furthermore, teachers also organized upper division students to teach lower division students. During the last several years, although the number of classes has been increased, the number of teachers has not. The quality of teaching has been raised nevertheless. Teachers have become the organizers of school, social, and family education, creating a lively and forward-looking educational environment.

Poor and lower-middle peasants determined through discussions the school budget and teachers' salaries. Teachers are paid by a work-point system under which they earn work points by the day, just like the commune members. The peasants said: "In this way, we and the teachers have the same thinking and the same attitude. We do things like members of a family."

Only recently Chairman Mao instructed us: "In rural areas we should depend on the most reliable allies of the working class, i.e., the poor and lower-middle peasants, to run our schools." And the poor and lower-middle peasants of the Sung-shu Production Brigade say: "Only when we have the power can rural schools be run well. If we let the bourgeois intellectuals usurp the power, we will surely have bad schools."

Thoroughly Serve the Poor and Lower-Middle Peasants

Because the primary school that is run by the people of the Sung-shu Production Brigade insisted on implementing Chairman Mao's proletarian educational policy that "education must serve proletarian politics and must be integrated with production work," it subjected itself to suppression and undermining by a small group of bourgeoisie, who attempted to destroy it completely. Some people who had been seriously influenced by the bourgeoisie also went all out to downgrade the school, saying, "the school is just like the tail of a rabbit; it cannot grow too much," and "youngsters who go to this school will have to spend their lifetime on the farm digging ditches"; and they did not allow their children to attend this school. To all these remarks, the poor and lower-middle peasants of the Sung-shu Production Brigade said: "This is the school Chairman Mao wants us to run, the school where we train our good younger generation. This is a road completely different from the one the landlords and rich peasants took." A production team leader said: "The fundamental principle is that after their schooling, our children will still have to devote themselves to farming."

When there are no regular classrooms, the homes of commune members, the compound of the production teams, the space near the iron furnace, and the area under the trees near the river bank are all classrooms. When there are no regular desks and chairs, small boxes, stools, old broken troughs for water buffaloes, old long tables, etc., serve as desks and chairs. In order to solve the old problem that small children are too small to be sent too far away to school, and big children are too big for other people to take care of, the school created, with what little means were available, four teaching centers in the immediate area of the eight production teams so as to accommodate the children of the poor and lower-middle peasants.

At the same time, the school abandoned all unreasonable rules. Students whose families have too much work to do may bring their brothers and sisters to school; students may come to school late and leave early; students may enroll in any season; and there is no age limit for admission. In order to better learn Chairman Mao's writings, two women leaders of production teams attended this school when they had free time.

Participation in productive labor is a required course for all students. In addition, digging medicinal herbs, collecting firewood, and various other work projects consistent with the half-work and half-study policy have been carried out on a regular basis. During the last four years the students have collected 60,000 catties of firewood, which not only solved the problem of providing heat in the school but also in the production brigade; the remainder was sold for over 200 yuan, which was spent for school supplies and other necessities. During the last four years the school has not taken one cent from the students; and prior to the Cultural Revolution, it did not receive one cent from the state. This is in sharp contrast to the so-called "regular" school. Therefore, the poor and lower-middle peasants proudly say: "This is the real Yenan spirit."

A New Type of School Educates a New Type of Man

All the students at the Sung-shu Primary School strongly love Chairman Mao and are loyal to Mao Tse-tung thought; they also have deep affection for their organization and they love manual labor. Every day when they come to school, the first thing they do is take part in the "three-loyalty" activity, and the first thing they do when they return home is to take part in productive work. Each student thus becomes an activist in propaganda, or an organizer for the study of Chairman Mao's thought, regularly working on the farms, in the streets, and in homes and production teams.

Last year, the series of directives that Chairman Mao issued during his inspection tour in North, Central-South and

East China were distributed among all the homes by these students. They also distributed the July 3 and July 24 announcements among all the people in their areas. The students displayed bitter hate for Liu Shao-ch'i. All of them attended [anti-Liu] criticism meetings, and they wrote posters and pasted them on walls, trees, and every space they could find. Poor and lower-middle peasants praised the students as propagandists for Mao Tse-tung thought, and the primary school as "the propaganda headquarters of the production brigade." Students of the Sung-shu Primary School are well-rounded and tough when it comes to manual labor. They are not afraid of getting dirty and exhausted. They pick up nightsoil; they carry farm produce for the production brigade. A member of the commune, who is a poor peasant, compared his two children, saying: "The one who goes to a public school learns very little, and the longer he attends that school, the lazier he becomes. The other one, who goes to the Sung-shu Half-Work and Half-Study Primary School, likes to work; he is good in doing political propaganda. He knows how to use whatever he learns in his school." An old poor peasant said: "Once I saw some insects on the field of our production team. I told my two daughters to catch them. The one who was going to a public school told me, 'It is very dirty. I don't want to do it.' The other one, who is attending the Sung-shu Primary School run by the peasants, enjoyed doing it. This is a real case of two kinds of schools, two different roads. Afterwards, I sent both my daughters to the peasant-run school to learn Mao Tse-tung thought."

The stages of the development of the Sung-shu Primary School are also the stages of reeducation of three women teachers by the poor and lower-middle peasants. Our great leader Chairman Mao not long ago pointed out: "Many or even most of the graduates of the old schools can integrate with workers, peasants, and soldiers. Some of them do have some inventiveness, or have done creative work. But it is necessary to put them under the direction of correct policy, to have workers, peasants, and soldiers reeducate them, and to thoroughly change their old thinking. Workers, peasants, and soldiers should welcome this kind of intellectual." During the last four years, teachers of the Sung-shu Primary School have very closely integrated with the poor and lower-middle peasants, and they have made a great contribution.

When Hsu Chin-fang, the daughter of a poor peasant, first walked into a classroom in a mud hut, a three-legged desk there reminded her of the modern school building where she used to attend classes. She became quite upset. At this time, Li Sen-wen, an old poor peasant, told her the plight of the poor and lower-middle peasants in the old society — persecution, exploitation, and no culture. He encouraged her to work hard to help them. Some poor and lower-middle peasants brought her inspiring books, including "Serve the People." All this taught her a great deal. So she made up her mind to serve the poor and lower-middle peasants the rest of her life. These last several years, she has regularly done manual work with poor and lower-middle peasants, learned from them, and accepted them as her teachers. As a result, she is teaching while she is learning. With deep feelings, she said: "The poor and lower-middle peasants are my good teachers." And the masses of peasants affectionately call her "the little servant of the poor and lower-middle peasants."

In 1967 the production brigade decided to give each of the three women teachers thirteen yuan. But they firmly refused and said: "We are also commune members like everybody else. If we accept this money, we will have received some extra money." All the poor and lower-middle peasants responded with great satisfaction: "When we have such a school and such teachers, our younger generation never will change its color."

After Chairman Mao issued his directive concerning the running of schools by the poor and lower-middle peasants, this primary school became everybody's Mecca. Those students who had been attending the so-called "regular" primary schools started to transfer in large numbers to this peasant-run primary school.

Joint Investigation Team of the Revolutionary Committee of Liaoning Province and a Certain Unit of the People's Liberation Army.

18

THE POOR AND LOWER-MIDDLE PEASANTS HAVE ACQUIRED SOCIALIST CULTURE

Investigation Report on the Educational Revolution in the Countryside by the Niu-t'ou-kou Brigade, Lin-t'ao *Hsien*, Kansu *

Red Flag

Summary of the Contents

The poor and lower-middle peasants of this production brigade, under the leadership of the Party branch, have gradually become able to grasp socialist culture by employing many different forms of school operation. Under the guidance of Chairman Mao's thought on educational revolution, they have established through their own efforts brigade primary schools, village schools, and people's schools, so that those youths who have practical hardships are still guaranteed an education. In this way the great majority of the poor and lower-middle peasants and their sons and daughters are able to study culture, thus promoting, through active learning and usage, the extensive development of the mass movement that Chairman Mao has prescribed. This is a most welcome new situation that has emerged from the Great Proletarian Cultural Revolution.

* * *

---

*"P'in hsia-chung nung yu-le she-hui-chu-i wen-hua — Kansu Lin-t'ao hsien niu-t'ou-kou ta-tui kuan-yü nung-ts'un chiao-yü ke-ming ti tiao-ch'a pao-kao." *Hung-ch'i*, No. 8 (July 21, 1970), 35-39.

In villages, especially in mountain areas where dwellings are scattered, a fundamental task of the educational revolution is to fully implement the "May 7 Directive" of our great leader, Chairman Mao, so that education truly serves proletarian politics, serves the poor and lower-middle peasants, and is united with productive labor, enabling poor and lower-middle peasants and their descendants to become cultured workers with socialist consciousness.

After two years of conscientious effort to implement Chairman Mao's guideline for educational revolution, the Niu-t'ou-kou Brigade of Hsin-tien Commune in Lin-t'ao hsien has achieved results and gained experience.

A Welcome Change

Before liberation, Niu-t'ou-kou had one traditional school. The students studying there were mostly sons and daughters of rich landlords. After liberation, the situation changed greatly. But due to the reactionary, revisionist educational line promoted by the renegade, hidden traitor, and scab Liu Shao-ch'i, a great many poor and lower-middle peasants still have not fully transformed themselves culturally. Niu-t'ou-kou Brigade, which includes six production teams, and covers about three square miles, used to have only one public primary school. Before the Great Proletarian Cultural Revolution, out of 155 school-age children in the whole brigade, there were less than 40 children in school (just 3 girls), only about 25 percent of the total. During the Great Proletarian Cultural Revolution, the poor and lower-middle peasants of Niu-t'ou-kou, following the directive of our great leader, Chairman Mao, that "In villages, schools should be managed by the most reliable ally of the working class — the poor and lower-middle peasants," recovered the power to make educational revolution in rural areas. They ran the schools and truly became the masters of educational revolution. They led revolutionary teachers and students in fundamental revolutionary criticism, promoted teaching reform, raised the quality of schoolteachers, made the old primary school into a five-year primary school, and thus started to change the whole educational scene.

However, the struggle between the two lines and the two ideologies was still heated. After the criticism of "the theory of studying to become officials," there appeared another phenomenon: very few school-age children, especially girls, came to school. To ascertain the reason for this, the brigade Party branch and revolutionary committee organized teachers and brigade cadres to visit the students' homes, door to door. Some people said: "Since graduates from universities and senior middle schools all end up with shovels in their hands, what's the use of children being able to read?" Others said: "Girls are going to get married sooner or later; what's the use of reading books?" and so on. The brigade Party branch attributed the attitude that "reading books is useless" to the fact that Liu's poisonous idea that "one studies to become an official" has not yet been eliminated. The Party branch also asserted that if the poor and lower-middle peasants wish to seize the power of educational revolution, they must continually and thoroughly criticize the counterrevolutionary revisionist educational line of Liu Shao-ch'i, and implant Chairman Mao's proletarian educational line deep in the mind of the broad masses. Afterwards the members went back to their individual production teams, and set up groups made up of production team cadres, heads of households, teachers, and students to study Mao Tse-tung thought. In particular they studied Chairman Mao's "May 7 Directive" and other important guidelines for educational revolution, and they waged a concentrated attack on the "theory of studying to become officials." The poor and lower-middle peasants and revolutionary teachers and students united the thoughts of this brigade, then wrote more than 180 pieces of criticism.

Once ideological knowledge was heightened, the school entrance rate quickly increased: in the latter half of last year the number of students reached 114. Eighty-three were school-age children, more than 60 percent of the total number of school-age children, and the number of girls greatly increased from 3, in the past, to 39. With this foundation, and in order to make things more convenient for the sons and daughters of poor and lower-middle peasants, and to push the entrance rate a step higher, the brigade Party branch and revolutionary committee built additional village school units for four production teams, which were quite far from the schools, thus enabling 48 more school-age and preschool children to be educated right in the village. At the same time, they employed forms for guaranteeing education to enable the 22 school-age children who could not go to school because of practical hardships to also study culture. In this manner, all school-age children began to read books.

Chairman Mao has instructed us: "In educational work, we should have not only centralized regular primary and middle schools but also decentralized, irregular village schools, newspaper-reading groups, and literacy groups" ("The United Front in Cultural Work"). The brigade Party branch and revolutionary committee realized that if the whole brigade wished to become a great school of Mao Tse-tung thought, it was not enough to have only school education and children studying. Since most youths and adults among the brigade's poor and lower-middle peasants were illiterate or semiliterate, and could not adequately read the writings of Chairman Mao, they proposed to eliminate illiteracy, both new and old. They extensively initiated remember-past-sufferings-and-think-of-present-happiness activities, in which the participants discussed the hardships of the past, when there were no rights and no culture, and the happiness of having rights today and the necessity of studying culture. The principle that "political rights are hard to maintain if cultural rights are not held" became clear in the course of the discussion, and many mistaken ideas were corrected. As a result each production brigade established a people's school and organized the members of the whole brigade to study politics and culture. At present there are already 243 youths, adults, and elderly members — or 80 percent of the brigade's entire work force — participating in the lessons.

Today this brigade has not only extended primary school education, but has made education available in villages over a broad area beyond what is usually referred to as the range of the school. This is the extraordinary change that has occurred since the poor and lower-middle peasants seized their cultural rights and took control of the schools. It represents a great victory for Chairman Mao's proletarian educational line.

Four Ways of Running Schools

Our great leader Chairman Mao, in his excellent work "Report on an Investigation of the Peasant Movement in Hunan," highly praised the revolutionary act of peasants managing their own schools, pointing out: "The peasants always disliked 'foreign style schools.'" "Now the peasants are establishing evening classes, which they call peasant schools." "They are very enthusiastic about these schools, for they realize that only this kind of school is their own." Since liberation, and especially today, after the victory of the Great Proletarian Cultural Revolution, the broad masses of poor and lower-middle peasants, by establishing their own schools in this way, have fully realized the revolutionary aspirations of socialist culture.

In accordance with Chairman Mao's "May 7 Directive," and with a series of major guidelines for the proletarian educational revolution, the Niu-t'ou-kou Brigade Party branch and revolutionary committee have, in general, practiced four kinds of school management.

1. The Brigade Primary School. Following Chairman Mao's guideline for students, "Make book-learning primary, but learn other things as well," books are studied in the classroom but also a base has been established for studying agriculture, and agricultural study has begun. In this field, the brigade has done two things.

First, it led the teachers and students in clearing an uncultivated hillside and filling in ditches and shallow-water areas, making a small farming area of four *mou*. This has enabled teachers and students to participate in productive labor and to begin scientific experiments in cultivation. In the classroom they discuss theories, while on the farm they put them into practice. By on-the-spot observation and by using their own hands, they united theory and practice. The more the students studied, the more they liked to study. This school-managed small farm also enjoyed a certain success in raising excellent seeds for the production team. The potato production of the brigade had decreased seriously. In drought years, production per mou was less than 100 chin, but even in normal years production had been very small. Last year, this small school-farm experimented with the Heilungkiang seed on one-fourth mou of land and, even under serious drought conditions, harvested 1,150 chin. The production team was very pleased, and this year the successful seed was used in most of the fields.

Second, outside of school, the brigade made the third production team, where the school is located, a place where teachers and students receive reeducation. Teachers and students go to the production team on a regular basis to study the works of Chairman Mao with the poor and lower-middle peasants, develop revolutionary criticism, and participate in collective productive labor. Last year, when the production team was working on a water conservation project, they organized teachers and students to lift more than 100 large stones from the bottom of ditches and line three ponds, all of which were more than 150 meters long. Thus they added 26 more mou of water-rich land. This spring, they swept the roads for the production team and gathered 24 fang of manure. During the peasants' busy season, the school reserved a certain amount of time for labor with the production team. The poor and lower-middle peasants happily said, "This is truly our own school."

2. The Village School. The village school, like the brigade primary school, is divided into several grades, and each grade separately studies the textbooks used in the schools. When they have no teaching staff, they use the method of "soldier teaching soldier," with students in the fourth grade or above of the brigade primary school taking the part of the teaching staff. These primary school students, having left school and returned home, have become the "little teachers." Since some poor and lower-middle peasants did not have anyone else to take care of the

children, they could not send their school-age children to the brigade primary school to study. After the establishment of the village school, they were very pleased and encouraged the children, saying, "We have been saved from the cruel sea by Chairman Mao; so you must diligently study Chairman Mao's books and become good children of Chairman Mao."

The teaching staff of the brigade primary school undertook the guidance and training of these students, taught them methods of teaching, assisted them in evaluating homework assignments, and indicated the problems of teaching as they arose. They have increasingly raised their teaching level.

3. Guaranteed Teaching. For those school-age children and youths who could not go to school because of practical hardships, they also adopted mass-line methods. They extended the work of "little teachers" by sending them after school to teach people in their own homes. In the third production team, there was an illiterate young girl who, after going through the guaranteed teaching system, can now read the "three constantly read articles" and more than sixty pieces from the Quotations from Chairman Mao. The poor and lower-middle peasants say: "Our school has come into our homes and penetrated our minds. Mao Tsetung thought has spread from house to house, has cleared people's minds and opened their eyes so they do not lose their way on the revolutionary road."

4. People's Schools. In addition to using Chairman Mao's "three constantly read articles" and the latest directives as the basic teaching materials, they combine them with newspaper reading to promote learning. At the same time, taking into account the actual situation in which most of the masses were illiterate or semiliterate, they used primary school language textbooks for learning characters and culture. As for study time, they use the evening in winter and spring, the time before and after the work in summer and fall. On rainy days they use the method of collective study with the help of specialists. In this way they keep abreast of the current situation, immediately study the latest directives, and repeatedly study their basic outlook. The sixth production team had a poor peasant who worked unusually

hard at production and was a model in learning. He said: "We all should learn characters and sweep away illiteracy so that we can all read the books of Chairman Mao better and thus sow a good field for revolution." There was a lower-middle peasant who was paralyzed since childhood, and the evils of the old society had made him "a seeing blind man." After the brigade established a people's school, he was especially pleased and diligently studied everyday. Now he can basically read the Quotations from Chairman Mao and the newspapers.

Through these four forms of school management, school education has been combined with social education and family education, spreading education throughout the whole brigade in a short period of time.

First Signs of Success

The broad masses of poor and lower-middle peasants of Niu-t'ou-kou Brigade, in the spirit of the proletariat, experimented with reforming the old education and making education widely available. In spite of the relatively short period of time, they have already achieved success.

First, they promoted the development of the mass movement to make a living study and living application of the works of Chairman Mao. In past years, because the poor and lower-middle peasants of Niu-t'ou-kou had long had no cultural and educational rights, the number of those who could read could be counted on one's fingers. This situation made it very difficult for "everybody to read the books of Chairman Mao." After people's schools were opened, most of the poor and lower-middle peasants were able to study politics and culture. Consequently, illiterates have opened their eyes, the uncultivated have picked up pens, and they have started to read Quotations from Chairman Mao, which they carry at all times and all places. Already thirty-eight persons are writing out their lessons and studying journals. Some poor and lower-middle peasants could even write their family history after studying. One poor peasant, whose job was to feed animals, quickly raised his cultural level after intensive study.

He wrote down in his notebook, "Though my body is in Niu-t'ou-kou, my mind encompasses the world. I will work hard feeding animals for the sake of revolution." Following the rise in the level of political thought, good people and good things continually emerged throughout the whole brigade.

Second, the poor and lower-middle peasants correctly seized their great right to education and became masters of culture and education. During the educational revolution, the brigade exercised unified leadership. Production team cadres grasped revolution, promoted production, grasped education, and studied culture. In October of last year, some students of the fifth production team, influenced by the argument that "reading books is useless," did not come to school to study. Once they were detected, a meeting was immediately held in the team to mobilize and educate heads of families and students. Then all the students came back to school. The people's schools and village schools in the six teams were all well managed, so the cadres called a conference of the whole brigade to promote the experience of the six teams.

The cadres of each production team are not only the leaders of people's schools but are also the students of the school. The leaders investigating their study situation make the same demands on them as on other members of the commune. In each brigade the cadre led and things were well done; there were many difficulties, but no one was frightened; although production work was busy, no one faltered; everyday work was maintained without failure.*

The revolutionary leader of the third production team, who is also the deputy head of a small team, used to be completely illiterate. He actively led the production team in establishing a people's school, and he himself sincerely participated in studying culture. The poor and lower-middle peasants, with deep understanding, said: "We grasped the right of education and we learned cultural knowledge well." This is an extremely advantageous step toward consolidation of the proletarian dictatorship and toward total reform through Mao Tse-tung thought.

*There are a series of rhyming phrases in the original that do not translate well — Peter J. Seybolt.

Third, it was advantageous to use the Three Great Revolutionary Movements to train students to become the successors of the proletarian revolutionary enterprise. The brigade primary school united education with productive labor. At the same time, by having children, from the time they are small, engaged in social activities — such as having school students go to the production brigade to be leaders in studying culture — it was possible for them to study the works of Chairman Mao together with the poor and lower-middle peasants, to work with them and criticize the bourgeoisie with them, and to be constantly reeducated by them.

Since the establishment of people's schools, village schools, and the system of guaranteed education, and since education by the poor and lower-middle peasants, there are already twenty-one students who have gradually become "little teachers" whose thoughts are Red, who study hard, who love labor, and who are welcomed by the poor and lower-middle peasants. Thus, very good conditions have been established for cultivating students to become workers who have socialist conviction and culture.

Fourth, the educational revolution promoted the development of agricultural production. The brigade Party branch and the broad masses of poor and lower-middle peasants adhering to the principle of living study and living application of Chairman Mao's works, have plunged into the hot tide of the educational revolution, aroused their revolutionary strength to the skies, and determined to effect a new leap in agricultural production. Since last winter, the whole brigade has been working on water conservation construction. It has repaired two water drainage lines, totaling seven and a half li, and chiseled out four water holes, changing eighty-eight mou of dry land into water-rich land, and opening sixteen mou of unused land among the ditches. This laid a very good foundation for progress in agricultural production. At present it is exerting a continual effort to study thoroughly methods of treating deep ditches to raise production. It is about to take another large step forward on the bright road of the "May 7 Directive."

19

A NETWORK FOR POPULARIZING SOCIALIST EDUCATION

Investigation Report of
Nanan *Hsien*, Fukien*

Red Flag

Summary of the Contents

In Nanan *hsien*, schools are run in front of the doors of the poor and lower-middle peasants, in the remote mountain areas, and on the offshore islands, as demanded by the poor and lower-middle peasants. This has changed the former irrational distribution of schools. Besides, spare-time schools and political evening schools of various types have been set up throughout this *hsien* by such means as are appropriate to the local conditions. In this way, popular education for school-age children and teenagers is basically achieved and 80 percent of the adult commune members can also take part in study. Experience of this *hsien* shows that it is entirely possible to popularize socialist education so long as we conscientiously carry out Chairman Mao's "May 7 Directive" and fully arouse the masses.

* * *

*"I-ko she-hui chu-i ti chiao-yü p'u-chi-kang — Fu-chien Nan-an hsien ti tiao-ch'a pao-kao." *Hung-ch'i*, No. 6 (June 1, 1971), 35-41.

Under the guidance of Chairman Mao's proletarian revolutionary line, Nanan hsien, Fukien Province — while performing in an all-round manner the various militant tasks put forth by the Party's Ninth Congress and with the brilliant "May 7 Directive" as the key link — carries out a spectacular and down-to-earth mass movement of educational revolution, causing deep-going change on the educational front.

Compared with the conditions before the Great Proletarian Cultural Revolution, the number of full-time primary schools has doubled, that of middle schools increased by more than ten times, and that of students increased to more than 18,000 in the whole hsien. Large numbers of spare-time schools of various types have been opened to meet the needs of the poor and lower-middle peasants, with more than 80,000 students enrolled. The development of full-time schools and spare-time schools has made it possible for 95 percent of the school-age teenagers and children in the whole hsien to attend school, basically popularizing secondary and elementary education. Political evening schools have been set up in over 90 percent of the production teams in the whole hsien, with 80 percent of the adult commune members participating in the study; many production teams have set up red nursery classes for children under school age. In this way, full-time schools, spare-time schools, and political evening schools are run simultaneously, and education for school-age teenagers and children, education for adults and education for young children are conducted at the same time. A network for popularizing socialist education has taken shape in the whole hsien.

Building a Network for Popularizing Socialist Education Is an Urgent Demand of the Poor and Lower-Middle Peasants

Chairman Mao has taught us: "The question of 'for whom?' is a fundamental question; it is a question of principle" ("Talks at the Yenan Forum on Literature and Art"). The fundamental question the proletarian educational movement seeks to solve is the question of 'for whom?' That is, for whom is a school opened, whom do we rely upon to run the school, who takes leadership, what should be learned in school, and what kind of people should be trained? These questions have long remained the focal point of the fierce struggle between the proletariat and the bourgeoisie.

Nanan hsien has a population of 850,000. Almost all of its land lies in mountain areas. Before the liberation, its few schools were monopolized by the reactionary politicians, landlords, and capitalists. Over 90 percent of the poor and lower-middle peasants were illiterate and suffered bitterly from illiteracy. After the liberation, the hsien took a big stride in its cultural and educational undertakings. Particularly in 1958, the year of the Great Leap Forward, the broad masses of poor and lower-middle peasants, guided by Chairman Mao's line of proletarian education, touched off an upsurge of operating schools. The whole hsien once had more than 560 schools with more than 90,000 students. It also had set up more than 40 agricultural middle schools and other intermediate technical schools, together with a great number of spare-time schools. But the renegade, hidden traitor, and scab Liu Shao-ch'i and his agents employed all possible means to sabotage these schools. Under the pretext that these schools were "irregular" and "poor in quality," they dropped 42 percent of the full-time schools and almost all the spare-time schools. The schools, particularly middle schools, which were left behind were located in townships and the seats of the commune headquarters, so the students in many areas still had to cross mountains and rivers to attend school, and quite a large number of the school-age teenagers and children were denied any chance of admission.

The Great Proletarian Cultural Revolution totally smashed the bourgeois headquarters with Liu Shao-ch'i as the leader. After its establishment, the Nanan hsien revolutionary committee sent a special investigation group to go deep into the mountain areas, the islands, and the fishing villages to get a clear picture of education in this hsien, so as to reform the old educational system. It was discovered from this investigation that the children of poor and lower-middle peasants urgently demanded that they go to read in school and that the poor and lower-middle peasants also had a strong desire to learn proletarian politics and socialist culture. But 7 of the 24 communes of this hsien did not have a middle school, and some 40 of the 247 brigades did not have a primary school. The old educational system was far from being enough to meet the needs of the socialist revolution and socialist construction. It had to be reformed without fail!

After Chairman Mao issued the directive that "In the countryside, the schools should be managed by the poor and lower-middle peasants — the most reliable ally of the working class," the Nanan hsien revolutionary committee immediately sent Mao Tse-tung thought propaganda teams, comprising poor and lower-middle peasants, into all the schools in the hsien. The entry and stay of the poor and lower-middle peasants' propaganda teams in the schools shattered the monopoly of the intellectuals. These propaganda teams tightly grasped class struggle, sharply criticized and repudiated the counterrevolutionary revisionist line of education, smashed the sabotage activities of the class enemies, surmounted the interference by the force of old habits, firmly grasped the leadership over the schools, and carried out the movement of educational revolution.

Vice Chairman Lin points out: "Whether or not the proletariat can firmly occupy the positions of culture and education and remold them with Mao Tse-tung thought is a crucial problem concerning whether or not the Great Proletarian Cultural Revolution can be carried through to the end." The hsien revolutionary committee took the educational revolution as a task of utter importance in the struggle-criticism-transformation campaign during the Great Proletarian Cultural Revolution, and its leaders personally grasped this task. They learned from practice that to meet the needs of the poor and lower-middle peasants, it was necessary not only to grasp school education but also to grasp social education; it was necessary not only to grasp the education for school-age teenagers and children, but also to grasp the education for adults and for young children; it was necessary not only to grasp full-time education but also to grasp spare-time education. Running a school in only one form is not sufficient; schools should be run in various forms, and it is necessary to vigorously grasp the popularization of socialist education. They advanced along the road indicated by Chairman Mao's "May 7 Directive," perseveringly put stress on popularization, adopted means appropriate to local conditions and ran schools in a flexible manner, setting up a new network for popularizing socialist education in townships and rural areas throughout the *hsien*.

Fundamental Methods and Experience

In the course of building the network for popularizing socialist education, Nanan *hsien* firmly acted in accordance with the series of Chairman Mao's directives on the proletarian educational revolution and tightly grasped the link of the struggle between the two classes, between the two roads, and between the two lines. Their fundamental methods and experience were as follows:

1. "Spread the points to the basic level, run schools in a decentralized manner," run the schools in front of the doors of poor and lower-middle peasants.

In the past, dominated by the counterrevolutionary revisionist line of education, the old schools were situated in townships and were run in the so-called "regularized" manner, keeping the children of poor and lower-middle peasants out of schools. The broad masses of poor and lower-middle peasants, feeling very indignant about this, pointed out straightforwardly: "The so-called regularization obviously aims at preventing the children of poor and lower-middle peasants from acquiring culture!" They strongly demanded that the schools be run in front of the doors of the poor and lower-middle peasants.

The *hsien* revolutionary committee firmly supported the just demand of the poor and lower-middle peasants, and obeyed

Chairman Mao's teaching: "There is no construction without destruction. Destruction means criticism and repudiation; it means revolution. Destruction means reasoning things out, which is construction. Put destruction first, and in the process you get construction." They sharply criticized Liu Shao-ch'i's counterrevolutionary revisionist line of education. On the basis of lowering the public primary schools in the hsien to be managed by the brigade, and after repeated study, they suggested the revolutionary measure of "spreading the points to the basic level, running schools in a decentralized manner," that is, decentralizing the existing schools, distributing them in a reasonable way, running the schools in front of the doors of the poor and lower-middle peasants, so the poor and lower-middle peasants might also go to study in school.

As soon as this happy news came out, the broad masses of poor and lower-middle peasants were filled with joy and rushed to inform each other of it. But the class enemies hastily jumped out to launch an attack and carry out sabotage, saying nonsensically that running schools in a decentralized way "was an irregular method and the students could never make a name even if they studied for their whole lives." Some teachers also objected to this way of running the schools. Influenced by the force of old habits, some commune members thought that "nothing could be learned from the school in a mountain village," so that they did not allow their children to attend the school. These phenomena, when reflected inside the hsien revolutionary committee, also caused doubts and worries among some comrades.

In view of this state of affairs, the hsien revolutionary committee first used Mao Tse-tung thought to unify the thinking of the leading group. Immediately after that, it held Mao Tse-tung thought study classes extensively among the masses and organized them to study Chairman Mao's directives on the educational revolution, to criticize and repudiate the erroneous ideas, and to uncover the sabotage activities of the class enemies. The broad revolutionary masses came to realize that "spreading the points to the basic level, running schools in a decentralized manner" was for the purpose of implementing Chairman Mao's proletarian line of education and popularizing socialist education. Accordingly, they unanimously and vigorously went into action and spread the existing middle and primary schools in the whole hsien to the mountain areas and islands and other areas where education was relatively backward. They also added classes of junior middle school to a full-time primary school were conditions permitted. Very quickly an upsurge of operating schools for poor and lower-middle peasants was whipped up in mountain areas, on islands and in fishing villages. There was in Huamei Brigade, Szushan Commune, a remote mountain village which had only six households of poor peasants. The brigade specially sent an educated youth there to run a class to teach its school-age children. The poor and lower-middle peasants said happily: "Now a school is brought to our door. We should attribute this wholly to Chairman Mao!"

After the measure of "spreading the points to the basic level, running schools in a decentralized manner" was adopted, the number of primary schools in the hsien increased to 621 as compared with 310 before the Great Cultural Revolution, that of junior middle schools increased to 258 (including classes of junior middle school affiliated with primary schools) as compared with 17 in the past, and that of senior middle school increased to 59 as against 7 in the past. Apart from these, more than 270 separate classes were set up. Basically, there was a primary school in a village, a junior middle school in a brigade (area), and a senior middle school in a commune. The rate of school attendance of the teenagers and children increased by 20 percent as against the past.

2. Spare-time schools of various types are run on a large scale, so the children of the poor and lower-middle peasants can study in school.

After the measure of "spreading the points to the basic level, running schools in a decentralized manner" was adopted, a very large number of children, in particular the girls, of the poor and lower-middle peasants could not attend school because of many real difficulties. How should the problem of schooling for these teenagers and children be solved? Following Chairman Mao's teaching, "In the field of educational work, there should be the centralized, regular primary schools and middle schools, and the decentralized, irregular rural schools, newspaper-reading groups, and literacy groups as well," the revolutionary committee of Nanan hsien aroused the poor and lower-middle peasants to conscientiously sum up the experience of the mass running of schools in 1958, the year of the Great Leap Forward, and ran spare-time schools on a large scale. In the past year and more, there have been set up in the whole hsien more than 1,350 evening primary schools, 258 evening middle schools, and 133 evening intermediate technical schools (of accountancy, medical and health service, farm machinery, electrical engineering, and other professions). As conditions vary with each village, mountain area and island, many good forms of education have been created to conduct spare-time classes, such as the herding-boy class (the boys grazing the cattle attend class by turn), the tea-picking girls' class (kept open to girls picking tea-leaves), the sea-tide class (in the coastal area, students attend class when the tide is in and carry out production when the tide is out), the mobile class (the teacher moves his teaching from one spot to another), the part-work part-study class, the morning class, the noon class, and the evening class. The number of students in spare-time schools was more than 70 percent of the total number of students in full-time schools, thereby basically popularizing secondary and primary education.

The teachers of evening primary schools and evening middle schools are chiefly the educated youths of the brigade. Some students of senior classes of full-time schools also serve as "little teachers." The teachers of full-time schools also teach on a part-time basis. The evening primary schools and evening middle schools do not deter production and the students can acquire culture from their books by a lamp. These schools are therefore warmly welcomed by the poor and lower-middle peasants. In some areas the girls, formerly burdened with household chores and left no time to attend school, now can acquire culture.

3. Political evening schools and Red nursery classes are operated on a large scale so as to put adult education and education for preschool-age children on the track of the proletariat.

After secondary and preliminary education has been popularized, how should education for adults and preschool-age children be carried out? Guided by Chairman Mao's "May 7 Directive," the poor and lower-middle peasants of Huamei Brigade, Shihshan Commune, and Yuanmei Brigade, Lunts'ang Commune, first established political evening schools with a production team as the unit and used Chairman Mao's works as the fundamental textbooks for learning politics, military science, culture, and agricultural and scientific techniques, and for criticizing and repudiating the bourgeoisie. Revolutionary songs were taught and revolutionary literary and art activities carried out. Because they were in accord with the characteristics of the rural areas, the political evening schools were welcomed by the poor and lower-middle peasants as soon as they presented themselves. The hsien revolutionary committee firmly supported this revolutionary newborn thing and called special on-the-spot meetings to popularize it. As a result, political evening schools, newspaper-reading groups, and literacy classes sprang up like mushrooms. More than 330,000 adult commune members took part in study regularly. Political evening schools were set up usually with a production team as the unit. Some of them were run jointly by a few production teams. Study was conducted from two to five nights a week.

Red nursery classes for preschool-age children of three to six have been set up in more than 2,000 production teams of the hsien. Here the children are taught Mao Tse-tung thought when they are young. This further liberates the labor force of women and lays a good foundation for shortening the term of schooling.

4. Rely on the masses, practice self-reliance, run the school with diligence and frugality.

Along with setting up schools in large numbers, there arose the question of insufficient outlays, school buildings, and equipment. What should be done? At first, some localities relied on the higher authorities for allotment of outlays. But the poor and lower-middle peasants said: "Now we hold the power of the schools and the schools are opened to us. We must run the schools self-reliantly!"

With revolutionary spirit, it would be possible to run the revolutionary schools. In Hout'ien Brigade, Fengchou Commune, 1,200 people had never attended school before. This time, the poor and lower-middle peasants were filled with joy when they heard that a school was to be set up in their brigade. They built two school buildings with self-reliance, spared two big sitting rooms and one thatched-roof hut and had them renovated, thereby solving the problem of classrooms. There were no desks and benches, but they made some with earthen blocks. They also selected four educated youths who had come from the city and who had always behaved themselves well, and posted them as teachers. In this way, the school was set up very quickly. Without spending a cent from the state, the poor and lower-middle peasants of Hsiawu Brigade, Shihching Commune, also set up a full-time primary school, with part-work part-study classes of a junior middle school affiliated with it.

The hsien revolutionary committee promptly summed up this experience of self-reliance and of running a school through diligence and frugality, thereby further exploiting the enthusiasm of the masses in running the school. In the past year and more, in the whole hsien, more than 1,000 school buildings have been newly built or renovated by the masses; more than 14,000 sets of desks and benches were newly made or repaired, and another 1,000-odd sets were made by piling up earthen blocks and stone tables. Some people said derisively that this school was "irregular" and "unpresentable." The poor and lower-middle peasants said: "Whether or not it is regular depends on whether it follows the correct orientation; whether or not it is presentable depends on whether or not the students it trains resemble the poor and lower-middle peasants!" In this way, the many difficulties in popularizing education were solved in the course of a school being run by the masses.

5. Shorten the term of schooling, reform teaching-learning, self-reliantly compile indigenous textbooks, conscientiously teach socialist culture.

Chairman Mao has taught us: "The term of schooling should be shortened. The curricula should be simplified. Teaching materials must be thoroughly transformed." Accordingly, the hsien revolutionary committee has, since the second half of 1969, enforced the new system of schooling in the whole hsien in a planned manner and step by step, shortening the term of schooling. Students of fifteen or sixteen may be graduated from a middle school. The content of teaching-learning is decided in accordance with the principle of "teaching fewer but essential things," and the part of content which is duplicated and pedantic is discarded and new content added in order to enable the students to develop morally, intellectually and physically and to develop them into socialist-minded, cultured laborers. In teaching every course of study, Mao Tse-tung thought is put in command, proletarian politics brought to the fore, and theory integrated with practice.

When the political evening schools for adults were established, the phenomenon of neglecting socialist culture existed for some time. Upon discovering this, the hsien revolutionary committee immediately organized all to study Chairman Mao's relevant teachings, carried out activities to recall past bitterness and think about present happiness, and heightened the students' understanding of cultural study. The poor and lower-middle peasants learned that after mastering the socialist culture, they could study Chairman Mao's works in a better way, gain more scientific and technical knowledge, and actively acquire culture while studying politics and military affairs. They generally adopted the method of acquiring culture through the study of quotations from Chairman Mao. In this way, they learned to read and consolidated their achievements in political study.

In the past year and more, various schools have been

conscientiously practicing the reform of teaching-learning and the teaching of socialist culture. They sharply criticized and repudiated the "theory of getting educated in order to become an official" and the "theory that to be educated is useless" and the "theory that it is a misfortune to be a teacher." The students learned for the revolutionary cause and the teachers taught for the revolutionary cause; they have greatly heightened their consciousness. Almost all schools have formed ties with factories and with production brigades, thereby building base areas for learning farming and industrial work. Many of the senior middle schools and some of the junior middle schools and primary schools also ran small factories and small farms and conducted scientific experiments self-reliantly. In the past year and more, Nanan hsien has compiled a complete set of textbooks ranging from primary school to senior middle school. The Party branches of some brigades also aroused the poor and lower-middle peasants to discuss problems together and have compiled supplemental teaching materials for primary school, giving prominence to proletarian politics and closely integrating theory with practice.

6. Build a contingent of teachers of the proletariat.

Chairman Mao teaches: "In educational reform, the most important problem is the teacher." In the course of popularizing education, Nanan hsien pays particular attention to building a contingent of teachers of the proletariat. The teachers who taught for some time have been rectified in an all-round manner and the handful of bad elements who sneaked into the ranks of teachers have been eliminated. Meanwhile, the method of training teachers locally has been adopted. More than 1,400 teachers have been selected, through recommendation by the poor and lower-middle peasants and with the approval of the commune and brigade revolutionary committees, to replenish the contingent of teachers. Among these teachers, 54 percent are poor and lower-middle peasants who have high political consciousness and an exceptionally high cultural level, 15 percent are demobilized armymen or armymen transferred to another trade, and 31 percent are educated youths who have labored for over two years in the countryside and conducted themselves well. After taking up their posts in education, these teachers not only have added fresh blood to the contingent of teachers as a result of popularization of education, but also have further consolidated the leadership of the proletariat over education. They bring to the schools the good experience of the poor and lower-middle peasants in the living study and application of Mao Tse-tung thought, propelling a mass movement of applying the experience in schools. They also bring the good experience of the poor and lower-middle peasants in learning from the Liberation Army, thereby strengthening political and ideological work in the schools. They take the lead in carrying out Chairman Mao's "May 7 Directive," often bring to the schools the poor and lower-middle peasants' opinions on educational revolution, and actively carry them out. They put daring in the forefront and boldly make creations. They have become a vigorous shock force in revolutionizing education. Apart from this, there has also been set up in the whole hsien a contingent of several thousand teachers who are poor and lower-middle peasants and not detached from production.

Nanan hsien pays particular attention to training and improving its contingent of teachers. These are the measures adopted: (1) The mass movement of the living study and application of Mao Tse-tung thought is carried out extensively among the teachers, and use is made of the winter and summer vacations to hold special study classes, so as to organize the teachers to study Chairman Mao's concepts of the proletarian revolution in education and so as to educate them in ideological and political lines. (2) Teachers are sent by turn and by group to be trained in the Three Great Revolutionary Movements and organized to make social investigations. They also maintain constant relations with some fixed production teams and take part in various political movements in the communes or brigades. In this way, they may continuously transform their world outlook in the course of integrating themselves with the poor and lower-middle peasants. (3) Newly-appointed teachers are organized to form "couples" with the teachers who have taken their posts for some time, so they all can learn from each other and make improvements together. (4) Short-term training classes and "exchange experience" meetings are held in order to continuously heighten the political and professional levels of the teachers. Revolutionary committees at all levels in this hsien conscientiously implement the Party's policy toward intellectuals, imposing stern demands politically on the teachers, giving them patient help ideologically, using them boldly in work, showing them warmhearted concern in everyday life, thereby further exploiting their enthusiasm for revolution.

A Tremendous Change

In Nanan hsien, the building of the network for popularizing socialist education has brought a tremendous change in various fields.

First, the hsien-wide mass movement for the living study and application of Mao Tse-tung thought has been pushed vigorously to develop in greater depth and width; a great impetus has been given to the revolutionization of man's thinking. "All work of the school aims at changing the students ideologically." Schools of various types gave preeminence to the living study and application of Mao Tse-tung thought and the use of Mao Tse-tung thought to train and educate man. The schools have become important points for extensively propagandizing Mao Tse-tung thought and the militant orders of the Party Central Committee, as well as crucibles for tempering successors to the revolutionary cause of the proletariat. With Mao Tse-tung thought popularized extensively, the masses of the people continuously increase their ideological consciousness. A younger generation of socialist new men is nurtured and growing up.

Second, a telling blow has been dealt to the bourgeoisie in the ideological sphere; Mao Tse-tung thought has been used to occupy the ideological and cultural fronts in the countryside.

In the past, dominated by Liu Shao-ch'i's counterrevolutionary revisionist line, the ideological and cultural front in the villages in Nanan hsien was flooded with the poison of feudalism, the bourgeoisie, and revisionism. After the network for popularizing socialist education was built, the masses, ranging from children to youths and from the middle-aged to the old, have found the form of study suitable to themselves and are learning politics, military affairs and culture in full-time schools, spare-time schools and political evening schools. There, they also criticize and repudiate the bourgeoisie, learn to sing revolutionary songs, carry out revolutionary literary and art activities, thereby wiping out the evil practice of feudalism, the bourgeoisie, and revisionism. In holding weddings or funerals, the commune members pay attention to breaking down old habits and customs and establishing new ones. Some political evening schools also organize women students to rebel against the feudal marriages of convenience, to break down outdated regulations, and to establish revolutionary new styles.

Third, favorable conditions have been created for wiping out illiteracy, thereby enabling the peasants to quickly heighten their cultural level. Meanwhile, a group of key elements have been trained for doing business accounting in the rural communes and brigades, carrying out business management for the poor and lower-middle peasants, enforcing cooperative medical service, and popularizing revolutionary literature and art on a big scale.

Fourth, an impetus has been given to technical innovation in the countryside and developing agricultural production. Schools of various types have paid particular attention to making scientific experiments in farming and doing farming by scientific methods. Many political evening schools organize their students to learn techniques of agricultural production and to learn the advanced experience of other localities. In 1970, Nanan hsien firmly grasped the measures of increasing agricultural output by double-cropping rice, popularizing short-stalk rice of a fine strain, transplanting seedlings to a rational density, and transforming the low-yield fields. Schools of various types vigorously worked in cooperation. Many schools also made experiments in transplanting seedlings with soil attached to the root and comparing crops of different strains and made the "920" new agricultural insecticide, bacterial fertilizer and carbohydrate fodder, directly serving agricultural production. Szushan Commune, situated in an extremely cold mountain area, formerly did not pay attention to scientific farming and its grain output remained very low. In 1970, the commune leadership organized the commune members, through the political evening schools, to repeatedly study Chairman Mao's teaching "In agriculture, learn from Tachai," and to learn the technique of agricultural production, thereby greatly arousing the determination of the poor and lower-middle peasants to fight against nature and to do farming by scientific methods. The 25 brigades of this commune have each built three-in-one posts for making experiments on agricultural techniques. They have made research and experiments on more than 70 items and cultivated new varieties of paddy suitable to the local environment, thereby defeating the cold waves, prolonged rains, torrential rains and insect pestilence, and reaping a bumper harvest in the whole commune. In the whole hsien, total grain output increased by more than 30 percent as against that in 1969, the level of 1,000 catties of grain per mou on the average was attained, and more than 1,000 grain-short production teams won their emancipation and reaped more than enough grain for their own consumption.

NCNA correspondent and NCNA reporter

VIII

Middle Schools, Physical Education

20

A MIDDLE SCHOOL SERVING THE THREE GREAT REVOLUTIONARY MOVEMENTS

Investigation Report of an Agricultural Middle School in Kuei Village, Hsü-ch'ang *Hsien*, Honan*

Red Flag

Summary of the Contents

This school takes the road indicated by Chairman Mao for managing schools. In the four areas of admissions, school system, examinations, and vacations, it has carried out transformation to solidify the proletarian dictatorship, build a new socialist countryside, and train a group of workers with socialist consciousness and culture.

* * *

The Agricultural Middle School of Kuei Village, Hsü-ch'ang *hsien*, was a school established personally by Comrade Yang Shui-ts'ai in September 1963. Ever since the establishment of the school the people there have followed Chairman Mao's great instruction that "education must serve proletarian politics and must be coordinated with production and labor." Under the supervision of the poor and lower-middle peas-

*"I so-wei san ta ke-ming yün-tung fu-wu ti chung-hsüeh — Ho-nan Hsü-ch'ang hsien Kuei ts'un nung-yeh chung-hsüeh ti tiao-ch'a pao-kao." *Hung-ch'i*, No. 8 (July 21, 1970), 50-54.

sants, they have trained a new force for the construction of socialism and pushed forward the development of Three Great Revolutionary Movements in the villages. The poor and lower-middle peasants say: "This is a school where a living study and living application of Mao Tse-tung thought has been made; it is a testing station where progressive experience in agriculture is promoted, and it is a good place for training agricultural technicians.

Take the Road Indicated by Chairman Mao for Managing Schools

This school was established and developed in the midst of violent struggles of the poor and lower-middle peasants against the renegade, hidden traitor, and scab Liu Shao-ch'i's revisionist educational line.

Since the beginning of the Great Proletarian Cultural Revolution, and especially since 1968, when Chairman Mao published the directive "In the villages, the most reliable allies of the working class — the poor and lower-middle peasants — should manage the schools," the poor and lower-middle peasants and the revolutionary teachers and students in the Agricultural Middle School in Kuei Village have been greatly encouraged. They raised high the flag of revolutionary mass criticism and relentlessly criticized the counterrevolutionary revisionist educational line of Liu Shao-ch'i. They moved a step forward in strengthening leadership over school affairs by the poor and lower-middle peasants' management committee and firmly grasped the great power of education. However, "the defeated classes will continue to struggle." When they criticized the counterrevolutionary and revisionist errors of the renegade Liu Shao-ch'i — such as "the theory that one studies to become an official" — and when the graduating students were actively preparing themselves to go back to their teams and participate in production, there arose an evil wind in the society. A small handful of class enemies took the opportunity to say that "Agricultural Middle School students can do nothing but labor; . . . this time we saw them shouldering a maise bar and grasping a graft knife when they went to take their examinations." Under the influence of this evil wind, some people who were quite strongly affected by the poison of the revisionist educational line complained that the Agricultural Middle School was "irregular" and that the things learned were "unsystematic," and they proposed to manage a so-called regular school.

In dealing with these conditions, the hsien revolutionary committee, along with the commune revolutionary committee and the committee managed by the poor and lower-middle peasants, immediately analyzed and studied the problem. They realized that this was a continuing struggle between the two classes, the two roads, and the two lines and that this reflected the fact that some people still had a lingering attachment to the old educational system. The hsien and commune revolutionary committees immediately grasped the problem and organized the poor and lower-middle peasants and the revolutionary teachers and students to make a living study and living application of Mao Tse-tung thought and to criticize the counterrevolutionary, revisionist educational line of the renegade, hidden traitor, and scab Liu Shao-ch'i. They recalled the process by which Comrade Yang Shui-ts'ai led the poor and lower-middle peasants in establishing the Agricultural Middle School, and greatly raised the class consciousness and consciousness of the struggle between two lines of the poor and lower-middle peasants and the revolutionary teachers and students. They said: "Our agricultural school is managed according to the educational policy of Chairman Mao; it serves the poor and lower-middle peasants and the Three Great Revolutionary Movements. This is excellent!" After revolutionary mass criticism, the broad stratum of poor and lower-middle peasants and the revolutionary teachers and students said that they would certainly follow the great instructions of Chairman Mao and proceed along the road of the "May 7 Directive" and make the Agricultural Middle School truly a school of the "K'angta" type. The slogans "Reading books is for revolution" and "Cultivating fields is for revolution" have become the new social style. The broad stratum of poor and lower-middle peasants made it their own responsibility to have school children do agricultural work and to train their children to guard against revisionism. They competed to send their own children to the Agricultural Middle School to study and labor.

Establishment of a New Teaching System

This school, in accordance with Chairman Mao's great instructions that "it is essential to shorten the period of schooling and revolutionize education," and "study is the main task, but other things should be learned also," transformed the old educational order and established a new teaching system.

1. Admission. The school invites applications from students, first, regardless of their cultural level; second, regardless of the particular season of the year; third, regardless of whether they were cadres or regular commune members. One can be admitted to the school only at the request of the poor and lower-middle peasants; or in accord with the demand of the Three Great Revolutionary Movements and with the consent of the committee managed by the poor; or with the recommendation for unqualified acceptance from the poor and lower-middle peasants. Students are chosen from the team and return to the team. There are primary school students of ten or so who are mainly studying lessons, but who are also studying other things; there are also poor peasants close to fifty years of age who are getting specialized technical knowledge (e.g., fruit-tree grafting, agricultural machinery techniques, and scientific agricultural experiments). When they enter school they first study the "three constantly read articles" and learn how to hold a discussion and application meeting, how to fight selfishness and criticize revisionism, and how to serve honestly the Three Great Revolutionary Movements. They also participated in collective production for a certain period of time. Only then are class levels arranged in accord with different circumstances, course emphases determined, and teaching begun.

2. School system. Their school system is unusually ingenious. It has long-term classes of two years, and short-term classes of several months to several days. The main determining factor is the needs of the Three Great Revolutionary Movements: if long, then long; if short, then short. Long and short are integrated. The long-term classes concentrate on study and make the learning of other things subsidiary. Besides the lessons on socialist culture, they also have classes on the techniques necessary for agricultural and forestry production. After graduation, the students go back to their original production team to participate in productive labor and to work in the team.

The short-term classes do not have systematic time restrictions. Priorities are based only on the needs of revolution and production; whenever it is necessary to send students to study, the students come, and whenever it is necessary to send them back to the team and let them work, they go back. For example, the seventh team of Kuei-hsi once needed an accountant. The school immediately graduated a student ahead of time and sent him to the brigade to serve as an accountant. He worked enthusiastically, his records were neat, and he was warmly welcomed by the poor and lower-middle peasants. In the past several years the school has graduated ahead of time, at the request of the poor and lower-middle peasants, thirty-seven students who went back to the teams as team heads, accountants, guards, and militia cadres. This has strengthened the foundations of the leadership group.

The short-term classes are also divided into many types of different training classes so that the students can train themselves for the production team as propaganda-agitation forces and as various types of technical personnel. Each training class puts proletarian politics to the fore. The first lesson is always on the "three constantly read articles," and the first meeting is on how to fight selfishness and criticize revisionism. As a result, in spite of the short period of study, students manage to acquire the idea of how to serve the people and become relatively good at a skill. Last winter, when there was an upsurge in the effort to provide electrical power for the villages, a large number of electrical engineers were needed. The Agricultural Middle School at once organized an electrical engineering training class, trained thirty-eight electricians for the fourteen brigades, and began to solve the problem of a lack of electrical engineers. When the masses requested that revolutionary songs be taught, the school quickly organized a short-term revolutionary music class, training more than four hundred singers for the twenty-eight brigades of the entire commune.

3. Examinations. This school does not have the old custom of having examinations in the classroom, but emphasizes instead the students' making a living study and living application of Mao Tse-tung thought in their daily lives, struggle against selfishness, and criticism of revisionism and its manifestations in productive labor. Implementing the principle of uniting theory with practice, the school holds examinations during practice, which demonstrates that practice determines the efficacy of study. For example, in the study of electrical engineering, a worker with practical experience was asked to become the teacher. He closely integrated teaching and practice, study and application, beginning with circuit design, installment, maintenance, and repair, and ending with electric lights on and motors running. Practice itself is the examination.

Another example: when the students study fruit-tree grafting, the whole process, from the selection of grain and the handling of the tender seedling to the planting of the mature seedling, constitutes one examination period. If a student is capable of taking full responsibility and successfully raising the growth rate of the seedling, then he is considered to have passed the course; otherwise he has to continue to practice through the second year grafting period. This kind of examination not only enables theory to lead practice and practice to enrich theory; it also trains students far more effectively, completely, and thoroughly to achieve the revolutionary spirit of service for the people.

4. Vacations. The vacation system of this school is not based on the cold and hot seasons, but is determined by the needs of the Three Great Revolutionary Movements in the villages. The principle of the vacation system is "the vacation period is not fixed, but depends on whether the village work load is heavy or light. When it is slack, they concentrate on studying; when it is busy, they do practical work." In winter, when rural work is slack, the students go to school as late as the twenty-eighth or twenty-ninth day of the twelfth month of the lunar calendar and resume classes on the third or fourth day of the first month. When the busy season comes to the village, vacations are given to let the students engage in labor and directly receive education from and examination by the poor and lower-middle peasants. The school considers vacation an extension of the classroom lessons on agriculture. The poor and lower-middle peasants evaluate whether the students' thought is good, whether their labor is active, and whether they are able to unite study with practice. The school considers the poor and lower-middle peasants' opinion of students as an evaluation of the school itself. When the poor and lower-middle peasants are satisfied, the school is going well and it will continue forward. When there are complaints, the school knows there are deficiencies that must be corrected immediately. Anything asked by the poor and lower-middle peasants and anything needed for the Three Great Revolutionary Movements is acted on right away. After the Party's publication of the report of the Ninth Congress, the school organized the students to study the report conscientiously, and then let them go back to the teams to initiate propaganda activities. During the last wheat-harvest vacation period, the cotton and maize became infested with vermin. Some production teams felt that the damage was not significant and did not try to overcome it; some tried but failed. Responding to the vermin conditions and to requests from the poor and lower-middle peasants, the school twice recalled the students from vacation, accompanied them to the fields to do research on the vermin conditions, discussed preventive methods, and then

sent them on vacation again. After the students went back to the teams, they launched, under the leadership of the teams cadres, a mass vermin-prevention campaign and swiftly eliminated the vermin problem. The poor and lower-middle peasants were completely satisfied with this result.

The Harvest of Seven Years of Running the School

During the past seven years, the long-term classes of this school trained 158 students; the short-term classes had altogether eight semesters. The number of people who have participated in study is 1,018. Most of the graduates of the Agricultural Middle School are already working as reliable successors to the revolutionary enterprise on various fronts. In the past several years, the Agricultural Middle School has selected 35 outstanding honor graduates and sent them to join the Chinese People's Liberation Army; 18 graduates went back to the brigades as basic-level cadres, having been recommended by the poor and lower-middle peasants and approved by higher levels; 11 graduates became leaders in the study of the works of Chairman Mao; others are teachers, agriculturalists, foresters, electricians, timekeepers, and so on. They are loyal to Chairman Mao, to Mao Tse-tung thought, and to the proletarian revolutionary line of Chairman Mao; they form a strong backbone for the solidification of the proletarian dictatorship in the villages and the construction of the new socialist countryside. Ta-yang Brigade was a backward brigade that had very complicated class struggle. One student of poor peasant origin who graduated from the Agricultural Middle School became the vice secretary of his branch after returning to the brigade in 1965. He firmly kept in mind Chairman Mao's instruction to "never forget class struggle." During the Great Proletarian Cultural Revolution, he led the masses in a courageous attack on a small handful of class enemies and discovered a sum of money illegally kept for over twenty years by rich peasants who hoped for the return of the old regime. They also disclosed the crimes of speculators who had ingratiated themselves with corrupt cadres. The poor and lower-middle peasants unanimously recommended that he become the secretary of the brigade Party branch, and head of the revolutionary committee. He made a living study and living application of Mao Tse-tung thought, took the lead in everything, provided a good example through his conduct, and stressed proletarian politics, so that the whole brigade changed markedly.

The revolutionary teachers and students of the Kuei Village Agricultural Middle School have inherited and developed the poor and lower-middle peasants' ideal of hard struggle, love for labor, and enthusiasm for collectivity. Their shoulders are never without baskets of soil, and their hands are never without a hoe. They uphold the real character of the poor and lower-middle peasants from beginning to end. They made Comrade Yang Shui-ts'ai a model of encouragement for themselves. They fear neither hardship nor death, and they compete to undertake important activities and vie to do heavy tasks. On one day last year, in the midst of fighting against drought, the chain of a machine suddenly dropped into a well. A student, despite the depth of the well and the coldness of the water, jumped into the well and retrieved the chain, guaranteeing the normal progress of the anti-drought activities. One student, who protected each blade of grass and piece of wood belonging to the group, was praised by the poor and lower-middle peasants as a "red caretaker." The poor and lower-middle peasants happily said: "The students trained in the old school ate more, dressed better, and were more extravagant, but the students of our Agricultural Middle School love to work and are not afraid of hardship. With such a good younger generation, we can put our minds at ease."

Since the Agricultural Middle School has clearly understood the school management policy for serving the Three Great Revolutionary Movements, the school has become in fact an experimental ground for the whole commune's agricultural science, and has promoted technological reform in agriculture and scientific cultivation. The new courses on reformed techniques of production in the field are first tested and experienced here; other advanced agricultural techniques from the outside are first demonstrated here; only then are they disseminated.

Some brigades had not customarily raised maize before. The Agricultural Middle School accepted the important task of searching for methods that would produce a high yield of the maize. Having experimented for many years, it finally produced the highest yield on record, more than 1,000 chin, the amount usually produced in two seasons. Production of cotton per mou reached 225 chin. In the past several years, the Agricultural Middle School has introduced wheat, sweet potatoes, and 70 other kinds of beneficial products. Through experiments, they have already made 26 of them widely available, effectively promoting the development of agricultural production. Students in the Agricultural Middle School have gained substantial skills. On returning to the team they have been functioning as agricultural technicians, in addition to doing their other work, and have become leaders in the renewal of agronomy. They are always working on experiments for high production of grain and cotton, fruit-tree grafting, installment of electric lines, maintenance and repair of machines, and other such projects.

At present, the Kuei Village Agricultural Middle School is in the process of a comprehensive summary of its experience, trying to extend its accomplishments, and overcome its defects. It is determined to continue to make new contributions to the construction of a new socialist countryside.

21

HOW DID WE INITIATE "INDUSTRIAL STUDIES" ACTIVITIES?

Tientsin No. 42 Middle School
Revolutionary Committee*

If we are to sustain and deepen the educational revolution and apply Mao Tse-tung thought to reform of the old schools, the most important questions are how to resolve the severe "three separations" phenomenon, how to make education serve proletarian politics, and how to unite education with productive labor.

How can education be united with productive labor? We, the revolutionary teachers and students of the No. 42 Middle School in Tientsin City, in accordance with the spirit of Chairman Mao's "May 7 Directive," and on the basis of the special characteristics of urban schools, have adopted the two methods of linking factories with schools, and of having factories managed by schools to learn about industry.

Linking factory with school means letting teachers and students go periodically to factories to learn about industry. In order to grasp typical experiments, we send students from one class to a factory. To learn about industry, we carry out the principle of "making study primary," proposed by Chairman Mao. Thus classes on cultural matters are also held in the factories. We have practiced this system for the last four months and have attained definite results.

---

*T'ien-ching shih ssu-shih-erh chung ke-ming wei-yüan-hui, "Wo-men shih tsen-yang k'ai-chan 'hsüeh-kung' huo-tung ti?" Hung-ch'i [Red Flag], No. 8 (July 21, 1970), 58-60.

Our great leader, Chairman Mao, has instructed us that "the working class must lead everything." Besides beginning to learn about industry outside of school, we ought to depend on the broad working masses who are associated with the factories. With the assistance of the factory, we have studied with the workers the directives of Chairman Mao, run a "May 7" study class, launched revolutionary mass criticism, exchanged experiences, and gained the support of the worker-instructors for industrial study activities. They said: "Chairman Mao directed that the proletarian educational revolution must be led by the working class and must have the participation of the working class. This is a splendid duty assigned to us by Chairman Mao, as well as an honorable responsibility of the working class. Since you came to the factory, we, the workers, can all participate in the educational revolution." The strong assistance of the workers has created for the students an excellent situation in which there are people controlling ideology, there are people taking cultural courses, and there are people teaching skills.

Because of the solid leadership of the working class and a close unity with productive labor, the classes on culture in the factory have two salient characteristics: the first is a class nature, and the second is a practical nature. A "three-in-one combination" of worker-instructors, teachers, and students prepared small group-discussion classes, which — through a successive process of remembering the hardships and recalling the pleasures, revolutionary mass criticism, and study of dialectical materialism — discussed theory while teaching about application. The students said, "We understand what we have studied, can apply what we have read, and are able to remember what we have heard. We have acquired cultural knowledge and at the same time elevated our socialist consciousness. We welcome classes of this kind."

For example, when an on-site class on the "motive power of lathes" was held at the Mechanical and Electrical Installation Company, the worker-instructor began by recalling scenes, when he was an apprentice at San-t'iao-shih, of human power replacing electric machines, of workers pushing a huge wheel to move the lathe, of dripping with perspiration, and of being totally exhausted. He then let the students calculate the horsepower of this kind of machinery to make them realize how capitalists used workers as bulls and horses. Another example: in dealing with three kinds of acid and two kinds of alkali, according to the old teaching method, one had to learn first the ferrous and nonferrous chemical components, and only then could one discuss acid and alkali. At present, however, we have introduced productive labor in a spice factory to students who have studied chemistry for only two weeks. As a result, the students have learned far better.

Our school's experimental class, which studied industry by going to a factory, had altogether fifty-two students. After only four months, they have grasped the basics of the various skills of using a winch, a roller, an electric welding tool, a riveter, a crane, and of doing electrical work and carpentry. In addition, the students' physical condition was strengthened; their faces became tanned, their muscles became strong, and each of them became an outstanding youngster.

"All work in the schools should serve to transform the students' thought." The teachers and students, having learned about industry in the factory, and having been influenced by the working class's progressive thought and the high quality of their education, have transformed their thought. Those students who were afraid of hardship and fatigue, and who did not like labor, have changed and now compete to work hard and even rush to get the heaviest hammer, which weighs fourteen pounds. With deep understanding, the students say: "In the past what we thought about at school was a small individual world, while today, in the melting pot of the working class, our hearts and minds are open, and we think about 'preparing for war, preparing for natural calamities, and serving the people,' and about world revolution. We ourselves seem to have changed."

In one class, originally, anarchist thought was rather serious, and very few students participated in the daily early morning military training. At present, however, most of the students go to the factory at seven o'clock, sweep the floor, polish the machinery, and make preparations. Their attitude toward labor and their collective feelings have been greatly strengthened. The easygoing and sloppy work style of the past has been replaced by a work style of unified struggle. When mass criticism and anti-selfishness meetings were held in the past, very few people spoke up. At present, however, they all speak up without hesitation, carry on spirited debates, and write drafts of criticism. Those who did not want to read books in the past are now rushing to the New China Bookstore in order to obtain handbooks on practical electronics, and are asking the worker-instructors to teach it and the teachers to discuss it. Those who disliked mathematics most in the past are now teaching mathematics and conscientiously preparing for the classes. Based on their own practical experiences, they have criticized the theory that "reading books is useless"; they have recognized that study is necessary for revolution. The whole class has become a revolutionized unit.

Having studied industry by linking factory and school, the revolutionary teachers and students of our school have realized deep feelings in the process of being reeducated by the working class and participating in productive labor, and a new type of revolutionary teacher-student relationship is being formed. Students respect teachers and are concerned with the progress of teachers, while teachers can now drop their pretensions and modestly study toward their educational goals.

Having experienced industrial study outside of school, we are now wondering whether it is possible to devote one year out of four years of middle school (preferably the third year) to going to factories and villages (half a year in a factory, another half a year in a village) to study industry and agriculture as well as culture. This would be beneficial for educating and training students. Naturally, this does not include a certain amount of time each year for going to factories and farms to study industry and agriculture.

The school-managed factory is another way of learning about industry.

Based on the needs of socialist construction and the school's special characteristics, we are running three factories. One of them is a metal-processing factory, which enables us to closely integrate teaching with the production of small-current transformers. The second is an insecticide plant, which has already begun trial production of the insecticide "920." It is beneficial for integrating the process of studying agriculture by teachers and students with scientific experimentation. The third is an electronics plant. This is a factory that our school established in a short period of time not long ago, relying solely on our own efforts and local resources.

At the time we started the electronics factory, we visited several electronics factories based on local methods in Tientsin. Although they were using local equipment, they had to spend more than 200,000 yuan to get the operation going. We studied the instruction in Chairman Mao's essay "The Bankruptcy of the Idealist Conception of History" which says: "Under the leadership of the Communist Party, as long as there are people, any human miracle can be performed." We have also studied Chairman Mao's important annotation on the essay "Who Said Chickens Can't Fly?" After that, everyone said: "We will follow Chairman Mao's directives, for they bring us strength and victory." With no tools and no capital, we struggled for over a month, being self-reliant, diligent, and frugal; we finally produced a semiconductor triode, which passed successfully the inspection of the Tientsin Semiconductor Factory. Running this factory, we have spent altogether only a little more than 200 yuan; what is more, this money was accumulated by the students selling abandoned iron and steel they had collected.

How did we solve the problem of equipment for this electronics factory run by the school? In order to make the semiconductor triode Model 3AX1-5, there are more than ten processes, requiring approximately seventy pieces of equipment. Most of them were teaching materials and tools that the school already had, which we either modified or repaired, and more than ten of them were modified from the abandoned materials that we obtained through other factories or from a company that supplied waste materials. For example, imported diffusion furnaces cost several tens of thousands of yuan, while buying homemade ones would still cost several thousand yuan. But we obtained two spare pieces of high-temperature magnetic tube from a factory, bought three pieces of small magnetic tube, found an abandoned iron tub, and made of them an electric furnace. Since the electric heat resistance of the K'ang-tai [?] wire was inadequate, we used a regular electric furnace wire instead, and we have carried out many kinds of experiments in wire wrapping methods. This way, spending only five yuan, we have made three large and small high-temperature furnaces, including a preliminary heating furnace [yü-jê lu], an incendiary finishing furnace [shao-chieh lu], and a diffusion furnace [k'uo-san lu]. The temperature in all of the furnaces reached more than one thousand degrees, and all had constant temperature areas. Using these furnaces, we baked semiconductor triodes.

When the first batch of triodes was completed, teachers and students were very elated. However, inspection proved that the quality was not satisfactory. After an analysis, it was found that it was due to inadequate welding (we used tin welding) and a lack of electrolysis. We took these problems to a factory for study and found that the factory's equipment for welding and electrolysis was all "foreign." Buying it cost a tremendous amount of money. So we observed Chairman Mao's instructions to "abolish inhibiting ideas," "liberate our thought," "be self-reliant," and "rely on local resources." In only one day we modified the "multiple-use transformers" that had been used as a teaching tool and solved the welding problem. At the same time, we solved the problem of electrolysis.

Our method of using local resources to solve the equipment problem has many merits, such as enabling us to break old bonds, relying on the masses for ideas, and relying on collective wisdom to solve problems. "There are many people, much discussion, high enthusiasm, and great energy" ("Introducing a Cooperative"). There was some key equipment, like quartz pipe and ion water purifiers, which the teachers and students, experimenting with hundreds and thousands of methods, provided by their own efforts. We mobilized the students to go to every hospital in the city to collect all kinds of surplus insulated thermal tubing. If one copies everything, nothing can be accomplished; but if one improves native methods, then everything can be accomplished. In this way — by self-reliance, using local resources, exploiting used and abandoned things, and adopting the simplest means — in a short period of time, despite obstacles, we succeeded in making semiconductor triodes. After visiting our electronics factory, our brother schools said in retrospect, "Having observed the Western manner of production in factories, we felt that we dare not do it. But having seen yours, based on local resources, we feel that we can do it too."

In the process of running this electronics factory, the teachers and students have shown a spirit of selfless labor and have actively devoted themselves to production. Whenever we failed, or quality was not acceptable, we studied the "three constantly read articles," and learned Chairman Mao's instruction to "be determined not to fear sacrifice; overcome every difficulty; struggle for victory." In everyone's mind is a determination to fight for the glory of the great leader Chairman Mao and for the glory of the great socialist fatherland, which gives them boundless strength to fight for victory against difficulties.

Establishment of out-of-school bases for studying industry and school-run factories has not only created products but, more important, has further tempered the broad range of revolutionary teachers and students. The process of learning about industry is also a process of receiving reeducation from the working class, and of reforming one's world view. The broad masses of teachers and students are now teaching and studying for the revolution, and they have taken a joyous step forward on the road of revolutionized thought.

Establishment of out-of-school bases for studying industry and school-run factories has promoted the transformation of teaching content and methodology. The contents of productive labor and lectures given by worker-instructors are excellent new teaching materials. Study of written experiences summarized from the study of industry is an excellent new teaching method.

The two methods of studying industry — going out of school, and staying in school — are mutually related and mutually supplementary. Studying industry by going out of school enables teachers and students to have broad contact with society, with workers and masses and, furthermore, enables them to study the superior quality of the working class. As for studying industry at school, you can quickly and flexibly allocate production and labor, according to the needs of teaching plans of different periods.

Chairman Mao has pointed out: "Our educational policy should enable those who receive education to develop ethically, intellectually, and physically, to become workers with socialist consciousness and culture" ("On the Correct Handling of Contradictions Among the People"). Having gone through these preliminary industrial study activities, we repeatedly review this instruction of Chairman Mao's and feel very close to it. Our industrial study activities have just begun. We are determined to carry the educational revolution in middle schools through to the end by unceasingly advancing in the direction indicated by Chairman Mao.

22

MASS PHYSICAL TRAINING

Peking Review*

Peking Review Editor's Note

Many readers have recently written to us for information about mass physical training in China. The general principles guiding such activity are Chairman Mao's teachings, "Promote physical culture and build up the people's health" and "Our educational policy must enable everyone who receives an education to develop morally, intellectually, and physically and become a worker with both socialist consciousness and culture." The following two reports show, in some respects, how Chinese physical culture workers put these principles into practice.

Physical Training in a Middle School

In last February's round-the-city race, a traditional mass sports activity in the capital during the Spring Festival, the Peking No. 26 Middle School had the most participants. Many gave a good account of themselves, and its girls' relay team

*Peking Review, No. 14 (April 7, 1972), 11-14. This article has been edited to conform with American spelling and punctuation.

placed fifth. Prior to this, more than one hundred boys and girls in the school formed some twenty teams to take part in a middle-school cross-country run held by the city's Chungwen District. One of the girls' teams won the championship and three others came in fourth, sixth, and eighth; and the boys' teams came in second, third, eighth, and tenth. Curious about these successes, which have won widespread acclaim, we paid the school a visit.

Upon our arrival at 6:30 in the morning, we saw some five hundred students training on the sports grounds — some practicing throwing the javelin, discus, hand grenade, and other objects; some running or practicing the high jump and long jump; and some playing ball games. At 7:30, the students gathered on the large field or in the courtyards, doing setting-up exercises to music broadcast over the radio. Classes began at 8. From 8 through 4 p.m., we saw over a dozen classes taking physical training lessons on the grounds. During the interval after lunch and after 4 o'clock in the afternoon, the students played ball games and engaged in various other activities. So keen are the youngsters on the ball games that they throng the sports grounds even on Sundays.

The No. 26 Middle School has 3,070 boy and girl students in fifty-four classes. The school has five full-time and three part-time physical training teachers and adequate sports facilities, including nine basketball courts, one volleyball court, one football field, and ten table tennis tables. Apart from school teams for football, boys' and girls' basketball, volleyball, table tennis, and track and field, many grades and classes have their own teams.

How to organize such large contingents in regular training? What ideology should be used to guide their activities? What results have been obtained from mass physical training? And what is the relationship between moral, intellectual, and physical development? Answers to these questions were given by a physical training teacher whom we interviewed.

"Through the Great Cultural Revolution," the teacher began by way of introduction, "we have come to understand that in physical training there is also the question of 'For whom?' Since the purpose is to build up the people's health, we should stress the mass character of such training. It is wrong to train just a few 'stars'; our duty is to help the majority of students take an interest in physical training and actively participate in sports activities.

"Having made this clear, we have bent our efforts in this direction.

"First of all, we do our best to popularize those sports that give a comparatively large amount of exercise but require no particular skill, such as running, tug-of-war, skipping, and throwing the hand grenade. We have introduced a kind of relay race with the participants running back and forth on a sixty-meter-long track. With twenty to thirty on a team, as many as forty to sixty can take part in each race. Everyone can run, so if we make proper arrangements, the students will all be willing to join. Tug-of-war also gives the body quite a lot of exercise. With twenty on each side, forty can join in each contest.

"Second, we pay proper attention to combining athletic meets with everyday sports activities, using competition to stimulate training. It is natural that an upsurge in mass activity precedes every such meet. However, we used to stress only getting good results and did not combine competition with everyday training. The result was that students started training only a few days before a competition and laid off when it was over. The accent now is on popularization. Before an athletic meet starts, every grade and class is required to hold trial competitions to select its representatives. To do this, it has perforce to start training two or three months in advance; and the net result is that there will be many small-scale athletic meets before the actual school meet is held, with over 90 percent of the students having taken part.

"To induce more students to take an interest in track and field, which lays a good foundation for other sports, we have made due arrangements in the rules of competition. Since placements are determined by the total number of points won by a team, which can field only a definite number of contestants, we have stipulated that points be given to everyone who has competed according to the rules, with only one point difference for each placement. In this way, all the contestants are encouraged to do their best for the team. Both in making preparations and in holding the school athletic meet, we have done away with the past practice of having only a few kept busy while the majority look on unconcerned. Now we mobilize the noncontestants to do various work, such as serving as umpires, judges, and timekeepers; and we ask the teachers to explain the rules to them beforehand. All this makes them doubly enthusiastic about learning the rules. Thus an increasing number of working personnel are trained, and more and more students take a great interest in athletics.

"Matches in various ball games are quite common between classes or grades and between teachers and staff members and students. In addition to athletic meets every spring and autumn, the school teams often compete in interschool tournaments.

"Increased interest, once sports have become popular among the students, spurs them on to raise their standards. Drawing on their initiative, we give them lectures on various sports during physical training classes and morning and afternoon training sessions and put them through a rigorous basic training course. Those grades or classes that have not done well in the previous athletic meet are all the more anxious to show improvement; and, after hard training, they often do better in the next meet. The other grades and classes are not complacent about past successes either, but continue to forge ahead. When such friendly emulation is the order of the day, steady improvement is assured for one and all.

"Students showing promise are sent in groups to the spare-time physical culture and sports school attached to the Peking Gymnasium for short- or long-term specialized training. With their standards raised, they constitute a major force in helping promote sports in our school.

"No effort has been spared to foster good sportsmanship among the students. Fine examples of this during competitions are frequently propagandized throughout the school. Equal attention is paid to using sports activities to educate the students ideologically and properly handle the relationship between physical training and study and between physical and moral development. Recently, to help the students take examinations seriously, we held a forum in which several students holding responsible posts in their grades or classes and sports activists discussed how they correctly handled this relationship. Their views, broadcast over the loudspeaker or made public in the wall newspapers, received the close attention of all the students.

"We always encourage the students to repair and make the sports equipment themselves. When table tennis became increasingly popular and there weren't enough tables, we called upon the students to build eight brick and cement tables in the open air. And whenever the wooden tables have to be repaired, the students always do it themselves. This helps them cultivate the habits of caring for public property and of taking part in physical labor.

"Practice over the past year or so has given us tangible results. As more and more students take part in sports, they have in general grown taller and put on weight, with much better health and stamina acquired through a period of training. In particular, girl students' physiques have greatly improved. Now more energetic, the students have shown better discipline and are keener in their studies.

Winding up his discourse, the teacher said: "We are now aware as never before of the benefits of promoting mass physical culture and sports. Chairman Mao's teaching, 'With us, therefore, the raising of standards is based on popularization, while popularization is guided by the raising of standards,' has given us the correct orientation. There are many shortcomings in our work, and we have to make still greater efforts in order to do a good job of promoting physical culture and sports among the masses."

The Peking Spare-Time Physical Culture and Sports School

It was a Sunday morning. Bathed in warm spring sunshine, the playgrounds were filled with hundreds of juvenile athletes having a training session under the supervision of coaches. On the running tracks, some were practicing the start and the spurt; others were clearing the hurdles. Basketball players were practicing shooting; volleyball players were volleying and smashing, pounding away at the ball without pulling their punches; and football players were tying out various kinds of shots at the goal. At a nearby cement rink, other youngsters were skating on specially made roller skates.

In the gymnasium, little girls were performing free exercises on a carpet, to the accompaniment of piano music; boys were tumbling on the mats; others, wielding swords and spears, were practicing the traditional Chinese wushu. In the table tennis hall, scores of young players, some hardly taller than the tables, were playing with skill and exchanging fast attacks. All around, spirited youngsters were practicing with concentration; and the coaches, genial yet serious, were giving directions or demonstrations to the trainees.

Such were the lively scenes we saw on our visit to the Peking Spare-Time Physical Culture and Sports School. Medium-sized but fairly well equipped, it has more than fifty experienced coaches, some of them quite well-known sportsmen. There are now over a thousand trainees, ranging from seven to sixteen years old, taking special training in table tennis, basketball, volleyball, football, track and field, gymnastics, wushu [Chinese boxing], skating, and water sports. So as not to affect their studies, they train during after-school hours, from 4:30 to 6:30 p.m. on weekdays and all of Sunday. Coming to the school three to four days a week, they get an average of two hours of training each time, free of charge.

The aim here is to promote mass sports activities in the middle and primary schools and to train prospective athletes for the country. The three-stage training that the school has adopted is an embodiment of the principle of raising standards on the basis of popularization.

The first stage is to send the school's coaches to the various middle and primary schools to organize training in different sports there. This is what is called establishing training centers, which may be run on a long-term or short-term basis. In other cases the coaches only help the physical culture teachers in these centers to give the students special training. In this way sports activities in these schools are promoted, and promising boys and girls are spotted.

The second stage is running short-term classes with selected trainees (from various schools) whose ideology and physiques are good and who have acquired rudimentary techniques in some kind of sports. Three to four months' specialized training during after-school hours helps these trainees greatly improve their physiques and basic techniques.

The third kind of training is for the best among the trainees. They continue training for another year in the so-called "long-term" training classes, where they receive further coaching. Most middle-school graduates who have attended such training courses will form the main force in promoting physical culture and sports among the masses, and some will be sent to higher institutes of physical culture and sports for further training.

Like other schools in New China, the Peking Spare-Time Physical Culture and Sports School requires that its trainees grow up to be working people with both socialist consciousness and culture. The accent, therefore, is not only on the youngsters' physical development but on their moral and intellectual development as well. Maintaining close ties with the teachers and parents, the coaches do their bit in educating the trainees ideologically in the light of their conduct both in the schools and at home. Very often the coaches are the bosom friends of the trainees, who are willing to say how and what they think so as to get help in improving.

In order not to affect their studies, the spare-time physical culture and sports school sees to it that the youngsters get only an adequate amount of exercise. Since middle-school students have more lessons to do than primary-school pupils, they accordingly get less training. Abundant facts have shown that after joining the spare-time school, the youngsters have made tangible improvements both in ideology and in health, and they have in general also progressed in their studies.

The first lessons the youngsters usually get at the spare-time school involve listening to the coaches talk about the exemplary deeds of outstanding sportsmen. How well-known table tennis player Chuang Tse-tung and high jumper Ni Chih-chin, cherishing high aspirations and undergoing painstaking training, won the men's singles world championship three times running and set a world record in the men's high jump, respectively, deeply impresses the youngsters, enabling them to understand that training and setting records are all for winning honors for the people, not for personal gain. Aware that they are training for the revolution, they take greater pains and are more tenacious than ever before in working to realize their ideal.

On Sundays or holidays, the school often takes trainees to factories or to villages on the city's outskirts to give exhibition matches or take part in physical labor. This gives them the chance to keep in close touch with the working people and to listen to veteran workers or poor and lower-middle peasants tell about their sufferings in the old society and their happy life in the new. All these effective methods help trainees foster the conception of serving the people. In day-to-day training sessions, the school encourages mutual help and unity. Practicing together with the youngsters, the coaches discuss with them how to master basic movements and tactics, and help everyone work out proper ways of overcoming shortcomings and raising his standards. Teaching and learning from one another, they have thus cultivated the spirit of working for the collective.

Last year the spare-time school ran 32 long-term classes, with 528 trainees, and 210 short-term classes, with 4,800 trainees, and established training centers in over 200 schools in the urban and adjacent rural areas. All the trainees, while in training or after finishing their courses, became activists in popularizing sports in their own schools.

The Tsaochang Primary School, where conditions and equipment are below average, is an outstanding example of popularizing sports among its 600 pupils, though it has only one physical culture teacher. Through the joint efforts of this teacher and coaches from the spare-time physical culture and sports school, table tennis has really taken root and blossomed there. Having established a training center in the school, the coaches come three times a week to demonstrate and explain the basic techniques and tactics of the game. The pupils there have physical training lessons twice a week, one devoted to table tennis. Now practically everyone in the school can play the game and, with the exception of the first grade, all the classes in the other grades have teams competing in interclass tournaments.

Many promising players have been discovered and sent to short-term or long-term classes for further training. Back in the school, these players are "little teachers" of their schoolmates. Playing for the school team, they often compete with other training centers and have friendly matches with teams from nearby factories. With many fine players having come to the fore, small wonder that one of their girls won the singles in the interprimary-school table tennis tournament last year.

The Tsaochang Primary School also has a *wushu* team of thirty members, all developed by their schoolmates who have been trained at the spare-time school. There are many other similar examples of such trainees in other schools passing on what they have learned at the special training classes to their schoolmates.

Established in 1958, the Peking Spare-Time Physical Culture and Sports School, which has been tempered in the Great Proletarian Cultural Revolution, is now clearer than ever about the question "Whom should it serve?"

IX

Higher-Level Technical Training

23

THE WAY TO TRAIN ENGINEERING AND TECHNICAL PERSONNEL AS VIEWED FROM THE SHANGHAI MACHINE-TOOL PLANT

Investigation Report*

People's Daily

People's Daily Editor's Note

We recommend the following investigation report to all proletarian revolutionary comrades, broad masses of workers, poor and lower-middle peasants, student youths, revolutionary intellectuals, and revolutionary cadres in the nation. This report vividly describes how the Great Proletarian Cultural Revolution has produced a great change in the ranks of engineering and technical personnel and has demonstrated the great vitality of new socialist ideas. It is entitled "The Way to Train Engineering and Technical Personnel as Viewed from the Shanghai Machine-Tool Plant," but it also points out the revolutionary direction of school education.

---

*"Ts'ung Shang-hai chi-chuang ch'ang k'an pei-yang kung-ch'eng chi-shu jen-yüan ti tao-lu — Tiao-ch'a pao-kao." Jen-min jih-pao, July 22, 1968.

Recently, Chairman Mao thoughtfully pointed out: "It is still necessary to have universities; here I refer mainly to colleges of science and engineering. However, it is essential to shorten the period of schooling, revolutionize education, put proletarian politics in command, and follow the road of the Shanghai Machine-Tool Plant in training technicians from among the workers. Students should be selected from among workers and peasants with practical experience and they should return to production work after a few years' study."

This great call of Chairman Mao's is our battle order to carry the proletarian educational revolution to the end. It is the great "antirevisionist" plan for the next hundred years. All true proletarian revolutionary comrades in revolutionary committees at all levels, factories, and schools, and on all other fronts in the country must firmly follow Chairman Mao's policy on proletarian education. They must criticize the revisionist education policy and destroy the old bourgeois educational system. And they must resolutely follow the worker-peasant-soldier road, as pointed out by Chairman Mao, in order to carry through the educational revolution to the end.

Scientific research departments and leading organs should also carefully study this report, for it is a sharp weapon to further criticize the antirevolutionary revisionist policy on science and technology advocated by China's Khrushchev.

The great historical significance of the Great Proletarian Cultural Revolution and its far-reaching impact on various aspects of our nation have just begun to be evident. The Great Proletarian Cultural Revolution is the prerequisite for a new industrial revolution in the nation. The tremendous creative force of the masses of people will continuously produce many miracles that the bourgeois fools and the rightist conservatives have never thought of. We would like to advise those nearsighted capitalist followers who have not yet become hopeless diehards to look ahead a bit further. We also would like to advise those college and university students who look down upon workers and peasants, and who think they themselves are so important, to discard their privileged status so as to quickly catch up with the millions of revolutionary people who are heroically moving forward.

The Great Proletarian Cultural Revolution Has Produced a Profound Change

The Shanghai Machine-Tool Plant is a large factory known for its production of precision grinders. It has over 600 engineers and technicians. There are three groups of personnel: forty-five percent are technicians promoted from among the workers, fifty percent are postliberation college graduates assigned to the plant, and the rest are old technicians who remained after the liberation. The storm of the Great Proletarian Cultural Revolution has produced a profound change in the technical work force at the plant. Primarily, this great revolutionary change is evidenced in the following ways:

1. The proletarian revolutionaries have actual control of the factory, including control over technical decisions. The reactionary bourgeois technical "authorities" who previously controlled the technical leadership of the plant have been overthrown. Many technicians who came from the ranks of workers, revolutionary young technicians, and revolutionary cadres have now become the masters of scientific research and technical design. All of them are proletarian revolutionary fighters, with deep class feelings for Chairman Mao and the Communist Party. This revolutionary technical team, which was suppressed in the past, now continuously demonstrates its creative wisdom and technical skill. With unlimited loyalty to Chairman Mao's proletarian revolutionary line, it is ceaselessly climbing new technical heights. During the first half of this year alone, it had already successfully trial-produced ten new models of precision grinders, including four that meet advanced international standards. The high speed and the excellent quality of the production are unprecedented in the history of the plant.

2. The antirevolutionary revisionist line in technical matters, as advocated by China's Khrushchev, and the reactionary

bourgeois world outlook have been severely denounced. As a result, the bourgeois technical "authorities" have become politically bankrupt, and the true "paper tiger" [i.e., superficial] nature of their technical expertise has been completely exposed. Previously, the capitalist-roaders did their best to build up these reactionary "authorities" and "idols" for young technicians to worship and urged them to "measure up" to these "authorities" and to "struggle hard to become engineers." Now, many of these young technicians have greatly changed their outlook. They realize that the idea of having fame and wealth is the beginning of revisionism and that the title of the bourgeois is something that they should not fight for. In the past, not a few researchers in the Grinder Research Department used to record technical data in their personal notebooks, which they treated as their "little private depositories"; but now, at their own initiative, they quickly submit such data to the department and compile them into handbooks for everybody's use. All technicians in the plant have volunteered to work in the shops alongside of the workers and to collaborate with workers in research and in improvement of designs. The old technicians, when they work in the shops, have also made conscientious efforts to shake off their pretentious manners and to humbly learn from the workers.

3. The relations between workers and technicians have changed. In the past, a handful of capitalist-roaders and reactionary "authorities" in the plant proposed a so-called "one and one" combination system — that is, one worker serves under one technician. This so-called "combination" meant that "the engineer works with his mouth and the worker with his hands," or the "engineer provides the idea, and the worker does what he is told to do"; and all this was nothing more than the old line that "mental workers rule, and manual workers are ruled." They also preached such reactionary theories as "workers and technicians must check on each other" and "workers and technicians must form two opposite groups." They put into effect a set of rules and systems that were designed to control, check on, and suppress the workers. The

"Handbook for a Productive Worker" alone has over 170 rules, which every worker had to memorize and follow. All this further widened the vast gap between workers and technicians. During the Great Cultural Revolution, this plant introduced a "three-in-one" combination system, consisting of workers, revolutionary technicians, and revolutionary cadres. Under this system, the ordinary workers now take part in designing, and the technicians also work on the production lines. Because theory and practical work have been closely integrated, the relations between workers and technicians have improved a great deal.

The Way to Train Engineering and Technical Personnel

Young technicians at the Shanghai Machine-Tool Plant (including personnel up to about thirty-five years of age) come from two sources: college and university graduates (numbering about 350, of whom ten percent are postgraduates or those who had studied abroad) and technicians promoted from among the workers (numbering about 250, a few of whom had studied at secondary technical schools for a few years). Experience indicates that the latter group is superior to the former. Generally, the former group is more backward in its outlook and less competent in actual work. The latter group is more progressive in its ideas and more able. At present, the overwhelming majority of the technicians who came from the ranks of workers are the backbone of the technical work force. And about ten percent of them are qualified to independently design high-grade, precision, and advanced new products. Six of the ten new precision grinding machines that were successfully trial-produced during the first half of this year were designed by technicians who came from the workers' ranks.

Promoting technicians from among workers is the way to develop a proletarian engineering and technical work force.

We can see a sharp contrast between two technicians of about the same age, but with different backgrounds:

The first one is a graduate of a university in Shanghai. After one year of study of a foreign language and four years of further study in a foreign country, he received an "Associate Doctor" degree. In 1962, he started to work in the laboratory of the Department of Grinder Research at the plant. Because of the separation of theory from practical work, and because of his failure to collaborate well with workers, with some twenty years of school behind him and after a long period of scientific research in the department, he failed to make any outstanding contribution.

The second is a worker. At fourteen, he was an apprentice. At eighteen, he was sent to a machine-building school in Shanghai for four years. In 1957 he was appointed a technician in the Department of Grinder Research. In April of this year, under his direction as the chief designer, a large surface grinding machine was successfully trial-produced. This machine, which comes up to advanced international standards, not only meets an urgent need of our industrialization but also fills a gap in our manufacturing of precision grinders.

Before the Great Cultural Revolution, a small number of capitalist-roaders in our Party and reactionary technical "authorities" had madly suppressed and prevented workers from taking part in designing. Around 1958 there was a group of workers who were promoted to technicians but, under various pretexts, reactionary "authorities" at the plant gradually transferred them out of the Department of Design. Despite all this, the technicians who came from the ranks of the workers overcame all obstacles and demonstrated their ingenuity and creativity. Statistics indicate that of all the new products designed at the plant, those successfully trial-produced by technicians from the ranks of workers, and by young technicians in collaboration with workers, amounted to sixty percent in 1958, seventy percent in 1959, and eighty percent in 1960. Since 1960, particularly since the start of the Great Proletarian Cultural Revolution, almost all of the new products were designed and successfully trial-produced by their joint efforts. Not a few of these products meet advanced international standards — for example, the universal cylindrical grinding machine for mirror surface grinding, the high center cylindrical grinding machine, and other major products.

Some young technicians with college degrees have gradually shaken off the influence of revisionist educational policy, cast off their privileged status, and collaborated with workers. After a period of practice, they also made some more meaningful contributions in designing and trial production. For instance, a 1964 college graduate always kept a foreign book on the thread-grinding machine when he first began work at the plant. (The fact that we mention his foreign book does not mean that we should not read such a book.) Proceeding from theory to theory, he did not accomplish anything at work. During the Great Cultural Revolution, he raised his class consciousness and understanding of the struggle between the proletarian revolutionary line and the bourgeois reactionary line, and he decided to follow the road of integrating with workers. Early this year, together with two technicians who came from the ranks of workers and a veteran worker, he successfully trial-produced an important electric device for grinders.

Why do technicians promoted from the ranks of workers develop faster and contribute more?

The most important reason is that they have deep proletarian feelings toward Chairman Mao and the Communist Party. They do not work for fame and wealth, they are not afraid of dangers and hardships, and they will not stop working until they reach their goal. They firmly remember Chairman Mao's teachings and always think about how to compete favorably, in speed and quality, with the imperialists, revisionists, and reactionaries. Furthermore, they constantly try to find ways to economize resources for the state and to make the production process easy and efficient for workers. Some of the young intellectuals, however, affected by the poisonous influence of the revisionist educational policy, have long ago separated themselves from productive labor, alienated themselves from the workers, and longed for bourgeois fame and wealth; and they accomplished nothing in the end. There was one technician who dreamed of achieving fame as an expert in one brilliant move; he worked on some sixty research projects over the last ten years, which he gave up one after the other, thus inflicting a great financial loss on the state. Aiming at building up a reputation for himself, a 1956 college graduate did experiments on grinding heads all alone, and he ruined altogether some thirty grinding heads. At long last he asked veteran workers to help him. With their assistance, he finally succeeded in his experiments. In retrospect, he said: "Trying to make a grinding head behind closed doors only makes one suffer from complete failure. By working together with the workers, one tastes the sweetness of success. In the final analysis, one has to grind one's own head first before one knows how to make a good grinding head.

There is a much sharper contrast between technicians promoted from the ranks of workers and the traditional fame- and wealth-hungry bourgeois intellectuals. There was a bourgeois "expert" who spent eight years and a large amount of state capital in designing a grinder, but he failed completely. In the process, he collected quite a bit of so-called "data," which he used as capital to create fame and wealth for himself. About this the workers said, "How can such people have any feeling for our new society?"

Chairman Mao says: "The wisest and the ablest are those fighters who have practical experience." This is because, in their long period of practical work, they have accumulated a great deal of experience and because, after a few years of study in the after-work schools or in spare-time specialized technical institutes, they have closely integrated theory and practical work. Thus they have achieved a "leap forward" in knowledge, enabling them to successfully conduct scientific research and make independent designs. This is an extremely important reason why they become creative so much faster. When they study, they do so to solve particular problems. Therefore they penetrate, understand, and know how to apply the things they learn. Using his rich experience in practical work, one technician solved very complex technical problems in developing a product. While working on his product and studying the theory of metal-cutting, which he rapidly absorbed, he developed his own methods and ideas in metal-cutting processing.

Before they integrate with workers, it is very difficult for technicians who have graduated from colleges and universities to produce anything because of their inadequate practical experience and the irrelevancy of their book knowledge to productive work. Once, for example, several technicians of this type designed an internal thread-grinding machine. Because of their inexperience, it was impossible for the workers to assemble the machine from the blueprint until experienced workers revamped some of the parts.

The combination of the revolutionary spirit, which calls for the courage to imagine, to create, and to break through, with a strict scientific approach is an extremely important prerequisite for engineering and technical personnel in scaling scientific and technological heights. Yet to do this is something closely related to one's world outlook and practical experience. Many technicians who come from the ranks of workers have dared to break away from superstitions and foolish traditions, and therefore have become the least conservative because of their freedom from the mental yoke of personal fame and wealth and because of their rich experience in practical work. A good example of this is the recently trial-produced precision grinder that meets advanced international standards. Because technicians who had come from the ranks of workers had the courage to break out from the obsolescent structure of operations, they reduced the time for making the prototype from eighteen months to six. They also raised the surface finish by four grades, and reduced the number of parts and the total weight by one-third. The product cost was only 15.5 percent of a foreign-made precision grinder. But some school-trained technicians find it hard to discard superstitions and foolish traditions and to develop new techniques because they ignore ideological reform, are always concerned about their personal gains and losses, such as the loss of face and the image of a specialist, and because they have more mental restrictions and reservations than other people. Even they themselves say, "The more books one reads, the tighter the yoke. The result is that one loses his initiative and drive."

Workers at the Shanghai Machine-Tool Plant prefer students from the secondary technical schools, if they have to choose between graduates from colleges and graduates of secondary technical schools. Although the latter have less book knowledge, they also have fewer self-important manners; they have more practical experience and fewer mental reservations and restrictions created by old or foreign ideas. For these reasons there are quite a number of graduates of secondary technical schools who have accomplished more than graduates of universities. A case in point is the design of two extremely efficient automatic production lines by two 1956 graduates of secondary technical schools.

The Direction of the Educational Revolution as Seen from This Plant

On the basis of an analysis of their current conditions and the route that the various types of engineering and technical personnel at the Shanghai Machine-Tool Plant have followed, we also can clarify the problem of direction in the revolution in education.

From their experience, veteran workers and many young technicians more thoroughly realize that Chairman Mao's instruction that "the control of our schools by bourgeois intellectuals must not be allowed to continue any longer" is unprecedentedly brilliant and correct. They all believe that it is urgent and significant to carry out the proletarian revolution in education according to Chairman Mao's educational thought. His series of directives on revolution in education point out our forward direction. Now our problem is to act firmly and thoroughly, as Chairman Mao instructs.

In accordance with Chairman Mao's ideas on education and the special conditions at the plant, workers and technicians have presented the following views and suggestions regarding the revolution in education.

1. Schools must educate, as Chairman Mao instructs, "workers with socialist consciousness and culture." This is unlike the schools under the control of revisionist educational policies, which trained "intellectual aristocrats" who were alienated from proletarian politics, the broad masses of workers and peasants, and production work. This is a fundamental question affecting whether revisionism is to be wiped out or not. Comrades at the Shanghai Machine-Tool Plant believe that in the past it was a mistake to assign new graduates of colleges and universities as cadres in factories and in the countryside. The integration of young students with workers and peasants and the participation of the former in productive labor are an important means of changing their world outlook and teaching them practical, technical knowledge. Therefore, they [workers and technicians] recommend that new graduates of colleges and universities should, first of all, be assigned as ordinary laborers in factories and in the countryside to take part in productive labor. They should earn their "qualification certificates" from workers and peasants and then, depending upon actual demands, some of them may be assigned as technicians; but they must still devote a certain amount of time to physical labor. The rest will continue as ordinary workers and peasants.

2. School education must be combined with productive labor. Chairman Mao instructs that "our main method is to learn how to fight from fighting." Judging from the conditions of some of the technicians at the Shanghai Machine-Tool Plant, one of the serious weaknesses of the old educational system was the separation of theory from practice and the overemphasis on abstract traditional doctrines and methods, which made those who read more all the more stupid. Only by doing practical work can one master theory quickly and thoroughly, and apply it creatively. For this reason, workers and technicians at this point recommend that schools appoint experienced workers as teachers; that workers be allowed to lecture; and that some of the subjects be taught by workers right

in the workshops. There was a young technician who was assigned to work in a research office right after his graduation from the university. All day long he devoured books and deeply immersed himself in theory and in studying foreign languages. Because he was completely isolated from production work, he felt frustrated all the time. In the early stage of the Great Cultural Revolution, he went to learn from workers at the machine tool plant who had had a lot of experience; he worked on the bench and things began to change for him. Recently, working together with ordinary workers, he made a meaningful contribution in the grinding of a mirror surface. He is now thoroughly convinced that he must have workers as his teachers.

3. With regard to the source of engineering and technical personnel, they [workers and technicians] believe that in addition to continuing to promote workers to become technicians, units should also select graduates of junior and senior middle schools who have sound political ideology and two to three, or four to five, years of experience in productive labor, and send them to study in junior colleges and universities. There is now every possibility to do so. Take the Shanghai Machine-Tool Plant as an example. Most of its workers have an education above junior middle school. The advantages of selecting these youths to study in colleges and universities are: (a) they have a better political background; (b) they have a proven ability to do practical work, and experience in productive labor; (c) after a few years of work, a graduate of junior or senior middle school is about twenty years old. After another few years of study he will be graduated at age twenty-three or twenty-four, and will be able to work independently. As of now, a graduate of a university generally will be able to work independently only after two to three years of internship. Therefore, it is entirely consistent with the principle of getting greater, quicker, better, and more economical results to send youths with practical experience to study in universities.

4. As regards the retraining and raising of the standard of the existing technical force at the plant, they [workers and

technicians] point out that a large number of technicians graduated from various schools have long been subjected to the evil influence of revisionist educational policy and revisionist policy in managing economic enterprises. In addition, there is a group of technicians who were trained before the liberation of China. Some of them naturally are patriotic, and are working very hard; they are not anti-Party or antisocialist, and are not loyal to any foreign country, but they do have many problems regarding their world outlook and work style. In accordance with the policy outlined in the "Decision of the Central Committee of the Communist Party of China on the Great Proletarian Cultural Revolution," the plant should hold high the great banner of revolutionary criticism, as advocated by Mao Tse-tung thought, and organize them to participate in the revolutionary criticism meetings. These technicians will learn, in their mass meetings, how to thoroughly denounce such fallacies of China's Khrushchev as "experts should manage the factories" and "putting techniques in command," as well as the attitudes of "go slow" and "unconditionally accept anything foreign as better." They will also learn how to thoroughly repudiate the bourgeois idea of seeking fame and wealth. Meanwhile, the plant should organize its technicians into groups and send them, from time to time, to work as ordinary workers; or just arrange for them to have more time to work in the workshops as part of their regular everyday job, so as to assist them to integrate with workers and to combine theory and practical work.

Correspondents of Wen-hui pao
and the New China News Agency

24

STRIVE TO BUILD A SOCIALIST UNIVERSITY OF SCIENCE AND ENGINEERING

Workers' and PLA Mao Tse-tung Thought Propaganda Team Stationed at Tsinghua University*

Due to the intimate concern of our great leader Chairman Mao and the Party Central Committee under the leadership of Chairman Mao and Vice Chairman Lin, the proletarian revolution in education at Tsinghua University is flourishing. For over a year now the working class has led the revolutionary faculty, students, and workers in the school in holding high the banner of unity and victory of the Ninth Party Congress. Following Chairman Mao's brilliant ideas for educational revolution, and taking as the key link the "May 7 Directive" to "take the road of the Shanghai Machine Tool Plant by training technicians from among the workers," they are currently striving to build a socialist university of science and engineering.

The Working Class, Through Struggle, Must Maintain Firm Leadership Over the Revolution in Education

Chairman Mao instructs us: "To accomplish the proletarian revolution in education it is essential to have working class

*Chu Ch'ing-hua ta-hsüeh kung-jen, chieh-fang chün Mao Tse-tung ssu-hsiang hsüan-ch'uan tui, "Wei ch'uang-pan she-hui-chu-i li kung k'o ta-hsüeh erh fen-tou." Hung-ch'i [Red Flag], No. 8 (July 21, 1970), 5-19.

leadership; the masses of workers must take part in this revolution and, in cooperation with Liberation Army fighters, form a revolutionary three-in-one combination with the activists among the students, teachers, and workers in schools and colleges who are determined to carry the proletarian revolution in education through to the end. The workers' propaganda teams should stay permanently in the schools, take part in struggle-criticism-transformation, and always guide these institutions."

Working class leadership will fundamentally guarantee the thorough destruction of the capitalist educational system and the establishment of a proletarian educational system. The proletarian revolution in education is a deeply penetrating revolution to assure the dictatorship of the proletarian class over the capitalist class in the realm of culture and education. Since July 27, 1968, when the working class mounted the political stage for struggle-criticism-transformation in the superstructure, a fierce struggle has been going on between the proletariat and the bourgeoisie to see who will transform and triumph over whom. The leadership of the working class is constantly being strengthened and consolidated by this struggle between two classes, two roads, and two lines.

Working class leadership means the leadership of Mao Tse-tung thought. The working class, under the leadership of its vanguard, the Communist Party, has entered the field of education in order to carry out Chairman Mao's great directive that "the length of schooling should be shortened, education should be revolutionized, and the domination of our schools by bourgeois intellectuals should be tolerated no longer." It is using Mao Tse-tung thought to take control of the schools and transform them.

In order to take control of the schools and maintain leadership in the educational revolution, the working class must criticize and repudiate the bourgeoisie, firmly grasp class struggle in the realm of ideas, and exercise leadership over the intellectuals politically and ideologically. Otherwise, working class leadership cannot be consolidated; indeed there is a danger of losing it again. In accord with Chairman Mao's great instruction that "there is no construction without destruction," we have begun deep and protracted revolutionary mass criticism. We have criticized the counterrevolutionary revisionist line and counterrevolutionary clique of the renegade, hidden traitor, and scab Liu Shao-ch'i; criticized rightist and extreme "leftist" bourgeois-reactionary thought trends; criticized feudal, capitalist, and revisionist education systems and revisionist thought in various academic areas; and criticized the comprador, foreign slave-mentality and doctrine of trailing behind at a snail's pace.

The overthrown bourgeoisie will never accept its defeat. It will invariably exert its influence in the intellectual realm, and make use of the weak points in the world view of the intellectuals to spread poison in a vain attempt to regain its lost "hereditary domains" and to contend with the proletariat for the allegiance of the intellectuals. Some have publicly proclaimed: "The working class is not capable of leadership in matters of advanced science." Others have taken on the appearance of the extreme "left," distorting the Party's policy toward intellectuals by saying that "working class leadership in everything means the intellectuals must stand aside" in a vain attempt to push the intellectuals into opposition to the working class and to carry out a countercoup. By mobilizing the masses and relying on invincible Mao Tse-tung thought, we resolutely exposed and criticized the small handful of class enemies for their criminal attempt to sabotage and weaken working class leadership. Their plot for restoration has been pulverized.

The struggle for leadership between the proletariat and the bourgeoisie often largely takes the form of a struggle against the force of bourgeois habits. As the revolution in education develops in depth, the bourgeois ideas of some intellectuals are constantly revealed in new forms. Some of them say: "You take charge politically while I lead in vocational work." Some feel that they have been sufficiently reeducated so that when they are encouraged to take the initiative they think that the working class is "turning power over" to them. Some feel that they are "old hands" at transforming education and in vocational work, so the working class can "quit." Still others think that developing the usefulness of the old teaching staff is tantamount to reverting to the old system.

These mistaken ideas, which are rightist or "leftist" in appearance, but rightest in essence, are all manifestations of the obstinate bourgeois world view and are extremely destructive. If they are not thoroughly criticized, old things will return and will be consolidated in new forms; working class leadership will greatly subside; and the revolution in education will take the wrong road of reformism. Experience shows that it is much more difficult to destroy the force of old habits than to eliminate the sabotage of a handful of class enemies.

The spiritual stronghold of reaction can only be destroyed by the spiritual weapon of revolution. Only by thoroughly criticizing and discrediting the small handful of class enemies and the force of old habits and cleaning out their poisonous residue can they truly be brought down and can the leadership of the working class fundamentally be consolidated. Therefore revolutionary mass criticism is a task of strategic importance in building socialist universities, an important course in the revolutionary curriculum, and a powerful weapon in prosecuting the long-term struggle between the proletariat and the bourgeoisie and in consolidating the dictatorship of the proletariat.

If the working class is to maintain firm leadership in the educational revolution, it must unreservedly mobilize the masses and thoroughly carry out the mass line. It must resolutely implement Chairman Mao's guideline to "Let a hundred flowers bloom, let a hundred schools of thought contend" and fully promote proletarian democracy to create an atmosphere in which people dare to criticize and argue. It must rely on the active elements who are determined to promote the educational revolution to its final conclusion, boldly trust the great majority of the intellectuals, and unite with all possible forces. Only in this way can it comprehensively establish the dictatorship of the proletariat over the bourgeoisie. If it fails to do this the working class will isolate itself and working class leadership will exist in name only. The revolution in education is like all other revolutionary work in that "unless the masses are conscious and willing, it will become a mere formality and will fail" ("The United Front in Cultural Work").

Working class leadership in everything does not mean the monopolization of everything or the use of crude methods to overwhelm everything so that the intellectuals are placed in a passive, "one-push-one-step" position. Relying on the many revolutionary intellectuals and fostering their initiative will not weaken the leadership of the working class; on the contrary, it will strengthen it.

In order to maintain its firm leadership of the educational revolution, the working class must "constantly raise its political consciousness through struggle," energetically make a living study and a living application of Mao Tse-tung thought, and be leaders in the ideological revolution. This requires that we conscientiously do the following: resolutely observe and implement all of Chairman Mao's instructions and proletarian policies whether we understand them or, momentarily, do not understand them; we "must be modest and prudent, and guard against arrogance and rashness."

As members of a propaganda team, we must learn from those we are reeducating, be modest pupils of the masses so as to learn what we do not know, and master the laws governing the struggle between the two classes and the two lines in the realm of education. We must work hard, regularly participate in physical labor, and closely relate to the masses so as to guard against rotteness and corruption. We must immerse ourselves in reality, carefully investigate and study, be able to grasp typical examples, and follow the principle of grasping well one-third of one's total work and conscientiously summing up that experience. Being loyal to Chairman Mao and continuing the revolution requires that we have a spirit of self-criticism and that we correct whatever mistakes we might make. Only in this way can the working class undertake the lead in the great historic task of struggle-criticism-transformation in the superstructure. Only in this way can it guarantee that the proletarian revolution will advance victoriously along the brilliant road of Chairman Mao's "May 7 Directive."

While Making Use of the Original Teaching Staff, Transform It; Form a Three-in-One Teacher Corps

"The teacher problem is the most crucial problem in transforming education." Establishing a proletarian teacher corps by forming a three-in-one combination of workers, peasants and soldiers, revolutionary technicians, and members of the original teaching staff is extremely important in putting a complete end to the domination of our schools by the bourgeoisie and the intellectuals and in establishing socialist universities.

The worker, peasant, and soldier teachers are the most vital revolutionary power in the teacher corps. They have the courage to innovate and abolish misleading beliefs.* And they have the ability to criticize. In addition, they create close ties between schools and factories by bringing the progressive experience of social production and the inventions of laboring people into the classroom. Students say their lectures are easy to understand and can therefore be readily used.

In the past year a number of workers, peasants, and soldiers on the front line of the Three Great Revolutionary Movements have been selected to be full-time or part-time teachers. They have matured through struggle and improved through experience. Their participation in teaching has advanced working class leadership in the schools, effectively assured the proper political orientation of teaching, and promoted the remolding of intellectuals and the transformation of education. By mounting the lectern in the universities, the workers, peasants, and

*"Superstition" is the usual translation of mi-hsin, but it does not convey the full sense in which it is used here — Peter J. Seybolt.

soldiers have effected something new in the fierce struggle between the two classes and the two lines on the educational front.

A very few bourgeois intellectuals have adopted a "wait and see" or a ridiculing attitude. Some planned to give the workers a feudal, capitalist, and revisionist load by saying, in effect, "I'll set the charge, you do the blasting." We waged a resolute struggle against this. Actually, workers, peasants, and soldiers have the best understanding of proletarian education. Universities in the past excluded workers, peasants, and soldiers. This is historically retrogressive. The mounting of the university lectern by workers, peasants, and soldiers today is historically inevitable.

The original teaching staff is an indispensable component of the three-in-one teacher corps. Chairman Mao has pointed out: "China needs the services of as many intellectuals as possible for the colossal task of socialist construction" ("On the Correct Handling of Contradictions Among the People"). Chairman Mao has also pointed out that the vast number of intellectuals in our country "want to remold themselves and are quite capable of remolding themselves" ("Speech at the Chinese Communist Party's National Conference on Propaganda Work"). This is also the situation with the teacher corps. Bad elements and counterrevolutionaries who have sneaked into the teacher corps, and those whose minds have ossified, are very few. Therefore, we must recognize that the great mass of teachers enthusiastically love the Party and Chairman Mao, but at the same time we must recognize that remolding their world view is a long-term, arduous process. The great masses of teachers, having been tempered in the Great Proletarian Cultural Revolution — especially since July 27, 1968 — under the leadership of the working class, and having been reeducated by the workers, peasants, and soldiers, have elevated their consciousness of class struggle and the struggle between the two lines. We must take full account of their revolutionary activism. We must also apply the principle of "one divides into two" to their professional knowledge. We must recognize that the old system has to be destroyed, but we must also recognize that some professional knowledge of natural science and experience accumulated in the past can be usefully developed if it is guided by the correct line and united with actual production. Our nation's Great Proletarian Cultural Revolution has opened the broadest horizons for fully developing the talents of all intellectuals who wish to serve the workers, peasants, and soldiers. We must have faith in the tremendous power of Mao Tse-tung thought. The great majority of the former teachers can continue to serve and can make a great contribution to proletarian education and to socialist culture and science if they are willing to engage seriously in political reeducation and to restudy their professional work. The extremely few teachers who really cannot do this must also be given a way out. They must still be educated, allocated appropriate work, and continually tested.

To help teachers meet the needs of socialist universities in the fastest possible time, it is necessary to conscientiously unite with, educate, and transform them while using them. The expression "first transform fully, then use" in fact recognizes neither the intellectuals' revolutionary activism nor the long-term process of their remolding. In his brilliant "Talks at the Yenan Forum on Literature and Art," Chairman Mao said: "This question of 'for whom?' is fundamental; it is a question of principle." In accordance with this teaching, we concentrated on solving for the teachers the questions "whom to serve" and "how to serve." We confronted their long-term weaknesses, manifest in the "three separations," and organized them to become tempered by participating in the Three Great Revolutionary Movements. They participated in establishing experimental farms; worked in different factories according to their talents; participated in physical labor in rotation and engaged in transforming education; remolded their thinking under relatively difficult conditions.

The world view of intellectuals is often reflected in the way they view professional knowledge. We must thoroughly reconstruct each professional field. Teachers participating in the Three Great Revolutionary Struggles must abruptly confront the old ideas deeply implanted in the souls of some of them, such as "knowledge is private," "theory is foremost," "strive for individual fame and fortune," and the foreign slave-mentality of "trailing behind at a snail's pace." This helps speed their thought transformation.

A complete change in the world view of the intellectuals cannot be effected spontaneously. A changed environment only provides the conditions for their remolding; we must also grasp the principle of being firm, strict, and meticulous in confronting their current ideas and reeducate them accordingly; use progressive examples among them so that they educate themselves, and inspire them to revolutionize their thought voluntarily. When they vacillate or retrogress in their thinking, we can provide strong and beneficial guidance through patient and conscientious ideological political work to transform their world view. We should correct their mistaken ideas by providing explanations and appropriate criticism.

"A correct policy toward the intellectuals is a prerequisite for victory in the revolution" ("Recruit Large Numbers of Intellectuals"). To effectively motivate the revolutionary activism of the vast number of teachers under the leadership of the working class; to encourage them to develop a revolutionary spirit of daring to think, daring to speak, daring to act, and daring to take chances for the proletarian revolution in education and to be bold in putting the educational revolution into practice, we must attend to the correct handling of the following questions in our work.

1. We must distinguish between those who are actively participating in the educational revolution, but whose thought is still fettered by old conventions as revealed in matters concerning the "three separations," and those who persist in taking the old road.

2. We must distinguish between those who earnestly want to integrate with the workers, peasants, and soldiers, but whose ideas on certain substantive questions about transforming education differ from those of their worker comrades, and those who refuse to be reeducated and boycott working class leadership.

3. We must distinguish between those who actively engage in professional work, and examine relevant Chinese and foreign books and reference materials relating to problems of educational revolution and technological innovation, and those who abandon proletarian class politics, who place theory above everything, who worship foreign things, and who want to restore the past.

4. We must distinguish between those who analytically and critically study domestic and foreign sources on things that we do not know or do not have in order to change backward aspects and fill in blanks, and those who have a foreign slave-mentality and would trail behind at a snail's pace.

We must not worry even though there is a small group of people who refuse reeducation and persist in taking the old road, for class struggle is a long-term process, and such people invariably exist. In the educational revolution we must persist in criticizing these outdated ideas and in educating and transforming these people.

5. Those whose political histories have been examined and cleared in the past must be enlisted to participate in the educational revolution in accordance with their different circumstances and their present behavior. We must educate and transform them while using them.

6. Those whose thought and actions can be characterized as "contradictions among the people" must be treated accordingly. Those bourgeois reactionary academic authorities who have been criticized by the masses and who have changed somewhat must continually be brought together with the revolutionary masses; they must criticize the revisionist educational line and feudal, capitalist, and revisionist academic thought so as to facilitate their voluntary revolutionization. At the same time, we must attend to the development of their "specific skills" in the service of socialist construction.

7. When specific questions of right and wrong in the natural sciences arise in the process of transforming teaching, it is "necessary to maintain a cautious attitude, to encourage free discussion and avoid hasty conclusions" ("On

the Correct Handling of Contradictions Among the People"). We must observe objective laws and settle these questions through practice.

The spiritual disposition of the vast number of teachers has changed in the course of the educational revolution: education by workers, peasants, and soldiers has become the conscious desire of many people, who enthusiastically serve the workers, peasants, and soldiers. Some have even made inventive creations. This is reflected in the attitude of the workers, peasants, and soldiers that "in the past these intellectuals and we were separated in our hearts and minds; we could hardly converse; now we are close and can converse intimately." Most teachers profoundly feel that reeducation reflects Chairman Mao's great concern for their well-being, and they are determined to be pupils of the workers, peasants, and soldiers all their lives and to be forever loyal to the Party's educational efforts.

A number of teachers who lived in the old society have also made great progress. Not a few of them have developed their usefulness during the educational revolution. A certain professor thought that there was no need to change a textbook which he had written in the past and which had been widely distributed throughout the country. He said, "If it is taken from the shelf and dusted off a bit, it will be usable." We let him join an educational revolution detachment. By confronting problems that had arisen when he taught workers, we were soon able to lead him to join the masses in criticizing the feudal, bourgeois, and revisionist education systems. By doing meticulous ideological and political work with him, we made him gradually realize that "my textbook, which put theory above all and made simple matters mysterious, did not satisfy the needs of the workers, peasants, and soldiers. It is not sufficient simply to dust it off or even to change it superficially. It must be thoroughly transformed. Later, he and other revolutionary teachers and students united with the workers, and in the process of solving important technological problems for a factory, they learned from the workers, elevated their consciousness, achieved results, and received the praise of the workers.

Revolutionary intellectuals who are armed with Mao Tse-tung thought and who are united with the workers, peasants, and soldiers are an important revolutionary force. At present, a three-in-one teacher corps shaped in the image of the proletariat is coming to maturity.

Establish a New Three-in-One System Combining Teaching, Scientific Research, and Production by Running Open-Door Universities, Linking Factories and Schools, Having Schools Run Factories, and Having Factories Guide Specialization

Establishing a new proletarian educational system is not simply a matter of organizational change, but is a revolution that comprehensively and thoroughly implements the policy that "education must serve proletarian politics and be combined with productive labor."

Whether a school is closely related to social practice and is run in an open-door manner is a question of principle, a question of what banner it upholds, what road it takes, and what orientation it maintains. The counterrevolutionary revisionist Chiang Nan-hsiang publicly opposed having students participate in class struggle and production struggle, and he loudly proclaimed that "Tsinghua University is a cradle for engineers," and "fighters in the Three Great Revolutionary Movements can be trained in the laboratories." This prevented many teachers and students from seeing how workers work and farmers farm. It also damaged their health. The school became ever more revisionist, and the students became more stupid. The propaganda team led the masses of teachers and students in a penetrating criticism of this revisionist line and helped them resolutely take the road indicated by Chairman Mao in his "May 7 Directive." They have established an experimental farm, gone to factories, to construction sites, to rural areas, and to army units to participate in class struggle, production struggle, and scientific experimentation, thus coming into extensive contact with social reality. They have extended the revolution in a number of ways by participating in industrial and agricultural production; by running full-time, part-time, and spare-time college courses and short-term training classes for workers; by carrying out technical innovation, scientific research, and social investigation.

The proletarian revolution in education is a deeply penetrating socialist revolution of a broad mass nature. It surely will not proceed well without the participation of the broad masses and the support of the leadership of all departments at all levels. Running schools in an open-door manner, linking factories and schools, taking universities into society as a whole, and giving a powerful impetus to the development of industrial and agricultural production by extending and elevating culture will fundamentally change the "three separations" situation in the old schools, which isolated them and made them shut their eyes and block their ears. It will harmonize school and society, give intellectuals even broader contacts with workers, peasants, and soldiers; it will enable them to participate actively and be reeducated and will hasten the transformation of their world view.

The teachers and students say with great feeling: "In the past we studied books behind closed doors; the 'engineer's cradle' rocked us until we were dizzy. Now that schools are run in an open-door manner, the furnace of the Three Great Revolutionary Movements has tempered us so that our hearts are red and our eyes bright." New techniques and innovations in social production continually enrich and renew teaching content and vigorously revitalize school education. At the same time, teaching and the fruit of scientific research directly serve socialist construction and promote the development of social production. Linking school and factory has opened broad new vistas in the educational revolution. We must persist in this for a long time.

A great, wise policy of Chairman Mao's is that "schools must run factories." It will not do for students to have only book knowledge and no working experience. "Besides meeting the needs of teaching and scientific research, all laboratories and affiliated factories of engineering colleges that can undertake production tasks should do so to the best of their ability." This is the passage from Chairman Mao's thought that directs schools to run factories. In the process of running factories, we developed fully a fierce struggle between the two lines and the two kinds of thought. We criticized the obsequious bourgeois work-style of seeking foreign solutions and going to the government for a handout. We criticized cutting production off from education and took cognizance of the mistaken idea that "production is everything." We resolutely and thoroughly carried out Chairman Mao's policy of "self-reliance," "hard struggle" and "eliminating inhibiting beliefs," "emancipating the mind." We persistently highlighted proletarian politics, and implementing the principle that "the main task is to study," we have made training people our foremost concern.

In conformity with the needs of socialist construction and teaching, and in keeping with the benefits of mutual promotion and development of various specialties, we fully utilized existing equipment and facilities, used simple, indigenous methods, and used our own initiative to set up a number of small and medium factories of various types — including a precision machine-tool plant, an experimental, multipurpose electronics factory, and a motor vehicle plant — all of which accept scientific research and production assignments from the national government. The experimental, multipurpose electronics factory, for example, was built by using the facilities of a former laboratory. It uses suitable old equipment and some new equipment. It has stimulated the use of automatic controls, radio technology, and electronic computers. It produces many different electrical products.

When production plans are made for school-run factories, the needs of teaching must be considered and given sufficient leeway. The products selected for manufacture should be typical, varied, and advanced. They should be products urgently needed for industry and national defense that can also satisfy the demands of teaching a specialty. There should be a certain amount of serial production, but at the same time research, experimentation, and the adoption of new techniques should be promoted vigorously.

On the basis of industrial and agricultural production, the development of scientific techniques, and the need to catch up with and surpass advanced world levels, we began to transform the old school system by having schools run factories and by linking factories and schools. We broke the barriers surrounding academic departments in the past by merging some faculties and adding others. Specialization is guided by the factories by having school-run factories, scientific research units, and systems of factory-school links include the study of specialties relevant to their regular work in scientific research and production.

At the same time, we are establishing a new type of basic theory group. The basic units of the new system are teams of specialists, which include workers, students, and teachers. School-run factories carry out unified leadership by seeing to overall coordination of teaching, scientific research, and production. In this way, what was once purely a teaching unit characterized by the "three separations" and dominated by bourgeois intellectuals has become a foundation for teaching that unites teaching, scientific research, and production, using workers, peasants, and soldiers as the principal group. For example, teachers and students specializing in metal-forming participated in labor in a forging and pressing workshop of a motor vehicle plant. They combined their study of "forging technology" and similar courses with producing various forged parts of a motor vehicle, thereby combining production technique with the study of scientific theory. The beneficial aspect of this procedure is that workers participate in every aspect of teaching, strengthening the working class leadership in the school; the teachers both teach and participate in production, which aids in the transformation of intellectuals; the students both study and produce, guaranteeing the unity of education and productive labor.

Scientific research is an important task that scientific and engineering universities must undertake. While running factories, we have strengthened the conversion and construction of laboratories. School-run factories and laboratories are closely related to society, making schools an important base for cultivating students' ability to do scientific research and for energetically initiating scientific research, for excelling in the most advanced technology, for creating new techniques and new products, for probing new theories, and for catching and overtaking advanced world levels.

The many specializations within our school, in accord with their defining characteristics, use the school-run factory as the main base; some others rely on links between the school and outside factories; while some rely on laboratories to unite scientific research with teaching. Nevertheless, school-run factories and laboratories cannot take the place of links between the universities and factories. All specialties must closely combine these three forms and, in particular, the university must face society, linking itself with factories outside.

In the past year and more, by running schools in an open-door manner, linking factories and schools, having schools run factories, and having factories guide specialization, we have trained a group of working class technicians and have completed a number of projects in technological innovation and scientific research. In addition, we have tested and produced for the nation a number of products urgently needed for industry and national defense.

In Training Worker, Peasant, and Soldier Students It Is Imperative to Maintain Class Struggle as the Principal Part of the Curriculum and to Maintain the Unity of Theory and Practice

Raising and educating new proletarian intellectuals is a matter of fundamental importance for consolidating the dictatorship of the proletariat for the next hundred years, and it is the fundamental task of a socialist university. Following Chairman Mao's instruction that "students should be selected from among workers and peasants with practical experience and should return to production after a few years of study," we have, since last March, enrolled as students nearly 600 workers, peasants, and soldiers with practical experience, and run experimental classes in various specialties; we have thus made some progress in selecting and training worker, peasant, and soldier students. The plan for this year is to accept 2,500 students. At present we have already enrolled over 800.

As soon as the worker, peasant, and soldier students entered the school, they raised the resounding slogan, "We study in the university, administer it, and transform it, using Mao Tse-tung thought." They actively plunged into the battle of the educational revolution and, together with the teachers, administrators, and workers in the school, created a foundation for a three-in-one combination of teaching, scientific research, and production. In addition, they greatly stimulated the educational revolution by determining teaching procedures and editing new teaching materials together with the teachers. We are confronted with a new subject in determining how to train this sort of new revolutionary force to become "cultured workers with socialist consciousness" ("On the Correct Handling of Contradictions Among the People").

Whether we persistently make political education the heart of all education for the worker, peasant, and soldier students is a question of whether we implement the proletarian educational line. When the experimental classes began some people thought: "Since worker, peasant, and soldier students have high political consciousness, it is no longer necessary for the school to change their ideology." Some teachers felt: "We are the ones to be reeducated; we are not qualified to change the students' ideology." Therefore some individuals thought that they should "discuss only mathematics, physics, and chemistry and not bother with revolution." Some students had the mistaken viewpoint that they were "born red" and had "entered school to learn an occupation and that they would patch up their politics after they returned home." We organized everyone to study intensively Chairman Mao's great instruction that "politics is the commander, the soul"; "in all of its work the school should aim at transforming the students' ideology." We combined this study with education on the struggle between the two classes and the two lines on the cultural and educational front, and we diligently sought to transform the students' world view so that all would realize that class struggle in the realm of political ideology is unending and that class struggle in society is necessarily reflected in the ranks of workers, peasants, and soldiers. The residual poison of bourgeois ideology, seen in the purely vocational viewpoint and the attitude that "one studies to become an official" and "theory above everything," can at any time infect worker, peasant, and soldier students, and especially young students. If we do not recognize this, and relax education in political ideology, worker, peasant, and soldier students are in danger of becoming contaminated by the bourgeoisie. In all of its work and in every class, a school is using either proletarian thought to educate the students or bourgeois thought to poison the students. There is no such thing as "teaching books and not teaching people." Teaching only vocational knowledge and ignoring politics will inevitably lead down the bourgeois road. The former teachers must strive not only to transform their thought and change their stand and their feelings but also to put Mao Tse-tung thought in command of educational work, and to boldly undertake the task of publicizing Mao Tse-tung thought. They say: "Participating in the work of changing the thought of students is a duty entrusted to us for the proletarian revolutionary cause. It imposes an even higher, more serious demand that we be reeducated by the workers, peasants, and soldiers."

We are persisting in making class struggle the main course in school and admonishing the students to observe the five requirements introduced by Chairman Mao for successors to the revolutionary cause of the proletariat. We are instilling Mao Tse-tung thought in them and making the primary task of the school the constant elevation of the students' consciousness of the need to continue the revolution under the dictatorship of the proletariat.

We are resolutely and fully carrying out Chairman Mao's instruction that "the same thing applies to the students. While their main task is to study, they should also learn other things; that is, they should study not only books but also industry, agriculture, and military affairs, and they should criticize and repudiate the bourgeoisie." We have persisted in studying the Liberation Army and regularly participated in industrial and agricultural productive labor; regarding class struggle as the key link, we have continually fought selfishness, criticized revisionism, and criticized and repudiated the bourgeoisie.

By proceeding in this way the worker, peasant, and soldier students, while spending most of their time studying and teaching vocational matters, have always put proletarian politics to the fore and steadily elevated their consciousness of the need to continue the revolution; they have "developed morally, intellectually, and physically" ("On the Correct Handling of Contradictions Among the People"). Although their environment has changed, the fine qualities they possessed as ordinary laborers have not changed; although their theoretical level has risen, their work style of relating theory and practice has not changed; although their capability has risen, their spirit of modesty and prudence has not changed.

Science and engineering universities, if they are to train laborers to serve the socialist cause by drawing on both scientific theory and practical experience, must enable worker, peasant, and soldier students to solve real and immediate production problems and undertake planning and scientific research in order to meet our national need for scientific and technological development. To attain this objective we must oppose tendencies toward dogmatism and empiricism, persist in uniting theory and practice, and cultivate the students' capacity for analyzing and solving problems.

Worker, peasant, and soldier students should concentrate on theory while they are in school because "perception only solves questions of phenomena, theory alone solves questions of essence" ("On Practice"). On the other hand, it is a mistake to overemphasize theoretical study. "Marxism emphasizes the study of theory precisely and only because it can guide action" ("On Practice"). All theory is derived from practice and in turn must serve practice. Therefore, teaching in school must not be separated from practice. However, the practical experience of worker, peasant, and soldier students is not entirely a substitute for the practical foundation derived from teaching and learning; but it must be continually enriched and developed in the process of teaching and learning.

In some experimental classes we have corrected the fallacious concept that "worker, peasant, and soldier students need only study theory because they already have practical experience." We see to it that the content of study and the teaching process are always closely related to practice and that theory is applied to practice so that the fruits of teaching are directly tested in practice. Using this method, the students not only can understand the world but also can "apply the knowledge of these laws actively to change the world" ("On Practice").

For instance, in a short-term training class dealing with a special problem, the students combined courses in "electronic technique" and "telecommunications technique" with the research and manufacture of an advanced type of telecommunications machine. In merely half a year, students with only a junior middle school education learned the rudiments of basic theory and, together with the teachers, applied the knowledge they had acquired to the manufacture of telecommunications equipment meeting advanced international standards. Those students who "left middle school and immediately entered college" in the past could never measure up to this performance. Experience proves that if the proletarian teaching policy is to be implemented fully, "left" and right tendencies must be opposed, for only then can theory and practice be truly united.

Those admitted to science and engineering universities should be selected by and large from among the workers and peasants (with special attention given to enrolling intellectual youths who have settled in the countryside or who have returned to their home villages), Liberation Army men, and young cadres, all of whom are active elements who have emerged in the course of the Three Great Revolutionary Movements and who, in general, have had three or more years of practical experience, are about nineteen years old, and have a cultural level corresponding to junior or senior middle school training. Older workers and poor and lower-middle peasants who have rich practical experience can enter school regardless of their age or cultural level.

Science and engineering universities are liberating higher education from the bondage of the original universities by undertaking the task of broadly disseminating education and of training engineers and scientific researchers from among the working people, and by adopting many forms of education both inside and outside of the school. In addition to the two- or three-year regular classes and the one year or so accelerated class, they also run scientific research classes, spare-time university classes, and short-term classes on special topics. All of these are established both inside and outside of the schools.

Destroy Slavish Comprador Philosophy and the Doctrine of Trailing Behind at a Snail's Pace; Compile New, Proletarian Teaching Materials

The transformation of teaching materials is a serious political struggle. It is a question of vital importance for raising a generation of new people. A slavish comprador philosophy and the doctrine of trailing behind at a snail's pace were very harmful characteristics of the teaching materials formerly used at universities of science and engineering. They pervaded every line of the teaching materials. Even today they are a spiritual yoke harnessing a small number of intellectuals. The key to thoroughly transforming teaching materials is the destruction of this slavish comprador philosophy and this doctrine of trailing behind at a snail's pace.

"A given culture is the ideological reflection of the politics and economics of a given society" ("On New Democracy"). Science and engineering textbooks in imperialist and social-imperialist countries discuss natural science, but they are written to meet their own political, economic, and military needs and are stamped with the brand of the exploiting classes because they summarize the world view of the bourgeois class toward scientific and technological development.

Liu Shao-ch'i and company frantically proclaimed the slavish comprador philosophy and the doctrine of trailing behind at a snail's pace. They introduced the whole package into China, allowing the foreign bourgeoisie to continue their dictatorship over the Chinese people through old teaching materials like these. Take a series of old teaching materials on electronics, for example. The "compact" system that it prescribes for this branch of learning is nothing but the epitome of the process of electronic development in bourgeois societies. But the textbook claims that everything it says is an eternal and immutable truth, and whoever wishes to develop an electronics industry and master electronic technology must creep step by step at a snail's pace along this old road. This attitude reveals the slavish and backward nature of the old teaching materials. The old teaching materials reverse history, plagerize the inventions and creations of laboring people, and proclaim "experts above everyone." They serve the desire of the bourgeoisie to monopolize science and technology. They propagate the attitude of "theory above everything" and commercialize education by turning simple things into mysteries and forcing up prices, serving the bourgeois intellectuals in ruling the schools. They propagate the attitude that material and technical conditions determine everything," denying that the human factor is primary and stifling the boundless creative capacity of the popular masses.

Old teaching materials like these have seriously poisoned many intellectuals and young students and produced sharp contradictions in our socialist politics and economics. They must be thoroughly transformed. We absolutely cannot take the reformist road and make patchwork revisions.

The transformation of teaching materials is a deeply penetrating ideological struggle. Serious attention must be given to changing the stand and feelings of the teachers so that they will come to stand on the side of the proletariat and to solve the problem of for whom to write and how to write textbooks. The propaganda team led the teachers and students in practicing the Three Great Revolutionary Movements. It organized the workers, poor and lower-middle peasants, Red Guard little generals, and teachers and students to cooperate in editing and writing teaching materials. It initiated revolutionary criticism and used the process of editing and writing teaching materials to make a living study and living application of Mao Tse-tung thought to carry out deeply penetrating reeducation of the intellectuals. Everyone came to the realization that it is a manifestation of slavish thought to maintain intact the old teaching materials for science and engineering. Those divorced from the working people will necessarily worship and be servile to foreign ways. Those who do not transform their idealist and metaphysical world view will always trail behind foreigners at a snail's pace. Chairman Mao long ago pointed out that "spiritually the culture of the Chinese people already transcends that of the capitalist world" ("Bankruptcy of the Idealist Conception of History"). In science and technology China has also performed many wonders that leave the Western bourgeoisie hopelessly behind. Conscious realization and full implementation of these superiorities will open a new phase in which the transformation of our teaching materials will shoot up like bamboo to commanding heights.

We deeply realize that the basic ideological weapon used in writing new teaching materials is invincible Mao Tse-tung thought. The needs of workers, peasants, and soldiers are our starting point, and the Three Great Revolutionary Movements are our source.

"Teaching materials must be thorougly transformed, in some cases beginning with the simplification of complicated materials." This is a complex and difficult task. It demands both a revolutionary spirit and a scientific attitude. We must strive to put politics in command of professional work, to employ a dialectical materialist viewpoint, scientific analysis, and penetrating exposition of scientific rules; we must unite theory and practice and observe the principle of condensing and concentrating so that our teaching materials will be revolutionary, practical, and advanced.

As for old teaching materials and foreign scientific and technical achievements still extant, we have maintained the principle of critical acceptance and implemented the policies of "making the past serve the present and things foreign serve China" and "weeding out the old to let the new emerge." In criticizing the general system of the old teaching materials, we have concentrated on the line by which it is guided, on which class it serves, and on the kind of world view that pervades it. We do not simply reject its specific natural-science content. On the other hand, we do not simply accept the useful parts; rather, we examine them with a critical attitude, discarding the dress and selecting the essence, discarding the false and keeping the true, thus inheriting the scientific content.

We divided "higher mathematics," which bourgeois experts lauded as "tested and flawless," into essential and dross categories, criticized its system of idealist and metaphysical "axioms," and absorbed its useful theorems and formulas. For example, proceeding from production activities, and taking as a clue the mutual contradiction in the struggle, development, and transformation of the differential and integral, we organized a new system and compiled new teaching materials in "calculus."

In the past, the concepts of differential and integral calculus were derived from piles of axioms and theorems and were very mysterious and unfathomable. Now the concepts are illustrated by familiar examples in production. For example, when a bench worker uses a file to round off a piece of metal, every stroke of the file makes short straight lines which finally combine to form curves. This process of turning the whole into parts and parts into the whole vividly illustrates the concepts of differential and integral calculus. After studying this the worker-students said: "There is nothing really mysterious about calculus; a mere file pierces the paper obscuring the window. Higher mathematics has again returned to the hands of we laboring people."

Transformation of teaching materials must also proceed from China's realities; we must enthusiastically and conscientiously sum up the inventions and creations of workers, peasants, and soldiers; we must raise new topics and introduce new generalizations. Chinese and foreign textbooks on water conservancy used to describe mountain torrents as completely harmful. But the poor and lower-middle peasants in the Chang-chia-kou area fully utilized the superior qualities of the people's communes to struggle with nature. Applying to the mountain torrents the principle that "one divides into two," they gained valuable experience in constructing a system that diverted the silt-laden mountain torrents to irrigate agricultural plots, thus changing harm to benefit.

Revolutionary teachers and students of an educational revolution detachment participated in this struggle and, together with the poor and lower-middle peasants, compiled a new textbook, entitled *Diverting Silt-Laden Mountain Torrents for Irrigation*. The poor and lower-middle peasants said: "When one learns the method of conquering floods from this book, one also learns Chairman Mao's revolutionary dialectics. It boosts the morale of the laboring people and deflates the arrogance of the bourgeoisie."

The transformation of teaching materials is a long-term task that cannot be accomplished once and for all. They must continually be transformed while being taught; they must continually be summarized, supplemented, elevated, and renewed so that they keep pace with and actively promote the rapid development of the socialist cause.

Practice New Teaching Methods by Combining Production and Scientific Research and Adhering to the Mass Line

Chairman Mao teaches us: "In the Great Proletarian Cultural Revolution, a most important task is the transformation of the system, principles, and methods of teaching." The question of teaching methodology is not just one of specific methods, but more importantly it is a question of principle concerning which class theory of knowledge and methodology will be employed in organizing the teaching process. Bourgeois teaching methods center on books and teachers, and divorce theory from practice. "The lesson is poured into students, who respond mechanically." This completely violates the principles regulating knowledge of truth. It can only produce bookish simpletons who are divorced from proletarian politics, from the worker and peasant masses, and from production.

When we first began experimenting with transforming teaching methods, because we had not eliminated the old teaching methods, some teachers were unable to put down their books and to stop mouthing formulas and whole sets of theories that had little to do with practice. Although they assiduously prepared their lessons, enthusiastically lectured, and patiently helped the students, worker and peasant students were still not satisfied. Practice made us realize that unless we thoroughly transformed the old teaching methods, the task of training proletarian intellectuals would remain an empty slogan.

In accord with Chairman Mao's teaching that in "unifying theory and practice" "the conception of practice is the primary and basic conception in the dialectical-materialist theory of knowledge," and his formula "practice, knowledge, again practice, again knowledge"; and in conformity with the special characteristics of the worker, peasant, and soldier students, we have united production and scientific research, using typical projects, products, and techniques and innovation. We have used the teaching method of going from shallow to deep step by step; we have correctly handled the relations between bringing out the key points, studying first what is urgently needed, and doing while studying, on the one hand, while systematically teaching, on the other; we have correctly handled the relations between specific and general, and the relations between basic courses and special courses.

The integration of systematic teaching with the process of learning while doing breaks down the former pedantic and confusing teaching system of going from theory to theory; at the same time, it conforms to the systematic and consistent characteristics of natural science. We have divided the teaching process into stages to accord with typical tasks of different types to be accomplished. Theoretical courses are planned and arranged in several stages and studied systematically following the principle of from shallow to deep, from easy to difficult. We have applied flexible methods such as "interlaced study" and "concentrated study," depending on differing circumstances.

Sometimes we concentrate on accomplishing tasks of production and scientific research by doing while learning in a planned way and making a penetrating study of typical cases in order to draw inferences from them. At other times we concentrate on learning theory. We elevate the students' theoretical level on the foundation of their rich perceptual knowledge, closely relate it to practice, and then apply what we have learned. In the process of teaching there must be assessments. Emphasis on independent study must be strengthened, the ability to do scientific research must be cultivated, and redoing work under the guidance of theory must be stressed.

The aim of integrating teaching with the performance of typical tasks is to grasp general laws by "dissecting a sparrow." Actually, each typical task has both a universal and a particular nature. The universal nature resides in the particular nature. Therefore, on the one hand, the selection of typical examples must be suitable, and, on the other, summarizing and elevating on the basis of "sparrow dissection" must be stressed — advancing from particular to general, from practice to theory.

Based on our practical experience in transforming teaching, we feel that the following principles should be strictly observed in selecting typical examples. They should emphasize proletarian politics, be oriented toward practice of the Three Great Revolutionary Movements, and embody crucial aspects of our nation's present scientific research and trends in technological development; they should be capable of promoting the main content of specialized courses and of illustrating general laws; they should accord with the cognitive process going from shallow to deep. The requirement for professional training will be met by achieving several typical tasks, proceeding from the simple to the complex.

Integrating teaching with the performance of typical tasks breaks the limitations imposed by the vast distance separating basic courses from specialized courses. Basic courses must be closely integrated with practice so as to strengthen their purposefulness. Some can be united with special courses to form new courses according to need. Those basic courses that are particularly useful for later courses, or are requisite for understanding later courses, should remain as separate courses.

Implementing this method of step-by-step integration of typical tasks with teaching is a relatively satisfactory method of solving the contradictions between the comprehensive nature of production and the specialized nature of teaching, and between the limited nature of a typical task and the encompassing demands of teaching. It unites book-reading and application, practice and creativity, the spots and the whole surface, the study of the written word with the study of labor. It accomplishes the objective of condensing, concentrating, and greatly refining the courses and shortening the study schedule.

It is necessary to maintain the mass line, "from the masses, to the masses," in implementing the new teaching methods. The teacher serves the students. His function is to raise the students' capacity to think for themselves, to study problems, and to engage in practice. Therefore the teacher must learn from the students and learn about them. The worker, peasant, and soldier students, with their high consciousness of class struggle and the struggle between two lines, have the capacity for sharp criticism and have rich practical experience. When they came in contact with teaching they immediately discerned the poisonous residues of feudalism, capitalism, and revisionism, the habitual force of rightist conservatism, and the supine adherence to old ways. They made penetrating comparisons between school and society. By comparing and making distinctions, they strongly criticized the foreign slave-ideology of trailing behind at a snail's pace, which had dominated the cultural and educational front for a long time. With this as a starting point, we vigorously developed "officers teach soldiers, soldiers teach officers, soldiers teach each other" activities. Those who were most capable acted as teachers, and all taught and learned from each other. Inspired teaching methods and discussion were used, which fully brought into play the initiative and creativeness of the worker, peasant, and soldier students and formed a new type of relationship between teacher and students.

In an experimental class on "binding tolerance" relating to the design of a piece of equipment, the teacher lectured on the basic principles and then the students eagerly expressed their own views. The classroom was lively during the whole period. The students who had been turners analyzed the influence of materials and processing conditions on tolerance; former bench workers explained the demands of fitting conditions on tolerance. The discussion was very enthusiastic. Those in the classroom not only clearly discussed the principles, they also brought up many ideas for improving the design. The superiority of the new teaching method was fully demonstrated.

Our great leader Chairman Mao instructs us: "China should make a greater contribution to humanity." The great task of thoroughly transforming the old teaching system and creating a proletarian educational system new in the history of mankind has already gloriously fallen on the shoulders of China's working class, poor and lower-middle peasants, and revolutionary intellectuals. The revolution in education is a hard struggle.

"We are confronted with many strenuous tasks, and our experience is far from adequate. So we must be good at study." We are determined to raise high the great red banner of Mao Tse-tung thought, strengthen Party leadership, resolutely accomplish all the fighting tasks set forth by the Ninth Party Congress, improve the living study and living application of Chairman Mao's thought on the educational revolution, and carry the revolution in education through to the end. For this we strive to build a socialist university of science and engineering.

X

Liberal Arts Colleges

25

LIBERAL ARTS UNIVERSITIES MUST CARRY OUT REVOLUTIONARY MASS CRITICISM

Shanghai Revolutionary Mass
Criticism Writing Group *

Revolutionary mass criticism must be carried out on all fronts, particularly by liberal arts universities.

Chairman Mao teaches us: Students "must also criticize the bourgeoisie." Chairman Mao has also said that the liberal arts should take all of society as their workshop. Society is a society of class struggle, and taking society as a workshop means linking the liberal arts intimately with the class struggle of society and with criticism of the bourgeoisie. Therefore, revolutionary mass criticism is not only the fundamental task of socialist liberal arts universities, it is also an urgent militant task in the current reform of the old liberal arts universities. We should not only criticize the bourgeoisie in society but also carry revolutionary mass criticism into the liberal arts themselves to criticize the reactionary bourgeois ideological systems in philosophy, history, literature, political economy, journalism, education, and other fields. Only in this way can the old liberal arts universities gain new life through criticism.

At present, however, there are still a small minority of people in the liberal arts universities who not only do not themselves carry out revolutionary mass criticism but who also

---

*Shang-hai ke-ming ta p'i-p'an hsieh-tso hsiao-tsu, "Wen-k'o ta-hsüeh i-ting yao kao ke-ming ta p'i-p'an." Hung-ch'i [Red Flag], No. 1 (January 1, 1970), 46-50.

stand in the way of others carrying out revolutionary mass criticism. They see in the distance the tense battle of millions upon millions of workers, peasants, and soldiers in the great struggle-criticism-transformation campaign, and hear the fierce sweeping and surging boom of revolutionary mass criticism, and yet they still are producing all kinds of negative opinions. They say things like "carrying out revolutionary mass criticism is irregular," "the articles written on revolutionary mass criticism in newspapers and journals have no bearing on our fields of specialization," and so on. In sum, what they are actually saying is: This liberal arts university of ours is sacrosanct, a regular "academy"; such matters as mass criticism have nothing to do with us specialized "academicians." Let the workers, peasants, and soldiers carry out mass criticism!

Is the liberal arts university after all a place of elegant seclusion where "books are read behind closed doors," or is it a battleground for studying and putting into practice Mao Tse-tung thought and criticizing the bourgeoisie? This question of orientation concerning the educational revolution in liberal arts universities must definitely be argued and clarified.

There is one argument that goes: "Carrying out revolutionary mass criticism is irregular." What then is "regular"? The Communist Manifesto proclaimed long ago that if the proletariat does not overthrow those parts of the old superstructure that the bourgeoisie uses to oppress the proletariat, then it cannot raise its head or straighten its back. After having gone through the Great Proletarian Cultural Revolution, the proletariat can indeed straighten its back and raise its head in liberal arts universities. However, true consolidation of its position and reform of the universities with Mao Tse-tung thought still call for bitter struggle. The so-called "regular" is nothing but restoring the old situation as it existed before the Great Proletarian Cultural Revolution, setting up a class schedule that is too full, having teachers cram lessons into students, while students are up to their ears in rote copying and while bourgeois thought is allowed to flow freely through the schools.

This sort of "regular" liberal arts certainly does not serve the proletariat; why should the proletariat set it up!

"We have to do research, therefore we have no time for carrying out mass criticism." This is at the very least a muddled viewpoint. The line, principles, policies, and methods of the proletarian education revolution have already been clearly set forth by Chairman Mao. There is no need for you to go out and do more "research" on this. If you are discussing how to seriously conduct the proletarian educational revolution and to sum up concrete experiences from practice, then one of the things you should not neglect is the carrying out of revolutionary mass criticism. What do liberal arts universities do? They study Marxism-Leninism-Mao Tsetung thought. "However, many among us, in studying Marxism, use methods that are directly contrary to Marxism." They do not understand that theory must be related to practice. The reason we study Marxism is to go out and solve practical problems, to carry out the class struggle and the struggle for production, and to criticize the bourgeoisie. Study and application are one. Liberal arts universities must without exception apply the fundamental principle pointed out by Vice Chairman Lin [Piao]: "In studying Chairman Mao's works one should have specific problems in mind, study and apply the works with full vigor, combine study with application, first study those things that can be immediately put to use, and achieve quick results. One must work extremely hard at 'application.'" Lecturing in a classroom and reading books are only one side of teaching and learning in liberal arts universities; the more important side is studying in the course of practice, in the course of struggle, and in the course of revolutionary mass criticism.

Of course we are not generally opposed to holding classes. In the future, new liberal arts universities will still hold some classes and will still have to compile some teaching materials. But all this must be coordinated with revolutionary mass criticism. Without carrying out revolutionary mass criticism, we can neither hold classes well nor compile good teaching materials. Some people do not carry out revolutionary mass criticism, and still compile teaching materials. This is the way they go about it: With scissors and paste they turn a thick book into a thin book, but leave untouched the erroneous viewpoint. Or they deliberately avoid analysis and criticism of major problems. On top of this, they do not work properly, but collect rumors everywhere, somehow assemble them together, and print and sell their material privately. They make hundreds of errors, deceiving not only themselves but also others, and they could be used by the small handful of class enemies. In fact they are trying to set up the "joint publishing houses" [t'ung-jen ch'u-pan she] that the bourgeoisie have been dreaming of. If you want to talk about the history of contemporary literature, you certainly cannot clearly explain Chairman Mao's proletarian revolutionary line on literature and art and Liu Shao-ch'i's revisionist black line on literature and art without criticizing Chou Yang, Hsia Yen, T'ien Han, Yang Han-sheng, and others. No matter whether you are talking about philosophy, history, or economics, if you do not criticize and repudiate the bourgeois ideological system in each academic field, then you cannot teach well in your field, and you certainly cannot successfully compile teaching materials.

Liberal arts universities train revolutionary troops for spreading Marxism-Leninism-Mao Tse-tung thought. They train proletarian fighters on the ideological and cultural fronts. How can we form such ranks? Can we rely on the old-style classroom, which is like a closely sealed tin can? No. The historical experience of the class struggle tells us that proletarian fighters are formed, and can only be formed, in the course of class struggle. If we turn away from class struggle and turn away from revolutionary mass criticism, then we will not be able to form a proletarian force with fighting strength. We need ranks in order to criticize the bourgeoisie, in order to struggle. If we do not use troops to fight, is it conceivable that we would use them as a guard of honor? Relying entirely on classroom learning, can we produce proletarian troops like these? Those who can recite Marxist theories word for word in their examination papers, but easily succumb and are poisoned when they run up against a bourgeois novel, are definitely not proletarian fighters. There is only one criterion for us: whether a person serves proletarian politics and the workers, peasants, and soldiers, or whether he serves bourgeois politics and the exploiting classes; whether he can defeat the bourgeoisie in their attack on the ideological and cultural fronts, or whether he will be defeated by the bourgeoisie. If liberal arts universities do not carry out revolutionary mass criticism, they are not only failing to train proletarian fighters, but they are training bourgeois "academicians."

The old concept of a "university" must resolutely be smashed. The ranks of revolutionary literature and art workers that emerged in the course of the work of Comrade Chiang Ch'ing in fostering revolutionary model operas under the guidance of Chairman Mao's revolutionary line, and with the help of Mao Tse-tung thought, have reformed, tempered, and improved themselves in the course of acute class struggle, in the course of penetratingly and persistently developing revolutionary mass criticism in connection with artistic practice, in the course of criticism of the counterrevolutionary revisionist line and foreign and conventional dogmas, and in the course of detailed scientific criticism against a batch of ancient and contemporary Chinese and foreign works. This sort of criticism is not only acute class struggle but is also very good study and self-transformation. It also includes the analysis, criticism, and lessons that can be drawn from "adapting ancient things to present-day uses, using foreign things for Chinese purposes, and eliminating the old to bring forth the new." And are there not thousands, tens of thousands of talented people who have burst forth from the masses of the workers, peasants, and soldiers, having gone through revolutionary mass criticism and other revolutionary practice during the Great Proletarian Cultural Revolution? The people who stress "regularization" are those most strongly opposed to setting up writing groups in the liberal arts. Nevertheless, thousands upon thousands of writing groups of workers, peasants, and soldiers have played their part as the main force in the struggle of criticism of the bourgeoisie and have also contributed valuable experiences for the educational revolution in the liberal arts. Is this not a fact? Why do people blaze up in great anger at the mention of the newborn things of the proletariat? Should they not delve deeply into their own thoughts?

A small number of people who call most energetically for "regularization" are frequently those who yearn for the academic life of the old-style liberal arts universities. In the past, first of all, they were incapable of productive labor; second, they could not distinguish fragrant flowers from poisonous weeds; and third, they did not do investigative research. But if you say that they have no ability at all, you are charging them falsely. They are capable of compiling lectures and delivering them in the classroom. If you suspect that their lecture papers have turned yellow, they feel, on the contrary, that the more these papers are on display the more fragrant they become! This bit of "ability" of theirs should first be criticized and then used. But we still hope that these people will drop their airs; honestly go among the masses to learn from the workers, peasants, and soldiers; seriously transform their thinking, begin their study again from the beginning, and thoroughly purge all bourgeois poisons in the old liberal arts universities. Only in this way is it possible to do something for the people. If these people still want to bring about the "regularization" of the old liberal arts universities, they will definitely reach a dead end.

"The articles written on revolutionary mass criticism in newspapers and journals have no bearing on our fields of specialization." True, old-style liberal arts universities were divided into many departments. There were philosophy, history, literature, economics, journalism, education, etc. Even within one department there could be still further divisions. Taking Chinese history as an example, it could be divided into ancient history, modern history, and contemporary history. Ancient history might be divided further into the history of the early Ch'in dynasty and the history of the Ch'in and the Han dynasties. Chinese history is so long that it can always be divided into periods. Once there was a professor who taught the history of the early Ch'in dynasty, but did not even entirely understand early Ch'in history. He only knew about the history of the Shang-Yin dynasty. But he did not even have a complete understanding of the Shang-Yin dynasty because he only understood oracle bones. And he did not even have a full understanding of oracle bones because he only knew how many pieces of oracle bones there were in the whole country and where they were stored. How much can this sort of "specialist," lost in a cul-de-sac, benefit the people and the country? Well, he did have some small use, in that he could find where the oracle bones were stored; but this is definitely not the orientation of our proletarian education.

You stress the division of special fields, and yet the class struggle and the onslaught of bourgeois ideology have never been divided into special fields. Recently, in a certain place, there was a technician of a gas company who, in trying to reverse the verdicts on the bourgeoisie in Shanghai, "broke down the door and rushed out," regardless of whether or not things were divided into special fields, and used the form of literature to attack the proletariat. Why then should the proletariat be restricted by the divisions of special fields in its criticism of the bourgeoisie? If you are going to talk about the division of special fields, then what fields do the masses of workers, peasants, and soldiers belong to? And yet, in the course of revolutionary mass criticism, they have been the main force. Nevertheless, it is also necessary to successfully carry out revolutionary mass criticism in one's own special field. Every special field has the responsibility of using Mao Tse-tung thought to criticize the bourgeois world outlook and to reform the old curriculum. But this is not to say that mass criticism should be confined only to special fields. For proletarian fighters the most important thing is the revolution and the criticism of the bourgeoisie; special fields are only secondary. The sound of gunfire is an order. Who can say that if the attack of the bourgeoisie does not fall within the scope of his own special field he should hold himself aloof, asleep on a pillow?

While we acknowledge the need for appropriate divisions into special fields, we oppose divisions that are too refined, and we especially oppose setting up special fields as above everything else. In fact, dividing up special fields in such a refined and dead manner is a metaphysical trick played by the bourgeoisie in their attempt to restrict the struggle of the proletariat against the bourgeoisie in order to make young people's thinking one-sided. Practice proves that in the development of science various special fields have been mutually coordinated. This is even more true of liberal arts. In the course of revolutionary mass criticism, to lay undue emphasis on the division of special fields does not strengthen the concerted fight for the great goal of the dictatorship of the proletariat, and we cannot achieve the goal of concentrating superior forces to annihilate the enemy.

"If the leadership does not make its intentions clear, then the task is not clear." How can the intentions of the leadership be made "clear"? Our great leader Chairman Mao has taught us all along that we should take full account of the struggle on the ideological and cultural fronts. In the "Circular" issued by the Party Central Committee, Chairman Mao has already set forth for us a clear-cut militant task: "Hold high the great banner of the Great Proletarian Cultural Revolution, thoroughly expose the bourgeois reactionary stand of that group of so-called 'academic authorities' who oppose the Party and socialism, thoroughly criticize the bourgeois reactionary ideas in the academic, educational, journalistic, literary and art, and publishing circles, and seize the leadership in these cultural spheres." Ever since the Great Proletarian Cultural Revolution we have waged a fierce struggle and done an enormous amount of work, but have we completed the task of "thorough criticism" against bourgeois reactionary ideas? Speaking of the literary and art front, in those years Lu Hsün had already criticized the four representative characters of Liu Shao-ch'i's counterrevolutionary revisionist line in literary and art circles: Chou Yang, Hsia Yen, T'ien Han, and Yang Han-sheng. But have we criticized them at all thoroughly?

Not yet. Is this not a "duty"? From this we can see that the question is not whether the leadership makes its intentions clear, but rather whether we really want to carry out revolutionary mass criticism or only pretend to want it.

"We are about to leave anyway; why bother carrying out revolutionary mass criticism?" They are lying when they say they are about to leave. What they are really after is bourgeois individualism. They have lived off the workers, peasants, and soldiers for so long that they should do a little something in their interest. Once they have left is it all right to stop carrying out revolutionary mass criticism? Can they avoid transformation of their bourgeois world outlook? No, they cannot. Whether you go to the factory or to the farm, or even if you change your occupation three hundred and sixty times, you still have to take part in revolutionary mass criticism, and there is still the question of world outlook. "Please, sirs, don't play the music of the previous dynasty"; decadent bourgeois individualism has no future in socialist society. Revolutionary mass criticism in liberal arts universities must be led by the working class and must fully arouse the masses. In places where conditions are favorable, universities can work with the workers and poor and lower-middle peasants in carrying out revolutionary mass criticism. The workers' Mao Tse-tung thought propaganda teams must resolutely carry out Chairman Mao's instruction: "The workers' propaganda teams must stay in the schools permanently, take part in the overall struggle-criticism-transformation task in the schools, and lead the schools forever." To accomplish this great historical task, the workers' propaganda teams should understand the history of the struggle between the two classes and the two lines on the ideological and cultural fronts. The class struggle and the struggle between two lines on the ideological and cultural fronts are extremely sharp and complicated. But the working class and the revolutionary intellectuals, armed with Mao Tse-tung thought, will certainly be able to temper and improve themselves in the wind and waves of revolutionary mass criticism, and be good at struggle. Let us raise higher the great red banner of Mao Tse-tung thought, unite all the revolutionary forces that can be united, intensively develop revolutionary mass criticism, and struggle hard to truly transform liberal arts universities into great red schools of Mao Tse-tung thought!

26

REFORM LIBERAL ARTS UNIVERSITIES THROUGH REVOLUTIONARY MASS CRITICISM

Investigation Report on Futan University's "May 7" Experimental Liberal Arts Class*

Red Flag

Summary of the Contents

This article dwells on the importance of revolutionary mass criticism and social investigation to the reform of liberal arts universities. Having conscientiously summed up what they learned in traversing a tortuous path, Futan University's "May 7" experimental liberal arts class resolutely carried out Chairman Mao's instruction that "liberal arts should take the whole society as its factory" and, focusing on revolutionary mass criticism, organically combined classroom teaching and the Three Great Revolutionary Movements. With respect to teaching material, they persisted in putting all courses of study under command of Marxism-Leninism-Mao Tse-tung thought. Taking Chairman Mao's works as the basic teaching material and opposing

*"Yung ke-ming ta p'i-p'an kai-tsao wen-k'o ta-hsüeh — Fu-tan ta-hsüeh 'wu/ch'i' wen-k'o shih-tien-pan ti tiao-ch'a pao-kao." Hung-ch'i, No. 6 (June 1, 1971), 67-74.

> the transplanting of the old teaching material, they overcame the lack of teaching material. In the course of revolutionary mass criticism they broke the old concept of "dignity of teachers" and built a new teacher-student relationship. Teaching presented an initial approach of "officers educate men, men educate officers, and men educate one another."

* * *

In September 1969 Futan University enrolled thirty worker-peasant-soldier students and set up a two-year "May 7" experimental course of liberal arts with literary and art comment as the main content of specialization study. Among these students, twenty-four were workers, four were PLA men, and two were poor and lower-middle peasants. The initial experience acquired by the experimental class over the past year shows that if the universities of liberal arts are to be reformed, it will be imperative to persevere in revolutionary mass criticism. Without revolutionary mass criticism, liberal arts will be nothing but a pool of stagnant water; with revolutionary mass criticism unfolded, the stagnant water can be changed into flowing water.

A Tortuous Path Serves as a Lesson

In what way should the socialist universities of liberal arts be operated? The "May 7" experimental liberal arts class debated this question extensively for a time.

At the time this experimental class was started a number of class heads and teachers expressed their views in these terms: "Ours is a regular university and it is charged with the tasks of raising education to a higher level." This view was taken as the starting point, and the curriculum was crowded with seven courses of study. Instead of taking class struggle as the main course of study and instead of doing everything to remold the minds of the students, teachers of the different courses taught in their own ways and gave prominence to their own courses of study. Cramming was the method of teaching adopted; the teachers "played the gramophone" while the students "served as the tape recorder," and many students did not even have enough time to take notes.

In the winter of 1969, when every front was criticizing and repudiating the big poisonous weed of an article reversing the verdict on the bourgeoisie, and the worker-peasant-soldier students were asking to join the battle, the teachers kept troops entrenched and watched the fire from across the river, emphasizing that their "teaching tasks are so heavy that they cannot join." When the movement for revolutionary mass criticism was rising in society against the "four men" — Chou Yang, Hsia Yen, T'ien Han, and Yang Han-sheng — the worker-peasant-soldier students lost their patience and, with the support of the school leading body, entered into a controversy about the orientation of the "May 7" liberal arts class, contending, blooming, putting up big-character posters, and holding debates. They broke the ice and the pool of stagnant water began to flow.

The students pointed out that the "teaching reform" as carried out at the time was like "wearing new shoes and traversing the old road" and that "receiving lessons is like going to a New Year's party with too many courses served." They demanded simplification of the curriculum. But some teachers said this: "These seven courses of study are already like condensed cod liver oil and cannot be compressed further." They emphasized that worker-peasant-soldier students must "adapt themselves to the law of the college." Worker-peasant-soldier students remarked: "We could write militant articles while in a factory and cannot do so in a college. If we go on 'adapting ourselves to the law' like this, goodness knows how we shall be 'remolded!' " They demanded that teaching be integrated with revolutionary mass criticism and opposed the indifferent attitude assumed towards mass criticism of the "four men." However, some people emphasized: "Ours is a university, and we should lay a good foundation before joining the battle." The students sharply pointed out: "To put stress on laying a good foundation behind closed doors is to fight with toy guns. We should criticize the 'four men' in all seriousness and traverse the road of the worker-peasant-soldier mass criticism writing class!" "Where will this way of 'elevation' go? Are we to be trained to be bourgeois academicians or to be proletarian fighters?" For three months the "May 7" liberal arts class traversed this tortuous path. Students of the class would not go farther along this tortuous path.

"Error is often the guide to truth." Under the leadership of the worker-PLA propaganda team, the "May 7" liberal arts class stirred up the hornets' nest. The whole class was given a living education in two-line struggle. They deeply realized that the question of holding what flag, grasping what key link, and traversing what road still existed in the new situation. To implement Chairman Mao's "May 7 Directive" it would be necessary to put "political studies" and "criticism of the bourgeoisie" in the leading position. Without criticizing and repudiating the revisionist educational line pushed by Liu Shao-ch'i's group in the old liberal arts and without criticizing the bourgeoisie, the new leading group will run counter to Chairman Mao's proletarian educational line. The working class leadership over the universities can be consolidated and strengthened step by step only through sustained and deep-going development of revolutionary mass criticism.

Conducting Revolutionary Mass Criticism in Society

Chairman Mao points out: "Liberal arts should take the whole society as its factory." To unfold revolutionary mass criticism, students of liberal arts must go into society to form a unity with the workers, peasants, and soldiers. After the "May 7" liberal arts class conducted this big debate, the students stepped out of the school in separate groups and began to throw themselves into the Three Great Revolutionary Movements.

Did the struggle come to a close? No. The practice of

taking society as the factory was repeatedly interfered with from the right and the "left," making it necessary to carry on the two-line struggle.

When we first went to the lower stratum some comrades strongly emphasized the need to "place the teaching base in the school," lest the "normal teaching order" be disturbed. But the majority of our comrades held that in conducting revolutionary mass criticism, students of liberal arts must go deep into society and come into contact with the actual struggle before they can gain specific perceptual knowledge, and that to operate the school apart from the Three Great Revolutionary Movements and behind closed doors was actually a manifestation of idealist transcendentalism. Once, the students tried to criticize reactionary stage despot Chou Hsin-fang's "theory of pleasing the audience" when they criticized the "four men." Some suggested that all they got to do was read written material. But the majority of our comrades did not share this view and insisted on conducting a survey in the factories. In the course of the survey, some workers came forward to bring one thing to light. A bad fellow went to the play Hai Jui Submits a Memorial, presented by Chou Hsin-fang. When "Hai Jui" carried a coffin to the stage, that fellow clapped hands and applauded. Later he made these vicious remarks: "It is a pity the coffin is not big enough." Facts of living class struggle brought it home to the students that Chou Hsin-fang's "theory of pleasing the audience" was one of pleasing the landlords, rich peasants, counterrevolutionaries, bad characters, and rightists and was aimed at creating public opinion in favor of counterrevolutionary restoration. With the survey conducted and a mass of data consulted on "all people's literature and art," this revolutionary mass criticism was enlivened. Talking about their experience, the teachers and students said: "'All people's literature and art' was criticized and repudiated in the past but not so penetratingly and forcefully as now."

A social survey was likewise conducted when revolutionary mass criticism was unfolded in the sphere of classic literature research. For example, when criticizing the bourgeois theory of human nature disseminated by the "four men" who conducted research in Dream of the Red Chamber, the experimental class persisted in conducting an extensive survey in factories, libraries, and theaters. Confronted with events of appalling class struggle, they came to realize that the bourgeois theory of human nature is opium for doping and eroding one's soul.

The "May 7" liberal arts class acquired this experience when taking part in social practice: In the primary units they must serve the Three Great Revolutionary Movements and create revolutionary public opinion; they may not behave like "guests" and may not expect other people to obey them or to compromise with them. The question involved here was whether one should proceed from the stand of the workers, peasants, and soldiers or from "one's own" stand. Where this question was correctly dealt with, the students would be welcomed by the workers, peasants, and soldiers; if the opposite was the case, they would not be welcomed by the workers, peasants, and soldiers. Prior to the National Day last year, a group went to State Cotton Mill No. 21, where revolutionary mass criticism was conducted with outstanding success, and investigated the class struggle in the sphere of literature and art. On their initiative the students conducted a survey in coordination with the central task of the mill. They were supported by the Party committee for the mill and welcomed by worker comrades.

While in factories the revolutionary teachers and students gained a clearer view of the relationship between the source and stream of liberal arts. Class struggle had always been acute in State Cotton Mill No. 21. Back in 1952 a reactionary "stayed at a selected point" in the mill and concocted a big poisonous weed, "Morning in Shanghai." In doing an investigation and study the experimental class emphasized the need for everybody to collect material and do specific work in propaganda and organization. Each forum or visit became an extremely lively course of class education and course of literary and art comment. For example, they investigated the promotive role played by the mill's literary and art propaganda team in presenting revolutionary literature and art. They also investigated the circumstances in which several youths embarked upon the criminal road after they were corrupted by feudal, capitalist, and revisionist literature and art. Applying Mao Tse-tung thought, they analyzed these positive and negative materials. In this way, they deepened their knowledge of the harm done by the counterrevolutionary revisionist line on literature and art pushed by Chou Yang's group, and deepened their understanding of the relationship between literature and art on the one hand and politics on the other. As their survey gradually made deep-going progress their knowledge gradually deepened. Survey outlines and writing outlines were correspondingly revised and supplemented. The whole survey process was turned into a process of studying and applying Mao Tse-tung thought in a living way and taking a leap from perceptual knowledge to rational knowledge. Formerly, some schoolmates had only an inadequate knowledge of the importance of taking society as the factory. Now they had this to say: "The old liberal arts had no need for the source but only for the stream. Study of old liberal arts became ever narrower in scope and lifeless. After we step out of the school and acknowledge the workers, peasants, and soldiers as teachers, we find that our study is becoming ever broader in scope and lifelike."

The "May 7" liberal arts class went to fifteen primary units to join revolutionary mass criticism and conduct investigation and study. At the same time, they threw themselves into the struggle within the school to criticize the "left" and right erroneous thinking and tendencies. Constantly going into the thick of social practice, the worker-peasant-soldier students made progress in varying degrees both as regards their ideological awakening and as regards their ability to analyze problems, and ability to do mass work and write. When they first came to the school some students found it difficult to express themselves in writing mass criticism articles; now they were able to write mass criticism articles of definite quality. Over the past year the students of the class wrote more than 600 criticism articles, survey reports, and ideological comments, of which 46 were carried in the press and broadcast over the radio.

Another tendency showed itself after the "May 7" liberal arts class overcame the tendency towards teaching behind closed doors. Some comrades sweepingly negated classroom teaching without making an analysis. They said: "Now that society is taken as the factory in each case, what is the use of classroom teaching?" To counter this vacillation to the "left" and to the right, the worker-PLA propaganda team led the students to draw a distinction between teaching guided by Mao Tse-tung thought and "centering on classroom teaching," pointing out that it would be necessary both to learn combat in combat and to proceed with the necessary classroom teaching and that the two should be closely combined. The former laid emphasis on practice directed by theory, while the latter laid emphasis on elevating practice to the theoretical plane. Teaching might be done in the form of presenting new ideas as related to what is already known. For example, the teachers gave the students some clue to two-line struggle over the question of research in Dream of the Red Chamber and brought up some questions to open up the students' minds so that the students might, with these specific questions in mind, conduct social surveys. Teaching might also be done in the form of summing up some questions. For example, when the students criticized the "theory of merging the spirit of the time" and the "theory of indistinctive state," the teachers explained and summed up some difficult and controversial questions, bearing in mind what the students wanted to know. The teachers gave lessons relevant to revolutionary mass criticism, while the students received lessons relevant to revolutionary mass criticism. Thus the students could understand, remember, and apply what they learned. The students expressed their views in these terms: "Teaching based on our practice can solve problems more effectively than a hundred lectures on concepts."

The experience of the "May 7" liberal arts class may be summarized as setting teaching in motion through revolutionary mass criticism. Conducting social surveys, summing up and exchanging experience, making self-study, and exercising teachers' supervision — these links were organically combined, centering on revolutionary mass criticism. As regards organization and arrangement, the principle of proceeding from realities and shooting at a definite target was adhered to, and attention was paid to providing examples and giving coherence (from the shallow to the deep, from the small to the big, and from the simple to the complex) to combat tasks.

Conscientiously Study Marxism-Leninism-Mao Tse-tung Thought, Take Chairman Mao's Works as the Basic Teaching Material, and Direct the Deep-going Development of Revolutionary Mass Criticism

Revolutionary mass criticism must be guided by revolutionary theory. Universities of liberal arts must resolutely take Chairman Mao's works as the basic teaching material and put all courses of study under command of Marxism-Leninism-Mao Tsetung thought.

The "May 7" liberal arts class followed a zigzag course in its approach to the problem of teaching material. At the outset it refrained from mass criticism and merely transplanted the old teaching material. After the big debate, the old teaching material was thrown overboard, but the refrain "it is difficult to compile liberal arts teaching material" was sung, and for a time teaching material was unavailable. The worker-peasant-soldier students were not satisfied with the "let the matter slide" approach. They had the need for teaching material. After debate and practice the teachers and students of the "May 7" liberal arts class came to realize that since the founders of Marxism-Leninism and Chairman Mao had long written systematic, integral, and direct works on each aspect of social science, their brilliant works should be the best teaching material and typical models of revolutionary mass criticism and that there was no reason to suggest that no teaching material was available. Marxist-Leninist works and Chairman Mao's works are weapons for directing revolutionary mass criticism in liberal arts. In particular, Chairman Mao's theory of philosophy, theory of political economy, theory of literature and art, theory of education, theory of historical science, and theory of journalism are brilliant crystals of struggle against the bourgeoisie in these spheres and should become the basic teaching materials on the fundamental theory and specialized theory of liberal arts.

Having determined the orientation, i.e., taking the works of proletarian revolutionary teachers as the basic teaching materials, the "May 7" liberal arts class stressed the need for conscientious reading and laid down the following principle: In receiving lessons in fundamental theory, the students must read thoroughly Selected Works of Mao Tse-tung, Vol. IV, and the principal works of Chairman Mao's publicly announced since the liberation, as well as several principal works of Marx and Lenin. In receiving lessons in specialized theory, the students must selectively read the relevant parts of the selected works of Marx, Lenin, and Chairman Mao. In line with revolutionary mass criticism, they also selectively read the relevant works of Lu Hsün. However, the controversy was still not concluded.

Before the controversy was over, a new controversy arose between two views. Comrades who laid "emphasis on specialized courses" held that the "part related to our speciality" in Chairman Mao's works should be studied and that it was not necessary to spend time on the "part not related to our speciality." On the other hand, some comrades held that to use the "specialized" criterion of old liberal arts to divide Chairman Mao's works into what should be studied and what should not be studied was to destroy the integral quality of Marxism-Leninism-Mao Tse-tung thought and to subordinate it to "one's specialized system," which was a reflection of the fact that the remnant pernicious influence of old liberal arts had not been eliminated. Practice proved that if one studied only the "part related to one's speciality" one would be unable to gain a thorough understanding of even the "relevant part." Marxism-Leninism-Mao Tsetung thought is a revolutionary, scientific, and proletarian outlook on the world and an integral theoretical system. It is inconceivable that one who does not understand and apprehend dialectical materialism and historical materialism can learn any special field of liberal arts with success. Nor is it conceivable that a student of literature and art who knows nothing about Chairman Mao's treatise on the history of the Chinese revolution or a student of history who understands absolutely nothing about the acute class struggle in the philosophical domain can learn his speciality with success. As a matter of fact, class struggle in one sphere is closely bound up with that in the other. Emphasis may be laid on one sphere, but if we confine ourselves to the narrow bounds of a specialty we shall be unable to understand thoroughly and master Chairman Mao's basic line, nor shall we be able to apply Mao Tse-tung thought accurately in criticizing the bourgeois ideology in each sphere of learning. For this reason, universities of liberal arts must take Mao Tse-tung thought as a subject to be studied in totality.

Chairman Mao's basic works should be studied and applied over and over again. Students of the "May 7" liberal arts class studied the brilliant work "Talks at the Yenan Forum on Literature and Art" many times. The first time they studied the "Talks," their teachers explained the content from the angle of criticizing the "four men's" counterrevolutionary revisionist literary and art thinking. The second time they studied the "Talks," their teachers went a step further and explained the content from the angle of proletarian transformation of the world and ideological construction of the proletarian party, linking it up with the practice of the Great Proletarian Cultural Revolution. Later, the students studied the "Talks" over and over again with reference to their combat tasks. According to the students, each time they studied they gained something new from the "Talks" and the more they studied the more they comprehended penetratingly the great development of Marxist-Leninist theory in the "Talks."

Taking Chairman Mao's works as the basic teaching material, we must study, from Chairman Mao's works, the clear-cut critical and militant spirit; study the Marxist-Leninist stand, viewpoint, and approach; and study and apply them in a living way during the struggle. The "May 7" liberal arts class studied and applied the "Talks" with respect to four aspects: (1) Comprehend, through study of model revolutionary operas, the brilliant idea of making literature and art serve the workers, peasants, and soldiers. (2) Deepen understanding of the "Talks" in the process of criticizing the "four men" and reactionary "authorities" of art. (3) Repeatedly apply Chairman Mao's stand, viewpoint, and approach in the process of investigating class struggle in the sphere of literature and art. (4) Systematically select and read some Chinese and foreign classic literary works of a representative nature; by "dissecting several sparrows," disclose the clue to the history of literature, study and grasp Chairman Mao's basic views on the question of cultural legacy. In short, everything was aimed at understanding the basic spirit of Chairman Mao's works, whether the positive side or the negative side was contacted and whether the present state of affairs was investigated or historical research was done.

The "May 7" liberal arts class began in May last year to take Chairman Mao's works as the basic teaching material. In more than ten months of practice the students read thoroughly Selected Works of Mao Tse-tung. They also studied the history of the Party, while the teachers purposefully let the students read some reactionary articles by Ch'en Tu-hsiu, Wang Ming, and Liu Shao-ch'i. From the contrast they understood the correctness of Chairman Mao's proletarian revolutionary line. By criticizing political charlatans like Liu Shao-ch'i and Wang Ming, they deepened their understanding of Mao Tse-tung thought.

Further, they paid attention to integrating study of Chairman Mao's works with study of Marxist-Leninist works. As a rule, in integrating study of Chairman Mao's works with study of Marxist-Leninist works, combat tasks were taken as a lever to set teaching in motion. For example, centering on the combat task of commemorating the centenary of the Paris Commune and the repudiation of modern revisionism, classic works like The Civil War in France, State and Revolution, and "On People's Democratic Dictatorship" were selectively read;

taking as the clue the struggle of Marxism against all shades of opportunism over the question of state power, they gathered together and studied the brilliant works of Marx, Lenin, and Chairman Mao on the dictatorship of the proletariat. Grasping the four links of study, application, lecturing, and writing, they developed selective reading and specialized study into thorough reading. The students were able to gain an integral understanding of the basic viewpoint of Marxism-Leninism-Mao Tsetung thought in this important respect, and to bring the important point to fore and achieve "less but better" results. Formerly, the students in the old department of Chinese language went through a five-year course, but some of them never read The Civil War in France. Now, in general, the students of the "May 7" liberal arts class read the work two or three times and, in some cases, seven or eight times. In the school and in nine units outside the school, five students dwelt on the history of the Paris Commune and delivered reports on study of The Civil War in France. They won favorable mass comment.

Chairman Mao teaches us: "All school work is aimed at changing the thought of the students." In the course of studying Marxism-Leninism-Mao Tsetung thought it is imperative to remold students' outlook on the world. At the initial stage the "May 7" liberal arts class paid attention to the teaching progress only, with the result that both the teachers and the students examined and sought progress and overlooked the question of putting the remolding of world outlook in the leading position. A number of students thought in these terms: "I have been chosen from among the workers, peasants, and soldiers, and I am not lacking in political consciousness. What I lack is only professional training." "If I fail to pass the hard test of professional training I shall be unable to achieve what my unit expects from me." Some sought to learn how to write articles but overlooked their ideological revolutionization. They even said this: "Having studied Chairman Mao's works I shall be able to write articles easily." This shows that the bourgeois idea of "taking study as a stepping-stone to officialdom" and "regarding professional training as the most important thing" was eroding the minds of the students at all times. This lesson reminded the leading body of the "May 7" liberal arts class of the need to grasp the style of study. The leading body emphasized that thorough reading of Chairman Mao's works may not be turned into a written language course in disguise, still less may study be evaluated from a purely professional viewpoint and a viewpoint of seeking personal fame and gain. It was emphasized that study must be integrated with practice and one's thinking. Repudiation of revisionism must be integrated with struggle against self-interest. Thanks to ideological contending and exposure of and struggle against their self-interest, the worker-peasant-soldier students were enabled to realize that "only a red heart means a red pen" and "while learning how to write with a pen one must ensure against change of one's heart." They said this: "If you want to be the spokesman for the workers, peasants, and soldiers you must intensify remolding of your world outlook. Only thus can you really occupy and transform the position of liberal arts."

Building a New Teacher-Student Relationship in the Course of Revolutionary Mass Criticism

In 1958 our great leader Chairman Mao pointed out: "The institutions of higher learning should grasp three things: (1) Party committee leadership, (2) mass line, and (3) integration of education with productive labor." But the old universities of liberal arts never carried out this great instruction. They relied only on a small number of bourgeois professors and reactionary academic "authorities." These people lorded it over others in the schools. Shortly after the "May 7" liberal arts class was set up, teaching reform was turned into a forlorn affair, and the role of the students was given no importance, the reason being that the revisionist educational line on the old liberal arts had not been sufficiently criticized and repudiated. Some members of the class Party branch even said this: "One teacher can easily guide two students." This being so, while representatives of the worker-peasant-soldier students also joined the three-in-one leading group, actually they served as a foil. The result was that "the students merely obeyed the teachers whose words counted." Mass debate gave an impetus to repudiation of the revisionist educational line on the old liberal arts and brought it home to the leading body of the experimental class that the "play safe and fear disorder" mentality was an indication that the leading body put no faith in the masses and dared not follow the mass line. Once revolutionary mass criticism was unfolded, those members of the Party branch who had misgivings in the past dispelled their misgivings and applied the methods of contending, blooming, putting up big-character posters, and holding debate in the practice of teaching reform. Practice proved that under the unified leadership of the Party organization, the worker-peasant-soldier students selected from among the workers, peasants, and soldiers were fully able to manage themselves and educate other people.

A new teacher-student relationship was built in the course of struggle. Once revolutionary mass criticism was unfolded, the old conception of "dignity of the teachers" was subjected to criticism and a new outlook of "officers educate men, men educate officers, and men educate men" began to appear in the teaching work. The mass criticism articles written by the students might be corrected by the teachers while the students might correct the mass criticism articles written by the teachers. The students corrected the articles written by each other. In classroom, the students might stand up to raise questions or debate any time they thought what the teachers taught was wrong or incomprehensible to them. As a result of ceaseless discussion and debate, the students heightened their initiative and enthusiasm for self-study and could, with specific questions in mind, do serious reading and look for positive and negative data, and gradually they acquired the ability to analyze and ponder over problems and improve their ability to criticize the bourgeoisie. Both the teachers and the students could do active thinking.

At the start, the teachers were not accustomed to this form

of teaching based on discussion and enlightenment. However, after a period of practice the teachers came to realize that the questions raised by the students and the arguments they made were very useful because they helped to correct errors and to supplement and enrich the teaching content on the spot. The present situation is such that if no question is raised during classroom teaching, everybody will have the feeling that the teachers and the students have not communicated with each other as regards viewpoint and feelings.

The "May 7" liberal arts class also let the students mount the platform to give lessons. In the case of a philosophy lesson in "On Contradiction," four students prepared lessons and gave lessons in separate sections. They prepared lessons with all seriousness. In giving lessons they proved themselves able to link up their state of mind and the class struggle in society and to criticize metaphysics and idealism. This way of teaching opened up the minds of the comrades who received the lessons. By letting the students mount the platform to give lessons, their consciousness and initiative in study were raised and great stimulation was given to the teachers.

"The question of teaching reform is mainly one concerning the teachers." The teachers of the "May 7" liberal arts class had not adapted to the new method of teaching. The methods of teaching to which they had been accustomed were not applicable now. And they were not accustomed to revolutionary mass criticism, social class struggle, and social survey. In teaching the course of literature and art, they were required both to carry criticism of the "four men" to the end and to reflect the prevailing state of class struggle. They were also required to debate with the students, to which they were not accustomed either. This kind of "inadaptability" reflected a great, new social revolution on the education front and made it necessary for the teachers to be reeducated politically and to study again professionally. The revolutionary teachers of the "May 7" liberal arts class spoke of their experience: "To change inadaptability into adaptability one must ceaselessly negate one's old self. The process of criticizing the 'four men' is the very process of remolding one's concept of literature and art." As for the bourgeois academic "authorities," the "May 7" liberal arts class saw to it that they were both "criticized and used" in the process of revolutionary criticism.

Worker-peasant-soldier students are the most vigorous force for revolution in the ranks of teachers. To conduct a mass movement the universities of liberal arts must recruit as part-time teachers the workers, peasants, and soldiers outside the school, who have rich practical experience, as well as practical workers so that the teaching content may reflect broadly and in a timely way the new problems, new experiences, and new trends on each ideological front in society and so that the pulse of classroom teaching may be exactly like that of class struggle in society. This is an important aspect of carrying out Chairman Mao's proletarian educational line. It will enable the universities of liberal arts to "obtain living water from its source."

Although the "May 7" experimental liberal arts class has achieved some success and acquired some experience over the past year in the practice of reforming the universities of liberal arts through revolutionary mass criticism, teaching is still not well planned and, in the process of organizing the students to join revolutionary mass criticism, some are given more tempering while others are given less. In handling the relationship between the two aspects of contradiction, it frequently happens that one tendency is likely to cover up the other. For example, the work of reforming the original ranks of teachers has two aspects, namely, unity versus struggle, use versus reform. This is also true of other relationships such as politics versus profession, theory versus practice, classroom versus society. These problems remain to be solved more fully through practice. It is intended, under the guidance of the great red banner of Mao Tse-tung thought, to go in the direction indicated by the brilliant "May 7 Directive," to learn the advanced experience from Tsinghua University, Peking University, and other fraternal institutions, to hold aloft the banner of revolutionary mass criticism and, together with them, to found new socialist universities of liberal arts.

CCP Committee of Futan University

XI

The Yenan Background

27

EDUCATIONAL METHOD AT K'ANGTA*

The Situation at the Resist Japan Military and Political University

In terms of its historical environment and the composition of its student body, "K'angta is the heroic historical product of a great age" (Wang Ming). A school for the anti-Japanese United Front, K'angta does not belong to any party or faction. Enrollment is not closed to members of any anti-Japanese party, nor to any classes of society, and at the same time no one is excluded on the basis of race, religion, creed, sex, or occupation.

In terms of its educational curriculum, K'angta is at the present stage a model wartime national defense educational institution. Its educational policy, courses, and methods are most suitable to the pressing needs of the current war of resistance, and it positively advocates that "today's school should be a work team, and a work team should be a school as well." In this sense it is necessary to take up "lively study of living books" in line with the principle "while studying, do not forget to fight Japan and save the nation." K'angta does not

*"K'ang-ta ti chiao-yü fang-fa." K'ang-ta ti tung-t'ai (published by the Mobilization Society of Wuhan, n. p., August 1939), pp. 81-97.

want to be like those schools of the past which kept students studying "with ears unable to hear what is happening outside the window, single-mindedly reading dead books," shirking the duty of real struggle, turning students into old and worthless "bookworms."

In terms of its mission and objectives, K'angta is a school devoted to filling the needs of the national war of resistance by creating elementary- and intermediate-level military and political cadres for the anti-Japanese war. This is fully consistent and in line with the guiding principle of all the nation's resistance schools, but K'angta is different from all types of specialized institutes, research centers, and church schools. Thus, the name, China Resist Japan Military and Political University, or K'angta for short, is nothing more than an accurate description of the reality of the school.

Precisely because it was born in an environment of armed struggle, the educational policy, courses, and student body of K'angta are not entirely similar to those of ordinary schools. By the same token, K'angta's educational method cannot help but be a little bold, betraying certain peculiarities. Some people have said these peculiarities are good qualities. I think there is some basis for saying so. I will now describe several aspects of K'angta's educational method for the benefit of the reader.

I. The Basis of K'angta's Educational Method

Educational method is meant to implement and realize educational policy and plans and to certify whether or not students have achieved thorough comprehension. It is a most fundamental and important type of method, not simply a question of educational technique but a question of the politics of education. The basis of K'angta's educational method is covered in the following points:

A. Educational Method as Based on K'angta's Own Educational Policy

The educational policy of K'angta, as can be seen from its courses, from President Lin (Piao's) theses, and from the trends of K'angta's history, may be summed up in three points:

1. Politically, a National United Front against Japan
2. Militarily, offensive warfare
3. Spiritually, a revolutionary tradition

From its creation to the present, although this period covers more than four semesters, the educational policy of K'angta has not undergone and will not undergo large transformations or changes in principle. Thus its educational method especially emphasizes the principles of the unity of theory and reality, few but essential courses, and teaching by example. K'angta is strongly opposed to that kind of formalistic education characterized by specious ostentation and preference of abundance over essence and quantity over quality; at the same time, it is opposed to study tendencies characterized by achievement-orientation, self-seeking, conceit, and vanity. K'angta uses the method of two-line struggle — opposing both formalism (idealism) and empiricism — to carry out its own educational plans.

B. Educational Method Based on Those Being Educated — the Special Nature of K'angta's Students

Although K'angta's educational policy remains constant throughout, its educational methods have changed and developed with time. At its inception K'angta did not establish a general theory or a systematic educational method. From time to time it was characterized by various inconsistent, independent phenomena. Now a complete educational methodology is being gradually formulated and defined by regulations. Bringing together the regulations for educational methodology was like a number of stones colliding and sending off sparks here and there; these sparks, amassed together, emitted a brilliant light. Not a single spark was dissipated, not a single educational experience was ignored. This is carried out by the following concrete method: When the enrollment in each semester is about full and before classes begin, a very thorough educational meeting is held. A careful analysis and theoretical discussion is conducted concerning the battle experience, political and cultural level, and theoretical understanding of the students and concerning what type of cadres are to be produced. The educational course is confirmed and those aspects of educational method which should receive attention or be revised are indicated, and class meeting hours are arranged as well, on the basis of this discussion. Thus determined by the needs of each semester and each squad in each semester, K'angta's educational method is not subject to mechanical or arbitrary formulation. Very strong emphasis is placed on solving all problems in terms of the concrete conditions and the concrete educational objectives of a given semester, and an efficacious educational method most suited to objective requirements is specified. For example, the first and second large squads of K'angta's first and second semesters were largely made up of high-level cadres of the Eighth Route Army. They had rich combat experience, a fairly deep understanding of political theory, and were highly sincere about studying. Thus the educational method applied in their case emphasized the self-study research format, with class attendance five or six times a week and the rest of their time being spent in self-study. Again, in the case of students of the second sub-squad of the first large squad in the fourth semester, all were Eighth Route Army middle- and low-level cadres; and the students of the fourth and sixth large squads were all workers and peasants. Although their struggle experience was relatively rich, their cultural level and theoretical grounding were comparatively weak. Therefore the educational method applied in their case stressed the 'enlightenment' [ch'i-fa] format, as well as discussion and cultural classes. Other general students have for the most part high school or college-level educational backgrounds, so their classes are taught mainly through the application of a mixture of 'enlightenment' and lecture methods.

C. Educational Method Based on the Situation of the School

The length of the period of instruction, the availability of teaching equipment and educational facilities, the financial resources available to the school, and especially the situation of the school in respect to wartime and peacetime and its location inside or outside of a war zone — all of these factors have a direct bearing on the type of educational method which the school adopts. K'angta exists under conditions of hardship: all of its educational facilities are extremely simple, its financial resources are very limited, and its educational semester is comparatively brief (from four to six months); as a result, K'angta's educational method is suitable for military preparedness and heavily emphasizes practical education. For example, military classes and particularly courses in tactical training are all carried out in the field. In addition, organized large-scale bivouacking exercises are often undertaken. (For example, this year, at the end of August, fourteen hundred persons took part in a large field exercise which lasted for one week; moreover, it was decided that in the future two such exercises would be held each semester.) In addition, each squad or even each small squad or group is supplied with a sha-p'an* for undertaking relatively concrete, practical military training. Another practical educational method is to raise to the level of principle the cultivation of thought and consciousness, habits, endurance, and the practice of physical labor to help students improve, transform, and discipline themselves so that they are able to make use of what they have learned.

---

*A sha-p'an is a four-by-six-foot box of wood or brick filled with sand or mud; with the use of model villages, bridges, forests, buildings, rivers, armored vehicles, warships, etc., friendly and enemy forces are distinguished and military operations simulated.

II. K'angta's Educational Principles

A. The Principle of Relating Theory and Reality

The relation of theory and reality is a basic principle of instruction and study at K'angta. It pervades all educational and study methods; K'angta is strongly opposed to reliance on formalism and pedantry and indeed has carried out an unrelenting struggle against pedantry. At the general concluding meeting of the third semester, the assistant head of the school, Lo (Jui-ch'ing), pointed out in a sharply worded statement: "Pedantry is the most malicious enemy of the unity of theory and reality in our educational policy. It is a 'fatal' element, and although now only vestiges remain, we must still carry out a severe attack against it, extirpating it by its very roots." Following this, pedantry was deprived of a foothold at K'angta, and the unity of theory and reality is being thoroughly effected. All teachers, administrators, and students at K'angta have applied the very valuable advice of Li-mi-te-jo-fu to their teaching and study method. He said, "We study Marxist-Leninism, not just to learn its alphabet, but to comprehend its ingenious revolutionary spirit," or as Lenin said, "theory is gray, but reality is ever green." This point is brought to the fore in all of K'angta's educational courses and methods. It is given special emphasis, canonized, and popularized; it is made concrete and sinified and used as a starting point for leading students to a grasp of theory and principles, for enabling students to concretely adapt theory to reality.

B. The Principle of Few But Essential Courses

"Few but essential" is one of the fundamental principles of K'angta's educational method. It is based on the accumulated experience of ten years of developing educational method under cannon fire. In particular, it is an educational method evolved in response to the present tense state of the war of resistance and the urgent need for resistance cadres. Everyone realizes that in the present state of uninterrupted warfare there isn't time for anyone to spend the proverbial "ten years by a cold window" mastering a variety of subjects; this is both completely impossible and unnecessary.

The purpose of the principle of few but essential courses is not to prevent scientific development and progress in a variety of fields, or to restrict people from studying all but a few circumscribed courses. Instead it is mainly intended to enable ordinary students to spend a very short time studying each course, not simply learning it and letting it go at that, but learning it and understanding it accurately, learning how to apply it. The point is that students should not go away with a half-baked or perfunctory understanding.

The implementation of the "few but essential" principle begins with extremely careful selection of courses, adhering to the "warehouse" model rather than the "department store" model, meaning that the number of courses taught at K'angta is not large, and all are extremely important. Each course is taught twice a week, each time for three hours continuously; in this way the understanding and receptive capacity of students is easier to systematize. Then the relative importance of the selected courses is weighed and, on this basis, the amount of time to be spent on a given course is determined; not all courses progress at the same pace or take the same overall amount of time. Again, the total amount of time does not exceed the time students spend studying on their own; this is one way of emphasizing the importance of students' independent study and intensive research. Thus, independent study hours are counted as part of formal course time and are not a time for recreation.

C. The Principle of Teaching by Example

First of all, teaching personnel make examples of themselves. Teaching personnel are education cadres. They teach students not only by explaining problems in the classroom and on the training grounds but also by everywhere making an example of themselves — giving the students an educational model in actual life, through the style of bitter struggle, in forging thought and consciousness and in independent study. Moreover, in each type of study group and extracurricular activity, teaching personnel take part actively and give assistance.

Second, students are taught organizational competency and method. This is completely antithetical to the past educational policy of keeping the people in ignorance and the traditional spirit that the people "can only be made to follow, they cannot be made to comprehend." K'angta's education is not intended only to instill in students an understanding of theory; it especially emphasizes educating students to be able to apply work methods and organizational techniques — as exemplified, for example, in the National Salvation Clubs and "People's Vanguard Corps" of each squad, all of which are operated according to the principle of independence and autonomy, carrying out their own work in a democratic fashion, undertaking exercises in leadership and other work. Another example may be seen in the August bivouacking exercises, one of the purposes of which is to provide students with organizational practice. From this one can get an idea of the importance which K'angta attaches to cultivating organizational ability in students.

The third mode of teaching by example is the use of applied education, teaching through the use of models. Because of the restrictions imposed on K'angta at present by material conditions, the use of models is very limited. For example, in explaining about artillery, the air force, warships, tanks, poison gas chemistry, etc., there is nothing to make models from, and the only recourse is pictorial illustrations.

III. Classroom Method

A. The Basic Method of Classroom Teaching Is the "Enlightenment Method"

What is the enlightenment method? It is not a method of simply pouring in information or lecturing; nor is it simple dialogical method. The simple dialogical method – that is, the simple asking of questions by the teacher – is inadequate because questions posed one by one only cover a small part of the larger problem, fail to express the organic interrelations to the rest of the problem, and omit the necessary premises which give rise to the question. Thus, excepting those listeners who know the question and can give an answer, the students are unable to reply easily; if they are simply told how to answer the question, their interest is not aroused. On the other hand, the enlightenment method begins with a discussion of the premises upon which a question is based, and then poses the question, breaking larger questions into smaller ones, establishing definite relationships among the questions, enabling the students, under the guidance of the teacher, to understand the whole problem from each of its aspects; from the process of the question's development, the rules and laws governing its development are understood.

The function of the enlightenment method is mainly to meet the concrete needs of students, at the same time motivating them to express their opinions positively and seek for themselves the truth behind questions raised. Its concrete method of application is as follows:

1. From the near to the distant.

For example, treatment of the Anti-Japanese People's United Front begins with a discussion of the necessity for eliminating factional strife among various political parties, sects and classes, overcoming friction, discussing the situation and seeking mutual understanding, moving toward unified action and unified opinion, rising from there to a common political platform, a unified political regime and a unified army, reforming the political system to realize a new democratic republican nation, etc. Now, in dealing with the history of China's revolutionary movement, the discussion at K'angta begins with the lessons of the first period of cooperation between the Republican and Communist parties during the Great Revolution of 1925-27. The May Fourth Movement, the Hsin-hai Revolution and the T'ai-p'ing movement are then discussed. In teaching general political knowledge, imperialism and colonial revolutions are first treated, followed by a discussion of capitalist and primitive society, etc. The advantage of this type of educational method is that it causes the students to understand easily and, even if they are transferred out of the course due to work exigency, the immediate, pressing problems will have been discussed, making the course more applicable to work.

2. From the concrete to the abstract — rules and principles.

If we want to discuss the principle "fighting Japan comes first," we must first explain that larger problems govern smaller ones, that the individual is subordinate to the group, that consideration of the nation and of the race supercedes consideration of all difficulties and all individuals; in this way we advance to the principle "fight Japan above all else, subordinate everything to the resistance."

3. From the parts to the whole, from the whole to its parts.

For example, in military training classes the tactical value of each type of drill and its importance as a factor in military victories is invariably explained. In the same way, discussion of military strategy and tactics must include explanation of the importance of always obeying orders, cultivating a disciplined military life-style, etc. This is just as Mao Tse-tung said: "The utility of each type of tactical action is comparable to the function of a person's ears, eyes, mouth, and nose; the importance of strategy may be likened to a person's brain. The two must cooperate mutually before a complete victory in battle can be achieved."

4. Grasping the laws of development from study of the process of events and projecting the future.

For example, in discussing how feudal society was able to develop into capitalist society, the internal contradictions of feudal society and the process and outcome of their development must be explained, which leads to an investigation of the laws of development of society based on private ownership as well as speculation on its future.

5. The question of describing key points.

When discussing a question, deductive and inductive methods

are used. In general, instructors are reluctant to explain a question in overly broad terms; they want to enable students to grasp the central and important points easily. After explaining each problem, a conclusion is made on the basis of review and clear, concise summary of the key points.

B. Making Associations During Instruction

There are several ways of making associations in teaching, for example, relating general principles with actual behavior, current problems with past and future problems, this course with that course; linking theory learned in school with actual experience at the front lines, one's individual thought and consciousness with theories one studies, daily life with education, important courses with supplemental education. The main advantage of making such associations is that they facilitate the enrichment and enlivening of the curriculum, warding off feelings of boredom and disinterest among students.

The main means of making such associations are giving concrete examples, drawing numerous metaphors, presenting hypothetical situations, especially leading students into a close relationship with current problems, etc.

C. Tests

In a formalistic sense, tests may seem similar to the examinations of the old school system. If, however, this apparent similarity is contrasted with the actual [functional differences], it will be understood that tests [as applied at K'angta] are not equivalent to the old examinations, even in principle.

The function of tests used at K'angta may be regarded as having twofold significance. In the first sense they serve to motivate and encourage study, stimulate those who fall behind, urge on those who are advanced, increase diligence, and awaken the positive nature of students' self-study. In another sense tests are used as a yardstick by which to measure educational progress and the students' degree of understanding, thus helping to improve educational methods. To fulfill these functions, therefore, K'angta uses a special format in giving tests which is unprecedented, accurate, independent, and creative. Before a test is given, a list of topics is drawn up. Students are permitted and encouraged to participate in lively collective discussion of these topics. Before the test a number of questions are selected from among the topics, and after some revision these become the formal test questions. Students assemble for the test – sometimes a whole squad participates – at a given time, but are permitted to consult among themselves, bring notes, and use reference books; sometimes the tests are handed over to the students to take to independent study rooms, to allow them more time to prepare answers.

Because the objective of tests at K'angta is only to promote studies and provide one means of measuring educational progress, there isn't the least bit of competition involved. Therefore, although importance is attached to detail and accuracy in answers, grading is not emphasized. The test papers are marked impressionistically with an A, B, C, D or Chinese letter grade, or some other abstract indication of score. It is quite apparent that these tests are, after all, rather informal; grading is somewhat a matter of luck and is not sufficient to indicate a student's overall educational accomplishments. In fact it is not exaggerating to say that test results are at most a basis for evaluating a student's grasp of a few questions; therefore arbitrary attention is not paid to the number of points scored. No doubt this is an accurate description.

The method of reading test papers is itself rather novel and not to be found at ordinary schools. Concretely, the method is as follows: those who conducted the exam prepare written answers to the questions, then organize a group of students who have a good grasp of the material. These students cooperate in examining and marking the papers. In this way the teaching personnel are spared a lot of trouble, and the results of the evaluation are more careful and rigorous than if the teacher had made them alone; in addition, this provides an extraordinary form of education for the students.

D. Supplemental Education

Aside from the courses determined in the educational plan, there are other forms of temporary educational activity which are included in the category of supplemental education. For example, the plan provides for regularly (once a week) inviting famous persons to lecture; collecting questions and suggestions from the "suggestion boxes" and "question and answer registers" of each squad and preparing written or oral explanations; soliciting large and small questions, doubts, etc., from graduating students of each squad before they leave the school. Responses to these, as well as other problems which the school considers important, form the basis for a week of lectures. This is a most valuable, systematic element of supplemental education and is most welcomed by the students. Other examples are all of the activities of the National Salvation Clubs, such as wall newspapers, self-examination and discussion meetings, singing and theatricals, etc., all of which are effective supplements to the main courses.

IV. How Teaching Personnel Prepare

A. Preparatory Educational Meeting

The preparatory educational meeting is a very good way of raising the quality of teaching and unifying the curriculum. It also serves as a "marketplace" for new teaching personnel.

1. General courses must hold one preparatory meeting per large squad for each stage or each week of every course, directed by the managing instructor (military or political); a representative appointed by the department of training attends and guides the meeting.

2. The main content of the educational preparatory meeting consists of determining the basic, key points which students must understand in each course, reviewing the achievements and failures of the previous week's classes, and indicating methods for taking care and making improvements in the future.

3. Discussing uncertainties, disputes, and controversies which have arisen or may arise, and how to solve them.

4. Determining the basic reference materials and the main themes of instruction in a given course. Generally, the main themes are proposed by the department of training; sometimes instructors themselves draft them.

B. Preparation Before Class

Because the enlightenment method is being used, thorough preparation before class is required of instructors. Preparation consists of:

1. notes on the material to be taught in a given class, including the scope and main points of the lesson, and necessary concrete examples, topics for discussion by small study group meetings after class, etc.;

2. estimating the total amount of time needed for the class and making firm decisions on what phases of the material are to be covered;

3. preparing equipment for the class, such as reference books, charts, appliances, etc.

C. Preparation in Class

1. Before presentation of new material in a given class, the instructor poses questions about the previous lesson, so that students may recall and review and the instructor can hear statements or arguments from the students; the opinions presented by students are never ridiculed or scorned. Instructors take a serious attitude and, according to the importance of the problem involved, provide a careful, concise explanation.

2. After each class is completed, instructors suggest a few (three or four) review or research problems for discussion in study groups; they also indicate primary and secondary reference sources for the material covered.

V. Extracurricular Assistance and Leadership by Instructors

There may still be some schools with the kind of teacher who, after class is finished, becomes absolutely indifferent to students' problems; in any case, this phenomenon is completely absent at K'angta. On the contrary, relations between teachers and students at K'angta are extraordinarily genial. There is no jealousy or reproach and certainly none of the turmoil of "student movements." This is of course because all leadership in the school is correct, and the educational system is able to satisfy the needs of students; but it cannot be denied that solidarity between teachers and students is an important factor as well. This solidarity can be seen first of all in the untiring and patient help which teachers give students outside of class.

First of all, teaching personnel or educational cadres living with the squads attend at least one meeting of a small study group each week, helping students understand questions and guiding their studies.

Second, teaching personnel frequently offer sincere and frank reprimands to students, urging them to reform infirmities in thought or consciousness and undisciplined behavior.

Third, teaching personnel attached to squads call regular meetings with leaders of small study groups, humbly receive and consider students' opinions, and discuss with them measures to be taken with regard to instruction.

Fourth, without regard for formalities, or constraints on their time, instructors patiently help students resolve their doubts or discuss their problems. Moreover, teaching personnel do not put on airs before students; nor are they addressed as "sir." Teachers and students mutually observe the rules while in class; after class they frequently go arm in arm like brothers, friendly and affectionate.

VI. Educational Organization and Courses at K'angta

A. K'angta's educational organization consists of the department of training established under the leadership of the school president; this encompasses the faculty of military education, faculty of political education, and the editing and translating section. Each large squad appoints a director of military education and of political education, and each squad has attached teaching personnel; military and political education cadres are under the department of training and the directors of military and political education. Some squads appoint cultural teaching personnel.

B. The apportionment of courses and class time at K'angta depends on whether a squad is military or political; generally, political courses in political squads occupy 70 percent of the total, with 30 percent for military courses. In the case of military squads the ratio is reversed.

In summary, K'angta's courses are as follows:

political courses: Chinese problems, general discussion of social science, general discussion of the Three Principles of the People, general political knowledge, philosophy;

military courses: guerrilla warfare, drill in deportment, infantry tactics and strategy;

cultural courses: general geography, natural sciences, arithmetic, Japanese language; etc.

...According to conversations with those in charge at K'angta and our own observations, there are still several shortcomings at K'angta, imposed by material conditions and financial problems which are regrettable and which impair the efficacy of education. For example, educational equipment is in very short supply, well-qualified professors are few in number, and a great many aspects of the educational program and system are still being worked out. Thus, it is hoped that patriots who support national defense education and are concerned about K'angta will offer assistance and guidance in respect to all of these problems.

28

THE PROBLEM OF TRANSFORMING GENERAL EDUCATION IN THE BASE AREAS*

Liberation Daily

Initial transformation of education in our anti-Japanese Base Areas began following the successive publication of Chairman Mao's speech "Reform Our Study" in May 1941; the Party Central Committee's "Decision on Investigation and Research" in August of the same year; the Central Committee's "Decision on Yenan Cadre Schools" in December; Chairman Mao's speeches "Rectify Study Style, Party Style, and Literary Style"** and "Oppose Stereotyped Party Writing"; and the Party Central Committee's "Decision on the Education of Cadres in Service" the following February.***

---

*"Ken-chü ti p'u-t'ung chiao-yü ti kai-ke wen-t'i." Chieh-fang jih-pao, April 7, 1944. This document was reprinted in Shen-Kan-Ning pien-ch'ü chiao-yü fang-chi [Educational Policy in the Shen-Kan-Ning Border Region], rev. ed. (edited and printed in the Civil Affairs Office of the Shen-Kan-Ning Border Region Government, September 1944), pp. 44-49.

**Now referred to in the official version of Mao's Selected Works as "Rectify the Party's Style of Work" — Peter J. Seybolt.

***All the articles here referred to can be found translated in Boyd Compton, ed., Mao's China: Party Reform Documents, 1942-44, Seattle, 1952 — Peter J. Seybolt.

Since the beginning of the Rectification [cheng-feng] Campaign in April 1942, this transformation has become a large mass movement which has achieved great success. However, the transformation has mainly been promoted for Party internal education and for political education, and its harvest has been greatest in these areas. Chairman Mao Tse-tung and the Party Central Committee have already stipulated basic principles for general education and cultural education, and there has been some progress in the past two or three years and during the Rectification Campaign. But the consciousness of Party and government propaganda and education organs in the various base areas has been insufficient in this regard. The old forms have not been fully destroyed and the new ones have not been well established. A thorough discussion of the way in which past education has been divorced from reality and from the masses was begun in the Shen-Kan-Ning Border Region following the middle school level education conference held last year. Total transformation is in ferment in middle and elementary schools in all locations: local cadre-training classes have been established in the majority of middle schools and normal schools, and especially worthy of notice is the transformation of elementary education in places like Sui-te and Yenan [two subregions in the Shen-Kan-Ning Border Region] and the activities of literacy groups and newspaper-reading groups in places like Ch'un-yao and An-sai [towns respectively in the Kuan-chung and Yenan subregions of the Shen-Kan-Ning Border Region]. If this movement is to continue to develop progressively, and the new system is to spread through all of the base areas and systematically be established, all Party and government organs in the base areas must give it their full effort.

There are two difficulties in carrying out transformation of a basic nature in general education: the first is the so-called new education being practiced in China today. Although it began only at the end of the Ch'ing dynasty, it has an international background and a history of several decades. Its system, courses, and methods constitute a complete package. It pervades all realms of human knowledge and social life, and therefore, although it has been criticized and attacked, it will take more than a day and a night to replace it with another package.

Second, old-style education is divorced from the people, and therefore a party and government that represent the welfare of the people cannot have much interest in it. Although we were quite creative in our education work during the civil war period [1928-1936], after the outbreak of the War of Resistance [1937], the base areas also did much difficult work which differed in principle in many respects from the old-style education. This transformation of principles was especially great during the civil war period, but because the old package still has not been thoroughly criticized and repudiated, and because there still has not been completely responsible and goal-oriented attention to the use and study of the new package as a weapon, there has, of course, been much wasted effort in trying to establish it fully. But no matter what the difficulties, this transformation must be and can be realized.

The strong point, as well as the weak point, of the current so-called new education is in its international background. We will not discuss now whether it is suited to the needs of foreign countries and foreign peoples; but in relation to our own situation, first of all, it is the product of capitalist countries at a high level of development and is not suited to China's needs. Second, it is the product of a ruling capitalist class and is not suited to the needs of Chinese democratic base areas. Third, it is the product of peacetime and is not suited to the needs of the anti-Japanese war. Fourth, it is the product of large cities and is not suited to the needs of agricultural villages (to say nothing of villages in extensive, sparsely populated areas like Shensi-Kansu-Ninghsia and Northwest Shensi). All of this is undisputable. We are in China, in democratic base areas, in wartime, in rural villages. Copying this system and these courses and methods offers no solutions to our problems.

For instance, what kinds of people are our elementary schools and middle schools supposed to train? They can train only four types of people. One type is the person who returns home to work after graduation. So-called national education was originally supposed to be for this purpose. But, at present, education trains people to advance to a higher educational level. Therefore, if one returns home, it is not worth the trouble to have graduated from elementary school, and worth even less to have graduated from middle school. When he returns home he is dissatisfied and cannot be a model worker. It is even worse than not having gone to school.

Another type is the "public person" who does various kinds of work for Party, government, army, and popular organizations. But education at present is not for this purpose; study is divorced from application. Furthermore, this need has its limits. If there are more than a certain number of public persons it reduces the necessary labor force and increases the unnecessary financial burden.

The third type moves on to the next educational level; but very few advance from elementary school to middle school. Even if all advanced and graduated from middle school, where would they advance from there? It is unnecessary and impossible for the base areas to run old-style universities; and the high-level cadre schools today have no connection with middle schools.

What other way is left? The only other way is to become vagrants and loafers. This is not a joke but a fact. It is evident therefore that a great transformation in lower-level education is both necessary and possible. The movement to transform Chinese education in the past several decades has not succeeded. The decisive reason for this has been the lack of democratic politics throughout the country; educational authorities cannot respect the needs of the popular masses. However, we have solved this problem. What we have not done well in the past has been the result of problems of thought, not political problems. If we can be thoroughly liberated from dogmatic methods of thought, thoroughly liberated from the old system, courses, and methods, and begin from the realities of the popular masses, we can certainly attain our objective.

Students who had studied abroad became the soul of the old educational system (the educational system after the abolition of the imperial examinations) due to the desire to learn from foreign countries. The nature of education within the nation was almost exclusively to train students to study abroad. Foreign countries were the model everywhere. Therefore the foundation stood not on its feet but on its head. The system of studying abroad has had its progressive uses. We should not totally deny it, as do those phony patriots who become increasingly incapable of abandoning foreign ways the more they talk about restoring ancient tradition. But we certainly must derive the educational foundation from the needs of the broadest mass of the people. One of the needs of the broadest mass of the people is for the broadest mass education; another is for mass cadre education. These two kinds of education that we have at present are fundamentally distinct from the old system. They are not of a preparatory and subordinate nature; they are not for advancing to a higher educational level. They have their independent and clear objective in actual life and actual work.

This kind of mass education should have its present and its future. It is its future to enable every worker to understand higher math, physics, and chemistry. It is its present to enable the masses to understand how to participate in guerrilla warfare, how to organize labor power, how to get the most necessary cultural knowledge. Cadres must understand how to become leaders. It is wrong to forsake the future for the present; it is especially wrong to forsake the present for the future. Between the present and the distant future there are, of course, several intermediate stages when the question of advancing to the next educational level will arise, but under present conditions in the base areas, this question should not arise. The system of general education in the base areas at present should be completely renovated and reorganized to accord with the particular needs of mass education and cadre education.

Since the family and the village are the foundation of the life of the masses in the base areas, our mass education, whether it be for children, adults, or women, should always be concerned with the family and village. Knowledge for the actual needs of family and village life should become the main or sole content of education. Forms of study appropriate to the conditions of family and village life — such as village schools, literacy groups, even the apprenticeship system of teaching production skills, etc. — should in part or entirely replace present elementary schools.

Since the central task of base-area cadres is war and production, our cadre education, regardless of whether in the past it was called middle school, normal school, university, academy, or training class, should have a sequence of courses in the knowledge required for actual leadership in war and production. These should partially or entirely replace the courses that exist for the purpose of examinations for educational advancement, or the courses that are the remnants of so-called standardization. We should recruit those who have experience in war and production, and appoint war- and production-work cadres as teachers and students to partially or completely replace those who have no knowledge of or interest in war and production. In this way we will perhaps get rid of the old forms of elementary and middle schools, and we will have mass education that is welcomed by the masses, and cadre education that is welcomed by the cadres. Only this kind of learning can give the masses and cadres true knowledge that will help the base areas achieve victory in war and production.

In order to solve all of the concrete problems in the process of transforming general education, we must correct all kinds of mistakes and tendencies that might arise. That is not within the scope of this article. This article only introduces a policy. Later we will separately discuss the question of systems, courses, and methods for mass education and cadre education in the base areas.

29

ON REGULATIONS AND CURRICULUM IN GENERAL EDUCATION*

Liberation Daily

In the April 7 editorial of this newspaper ("The Problem of Transforming General Education in the Base Areas"), we suggested a general principle for the reform of education in the base areas. We will now attempt to express our opinion again, this time with regard to the question of regulations and curriculum.

In the educational system of every age and every society there are always different educational regulations and course curricula. What are the things that determine these regulations and curricula? There are two determining factors: one is the class-oriented desires of the rulers or educators; the other is the level of development of productive technology and the social division of labor at a given time. Why do highly developed capitalist nations find necessary ten or twenty years of education from primary school to university, with each grade and year

*"Lun p'u-t'ung chiao-yü chung ti hsüeh-chih yü k'o-ch'eng." Chieh-fang jih-pao, May 27, 1944. This document was reprinted in Shen-Kan-Ning pien-ch'ü chiao-yü fang-chi [Educational Policy in the Shen-Kan-Ning Border Region], rev. ed. (edited and printed in the Civil Affairs Office of the Shen-Kan-Ning Border Region Government, September 1944), pp. 50-59.

tightly coordinated, covering dozens of compulsory general courses, dozens of departments, and hundreds of specialized courses? Of course, such a situation did not exist in ancient China or in old Europe. This is a reflection of mechanized production under capitalism. In a socialist society, educational needs are similar, but due to differences in the class-orientation and methods of production, educational regulations (e.g., requirements for school admissions) and curricula (as in the social science curriculum) under socialism are different from those of a capitalist society. In China's Great Rear areas [controlled by Chiang Kai-shek's National Government], the level of industrialization is far below that of America, Europe, or Japan, but in general, educational rules and curricula imitate those of the industrialized nations. This is a reflection of the semicolonial character of Chinese education. But those in control of the Great Rear areas are still not satisfied with this type of foreign education; they call it "education for the death of the nation and the extinction of the race" and advocate "supplementing this impoverished education with (Confucian moral) training." But their so-called training is even further from the needs of the race and the people. This is a reflection of the semifeudal nature of the rulers. The base areas are fighting Japan and they are democratic; in this lies their qualitative political difference from Europe, America, and Japan, from semifeudal, semicolonial areas, and from socialist areas. The base areas are also technologically backward villages with only a limited degree of social division of labor (the urgency of the War of Resistance limits this further); in this respect, too, the base areas are different from socialist and capitalist countries, as well as from several large cities in China. If these two basic points are missed in the process of formulating school regulations and curricula for the base areas today, it will be impossible to avoid mistakes.

But we have erred in exactly this respect. Because we have overlooked the first point (the political differences), our schools have, in the course of deciding who should be the educators and who should be the educated, lost touch with the principles of the War of Resistance and of democratic control, with the result that those who have the responsibility for the resistance and for production have no status in the schools, and their activities and needs are not seemingly reflected in the curriculum of the schools.

By overlooking the second point (economic backwardness), we have simply followed along in imitation of school regulations and curricula imported from Europe, America, and Japan (with greatly reduced competence, of course); we have not recognized that the so-called question of educational system only reflects a vertical cross section of the social division of labor, and the so-called question of curriculum only reflects a horizontal cross section of the social division of labor. The depth and breadth of what we are able to achieve and what we have achieved at present in social division of labor should be reflected in the length of our schooling and in the complexity of our range of courses. The experience of both the base areas and the Great Rear areas proves that to simply rely on education to promote industrialization is to fall for the fallacy of putting the cart before the horse.

In that case, what should regulations and curricula consist of in the base areas at the present time?

First, we will discuss regulations. Following from the concrete situation in the base areas, school regulations should incorporate the following special points:

First, cadre education should be given more weight than mass education. This is not only because cadres are the vanguard of the masses and as such are in greater need of cultivation and improvement — the objective of their cultivation and improvement is to benefit the masses — but also because there are, after all, limits on the nature of the popular education that can be provided in the environment of the peasant villages; regular, school education at the level of upper primary [grades 4-5] or above falls within the scope of cadre education (that is, we cannot now hope that all children or adults will receive upper primary "citizen's education"; all students graduating from upper primary level or higher-level schools should, as much as possible, be assigned to definite tasks; education in such schools should also suit the objectives of our work). For the above reasons, the education department of the government must devote more of its attention to cadre education, and mass education must be carried out to a large extent by the people, with the role of the government limited to that of giving leadership and assistance.

Second, in the education of cadres the improvement of cadres in service should be more important than the cultivation of future cadres. Previously, the standard educational system upper-level primary schools accepted as a rule only graduates from the one school level directly below; these students, under an educational policy correctly linked with practical needs, could of course learn to take on the responsibilities for various appropriate tasks but, after all, they lack experience. On the other hand, the numbers of cadres who already had experience failed to receive supplementary education; they were not regarded as an important element of the student body of schools at the upper primary level or above, and at most received simple training administered by government departments other than the education department, or through the party or military system. This is a completely backward situation and is in urgent need of correction. We must make sure that each level of school above the upper primary level absorbs active cadres for study; ordinary students will of course study with them and learn through contact with them, and instructors will also learn through contact with them, thus helping school education respond more directly to real needs.

Third, in mass education the education of adults should take precedence over the education of children. Adults in the peasant villages are currently the main bearers of the serious responsibilities of the war and production. Although educating them is unavoidably difficult, by improving their situation one step through education, we can improve the situation in the war and in production one step, and the results will be immediate — unlike educating children, the applications of which have several limitations. In the past, the base area educational departments regarded children's education as their main responsibility; on the one hand, this is imitating the approach of Europe and America, where there is no major problem of adult illiteracy and where there is no war being fought, or imitating the approach of feudal China, where no responsibility was taken for the education of adults, and where the education of children was simply a way of buying off the masses; on the other hand, it is running away from the problem, avoiding reality, and bowing to convention (this is not to say that the education of children is in itself of no value). On the whole, this too is a completely backward situation and is in urgent need of correction.

Fourth, in the case of either cadre education or mass education, the teaching of knowledge and skills directly necessary for the war and production must take precedence over other so-called general cultural education. Actually, all cultural knowledge is in some way applicable; the distinction made between "pure science" and applied science, between pure art and practical art, is at best constrained. But it cannot be denied that if we select on the basis of class differences and according to how much time we have, some things will be more directly applicable than others. Education in the base areas is for the people, for the people's war, and for production; therefore we must give emphasis to the knowledge and skills that are needed for the war and for production, not only in classes in political science and in political schools but also in classes in culture and cultural schools. We are in favor of cultural education, especially for workers, peasants, and cadres, but we do not favor that form of so-called cultural education that is irrelevant or barely relevant to the needs of the people's war or production. Past practice has already proved that such an education is ineffective and unwelcome. Of course it would be nice if the people and the cadres could learn some purely interesting things — from China or the West, old or new — but under the present circumstances we must for the most part restrict ourselves to that which is necessary. Even in teaching reading and writing we should restrict ourselves to what is necessary; certain worker and peasant cadres and cadres of the army corps go straight to the K'ang-hsi dictionary* when they wish to study culture, which results in precisely this sort of superfluous cultural education. In other cases there are educational workers who limit their teaching to the classroom, to what lies between the covers of books, who regard the teaching of a great many important skills as beyond the scope of educational work and do not study or teach these subjects. This kind of mistake is another result of the past emphasis on purely general cultural education.

Fifth, from what is described above, it can be seen that the grade levels, admission requirements, and scheduling of the school year in our school system cannot be arranged and managed in the way the old school system was. Generally speaking, we will have a three-level system: mass education (adult and child education in the villages, towns, and cities); primary-level cadre education (improvement and cultivation of district personnel and subdistrict and township cadres conducted on the district or subregion level), and middle-level cadre education (the improvement and cultivation of border region personnel and district and subdistrict cadres, as well as cadres engaged in agricultural, industrial, commercial, medical, artistic, and cultural work conducted at the military region and border region levels). As to high-level cadre education, because it is beyond the capacity of the base-area standard educational system, we will not discuss it here. Schools on these three levels, although they may sometimes take the names primary school, middle school, or university, are obviously substantively different. The length of the total course at each school level may differ according to local conditions; at any one level it may be as little as less than one year or as much as three or four years; the highest two years of primary school under the old six-year system may, in consideration of local circumstances, be included as part of elementary cadre schooling, made into preparatory classes for standard middle school, or

*Compiled in the Ch'ing dynasty during the K'ang-hsi Emperor's reign, 1662-1723 — Peter J. Seybolt.

set up as independent classes. In principle, mass schools will be run by the people; whether or not students pay fees is of course to be decided by the people, but we must persuade and assist the masses to give poor children an opportunity to enter school. In government-operated cadre schools, students covered by the government quota should as a rule not pay for schooling; but, at the same time, students outside of the quota should be allowed to study if they pay their way. In any case, under this type of school system it will be impossible to avoid putting students of different levels of advancement in the same class in some cases, and for this reason it will be almost impossible to coordinate rigorously all grade levels in the schools; but this should not be a source of concern. In peacetime, such a situation would certainly not be ideal (although in peacetime as well such a situation is not entirely avoidable); but in time of war, it is both consistent with our overall regulations and in line with our ideals — if our schools are capable of nothing more than taking a group of six-year olds and shutting them up in the same class until they are twenty or so, cutting them off from any close contact with the various people around them because of their "unequal degree of learning" (there are two sides to this so-called "unequal degree of learning": although children in school may have a higher degree of general cultural knowledge than the people, their knowledge of the war and of production is considerably lower) — if this is what we call being educated, then it would be more to the point to say they are being wasted than to say they are being educated; to be "educated" in such a way is to become a waste product of the times.

Sixth, as can also be seen from the above description, our in-school education cannot be separated from the various practical activities of the war and of production. For this reason the organizational form of our schools will be changed in many ways; the gap between in-school education and in-field or in-office education is by no means too large to be spanned. If popular education is to become widespread, then it must adopt several forms — winter school, half-day school, night school, weekly school, circuit schools, short-term training classes, literacy groups, a little teachers system, an apprenticeship system, and so on. In the same way, cadre education can also adopt a variety of approaches — winter school, part-time school, night school, weekly school, a rotation system of training, a work-group system, a practical study system, a work-aid system (a school assists a work agency study a certain problem or participate in carrying out a certain task). In all our schools and especially in our cadre schools, we should also do our best to promote and lead students in self-study, so that students become capable of solving problems and cultivate correct habits; this will also be a factor in linking our schools closely with both in-field and in-office education.

What sort of curriculum should these schools have? This must be decided in the light of conditions in the various base areas, the composition of the student body, and the nature and format of the schools; a fixed course schedule is of no value. Generally speaking, there are some courses we should cut down, some we should change, and some we should increase. Which courses should be cut down? The general objective of the popular schools is to teach reading, writing, and accounting; therefore our primary schools should have as their main courses only reading and arithmetic (first of all, abacus), with the goal of increasing the rate of efficiency of learning, shortening the term of study, and expanding the number of students. The more important these goals are, the shorter and more concentrated the curriculum should be; if there is only one course, that is fine. A complex primary school curriculum reflects the fact that in a capitalist country, because they wish to take part in the industrial life in the cities, the children (but not all the children) must have a great deal of general knowledge; because they do not wish to participate in the domestic labor of an agricultural society, the time they spend studying is greater; in this respect the peasant villages of China's base areas at the present do not "measure up." In the past, cadre schools — that is, those that correspond to middle schools and universities under the old system — taught many attractive but useless courses. In the Great Rear areas, those kinds of courses are the main, or at least the partial, reason why education is divorced from use and graduates are unemployed. In the base areas it is even more important that those courses be completely eliminated; those that still have some usefulness should be made electives for a minority of students. On the other hand, there are a number of courses that are basically quite useful, but in the past their content has been very poorly worked out; the content of such courses should be reordered. For example, literature and mathematics have always been considered important courses, but very often middle school students who had studied for five or six years were unable to act as reporters for a wall newspaper or keep accounts for a cooperative. This is because the old educational policy was aimed at training minor litterateurs and mathematicians, not at training propaganda and accounting workers who knew how to function in real life. The record of the social science curriculum of the base area schools in the past was even worse. All this must be reformed. In addition, some courses must be added to the curriculum. First of all, all cadre schools must teach courses on the general situation in the base areas, or on reconstruction in the base areas. Moreover, these courses should be made the soul of the entire curriculum and learning process. Wherever there are relatively complicated techniques required for specific forms of work, which must be taught separately, then such instruction should become the basis for important courses or even special training programs or schools, so as to thoroughly undermine the unwillingness of some students to engage in technical work. As for popular schools, generally speaking, where necessary and possible, courses in skills related to the war or to production should be taught in addition to the courses in reading and arithmetic. Under special circumstances, specialized training programs or schools may be established for popular education as well; for example, training for the people's self-defense militia, schools for women to learn weaving and sewing, etc.

In sum, the incompatibility of the old course curriculum with our new educational principles and regulations and the need for a new course curriculum cannot be questioned. But since any specific course curriculum represents a specific range of knowledge, we must give a great deal of careful thought and consideration to this new curriculum. Although our chief mistakes in the past in this matter were characterized by dogmatism, this is certainly no basis for saying that we can now approve of empiricism; yet this tendency is already incipient. For example, there is one type of opinion that favors practical activities alone and does not respect even essential academic knowledge. Another type of opinion is satisfied with sketchy and fragmented reports and lectures and does not emphasize systematizing and theorizing about experience and its conclusions and putting them into shape as courses and teaching materials. A third type of opinion assumes that as long as we emphasize the present we need not worry about the future at all, or it assumes that each base area can be completely ignorant of the situation and experiences of the nation as a whole, even to the extent of maintaining that each subregion or district should have a completely unique and self-contained set of courses and teaching materials, or that these should be changed with each year and each season. These opinions are evidence of another type of danger, and we must reject them. No single truth should be one-sidedly overstated; our model in carrying out all our work is that of the struggle between two lines of battle; this applies also to problems of education.

30

BORDER REGION GOVERNMENT DIRECTIVE ON PROMOTING THE STUDY OF MODEL SCHOOLS AND ON EXPERIMENTATION WITH POPULAR-MANAGEMENT PRIMARY SCHOOLS (April 18, 1944)*

Educational Policy in the Shen-Kan-Ning Border Region

Subregion commissioners and district chiefs:

Past primary education in the Border Region, compared with the situation before the revolution, has shown very great progress; but it still retains several shortcomings left over from the old style of education, especially in having educational policies that are still not suited to the needs of society and the masses in the Border Region. First of all, in terms of its content, the new education does not make use of the experiences and problems in the actual lives of the Border Region population. On the contrary, its content is a complex curriculum not relevant to the urgent needs of the villages. As a result, students are cut off from production and alienated from their

*"Pien-ch'ü cheng-fu kuan-yü t'i-ch'ang yen-chiu fan-li chi shih-hsing min-pan hsiao-hsüeh ti chih-shih hsin." Shen-Kan-Ning pien-ch'ü chiao-yü fang-chi, rev. ed. (edited and printed in the Civil Affairs Office of the Shen-Kan-Ning Border Region Government, September 1944), pp. 4-9.

families; when students return to their homes they are unable to "look after the homestead." After graduating from primary school they look down on manual labor and are unwilling to serve the peasants. Female students entering the primary schools become estranged from their families, clamor for divorce, and create other problems. These influences hinder the development of production among the masses, destroy family relationships, and are contradictory to the present need to build up production in the Border Region. Because of this, the populace in a large number of areas is unwilling to send its children to school, thus putting severe limitations on the projects to achieve universal education and to eliminate illiteracy. Since undergoing rectification last year, the government and cadres at various levels have gradually come to realize these facts. In different areas, the policy and content of education have begun to be newly transformed. For example, the Sui-te Subregion has put forward a policy of "uniting labor units, social organizations, government, and families with the schools" and has, moreover, already begun to move in the direction of reform. In other areas, since last fall, certain schools have begun to focus on combining the content of education with production and family life. For example, the Yenan City Complete Primary School, beginning in the latter half of last year, has added, above the fourth grade level, instruction in accounting, letter-writing, map-making, contract-writing, and abacus; it has in addition begun advising the students to pay attention both to their studies and to manual labor; students are encouraged to return home and help with household work. Students are taught to understand manners and to respect their parents; during New Year's, they participated in the *yang-ko* drama and joined in anti-epidemic propaganda work; all this was a first step forward, and it earned the support of the masses. This spring, therefore, a great many among the masses in Yenan City changed their earlier attitudes toward the schools and sent their children to register. As a further example, at the most recent combined teachers' meeting in Yenan District the policy of "combining production with education" was put forth. The Fu-hsien [Shensi] First Complete Primary School and the Tzu-ch'ang First Complete Primary School specified definite responsibilities for production, bringing about a combination of education and production; similar developments have taken place elsewhere. All this makes it very clear that primary education in the Border Region is already moving in a new direction, and this development makes us very happy. In this we have further proof that if only we think of the masses, plan for the masses, and adapt to the needs of the masses, our schools will be run well and the people will certainly welcome them. Naturally, as of today this transformation has not yet become widespread, but has merely started.

Our second problem is that the form of the Border Region primary schools has in the past also been unsuited to the needs of the masses in the Border Region. Because it is very difficult to broaden the attack on the old system, curricula, and schools, we sometimes find only a single school on the township level or even on the subdistrict level or above. Thus most of the students must leave home and live at school and are therefore unable to participate in household production; instead they increase the financial burden of their families. Moreover, because they have no way of learning of activities at the schools, and because the school year is long, members of the students' families become suspicious, thinking that once their children enter school they will become "public personnel." The result is that the majority of families are unwilling or unable to send their children to school, thus greatly inhibiting the spread of education in the Border Region. In addition, the standards of our teachers are not high enough, we are out of contact with the masses in the villages, and district- and subdistrict-level governments are deficient in ordinary leadership; therefore it is not easy to run our schools well. We only know how to have the government come in and operate the schools; we do not understand how to apply correctly the force of the masses, how to have schools run by the people themselves in accordance with their own ambitions; therefore, both the form and content of education are decided by the people. Formerly, in fact, there were popular-management primary schools in various areas, but in those cases the government was always either applying restrictions or simply letting the schools run themselves without even offering guidance. Now we must have a great transformation; we must take the majority or perhaps all of the primary schools and turn them over to the local masses to run by themselves; the government will then give material assistance and will offer guidance in matters of policy. Under this program, we must work in the future toward having a popular-management village school in every village; through cooperation, the village schools will be able to run winter study programs, night schools, and reading groups so as to achieve the goal of completely eliminating illiteracy in the Border Region. This new form of popular-management, government-assistance primary school has already begun to appear this year in Yenan City and Yenan District; there they have already accumulated a certain amount of valuable experience, which we must do our best to circulate.

At each level of government, attention should be paid to reforming primary education, promoting the study of models in each area, commending improvements in schools and teachers, finding heroes of education, collecting materials, consolidating experience, and preparing all this information to present at the National People's Educational Conference, which is being readied for the latter half of this year; our hope is that a draft program for thorough reform may be put together and carried out on a broad scale next spring. In addition, in response to this program for popular-management, government-assistance education, popular-management primary schools should be promoted, with each district experimenting in at least one locality; moreover, currently operating government-management primary schools should gradually be transformed into popular-management primary schools; this is one element of citizens education to which government at each level should pay serious attention in the first half of this year. Regarding the popular-management, government-assistance policy, we wish to clarify the following points:

1. The format of popular-management primary schools and the rate of implementation of this policy should be determined in all cases according to specific conditions in each area; no single rule will apply. At present there is a great demand among people of different areas to start primary schools; according to information now available there are among newly opened primary schools both those completely operated by the people as well as those jointly public and private. In general, if the people want to make ordinary primary schools into popular-management schools, in cases where the masses actually have the capability for operating them, they should be turned over to popular management; eventually the point should be reached where all primary schools from the central ones on down are run by the people.

2. Regarding the system, content, etc., of education in the popular-management primary schools, the opinions of the masses should be respected. Neither the overall amount of time spent in school nor the hours of class attendance (full days or half days, length of the school year) need follow a consistent rule. Course curricula may be accomodated to the desires of the people, and those courses that for the time being are not urgently needed may be abolished. If the masses wish to have instruction in only reading, writing, and abacus and do not want other subjects taught, then this also may be permitted. (In principle, we hope it will in any case be possible to teach an understanding of such political and production activities as students will come in contact with in the course of their daily life in the villages.) As for teaching materials, if the people are unwilling to use the textbooks we have used in the past, if they wish to use the traditional primers and character books, we can discuss it with them and write some texts in the old format but with the new content. (The Border Region Department of Education is drafting new textbooks especially for the latter possibility.) However, the people should be informed that excessively old-fashioned materials are impossible for young children to understand, and that to study them in this day and age is of no use anyway. In the employment of

instructors as well, the people may be allowed to choose those whom they trust, as long as they are good people; it doesn't matter, moreover, if they are somewhat old; in this the government should give guidance and assistance. If the people wish us to hire teachers for them, then we can make introductions. In other respects, it is not necessary for us to become involved; for example, in specifying the number of students, as few as ten or eight is fine. Recently, some district governments have suggested that only if there are more than thirty students and certain equipment will popularly managed schools be permitted; this is inappropriate. Selection of sites for schools, expenses, instructor's salaries, etc., may all be left up to the people to decide.

3. The policy of popular management cannot be divorced from that of government assistance. Popular-management schools cannot be allowed to run their own course; it is incorrect to think that we will lighten our responsibilities through popular management; in fact the reverse is true; we must strengthen our leadership. At the beginning of the period of popular management, district-level officials must pay especially close attention; there should be persons taking regular responsibility for supervision, inspection, lending assistance, and solving the problems of the people at any time, rectifying errors without bias. But the responsibility for direct and specific leadership must gradually devolve to the subdistrict heads and township chiefs. In the future, investigation of popular-management primary schools should be part of the administrative responsibilities of township and subregion heads, with district-level governments taking overall responsibility. Only in this way will popular-management schools be run well and develop in the future. We must be critical of the fact that in the past, subdistrict and township chiefs did not raise many questions about education. Before the policy of popular management and government assistance can be carried out, the subregion special commissioner's office and leaders in district governments must discuss it carefully at the political affairs conference; moreover, subdistrict and township cadres

should be called together to meet and discuss this directive and pass it down; it is essential that each cadre understand it if we are to effect a thorough transformation of primary school education in every area in the future. Please accept our regards.

Chairman Lin Po-ch'ü, Vice Chairman Li Ting-ming, Director of the Education Department Liu Shih, Vice Director of the Education Department Ho Lien-ch'eng

31

REGARDING THE NEW CURRICULUM FOR MIDDLE SCHOOLS*

Liberation Daily

The Northwest Bureau Propaganda Department [of the Communist Party] and the Provincial Department of Education of the Border Region Government, with the assistance of the [Party] Central Propaganda Department, have already decided upon the main content of the curriculum and fields of study for a three year (six semester) course in the secondary level normal schools in the Border Region, and have assigned special personnel to edit the teaching materials. The basic points of the curriculum and the time apportioned are as follows:

Border Region construction (1st through 3rd semesters, 4 hours per week); general political knowledge (4th through 6th semesters, 3 hours per week); national literature (1st through 4th semesters, 5 hours per week – 5th and 6th semesters, 4 hours per week); mathematics (1st through 4th semesters, 4 hours per week – 5th and 6th semesters, 3 hours per week);

*"Kuan-yü chung-teng hsüeh-hsiao hsin k'o-ch'eng." Chieh-fang jih-pao, May 27, 1944. This document was reprinted in Shen-Kan-Ning pien-ch'ü chiao-yü fang-chi [Educational Policy in the Shen-Kan-Ning Border Region], rev. ed. (edited and printed in the Civil Affairs Office of the Shen-Kan-Ning Border Region Government, September 1944), pp. 24-26.

history and geography (1st through 4th semesters, 3 hours per week); natural science (1st through 4th semesters, 3 hours per week); production (5th and 6th semesters, 3 hours per week); medicine (5th and 6th semesters, 3 hours per week). The schedule of classes for each semester is as follows (number of hours per week in parentheses):

1st semester: Border Region construction (4), national literature (5), mathematics (4), history and geography (3), natural science (3);

2nd semester: Border Region construction (4), national literature (5), mathematics (4), history and geography (3), natural science (3);

3rd semester: Border Region construction (4), national literature (5), mathematics (4), history and geography (3), natural science (3);

4th semester: general political knowledge (3), national literature (5), mathematics (4), history and geography (3), natural science (3);

5th semester: general political knowledge (3), national literature (4), mathematics (3), production (3), medicine (3);

6th semester: general political knowledge (3), national literature (4), mathematics (3), production (3), medicine (3).

There are four special characteristics of this schedule:

1. It is practical. Making Border Region construction the first item and production and medicine the last two items develops in the students, upon entering school, an orientation toward serving the people of the Border Regions, and toward the end of the course they will acquire a grasp of the technology necessary for serving the people of the Border Region. This is a change from the dogmatic old style of teaching students 10 or 20 courses, none of which were relevant to the Border Region.

2. It is simple. There are only eight subjects in three years; in the first three semesters class time is only nineteen hours per week; in the fourth semester, only eighteen hours; and in the last two semesters, only sixteen hours; this is a reduction

by half of the old system, which eliminates an unnecessary burden on the students so they have more time to carry out extracurricular study and activities.

3. It is concentrated. By studying only eight subjects in three years, only five at one time in any single semester, with at least three hours per week per subject, the students will be able to focus their powers of concentration on the work they are covering; this is unlike the old system, where students were burdened with an overly complex curriculum and most of the subjects were studied only one or two semesters, with perhaps an hour or two per week for each subject, and each student trying to pursue two or three majors; as a result, they were unable to get a deep impression of what they had studied — they would have been better off not studying at all.

4. It is integrated. For example, Border Region construction and history and geography are studied first, and political knowledge later, which is moving from the concrete to the abstract; natural science and some mathematics are studied first, followed by production and medicine, moving from basic principles to applications. Mathematics, history and geography, natural science, and political knowledge are not subdivided, as under the old system, into several smaller sections; this is intended to help the students achieve an integrated concept of what they learn.

The contents of each course have been researched carefully so that they are based on practical needs. According to our understanding, Border Region construction includes the history and geography of the Border Region, its political policies, and its organization; general political knowledge includes general knowledge of economics and politics, knowledge of the War of Resistance Against Japan and of the Three Principles of the People, and methods for organizing life and work; the main point of national literature is to cultivate the ability to read and write correctly, applying the practical vocabulary used in daily work; the purpose of the mathematics course is to develop necessary skills in accounting and statistics for the finance and economics of cooperatives and other departments; history and geography will teach Chinese history before the Opium War in the first semester, and Chinese history of the last hundred years, with an emphasis on recent history since the May Fourth Movement, in the second semester; only what is essential in world history will be taught during these two semesters; the third semester will cover Chinese geography, and the fourth semester, world geography, in both of which the emphasis will be on economic and political geography; the course in natural science will, relative to what is necessary for the War of Resistance and for production, provide the students a comprehensive and systematized general understanding of natural phenomena and the laws of nature. Production will be weighted in favor of agricultural studies, also covering elementary concepts of industry and commerce; medicine will concentrate on simple useful techniques of midwifery, first aid, preventive and veterinary medicine, etc., as well as including the study of the nature of some commonly encountered Chinese and Western medicines; these studies will be aimed at broadening the popular hygiene movement in the Border Region.

32

YENAN UNIVERSITY EDUCATIONAL POLICY AND TEMPORARY REGULATIONS (May 21, 1944)*

Educational Policy in the Shen-Kan-Ning Border Region

I. General Educational Policies

1. The objective of this school is to train and raise the capacity of New Democratic and Revolutionary Three People's Principles cadres to do the actual work of political, economic, and cultural construction in accord with the needs of the War of Resistance and Border Region construction.

2. This school will promote education on Chinese revolutionary history and on the present situation in order to improve the students' knowledge of revolutionary theory and their ideas for establishing New Democracy, that is, the Revolutionary Three Principles of the People. It will also promote education in the way in which one views life and in methods of thought, so as to

*"Yen-an ta-hsüeh chiao-yü fang-chi chi chan-hsing fang-an." Shen-Kan-Ning pien-ch'ü chiao-yü fang-chi, rev. ed. (edited and printed in the Civil Affairs Office of the Shen-Kan-Ning Border Region Government, September 1944), pp. 27-36.

cultivate in the students a revolutionary stand and a work style of seeking the truth by relying on facts.

3. The following methods should be used to correlate the education of this school with the actual working offices and actual activities of the Border Region, so as to elevate practical experience to the level of theory and to achieve a unity of theory and practice and a balance of study and application:

a) A specific organizational or working relationship with appropriate offices doing actual work should be established. Those in positions of responsibility in the appropriate offices doing actual work should, in accord with the concrete situation, directly participate in the leadership of educational work in relevant academies and departments of this school.

b) The principal teaching content of this school should be the specific and general plans and the summarized experience of all aspects of Border Region construction. The rule for technical courses is that they must meet the immediate needs of Border Region construction.

c) Those doing research in this school should carry out planned and systematic research on all aspects of the real problems of Border Region construction; in accord with the concrete situation, they should establish a time and place for participating in the work of appropriate offices doing actual work.

d) During their period of study, the students at this school should be sent for an established period of time to specific offices doing actual work in order to practice what they have studied.

4. This school should combine education and production to cultivate in the students a constructive spirit, a habit of labor, and a labor viewpoint through organized labor.

5. This school should carry on teaching through collective mutual aid on the foundation of independent study; faculty and students should learn from each other so that among them book knowledge and practical experience will merge. At the same time, democratic teaching should be promoted to encourage students to ask questions when they are having difficulty, and

to encourage a spirit of heated debate. The object is to cultivate a capacity for independent thought and criticism.

II. Study System

1. This school consists of the Administration Academy, the Academy of Natural Sciences, the Lu Hsün Academy of Literature and Art, and the Medical Department.* In accordance with these distinctions, all types of technical cadres will be trained. The Administration Academy shall have departments of administration, law, finance, and education. The Academy of Natural Sciences shall have departments of industry, agriculture, and chemistry. The Lu Hsün Academy of Literature and Art shall have departments of drama and music, art, and literature. Each department shall be further divided into classes and groups reflecting the nature of their specialized studies.

In addition, this school should also establish all types of supplementary training classes in accord with temporary or special needs.

2. The period of training in the various academies in this school is temporarily set as follows: Administrative Academy, two years; Academy of Natural Sciences, three years; the Lu Hsün Academy of Literature and Art, two years; the Medical Department, one to two years. However, the periods of study definitely should not be arbitrarily determined. The main standard is to finish study of the stipulated course.

3. In carrying on education in this school, study within the school (including lectures, reading, discussions, debates, etc.) and practice out of school are equally important. Of the total study time, study within the school should occupy sixty percent and practice should occupy forty percent. Each academy and department can adjust this ratio in accord with its concrete situation.

4. All faculty, staff, and students in this school must regularly

---

*Earlier in the Yenan period these were all independent institutions — Peter J. Seybolt.

participate in productive labor. The time spent, compared with study time, should be eighty percent for study, twenty percent for production. For faculty and staff this proportion can be increased or decreased according to their specific work.

III. Courses

1. Course design.

a) There are two kinds of courses in this school: general courses for the whole school, and special courses in the various academies and departments. There are also supplementary aid courses to meet the special needs of a portion of the student body.

b) The content of the general courses for the whole school shall be the history of the Chinese revolution, study of the current situation, and cultivation of a revolutionary view of life and methods of thought. The content of the special courses of the various academies and departments shall be the study of theories and policies related to a particular occupation, training in knowledge and skills, etc. The content of the supplementary aid courses shall be supplementary study of culture [i.e., literacy], etc.

c) Of the total period of study in the school, the general courses for the whole school should occupy thirty percent of the time, and all of the special courses of the academies and departments, seventy percent. Of the special courses, theory and policy courses should constitute thirty percent, and courses in occupational knowledge and skills, seventy percent. These proportions can be adjusted by the various academies and departments in accord with the concrete situation.

2. Courses.

a) General courses for the whole school

(1) General principles of Border Region construction

(2) History of the Chinese revolution

(3) Revolutionary view of life

(4) Current affairs education

(4) Agriculture Department
   (a) Agricultural botany
   (b) Agricultural chemistry
   (c) Soils and fertilizer
   (d) Genetics
   (e) Plant diseases and insect damage
   (f) General discussion of Border Region agriculture
   (g) Organization and management of agricultural production
   (h) Study of plants
   (i) Study of animals
   (j) Forestry
   (k) Gardening

d) Lu Hsün Academy of Literature and Art
(1) General courses for the whole academy: Discussion of literature and art (includes all questions on the history, present situation, and theory of literature and art
(2) Department of Drama and Music
   (a) Speech
   (b) Dance
   (c) Pronunciation and singing
   (d) Instrumental music
   (e) Folk songs
   (f) Study of famous compositions
   (g) Rehearsal and practice
   (h) Folk drama
   (i) Selective reading of famous plays
   (j) Present situation of the drama campaign
   (k) Present situation of the music campaign
   (l) Composition practice

Note: Two courses should be chosen from items (f), (i), (j), and (k).

(3) Art Department
   (a) Drawing
   (b) Sketching
   (c) Study of Chinese folk art
   (d) Study of world famous paintings

(e) Present situation of the art campaign
(f) Composition practice

(4) Literature Department
(a) Chinese literature
(b) Practical writing
(c) Study of the present situation in literature
(d) Selected readings of world famous writers
(e) Writing practice
(f) Journalism
(g) Border Region education

Note: Either (f) or (g) should be selected.

e) Medical Department (courses omitted)

IV. Teaching Methods

1. The first special characteristic of the teaching methods employed at this school is the unity of study and application; that is, on the one hand, study, and on the other, do. Go from the process of studying to doing, and from the process of doing to studying. Therefore:

a) The faculty and the students in this school who have the ability to work should actively participate in all aspects of relevant practical work and pursue research on all kinds of practical problems. In their practical work they should both immediately and directly serve the Border Region and carry on teaching. One of the main duties of the faculty is practical participation and practical research.

b) When the students have completed a period of study within the school, they should, as a general rule, go to the countryside for three months of practical training and then return to school to summarize their experience and to carry their study a step further. During their period of study in school, they should use the area near the school as a location for practical training.

c) In technical courses, practical training (or experimentation) is most important.

d) The main standard for testing the results of study in

this school is the ability to use what one has studied, the ability to implement knowledge (emphasizing practice and reflection).

2. The second special characteristic of teaching methods in this school is that independent study is primary and instruction by the teacher is supplementary. Collective mutual aid is carried out on the basis of independent study; mutual study between teachers and students is advocated. The whole school is organized for mutual aid in study among students at different levels and with different abilities. In general, teaching should be carried out by the following procedures:

a) Lectures: The teacher should lecture on only the main points in the content of a course. Emphasis should be on raising questions and stimulating the students to do research and follow leads.

b) Research: The students should do research, take notes, and hold discussions (conversations, debates, wall reports) based on practical materials indicated by the teacher.

c) Summarizing: After research is completed the teacher should gather the disputed points and the difficult problems that arise in the process of research and answer them separately, or make a relatively systematic summary of the whole course.

3. Fostering a spirit of democracy in teaching is the third special characteristic of the teaching methods of this school. Teachers have freedom to lecture, study, and do research. Differing ideas can be mutually debated and criticized. Students also can raise their views and criticisms of the teacher's lectures. In leadership, the emphasis should be on leadership in thought. Use of administrative methods to settle problems should be strenuously avoided.

Appendix

Biographical Guide

The following is a selected list of individuals that appear in the documents. Most of the information in this guide was taken from: Donald W. Klein and Ann B. Clark, Biographic Dictionary of Chinese Communism, 2 vols. (Cambridge: Harvard University Press, 1971); Chinese Communist Who's Who, 2 vols. (Taipei: Institute of International Relations, 1970); Who's Who in Communist China (Hong Kong: Union Research Institute, 1966). The following abbreviations are used: CCP (Chinese Communist Party), CCPCC (Central Committee of the CCP), GPCR (Great Proletarian Cultural Revolution), PLA (People's Liberation Army), PRC (People's Republic of China).

CHANG CHI-CH'UN 张际春

CCPCC member, 1956; deputy director of CCPCC Propaganda Department, 1954; director of Culture and Education Staff Office of the State Council, 1959. Criticized as revisionist in GPCR.

CHANG P'AN-SHIH 张盘石

Deputy director of CCPCC Propaganda Department, 1954; member of Presidium of National Conference of Advanced

Workers and Units in Education, Culture, Health, and Sports, 1960; Criticized in 1966 as follower of Lu Ting-i.

CH'EN HO-CH'IN 陈鹤琴

Prominent university educator before 1949; author of books on children's education and child psychology. Received B.A. at John Hopkins, M.A. in education at Columbia. Dean of Teachers College, Nanking University, 1949; president of Nanking Teachers College, 1954; vice chairman of Kiangsu Provincial Committee, 1956. Criticized as bourgeois educator in GPCR.

CH'EN TSENG-KU 陈曾固

Vice minister of education, 1954-1959; alternate member of Control Committee, CCPCC, 1962. Criticized for praise of Soviet education.

CH'I PEN-YÜ 戚本禹

Historian and author. Early critic of P'eng Chen (1961) and Liu Shao-ch'i (1963). Member of Central Cultural Revolution Group, 1966; deputy editor-in-chief of Hung-ch'i (Red Flag), 1967. Fell out of favor with Mao later in GPCR.

CHIANG NAN-HSIANG 蒋南翔

Alternate member of CCPCC, 1957-1966; member of Communist Youth League Central Committee, 1957-1966; vice minister of education in the State Council, 1960-1965; minister of higher education, 1965-1966; president of Tsinghua University, 1952-1966. Dismissed from all offices in 1966.

CH'IEN CHUN-JUI 钱俊瑞

Alternate member of CCPCC, 1956; vice minister of culture, 1959-1963; deputy director of Commission on Spare-Time Education. Fell from favor and lost official posts by 1964, probably for close association with USSR.

CHIEN PO-TSAN 翦伯赞

Historian and author of numerous books and articles. Chairman of History Department, Peking University, 1954; member of Standing Committee of Department of History and Social Sciences, Chinese Academy of Sciences, 1955; vice president, Peking University, 1959; member of Editorial Board of Li-shih yen-chiu [Historical Research], 1953. Condemned in 1966 for his bourgeois and feudal interpretations of history.

CH'IEN WEI-CH'ANG 钱伟长

Scientist, author of numerous books and articles. Professor of physics and applied mathematics at Tsinghua University, 1949; dean of instruction and member of Administrative Council, Tsinghua University, 1953; member of Secretariat, Chinese Academy of Sciences, 1954; vice president, Tsinghua University, 1956. Accused of being a rightist in 1957 and dismissed from all posts in 1958; cleared of rightist charge in 1960 after extensive self-criticism; came under attack again in GPCR.

CHOU EN-LAI 周恩来

Premier, PRC. Member of Standing Committee of CCPCC Politburo. Supported GPCR and emerged as No. 2 man in China after Lin Piao's fall.

CHOU YANG 周扬

Writer and translator. Alternate member of CCPCC, 1958-1966; deputy director of CCPCC Propaganda Department, 1954-1966; vice chairman of All-China Federation of Literature and Art, 1949. One of the "four men" criticized for bourgeois views on literature and art in 1966; dismissed from posts.

FENG TING 冯定

Member of Department of Philosophy and Social Sciences, Chinese Academy of Sciences, 1955; professor, Peking University, 1958; Studied in Moscow in 1930; very active in CCP activities during the war with Japan, 1937-1945. His three published books, especially Communist View of Life, have been severely criticized since 1964 for their bourgeois views.

FENG YU-LAN 冯友兰

Philosopher and author of many philosophic works. Director of research work, Department of the History of Chinese Philosophy, Peking University, 1953; member of Department of Philosophy and Social Sciences, Chinese Academy of Sciences, 1955. Criticized in 1957 rectification, reinstated, criticized for reactionary views in 1966.

HO LIEN-CH'ENG 贺连城

Vice director of Education Department of Shen-Kan-Ning Border Region, 1944. Not prominent after 1949.

HO WEI 何伟

Minister of education, 1964; diplomat in Foreign Ministry; ambassador to Hanoi, 1955-1962; Mayor of Canton, 1952-1955. Criticized in 1966 as anti-Maoist and executer of Liu Shao-ch'i line.

HSI CHUNG-HSÜN 习仲勳

Member of CCPCC, 1956; director of CCPCC Propaganda Department, 1953-1954; secretary general of State Council, 1953-1962 (officially removed in 1965); vice premier of State Council, 1959-1965. Criticized in GPCR, had been close associate of Liu Shao-ch'i and P'eng Te-huai.

HSIA YEN 夏衍

Playwright. CCP official in various posts; vice minister of State Council Ministry of Culture, 1954-1965 (dismissed in 1965); vice chairman of All-China Federation of Literature and Art, 1960. One of the "four men" criticized for bourgeois views on literature and art.

HSÜ LI-CH'ÜN 许立群

Deputy director, CCPCC Propaganda Department, 1961-1966; deputy editor-in-chief of Hung-ch'i [Red Flag], 1958; member of CCPCC Fourth National Committee, 1965. Criticized and removed from posts in 1966; worked with P'eng Chen to counter Mao.

HU CH'IAO-MU 胡乔木

Deputy director of CCPCC Propaganda Department, 1953; member of CCPCC, 1956; member of Department of Philosophy and Social Sciences, Chinese Academy of Sciences, 1965. Criticized for feudal intellectual attitudes and as backer of Liu Shao-ch'i in 1966 and removed from all posts.

LEI FENG 雷锋

An emulation model whose name has become synonymous with selflessness and hard work. Said to have been a common soldier who died on duty, leaving a diary in which he recorded his efforts to learn from and apply Chairman Mao's thought. A nationwide campaign to "learn from Lei Feng" began in January 1963.

LIN FENG 林枫

Specialist in cultural and educational affairs. President of Higher Party School, 1963-1966; member of CCPCC, 1945-1966. Criticized and dismissed from posts in 1966.

LIN MO-HAN 林默涵

Deputy director of CCPCC Propaganda Department, 1964; vice minister of culture, 1959; member of Presidium of National Conference of Advanced Culture and Education Workers, 1960. Criticized in 1966 for supporting Chou Yang's views on literature.

LIN PIAO 林彪

Named Mao's chosen successor at Ninth CCP National Congress, 1969; minister of national defense, 1959; member of CCPCC Politburo, 1955, and Politburo Standing Committee, 1958; vice premier, 1954. Fell from favor in October 1971 for reasons still not entirely clear.

LIU CHI-P'ING 刘季平

Vice minister of Ministry of Education and State Council, 1963; former deputy mayor of Shanghai and director of Health and Education Department of CCP Shanghai Municipal Committee, 1957. Criticized in GPCR for opposing Mao's plans for education.

LIU AI-FENG 刘皑风

Vice minister of education, 1958; Presidium member and

deputy secretary general of All-China Conference of Cultural and Educational Advanced Workers, 1960. Criticized in GPCR for worshiping foreign and ancient things.

LIU SHAO-CH'I 刘少奇

Vice chairman of CCPCC; CCPCC Politburo member since 1927; chairman of the Government of PRC, 1959; chairman of National Defense Council, 1959. Highest-ranking target of GPCR, dismissed from CCP in 1968 as principal person in authority taking the capitalist road. Often referred to as "China's Khrushchev."

LIU SHIH 柳湜

Director of Education Department of Shen-Kan-Ning Border Region, 1944; vice minister of education, 1952-1959. Labeled a rightist in 1957, label removed in 1961, reapplied in 1966.

LO JUI-CH'ING 罗瑞卿

CCPCC member, 1956; member of CCPCC Secretariat, 1962; full general in the army; vice premier, 1959; vice minister of national defense, 1959; chief of General Staff of PLA, 1959. In 1966 became major target of GPCR.

LU P'ING 陆平

CCP member; president of Peking University, 1960-1966. Removed as president of Peita after attack by Red Guards in 1966.

LU TING-I 陆定一

CCPCC member; alternate member of CCPCC Politburo; director of CCPCC Propaganda Department, 1946-1953,

1954-1966; minister of culture, 1965-1966. Criticized in 1966 as "king of the Palace of Hades" (Propaganda Department) and removed from all posts.

MA HSÜ-LUN 马叙论

Minister of education, 1949-1952; minister of higher education, 1952-1954; vice chairman of National Committee of Chinese People's Political Consultative Conference, 1965; member of Department of Philosophy and Social Sciences, Chinese Academy of Sciences. Criticized as bourgeois reactionary in 1966.

MAO YÜAN-HSIN 毛远新

Received one of Chairman Mao's major instructions on education when a student in 1964. No other information available.

NIEH YÜAN-TZU 聂元梓

Secretary, CCP Branch Committee, Department of Philosophy, Peking University, 1961-1962; lecturer in philosophy, Peking University; vice chairman of CCP Peking Municipal Committee, 1967; alternate member of Ninth CCPCC, 1969. One of seven people credited with writing the first "big character poster" in GPCR, she was particularly singled out by Chairman Mao.

P'ENG CHEN 彭真

Member of CCPCC Politiburo and Secretariat; mayor of Peking. Dismissed from all posts in August 1966.

P'ENG TE-HUAI 彭德怀

CCPCC member, 1945-1959; alternate member of CCPCC

Politburo, 1945-1954, full member, 1954-1959; Marshall of PLA, 1955; minister of national defense, 1954-1959. Policy conflict with Mao in 1959, removed from all offices; replaced by Lin Piao as minister of national defense.

PO I-PO 薄一波

CCPCC member; alternate member of CCPCC Politburo, 1956; vice premier, 1956; chairman of State Economic Commission, 1956. Criticized as revisionist in 1966 and removed from all posts.

TAI PO-T'AO 戴伯韬

Member of work group appointed by Lu Ting-i to draft new middle and primary school teaching materials, 1961. Criticized in GPCR as a reactionary academic authority. No other information available.

T'AO CHU 陶铸

CCPCC member, 1956-1967; member of CCPCC Secretariat, July 1966; replaced Lu Ting-i as director of CCPCC Propaganda Department, 1966. August 1966 ranked fourth in CCPCC Politiburo; 1967 dismissed from all posts.

T'AO HSING-CHIH 陶行知

Educational reformer, former student of John Dewey. Experimented with new forms of rural education later adopted by CCP, but considered bourgeois in his general orientation. Died in 1946.

TENG HSIAO-P'ING 邓小平

Member of CCPCC Politiburo 1955, and Politburo Standing Committee, 1956; general secretary of CCPCC, 1954-1956;

vice premier of State Council, 1954; vice chairman of National Defense Council, 1954. Dismissed from all posts in mid-1967 for "taking the capitalist road."

T'IEN HAN 田汉

Playwright. Vice chairman of All-China Federation of Literature and Art, 1960-1966. One of the "four men" criticized for bourgeois views on literature and art in 1966; dismissed from all posts.

TUNG CH'UN-TS'AI 董纯才

Vice minister of education, 1952-1965; secretary of CCP Committee, Ministry of Education, 1958. Criticized in GPCR for indiscriminate borrowing from USSR.

T'UNG TA-LIN 童大林

Associate of Lu Ting-i. Criticized as bourgeois reactionary in GPCR. No other information available.

WANG CHIA-HSIANG 王稼祥

Secretary of CCPCC Secretariat, 1956-1966; vice minister of Ministry of Foreign Affairs, 1949; ambassador to USSR, 1949-1951. Criticized as counterrevolutionary revisionist and removed from all posts in 1966.

WANG HAI-JUNG 王海蓉

Student when GPCR began; Mao Tse-tung encouraged him to promote student rebellion. No other information available.

WU HAN 吴晗

Historian, primarily of the Ming dynasty. Vice chairman of the CCP Peking Municipal Committee. Author of The Dismissal of Hai Jui, anti-Maoist play that sparked GPCR. Dismissed from all posts in 1966.

YANG HAN-SHENG 阳翰笙

Playwright. CCP member, 1925; vice chairman (1953) and general secretary (1960) of All-China Federation of Literature and Art. Criticized as antisocialist in 1964, one of the "four men" criticized for bourgeois views on literature and art; dismissed from all posts in 1966.

YANG HSIEN-CHEN 杨献珍

CCPCC member; president of Higher Party School, 1955-1961? Attacked in 1964 for his theory "combine two into one" (see glossary).

YANG HSIU-FENG 杨秀峰

A top educational official from 1952 to 1965. CCPCC member; president of the Supreme People's Court, 1965; minister of higher education, 1964; criticized as revisionist in 1966. Died in 1968.

YANG SHANG-K'UN 杨尚昆

Deputy secretary general of CCPCC, 1955-1956; alternate secretary of CCPCC Secretariat, 1956. Criticized in GPCR for colluding against Mao with USSR.

YANG SHUI-TS'AI 杨水才

Founder of an agricultural middle school in 1963 which has

become a model for others to follow. No other information available.

YAO WEN-YÜAN 姚文元

Journalist and writer. Member of the Central Cultural Revolution Group, 1966; member of the CCPCC and the CCPCC Politiburo, 1969. Achieved prominence only after start of GPCR.

YEH SHENG-T'AO 叶圣陶

Vice minister of education, 1954; member of All-China Federation of Literature and Art, 1949; director of People's Literature Press, 1962. Criticized for bourgeois views in GPCR.

YUNG WEN-T'AO 雍文涛

Secretary of Secretariat of CCP Peking Municipal Committee, January 1966; deputy director of CCPCC Propaganda Department, August 1966; deputy director of CCPCC Culture and Education Department, August 1966. Dismissed from all offices in January 1967, charged with being T'ao Chu's agent.

Glossary

"Academic Authorities" [hsüeh-shu ch'üan-wei 学术权威]

pejorative reference to those in higher education who do not adhere to Mao's mass line.

"Anti-Adventurism" [fan-ch'ang-chin 反冒进]

said to be Liu Shao-ch'i's position in regard to Mao's education policies in 1957.

"Both Criticize and Use" [i p'i erh yung 一批二用]

refers to proper handling of teachers, directed especially at those who mistakenly feel that teachers must conform completely to the Maoist line before resuming their teaching.

"Bourgeois Theory of Human Nature" [tzu-ch'an chieh-chi jen-hsing lun 资产阶级人性论]

assumes that all people, regardless of time or place, are basically the same; contradicts the theory that human thought, inclinations, interests are shaped in very important ways by social and material conditions.

"Cadre" [kan-pu 干部]

a person holding an official leadership position in Party, army, or government.

"Combine Two into One" [ho erh erh i 合二而一]

the philosophic theory, associated particularly with Yang Hsien-chen, which contradicts Mao's theory that "one divides into two," q. v. The theory is especially reprehensible to Maoists for counseling class harmony rather than class struggle.

"Compradore Foreign Slave Mentality" or "Creeping Along on All Fours" or "Creeping Along at a Snail's Pace" [mai-pan yang-nu p'a-hsing che-hsüeh 卖办洋奴爬行哲学]

refers to the attitude of those who look abroad for solutions to China's problems, use foreign textbooks in schools, etc.

"Creative Study and Application" (of Mao's Works) or "Living Study and Application" or "Active Study and Use" [huo-hsüeh huo-yung 活学活用]

instructions for combining theory and practice, making one relate to and enrich the other — admonishment to avoid abstract study or random activity.

"Dissect a Sparrow" [chieh-p'o ma-chüeh 解剖麻雀]

to experiment with something on a small scale before applying it widely.

"Experts Should Manage Schools" [chuan-chia chih-hsiao 专家治校]

a bourgeois revisionist concept.

"Fewer but Better" or "Few but Essential" [shao erh ching 少而精]

refers to Mao's directive to reduce the course load and concentrate on essentials.

"Fight Self, Criticize Revisionism" or "Fight Selfishness. . ." [tou ssu p'i hsiu 斗私批修]

Mao's instruction to all cadres, school personnel, etc.

"Five Fixes" or "Five Determinations" [wu-ting 五 定]

"determine the leadership, instructors, system, location, and activities" of newly established schools: instructions to those helping to establish schools in backward, rural areas.

"Four Men" or "Four Fellows" [ssu-t'iao han-tzu 四条汉子]

refers to Chou Yang, Hsia Yen, T'ien Han, and Yang Han-sheng, whose views on literature and art were not in accord with those of Mao Tse-tung.

"From Theory to Theory" [ts'ung li-lun tao li-lun 从理论到理论]

bourgeois revisionist educational method that removes theory from practice and is of no benefit to workers and peasants.

"General Line" [tsung lu-hsien 总路线]: "Go All Out, Aim High, and Build Socialism with Greater, Faster, Better, and More Economical Results" [ku-tsu kan-ching, li-cheng shangyu, to k'uai hao sheng ti chien-she she-hui chu-i 鼓足干劲力争上游、多快好省地建设社会主义]

Mao's formula for building socialism, announced to the Third Plenum of the Eighth CCP Central Committee in 1957, a key phrase frequently applied in educational and economic enterprises.

"Intellectual Aristocrats" [ching-shen kuei-tsu 精神贵族]

refers to those trained in bourgeois schools who exemplify the "three separations," q.v.

"Knowledge Is Private" [chih-shih ssu-yu 知识私有]

a bourgeois individualist, unsocialist conception.

"Long March" [ch'ang-cheng 长征]

the march from Kiangsi to the Northwest in 1934-1935, during which the CCP overcame enormous obstacles to survive and regenerate their movement. The march has become the great epic of CCP history, symbolizing the dedication and courage of the early revolutionaries. During the GPCR youth were encouraged to make their own long marches to see the country, learn from the people, and steel themselves against hardship.

"Looking to the Government for a Handout" [hsiang kuo-chia shen-shou 向国家伸手]

revisionist attitude contrary to Mao's emphasis on "self-reliance," q. v.

"Mao Tse-tung Thought Propaganda Teams" [Mao Tse-tung ssu-hsiang hsüan-ch'uan tui 毛泽东思想宣传队]

teams of workers chosen for their high political consciousness which, during the GPCR, entered colleges, secondary schools, literary and art groups, scientific research offices, and other units controlled by intellectuals. Under the guidance of provincial revolutionary committees of PLA units, they were given the task of uniting disputing factions, getting rid of hidden rebels and die-hard reactionaries, educating people in Mao's thought, and generally making sure that the proletarian line was being followed.

"May 16 Elements" [wu i-liu fen-tzu 五一六分子]

radicals criticized by Chairman Mao for anarchist and nihilist tendencies; the name is derived from the directive which initiated their activities, the May 16, 1966, directive by Mao Tse-tung which launched the inner-Party attack on revisionism.

"No Construction Without Destruction" [pu p'o pu li 不破不立]

an expression of Mao Tse-tung's: in education it refers to criticism and self-criticism and repudiation of revisionism, all a necessary part of creating a new, revolutionary order.

"One Divides into Two" [i fen wei erh 一分为二]

Mao's theory of contradiction: a method of analysis in dialectical materialism; in the Cultural Revolution it has been applied particularly to the promotion of class struggle (contradictory theory, "combine two into one," q.v.).

"One Studies to Become an Official" [tu-shu tso-kuan 读书做官]

a reactionary concept recalling the objective of Confucian education.

"Operate Open-Door Schools" [k'ai-men pan-hsüeh 开门办学]

admonition to let the public in on the management of schools, bring in teachers from the community, link up with factories and farms.

"Poor and Lower-Middle Peasants" [p'in hsia-chung nung 贫下中农]

in CCP class analysis, poor peasant families were those which, prior to 1949, owned too little land to be self-supporting and had to work as part-time tenants. Lower-middle peasant families were barely self-supporting and constantly in danger of becoming poor peasants. CCP estimates that these two groups constituted about 80 percent of the rural population.

"Popular Management, Public Assistance" [min-pan kung-chu 民办公助]

decentralization of financial and administrative responsibility emphasizing local option, and giving the civilian population considerably more control over their lives while reducing the costs and bureaucratic load of the government.

"Production Is Everything" [sheng-ch'an chiu-shih i-ch'ieh 生产就是一切]

a bourgeois revisionist concept that ignores class struggle and social objectives.

"Regularize" or "Standardize" [cheng-kuei-hua 正规化]

refers to the revisionist tendency of judging quality by a set of standards and trying to make all schools conform or be abolished; conflicts with Mao's emphasis on diversity, using methods suited to conditions in a particular area, etc. "Irregular" [pu cheng-kuei 不正规] is an epithet used by revisionists.

Revolutionary Mass Criticism and Repudiation" [ke-ming ta p'i-pan 革命大批判]

a task for everyone in schools and elsewhere to expunge revisionists and reactionary thought.

"Revolutionary Spirit of Daring to Think, Speak, Act, Take Chances"(sometimes "speak" is left out) or "Daring to Imagine, Create, and Breakthrough" [kan hsiang, kan shuo, kan tso, kan chuang ti ke-ming ching-shen 敢想、敢说、敢做、敢闯的革命精神]

a Maoist slogan directed particularly at those who become inactive for fear of criticism.

"Seek Fame and Wealth" [ming li ssu-hsiang 名利思想] — a variation is "Individual Fame and Fortune"

a bourgeois revisionist aspiration.

"Seek Tranquility, Fear Disorder" or "Go Slow. . ." [ch'iu wen p'a luan 求稳怕乱]

mentality of cadres who have no faith in the masses and fear to apply the mass line.

"Self-Reliance" [tzu-li keng-sheng 自力更生]

Maoist admonition to use initiative and local resources to do a task, and not wait for others to lead the way or provide materials.

"Self-Reliance, Hard Struggle, Eliminating Inhibiting Beliefs, and Liberating Thought" [tzu-li keng-sheng, chien-ku fen-tou, p'o-ch'u mi-hsin, chieh-fang ssu-hsiang 自力更生、坚固奋斗、破除迷信、解放思想]

four Maoist slogans often used together.

"Social Education" [she-hui chiao-yü 社会教育]

spare-time or part-time education, including literacy classes, newspaper-reading groups, etc., particularly for adults but also for children not in regular schools; the term was used more frequently before 1949 than after.

"Struggle-Criticism-Transformation" [tou-p'i-kai 斗批改]

struggle against those in authority taking the capitalist road; criticize and repudiate bourgeois and feudal ideas in oneself and others; transform education, literature and art, and other aspects of social endeavor to make them correspond to the socialist economic base.

"Teaching Behind Closed Doors" [kuan-men chiao-hsüeh 关门教学]

separating school from society and social tasks, causing the "three separations," q.v.

"Teaching Books, Not Teaching People" [chiao shu pu chiao jen 教书不教人]

refers to poor teaching methods attributed to bookish intellectuals of the old school.

"Technique Is Primary" [chih-shu ti-i 技术第一]

a bourgeois revisionist concept opposed to the Maoist emphasis on the primacy of politics and ideology.

"Theory Is Foremost" [li-lun chih-shang 理论至上]

a bourgeois revisionist conception that fails to relate theory to practice, manifest in schools in book-learning to the exclusion of application.

"Theory That Study Is Useless" [tu-shu wu-yung lun 读书无用论]

a leftist reaction to the attack on the education system, which Maoists condemned as a fallacy that is "left in form, right in essence."

"Theory That Teachers Are Doomed" [chiao-shih tao-mei lun 教师倒霉论]

apparently a rather prevalent attitude when teachers were widely attacked during the Cultural Revolution; attributed to reactionaries and contradicted by Maoists.

"Three Constantly Read Articles" or "Three Venerable Articles" [lao san pien 老三篇]

"In Memory of Norman Bethune," "Serve the People," and

"The Foolish Old Man Who Removed the Mountains": written by Mao Tse-tung in the Yenan period, they were chosen as representative of his thought during the Cultural Revolution and used widely in schools (all are found in Selected Works of Mao Tse-tung).

"Three-Good Policy" [san hao cheng-ts'e 三好政策]

education policy formulated by Mao Tse-tung in 1953: good health, good study, good work.

"Three Great Revolutionary Movements" or "...Struggles" [san ta ke-ming yun-tung 三大革命运动]

class struggle, production struggle, scientific experimentation.

"Three Separations" [san t'o-li 三脱离]

separation from proletarian politics, from the workers and peasants, and from production.

"Three Red Flags" [san-mien hung-ch'i 三面红旗]

General Line, People's Communes, Great Leap Forward.

"Transplant First, Transform Later" [hsien pan hou hua 先搬后化]

said to be Liu Shao-ch'i's policy regarding Soviet education.

"Two Kinds of Education System, Two Kinds of Labor System" [liang-chung chiao-yü chih-tu, liang-chung lao-tung chih-tu 两种教育制度 两种劳动制度]

allegedly Liu Shao-ch'i's proposal to establish an elitist system.

Chinese Education and Society: A Bibliographic Guide
The Cultural Revolution and Its Aftermath

Compiled with an Introduction by Stewart E. Fraser and Kuang-liang Hsu

"An important tool for students and scholars doing research on contemporary Chinese education." — CHOICE

This bibliography is the most comprehensive and up-to-date reference work available on developments in Chinese education since 1966. In addition to primary materials from the People's Republic of China, the entries are drawn from other Asian sources, as well as from American and European studies.

All areas of education are covered, including elementary, secondary, and higher education, teaching and teacher training, and Mao Tse-tung's educational thought. Most entries are fully annotated, and many are cross-listed.

The introduction provides valuable information on the research centers, journals, and publishing/translating agencies active in the field.

Stewart E. Fraser is Director of the International Center, George Peabody College for Teachers. Kuang-liang Hsu is a professor of library science at East Texas State University.

The People's Liberation Army and China's Nation-Building

Edited with an Introduction by Ying-mao Kau

"Students of contemporary Asian affairs should welcome [this volume] not only for its lucid analysis, but also for its wealth of documentation on the role of the PLA in China's nation-building."

— JOURNAL OF ASIAN STUDIES

This collection of articles and documents from mainland Chinese sources focuses on the role played by the PLA in China's modernization process. The volume documents and analyzes the activities of the PLA in key areas of political control and integration, manpower training and education, social reform, cultural change, and economic development.

Ying-mao Kau is an associate professor of political science at Brown University.

International Arts and Sciences Press, Inc.
901 North Broadway, White Plains, New York 10603

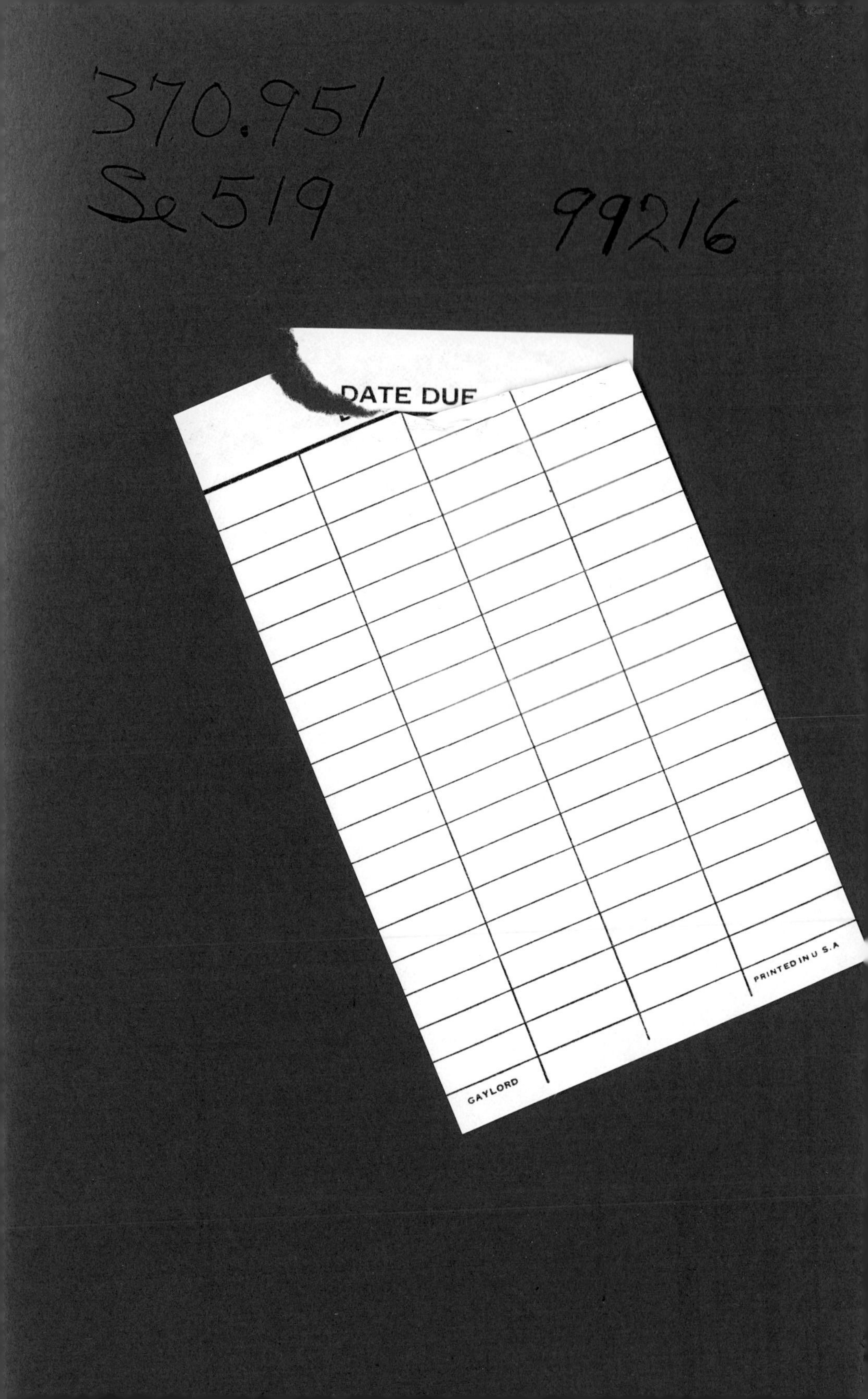
370.951
Se519
99216
DATE DUE
GAYLORD
PRINTED IN U.S.A.